The Crew Book

By Bruce Alger

The Crew Book
Of Crew 2409

24th Squadron
6th Group
313th Wing
21st Bomber Command
Of the 20th Air Force

By Bruce Alger
1945

Crew 2409 Roster

(Rank At End of Duty)

Position	Rank	Name	Number
Airplane Commander	Capt	Alger, Bruce R.	662 720
Pilot	1st Lt	Higgison, William F.	823 580
Navigator	1st Lt	Griesemer, Harold A.	086 383
Bombardier	1st Lt	Kagan, Jacob	783 013
Engineer	M/Sgt	Mount, Frank N.	371 184
Radio Operator	S/Sgt	Horvath, Albert E.	107 644
CFC Gunner	T/Sgt	Jones, Harold V.	593 102
Radar	S/Sgt	Gabriszeski, John F. Jr.	072 387
Right Gunner	Sgt	Blatt, Darius C.	833 988
Left Gunner	S/Sgt	Bush, Richard G.	374 833
Tail Gunner	S/Sgt	Helland, George W.	421 260
Crew Chief	M/Sgt	Patterson, Wilbur R. Jr.	273 834

In Memoriam
1994
Gabriszeski, John F. Jr.
Blatt, Darius C.

Gabby Al Charlie Dick Nick George Harold
   Hal   Bruce   Bill   Jake   Pat

MISSIONS

NO 1	Dress Rehearsal	6-1
NO 2	First Enemy Fire	7-1
NO 3	The First Big One	8-1
NO 4	Low Altitude "Blitz" Begins	9-1
NO 5	The Three Engine Return	10-1
NO 6	Our Own Dive-Bombing	11-1
NO 7	We Get Our First Fighter	12-1
NO 8	Lost Over Enemy Territory	13-1
NO 9	First Medium-Altitude Daylight	14-1
NO 10	The Big Thermal	15-1
NO 11	Flak-Alley	16-1
NO 12	First Okinawan Help	17-1
NO 13	Near Perfect Assembly and Bombing	18-1
NO 14	Rendezvous In The Clouds	19-1
NO 15	Phosphorus Bombs	20-1
NO 16	No Gas Reserve	21-1
NO 17	Incendiaries Again with "Ditchings"	23-1
NO 18	What a Send Off	24-1
NO 19	Secondary Target	25-1
ABORTED MISSION	Miss America - '62 Quits	26-1
NO 20	Formation Flying Inside Clouds	27-1
NO 21	Three Squadron Teamwork	28-1
NO 22	Iwo Jima	29-1
NO 23	One Too Many	31-1

TABLE OF CONTENTS
CHAPTER 1 INTRODUCTION
CHAPTER 2 THE PLANE
CHAPTER 3 TRAINING
CHAPTER 4 THE TRIP OVER
CHAPTER 5 COMBAT
CHAPTER 6 TRUK
CHAPTER 7 SEARCH MISSION
CHAPTER 8 TOKYO
CHAPTER 9 TOKYO
CHAPTER 10 KOBE
CHAPTER 11 NAGOYA
CHAPTER 12 SHIMONOSEKI STRAIT MINING
CHAPTER 13 INLAND SEA MINE LAYING
CHAPTER 14 NAGOYA
CHAPTER 15 TOKYO
CHAPTER 16 YOKOHAMA-KAWASAKI
CHAPTER 17 KANOYA AAIRFIELD EAST
CHAPTER 18 KANOYA AIRFIELD WEST
CHAPTER 19 MATSUYAMA AIRFIELD
CHAPTER 20 KANOYA AIRFIELD
CHAPTER 21 USA
CHAPTER 22 AIRMAN TO FAMILY
CHAPTER 23 NAGOYA
CHAPTER 24 NAGOYA
CHAPTER 25 HAMMAMATSU (TOKYO)
CHAPTER 26 TOKYO
CHAPTER 27 OSAKA
CHAPTER 28 KOBE
CHAPTER 29 OSAKA
CHAPTER 30 STATESIDE INTERLUDE
CHAPTER 31 KUMAGAYA
CHAPTER 32 POST WAR COMBAT
CHAPTER 33 APPENDIX

Chapter 1 Introduction

The following account is the story of a particular B-29 combat crew during training and combat. As to be expected, it includes many of the author's personal experiences and observations intermingled with the accounts of the experiences and activities of the crew as a whole. To a great extent, since crews are closely related within Squadron and Group, it is representative of all combat crews.

The combat section was written while participating in the raids against Japan. The brief training section was added as a background for the combat duty.

In the mind of the author, the soul-gripping experiences overseas provoke many thoughts, philosophic conclusions, and deduced morals in the fields of human relations, politics, religion, science, and human affairs in general. Life is reduced to its common denominator -- to stay alive. From this viewpoint life is often seen more clearly, as the individual pierces the haze obscuring human customs and morals. Further, it is one thing to be a member of a protective democratic way of life and another to be plunged into a totalitarian state whose profession is destroying.

In this account I have written only my observations and those of the men around me, of my crew and the other crews. The reader may deduce as he sees fit.

The "mission reports" were originally intended solely for those crew members about whom they are written. I have purposefully evaded the temptation to expand on the dangling bait of "morals to be deduced" about which long-winded philosophic discussion could be written.

Bruce Alger

Chapter 2 The Plane

On a sultry Nebraska day I get my first sight of the B-29. Over the top of a flight line building I see the top of the tail, much taller than an airplane tail should be, and then rounding the corner there it is, all 40 tons of it. What a plane! So this is the Air Corp.'s new weapon.

From a distance the airplane appears somewhat squat, resting low and long on its tri-cycle gear. The fuselage, like a long cigar, stretches parallel to the ground. The thick body becomes gracefully slender toward the tail, giving the impression that the tail actually sweeps into the sky-reaching vertical stabilizer and rudder. The entire body seems to balance nicely around the wing, dividing the heavier nose section and engines from the longer extent of rear fuselage and tail. As a result the nose section seems to be reaching out ahead, almost out of sight of the engines for those sitting forward -- a beautiful sight.

There is a guard with a gun slung over his shoulder standing at the nose of the plane. The lowest part of the under side of the fuselage is waist high while at the nose it reaches his shoulder. It is apparent that if he were standing under the tail he couldn't even reach it. As if to bear this out there is a tall ladder from the ground up to the rear door and another up into the nose wheel well, no doubt the entrance to the cabin. Without a basis of comparison the plane is difficult to size up because it is so well proportioned.

By this time I have come so close to the plane that I seem to be surrounded by it stretching indefinitely in all directions. I recall the dimensions -- 99 feet from nose to tail, 141 feet from wing-tip to wing-tip, 30 feet high, and 9 and ½ feet in diameter, and it looks every bit that big.

And here are the huge engines with their four-bladed propellers each capable of replacing 2200 horses. The props with an arc of 16 feet are the largest, most efficient blades yet devised. The B-29 has one-seventh the weight of a locomotive and four times the power. It is twice the B-17 in weight and power.

The guard apparently is accustomed to members of the air crews looking the plane over. It must be an old story to him and his disinterest contrasts sharply with the enjoyment I feel.

The main gear consists of dual wheels supported by steel members similar to the huge H-shaped steel beams used in the construction of bridges. The cylindrical electric motor that raises and lowers this massive gear is only 14 inches long and 6 inches in diameter. The doors that enclose the gear when retracted now extend vertically down on each side of the gear. I am now standing in the wheel well, as it is called. The top is several feet above me. The whole gear is supported by the large wing girders that extend through the fuselage to beyond the outer engine on either side, at which point the outer wing panels are attached. The wing whose construction I can see from the wheel well appears massive and strong. The gear has a combination oil-air oleo shock absorber to absorb the impact of landing and the roughness of the ground while taxiing.

The dual engine superchargers in the exhaust stack catch my eye next. These comprise another new feature on the B-29. A turbo supercharger is simply an air compressor driven by the exhaust directed through the wheel. The wheel in turn is connected to a duplicate wheel located in the air intake and in spinning it compresses the air that goes into the carburetor. Gasoline mixed with the air under pressure is admitted to the engine. The exhaust gases are controlled by a gate which when closed directs all the exhaust through the turbo supercharger. In the cabin of the plane the pilot opens and closes this gate by means of a knob connected to both gates of all four engines. So the power output is controlled. The turbos are needed on take-off and at high altitudes, the latter use permitting powerful operation up high even though the air is thin. The system is all the more wonderful because control of the gates is electronic. In practice it means just one knob to actuate all engines simultaneously.

The flaps next claim my attention. The flaps on a plane perform the task of slowing it down without loss of control by the pilot. A plane needs the rush of air over the wing and tail to make the controls effective. This rush of air is obtained through high speed, yet control is needed even when landing at slow speed. The flap is the last portion of the wing or "trailing edge" of the wing and extends from the fuselage to the aileron. When actuated it pivots where hinged on the top edge so that it slants down below the wing. In this position it accomplishes the necessary slowing down yet does not take away control. The stalling speed, the point at which the plane ceases to fly and fails, is lowered so that the ground is approached more slowly without danger of "stalling out." The B-29 flap is more efficient because it not only pivots down but slides back thus actually increasing wing area, permitting even slower speeds.

As I stand here thinking that I will soon be flying this huge plane, I recall that the army made my choice for me when, during cadet days, my friends and I were assigned to fighters or bombers according to our size, taking into consideration height and weight, and here I am looking at this giant craft -- the end of the line in bombers. Where does the line go from here?

But reflection gives way to the attraction of the cabin. The doors that enclose the nose wheel, when extended, permit a ladder to be fastened up the side. I climb up the ladder, still surrounded by a plane known only through pictures and print. It closely resembles the pictures. The top of the wheel well, beside the engineer's position, may be covered by a hatch, lowered during flight. Forward of this point is that part called the "flight-deck", including the engineer, pilot and copilot positions.

For the first time I slip into the pilot's left-handed seat. This is for me! Apparently the comfort of the members of the crew has been considered, for the seat will slide fore and aft, up or down, and tilt, which is particularly good for long legs. The rudder pedals may be adjusted forward or backward and the control column (the old familiar "stick") is comfortably within reach. Under the left hand are located the throttles and beside them the elevator trim tab. Rudder and aileron trim tab controls are located beside the seat to the left.

Trim tabs are miniature controls on the larger controls of aileron, rudder and elevator. By using these, the controls are neutralized and the result is greater ease in maneuvering the plane. The oxygen is to the left along with several emergency releases for bomb bay doors and cabin pressure.

To the right, conveniently placed below the right hand and beside the seat, is the "aisle stand". Here are found the other controls. There are toggle switches for changing the propeller pitch and also the feathering buttons. The feathering button actuates an electric motor which, through use of oil pressure, revolves the four prop blades in their sockets until the edge of the blades face into the wind. This might be compared to a knife whose edge is pointed forward while the knife is held vertical to the ground. In any other position the propeller will be forced to "windmill" by the rush of air against tilted blades, as when the engine is inoperative. The pilot feathers the engine only when it has ceased, because of malfunction, to operate properly, in which case it would idly windmill, slowing down the plane."If it can't help it mustn't hinder" – thus the feathering prevents dragging and permits greater speed. Also, an engine may be cut off and feathered if it is damaged and likely to suffer further harm by running. The toggle switches used for normal operation are used to actuate the oil pressure system which revolves the blades simultaneously in their sockets. By this method the "bite" of air it takes is regulated. If the bite is big the blade turns slower to do the work, but if you decrease the "pitch" until the bite is smaller it will revolve faster. The quickest way to get power is by using a small bite or low pitch as it is called. That is why on take-off the RPM is set at 2800 -- attaining speed faster by using a smaller bite and quicker turning, similar to shifting gears in a car.

To the right of the pilot's seat on the aisle stand are the light switches for the red and green wing-tip lights, the blue formation lights along the wing, the red, green and amber lights on the underside of the fuselage, and the white recognition lights on top. There is also the turbo supercharger knob and the gear and flap "up-down" switches. Toward the rear of the stand is the autopilot with its various switches and control knobs, all very convenient to reach.

The instrument panel is easy to see over the control column. There are the flight instruments of artificial horizon, directional gyro, needle and ball, airspeed, rate of climb -- all compactly arranged. The only engine instruments are the manifold pressure gauges and tachometers (the former represents power -- that is the fuel fed the engine, the latter the revolutions per minute of the propellers).The rest have been removed to the engineer's position.

Across the aisle is the copilot's position with similar seat, instruments and duplicate controls. He also has the radio compass and the flap position indicator and propeller lights which indicate maximum and minimum propeller pitch settings. Each panel has a clock and an ashtray -- all the comforts.

Looking at all of this equipment I have the premonition, understandable perhaps, that in spite of my present scant knowledge, the future will teach their purposes and uses. Further it is obvious that highly developed team work by the crew is necessary to get all this into the air.

Curiosity still holds me, so I continue this tour of first acquaintance undisturbed by the outside world.

The bombardier's position is next in line of scrutiny, being located ahead of and between the pilot's and copilot's seats. At least "he gets there first". His seat is lower than the flight deck and at the base of the pilot's and copilot's instrument panels. The all-glass nose permits excellent visibility, only the strong cross ribs offer obstruction.

The bombsight is directly ahead of the bombardier, ready for use when energized. To the right is the gunsight which, when unstowed, pivots out above the bombsight and at eye level for efficient use. On the right hand are the gun powder switches. To the left are the switches for the bombing circuits, master circuit switch, rack selector, bomb bay doors, salvo switch, and indicator lights. This position has a strictly business-like appearance and is not very roomy, yet with bent knees can be fairly comfortable.

Going back between the pilot and copilot seats I climb into the engineer's seat directly behind the copilot. The engineer has his back to the armor plated bulkhead behind the copilot, so he is in the position of seeing "where he's been" instead of where he is going. A window on his left permits his seeing No. 3 and 4 engines, while across the cabin at an angle he can see No. 1 and 2 through the navigator's window. Judging from the difficulty involved in seeing out of those windows it appears the engineer is supposed to stick with his instruments, and it's no mean job.

If there are any instruments missing on the engineer's panel it would be hard to tell what they'd be. There is the fuel mixture which determines whether a rich or lean fuel-air mixture is to be used, rich meaning more fuel per volume than lean. There is a duplicate set of throttles. There is also the cabin pressure regulator.

And this points out another new feature of the "big bird," namely, pressurization. The inboard superchargers are used to blow air into the cabin and in this manner keep the air pressure built up to similar to low altitude conditions. No matter how high the plane flies, the passengers and crew are able to breathe the atmosphere comfortably without the old oxygen mask. The engineer's position also can control the cabin heat thermostatically and manually.

There are fuel transfer levers used to shift fuel from one tank to another, depending on which engine needs fuel. This allows carrying of fuel in the center wing tank or bomb bay, for it can be transferred to the engine tanks when needed. There are switches for the six engine driven generators, two for the outboard engines and one each for the inboard, supplying electricity for the many electrical devices. The voltmeter and ammeter tell whether the generators are functioning properly. The engineer's levers are located at the bottom of the panel. On a desk-like top are the switches, while the instruments are mounted in the vertical panel, all very convenient.

Cowl flap switches are to the left. These control the cooling of the engines if the cylinder-head temperature gauges read too high, showing the engines are too hot. Oil cool switches permit cooling of the oil as needed. The master switch and magnetos are located on the face of the panel. There are fuel boost rheostats which actuate auxiliary motors to supply fuel at high altitudes or whenever the engine-driven fuel pump fails. As for the instruments, there are two manifold pressure gauges, with needles numbered 1 and 2 on the right gauge and 3 and 4 on the left, the numbers specifying the particular engine. There is the air speed meter, two altimeters and rate of climb indicators, one for outside air changes and the other for cabin pressure changes.

Fuel, oil pressure and temperature gauges are all located on the panel, each engine having its own set. There are cowl flap position indicators. There are also other gauges, but these are the most important. To the left is the oxygen equipment, radio, and fluorescent lights to illuminate the panel at night.

Sufficiently confused at this maze of instruments and levers, and with my book-learning strained to the breaking point, I move on to the right of the upper turret which extends into the after cabin. It's quite a squeeze. Every inch of space has been utilized. The folding table top, when clamped into place is wedged against the top turret which extends down to meet the protruding lower turret housing. The seat faces forward with an angle view ahead of the engineer, then the copilot. Just above the table and directly ahead are the flux gate compass and air speed meter. There is a chart case to the left for maps. To the rear, reached by pivoting the seat, is another cabinet for charts. Beside this is the drift meter, used to determine the airplane's drift right or left from a straight course as caused by cross-winds.

Beyond the navigator's position, aft, is the astral dome through which the navigator takes sun and star shots to determine position. It has a hook on which the sextant may be hung. On the side, behind the chair, is the "handset" for the gun data. The navigator must put the air speed, altitude, and outside air temperature into this computer so that the gun sights will solve the gunnery problems accurately. The navigator has a window to the left through which he can see almost 90 degrees from the wing to the nose.

Becoming progressively more impressed and confused, I slip around the back of the turret to find the radio operator's position. He is very cozy with the turret on his left and the forward bomb bay bulkhead on his right. The seat faces the "starboard" side (as the Navy would have it) and is aft of and in line with the copilot and engineer.

The Laison receiver is directly in front of his chair on a table. This is a powerful long range radio receiver for both short and long wavelengths. There is also a transmitter in conjunction with it, and a transmitter key for sending code. There is the antenna reel control through use of which the operator can release trailing antenna behind and below the plane for better communication. Numerous other technical radio units are here too; the modulator, dynamotor, amplifier -- but it's not necessary at this point, I feel, to be on speaking terms with all this equipment.

Befuddled, but not ready to quit, I crawl on hands and knees an interminable distance through the tunnel which connects the forward cabin with the blister section. It's the longest thirty-five feet I've encountered. The tunnel extends atop the bomb bays to connect the forward cabin with the blister section. In this way the forward and blister are accessible to each other during flight.

Arriving in the blister section I look down on another marvel of compactness. In the center on a raised, throne-like dais, is the ring sight gunner's position, manned by the Central Fire Control gunner, or CFC gunner, as the good book calls him. He is the key gunner, having a clear sweep of the upper reaches of air, fore and aft. His seat, sight, and equipment are on a 360 degree pivot. He is able to turn at will his entire position and with it the turret and guns he is controlling. His head space is in the blister, giving excellent visibility. It is a business-like location, giving the gunner a feeling of sitting almost outside, all alone. His interphone equipment is right there so he can communicate with ease with the rest of the crew.

Flanking this central pedestal and much lower are the side blister positions. The seats face aft with foot room aft below the level of the floor. The gun sight is placed in the blister reaching up half way, permitting the gunner to look over it as he desires to see even more at an angle. Looking down with my head against the glass, I feel almost out-of-doors. The right and left positions are similar. The usual oxygen, radio, equipment and ashtray are on the side near the blister. The cushions are fairly comfortable, suggesting that sleep on a long flight would not be bad, tho' legs cannot be straightened.

By moving to the left, going aft around the upper aft turret, I go through an opening into the radar room. This room originally had two or four bunks, but now these are replaced by loose equipment in addition to the complete radar equipment on the port side (facing forward) where the radar operator sits sideways facing the equipment. There is also a lavatory, but without modern plumbing. This room is the largest open space inside the pressurized section.

Beyond the bulkhead, aft, I enter the "rear unpressurized section", as it is called. To the left as I face aft is the rear entrance door. To the right is the auxiliary power unit or "put-put" as it's called. This generates electricity. It is a gasoline engine with generator attached. There's the battery, too, beside the put-put. An opening or escape hatch, as it's called, is overhead, high on the side.

Further aft is the lower turret. Oxygen bottles line the sides. In the middle is a catwalk to the tail position. This is a crowded crawl but finally inside the tail with door closed it is roomier, like getting out of a straight jacket into a bushel basket. The tail gunner is all alone. His seat slide up or down and the oxygen, interphone, and radio equipment are on the side. Directly facing the seat is the gun sight. Side and rear windows permit good visibility. An escape hatch is located on the right about shoulder height. This position is over 90 feet from the pilot. I can see the imperative need for interphones in this situation.

Chapter 3 Training

An airbase near a fair-sized city in Nebraska is the headquarters for our group's part in the B-29 training program, both on the ground and in the air. A group is composed of three squadrons, the first, second and third, by name. Ours is the first squadron, within which we do all our work. In addition to the flying done at this airbase, the flight training is accomplished at Batista, Cuba, and Borinquen Field, Puerto Rico. Beginning in July of 1944 our group training continued until the middle of December.

When the crews are being assembled man by man, much of the flying is done by skeleton crews in the B-17. Later, in the B-17 and B-29, we operate as full eleven-man crews, that is, after our crews are entirely formed. Both the ground school and the flying are directed to developing the crew members first as specialists and then progressively more as a combat team whose weapon is the B-29. The general objectives in the training of the individuals are as follows:

The pilot, my own position, is trained to know the airplane and to operate it in normal or emergency situations, in fair weather or foul, and to land or take-off under adverse conditions. He has to be able to fly by instruments, navigate by radio aids, and find his position by radio aids if lost. He must be proficient at formation flying, and be able to get the most out of the airplane at all times. In addition, he is the leader of a team whose training must be as a team. Since the plane is an eleven man weapon it must be operated by an eleven man unit to the best of their combined abilities, each as a specialist in his department. The pilot is told that he must bring out the best in each man by taking a personal interest in the work of each, by having their welfare at heart, and by keeping abreast of their training. The copilot is the second in command and must be able to do everything that the pilot has to do and to take over when necessary. He is the executive officer. Everything that applies to the training of the pilot also applies to the copilot. In our crew this position is filled by Bill Higgison.

To develop their skills and knowledge the pilot and copilot attend numerous classes on the technical side of the B-29 airplane, describing the structure of the fuselage, wings, gear and controls, as well as the engine, engine controls and the many instruments and accessory equipment that is included. They both have hours in the Link Trainer, a mock-airplane whose equipment duplicates the instruments, controls, and radios of a real plane, thereby permitting the pilot to develop his "blind-flying" ability without actually getting off the ground. In addition, they participate in a certain amount of similar training to that received by the other members of the crew so that they will better understand the other skills within the crew.

Hal Griesemer, the navigator, has classes and works on training devices which are directed toward strengthening the skills he already possesses, as well as preparing him for additional work as a member of the combat crew. His professional skills include piloting, dead reckoning, celestial navigation, an understanding of all radio and radar equipment used in navigation and bombing, and proficiency in target identification. As a training aid he does problems in the "Navitrainer" which simulates actual flights of an airplane, presenting all the attendant navigational problems. In addition he "doubles in brass," participating in many of the bombing classes.

Jake Kagan, as the bombardier, has a full program in his department. He endeavors to learn the bombsight, radar equipment, and automatic pilot insofar as they pertain to bombing. He studies the normal and emergency operation of bombs, bomb racks, switches, controls, releases, doors, and the like. As the nose gunner, he learns the gunnery end, including the manipulation of the computing CFC sight. In addition, as a DR navigator, he works in the navigation department to become proficient in pilotage and dead reckoning. Finally, he studies target identification. As a training aid, Jake does problems on the bomb trainer, a tall electrically driven platform with an attached bombsight which duplicates the bombing problem encountered when airborne.

Nick, the engineer, has the extensive task of learning the operation and maintenance of all the mechanical equipment. It is his duty to be thoroughly familiar with the engines and fuel, the electrical and oil systems, normal and emergency operating conditions, and the pressurization system for keeping normal breathing conditions in the cabin at high altitudes. Further, Nick studies the cruise control which concerns fuel consumption, the mileage considering the weight of the plane, load distribution within the plane, and the power used. His duties are many both in the air and on the ground in the maintenance of the plane.

Al learns the radio end. That means learning the operation and maintenance of all the radio equipment aboard the plane including the Laison set, the VHF set (very high frequency) for interplane communication and pilot air to ground, the radio compass, and the IFF (identification friend and foe). He also learns the use of all radio navigational aids. He practices receiving and transmitting code until fast and skillful. In addition, he studies radio procedures and codes used in authentication of radio messages, sending or receiving weather codes, and using blinker and call signals. The communication end is highly complicated and difficult because of its secretive nature in the combat area.

Jonesy, as the CFC (central fire control) specialist gunner, has the technical study of everything and anything pertaining to the care, maintenance, and operation of the entire fire control system. This means that he studies the wiring of the electrical circuits, he studies the handset and the automatic computing sight. He takes the guns apart and reassembles them with an eye to proper functioning and defective parts. He is to be the authority in the plane on the entire gunnery system.

Dick and Charlie are assigned to the left and right blister gunner positions, and George to the tail position. Each has particular techniques to master with regard to their location, but they each have the same general jobs as gunners, to learn the guns, the computing sights, and how to use this equipment skillfully. In the team, they each have electrical, mechanical and structural jobs, respectively, in working with the engineer in the care and maintenance of the airplane. They specialize in these departments.

Gabby, the radar gunner, also "doubles" in other duties. First of all, he trains to learn the radar operation and maintenance. Then he learns the navigational end so that he can better use the radar set. To this end, he takes some of the navigational training and works with the navigator in and out of class. In the same way, he works with the bombardier, doing much on his own to learn more about the radar end. In addition, he is expected to know the gunnery so that he can fill any of the gunners' positions.

The entire crew attends a large number of classes of a general nature concerning combat survival, overseas living conditions, enemy identification and characteristics, and, along the medical end, to protect and care for themselves in the midst of diseases, fevers, and other unsanitary conditions.

The crew members learn many things about their jobs from the ground school part of the training. At times we are almost buried with the paper work sent out by 2nd Air Force, under whose jurisdiction the training is received. Countless directives and pamphlets are sent out, then the revisions of these training aids, then revisions of the revisions or orders rescinding all the foregoing and substituting an entirely new set of directives. So it is, for example, that a complete B-17 training phase with exacting requirements is discarded when almost complete, replaced by another B-17 phase. As for the class work, countless times the subject matter is poorly prepared, incomplete, inaccurate or the instructor is not present. On paper we are credited with all these hours of excellent training. For example, at one class in "Carburetion of the B-29" we have a substitute teacher who admits to lack of knowledge on the subject matter, and says he had just been asked to teach. Furthermore, he has no model of the carburetor or pictures with which to illustrate, which he says are necessary to make the subject understandable. We are dismissed and credited with an hour on the "carburetor". It does not bother us particularly, since we know we'll learn it elsewhere, probably in connection with flying, yet we know we will be held accountable on paper for these many class hours.

From appearances it would be easy to judge that we are here ahead of time, before the necessary facilities have been prepared, but this couldn't be the case. We do remember the day, many weeks ago, that General "Hap" Arnold conducted a meeting which we attended together with our Commanding Officer. At the time, General Arnold stressed the importance of our training. He asked our Commanding Officer in our presence if we needed any help in men or materials, anything at all, and our Commanding Officer, instead of requesting the help that we needed, confidently stated that we were self-sufficient. Later we recalled this meeting and wondered why we weren't being trained as the General apparently intended.

However, we do learn much, and steadily, through our own efforts in flying, when we are allowed to go out and practice our specialties in the air. At first, we fly in the local area, learning the lay of the land, prominent landmarks, nearby fields, and generally becoming oriented as we do when transferred to a new locality. The pilot and copilot practice take-offs and landings. The skeleton crew consisting of Higgy, Hal, Jake, Nick, and I, drop bombs on the Broken Bow, Nebraska, bombing range. Jake practices his technique with the bombsight to improve his accuracy and develop team work with his new companions. The altitude, airspeed, and outside air temperature all make a difference to the bombardier. It's most important that he have a steady platform from which to bomb. If he does not, he will assume that the gyrations of the plane are actually true changes of speed across the ground and he will alter his manipulation of the rate and course knobs of the bombsight. Using this inaccurate data will make the bombsight's solution to the problem inaccurate and the bomb will miss the target.

The cooperation between the crew members is doubly important on the bomb run. Hal works simple dead reckoning problems figuring the distance, speed and wind to get an estimated time of arrival (E.T.A.) and at the same time keeping the plane on the proper course for the destination. The Bombardiers of the various crews are placed on a competitive basis in determining their hits on the target.

The Navigators are given a difficult night celestial navigation problem of over 1000 miles. On our hop, we go to Memphis and return. On this trip we are squarely over the city of Memphis, Hal says, "I'm not sure, but we should be in the vicinity of Memphis."

After this period of becoming acquainted, skeleton crews are sent to Batista Field near Havana, Cuba, for several days of over-water flying. Higgy, Hal, Al, Nick and I represent our crew. Realizing the importance of this early teamwork in determining if we have a combination that will click, I manage to have Nick included on the trip although it is against the specifications. The trip to Batista is designed mainly as experience for the Navigator and Radio Operator, since their work is emphasized. However, all who go may benefit, we figure. Such proves to be the case. We share a plane on the trip down and back with Preston's crew.

We find that men as well as planes take to flying over water quickly and comfortably. After the first few hours of uncertainty, with great expanses of water in all directions, the strain disappears and is replaced with confidence in the engines which keep right on going. Somehow Higgy and I, both terra firma pilots, are afraid the plane may know we are over water and not like it.

Hal and Al in navigation and radio, respectively, distinguish themselves. They both receive grades as high as are given, and rightly so. The first mission we go during daylight to Swan Island. Except for crossing the width of Cuba and the Isle of Pines, we are entirely out of sight of land. Both ways Hal guides us into our objective, giving the time of arrival quite accurately in advance. Going south on the 750 mile trip, our objective is the pinpoint island which consists of only enough land to support a radio station and is so small it doesn't rate the space it takes on a map. Hal, using dead reckoning and shots of the sun taken with the astro-compass, came mighty close. Later, we learn that Al had gotten in all his position reports accurately and on time, and sent in code to the Base. The second mission is of a different nature, being a night trip to Shreveport and return, a trip of 1100 miles. Hal uses celestial navigation again, in addition to dead reckoning, through the help of star "shots" taken with the sextant. A line position can be established across the earth's surface as a result of a star shot, which places the position of the plane with relation to the star (with the help of almanacs). By crossing two or more lines of position, each in relation to a particular star, the approximate position of the airplane on the Earth's surface may be obtained. Since there are no landmarks, Hal is forced to rely on his dead reckoning and celestial navigation and we, in turn, rely on Hal. We are hoping and happy to learn that Al knows his trade. On this trip, Al sends in regular position reports and also weather reports in code.

As the climax to the Batista work on the third mission, we do a "lost" procedure. This consists of flying for two hours away from the Base in any direction and then turning the Navigator loose to find himself and direct us back to Base without any outside help, only by use of his skill as a navigator. Unbeknownst to Hal, we take a sight-seeing trip up the Florida Keys to Miami, circle there and then head out east to sea. Just before we let Hal out of the curtained radio room we head south. He now goes to work and starts taking "shots" of the sun with the astro-compass. In thirty minutes he takes two shots during the difficult noon period and gives us a tentative position which is not far wrong. Shortly afterward, he gives us a heading to fly to the Base. We are surprised and pleased to find ourselves near Havana and then beside the field as the E.T.A. runs out.

The concluding flight of the Batista trip is the return to the Grand Island, which we make nonstop with the coordination of an established team. We know that the trip has been extremely worth-while and that we have the makings of a first rate combat crew, at least in their departments. We remember, too, many amusing little incidents which are already building up our team spirit. One in particular we enjoy recalling. The afternoon we returned from Swan Island was sultry and warm. Higgy and I were alternately snoozing and staring at the hypnotizing expanses of shadows and sunlight across the water. Like most posterior-weary pilots, we enjoy putting our feet on the rudder bar for a change of position. Now the pilot's left foot in this position is right beside the electrical switch panel containing the generator switches, light switches, and the alarm bell which is rung only in extreme emergencies such as "prepare to abandon ship".In this case, the sleeping foot came in contact with the alarm bell. As we nodded the floor hatch was violently thrown open and Hal appeared with his Mae West on ready to leave the plane, apparently with one foot out already."What's wrong?" he shouts at our sleepy faces and then realizes that we don't know either. So we trace the trouble to the errant foot and the alarm bell. We all get a big kick out of how worried he looked as he popped through the floor, like a rabbit out of his hole. He was really ready to leave.

After our return and a bull session with Jake, Jonesy, Dick, Charlie, Gabby and George about our experiences, we begin in earnest with a full crew. The ground school schedule goes on and we all participate in the training devices. The entire crew participates in the gunners' training aid, and the "Jam Handy". A motion picture projector throws pictures on a screen of enemy fighters attacking while the participant tracks and fires at the plane using the gunsight.

We finish the B-17 phase and start to fly the B-29 on practice missions. Prior to this, Higgy and I had been checked out in a B-29, that is, rated by the instructors as competent to fly it alone. Bill and I are pleased with the "big bird". We have eagerly anticipated flying the B-29.It is not disappointing either. It is fast, cruising at 200 or more and handles easily, although it takes strength to bank sharply or turn quickly. On landings, we sweat like troopers to place the plane squarely on the "first third" of the runway. The tri-cycle gear is new to us and we work much harder as beginners than is necessary after we get the hang of it; we "over-controlled". We find the B-29 stable, a good instrument plane, since only the flight instruments face the pilot, not the many engine instruments as on the B-17.Unlike the B-17, the B-29 will not hold itself level, but constant control is required. It hardly seems like flying any more, the plane is so steady and solid. As for the engines, we optimistically assume that the excessive oil leaks and engine temperature will be corrected.

Now we take the crew on missions. At the local ranges, we drop bombs giving the bombing team practice. Jonesy, Dick, Charlie and George are our eyes much of the time, developing rubber necks and swivel heads in calling out other planes, an important part of a good gunner's procedure. Later, the gunners load the guns with film and take pictures of the P-63s which attack us. This develops our air work in the gunnery department, increasing the gunners' skill and coordination on their gunsights, and among themselves in working over the fighters. The interphone procedure develops until we automatically recognize the Boston or Georgia accent and can hear everyone's message, no stuttering or stammering, and that took practice. It's a long way from Dorchester to Macon, particularly on the interphone. Loading our guns with "live" ammunition we go out to Broken Bow and fly at strafing altitude to fire on painted fences constructed for that purpose. It is good practice. Further, we learn to distinguish between the times for formal interphone procedure and the humor in our banter.

Then we combine all the skills into each flight. We fly to St. Louis by way of Des Moines, beat off fighter attacks and bomb the Union Station in formation. Sometimes we fly formation in the area for hours, assembling, changing position within the formation, and breaking up then forming again. Day or night, high or low altitude, alone or in formation, within a few miles of base or on a long cross-country flight, we practice until our jobs become almost automatic. The Denver Highway Bridge, Omaha Light and Power Company, Kansas City Packing House, Lincoln Army Air field and other strategic targets are camera bombed, and the pictures studied for bombing accuracy. In our impatience to complete the training, we sometimes forget how valuable this flying may prove to us later.

But it is hard to visualize bombing Japan while peacefully cruising over Nebraska. Nor is there much to remind us of war when we circle St. Louis and see the lights of Sportsman Park at night. It is all an adventure necessary during war. We are doing jobs that we have been trained to do for years, and occasionally realize that we enjoy exercising the skills so arduously learned. As a team, we are finding these skills more enjoyable, but most of the time it is just a job that we have to do. We can't change the pattern. We have tried hard to get where we are and occasionally, on reading current events, we can see where we fit into the scheme of things. It seems like a prosperous war, the way the U.S. can afford to train us for endless months when we could be in the fight. But no doubt it means life insurance to us in the end, thus permitting us, as my grandfather used to say, "To fight and get away, to live to fight another day."

Generally, we are quite fortunate in the performance of the planes. The early B-29s that we fly tend to heat up excessively, but this characteristic improves as winter comes and new cooling methods are used. Of course we have scares, but they only serve to teach us the "easy way" without incident. There is the night when the landing gear won't come down, and it looks like we might have to belly her on the runway. The wheel well doors won't come open and the emergency release won't force them open, so we take a chance on it and use the emergency motors without opening the doors. The motors force the doors open by driving the gear into them and we are able to come in safely. At the same time, we pull a boner by leaving the electrical power on the "emergency" side, so that the normal system is not getting any juice. As a result, after we land all our lights go out and the brakes fail to hold. Once again, the emergency system comes to our rescue. In both cases we learn. Another night, while flying to Denver, the electrical system goes hay-wire and we have no lights and no radio. So we fly even closer formation and send a code message to the flight leader, McElroy, by flashlight concerning our trouble. We manage to fly home safely with them, protected from other planes by their lights, and securing landing permission and instructions through them.

As a finale to the training program, we go in our turn to Puerto Rico. Flying down there, we accomplish the required 3000 mile navigation trip. The work at Puerto Rico is designed to permit our finishing up the missions not yet entirely completed. Mainly, this means the radar portion of several missions are not completed because of faulty radar equipment. Again, we have fighter interception and formation work as a part of the missions. However, the radar sets are still inoperative through lack of proper maintenance and we complete the missions on paper without flying them entirely. We are informed that it is imperative that the missions be finished up and we will be scheduled until they are completed. After seeing a sample of the "pressure" put on us, we realize that we are not able safely to fly that much. Since we know that we have learned the lessons the missions are designed to teach, we do the obvious thing -- we complete the paper work and write finis to our training.

In the department of the Inter-American Friendship, there are our memories of the Cuban girls who worked in the Army P-X at Borinquen Field. Naturally loquacious, they looked at Hal and his navigator's wings, rolled their eyes, and classified him as a "Star-gazer". Passing to Higgy and me, one Senorita looked us over and significantly intoned "Trrruck drivers, yes?" We agreed, startled by her perceptiveness and humor. So we added to their store of knowledge by pointing out Nick to her and saying "Meter-reader", and then Al saying "Static-chaser", then Jake the "Toggle-pusher". And then we all stood back and laughed at Sully, who arrived with a grin. The Senorita took one look at Sully, clapped her hand over her mouth and exclaimed, "That wan, he's how you say it -- story teller?" Then she explained for our edification that the gap between Sully's front teeth made the appellation obvious that Sully was untruthful. We enjoyed this and Sully admitted her accusation, seeing that he is the "weather man" in our Group.

We will never forget the gross mismanagement and confusion surrounding those days at Borinquen Field caused by our superior officers, including our Squadron Commanding Officer, trying to satisfy the paper requirements laid down by higher headquarters. Being afraid of taking a stand against these requirements, they try to force the impossible on the combat crews. Somehow we manage to get by, all of us here, without any crack-ups.

Meanwhile, another mean situation has developed concerning the crews who are scheduled to go on their last furlough and leave before going overseas. As in our case, we have worked all summer and fall without time off while others are being granted time off. We hope to finish up as a crew and then take our vacation, and this was agreed to by the authorities. Now we are finished but we're at Puerto Rico and someone forgot to provide transportation home. So we wait and wait and there are several crews in the same predicament. Finally, we are assigned to a B-17, a returned European war-weary. Our crew of eleven and nine from Maki's crew are put under my care and jammed into the old, tired plane. It is something of a miracle that we make it. Only the thought of that last visit home, so long awaited, before going overseas, keeps us going in the face of the odds against us. By the time we pass Cuba and cross the Gulf, our plane is about ready to quit. At Dallas it is necessary to have repairs. The authorities, in looking at the plane, are surprised that it can be flown. Just after midnight on December 13th, we arrive at Grand Island from the tropic south, amid ice and snow. Being late for the beginning of our time off, the crew scatters to visit families throughout the East. Combat duty is just over the horizon.

In retrospect, we realize how lucky our entire Group has been. In our Group's entire training program with the B-17 and B-29, there has been no major accident and no one hurt, a phenomenal record. We look beyond our own puny power to give thanks. Looking ahead we know something of our future combat prospects, gleaned from the Intelligence Reports of the scattered B-29 raids already being made on Japan. The bomb load carried is small, the damage inflicted on the enemy is slight, and our losses heavy considering the number of planes engaged. It doesn't look too good, but we are eager. Nor have we overlooked the possibilities. At every opportunity we have taken advantage of the training to learn the emergency procedures. Frequently, we practice "abandon ship" drill when parking on the ramp after a mission. The gunners try to improve their ability to recognize Jap fighters from slides and photos. We know that these skills will make all the difference one day.

Collectively and individually, the crew members have come to realize the all-importance of team work and are taking a pride in their work and in the way we do the job. We are building confidence and belief in each other and, factually, we are learning our jobs and we realize the value of knowing the facts as the means of doing a good job and, God willing, returning home after it is over.

As pilot and leader of the crew, I learned that "crew discipline" in the air and on the ground appeared to be no problem, with men such as make up our crew. My goal is to be the kind of commander they'd be glad to have, through setting a good example. Our crew organization is set up on principle that each man is considered an authority in his department and we would not doubt him unless he failed us.

He would have the responsibility commensurate with his job, a job that made each man, at one time or another, the key man. The copilot would be the executive officer and right-hand man of the pilot, whom he could replace and whose duties he would share. Both of them, by their professional ability, would keep the confidence of the crew. The crew would do their respective jobs and stick together because of their friendship and mutual respect. Whole-hearted teamwork would be our continued goal.

1. **Bill Higgison** is our copilot. He shares our enjoyment of having a Georgia "cracker" on the crew. His pronounced accent always flavors words of good sense and homely similes like "black as the inside of a cow," and he willingly enters arguments about the Civil War which are the height of good natured joshing. Seldom does anyone get the better of him. Bill is twenty-two years old, and is married to his Georgia sweetheart. About six feet tall and sturdily built, he has a fair to ruddy complexion on the "brownette" side. Good-natured, dependable and conscientious, we all feel glad to have him on the crew. Bill was studying insurance underwriting when he joined the service.

2. **Hal** hails from Reading, PA, where his parents, sister and dog reside. His nature and job complement each other. Painstaking, clear-thinking, and accurate, he is able to work under pressure, methodically getting the job done. Possibly his work as an apprentice draftsman before the war trained him this way. In appearance, Hal is nearly six feet tall and stockily built, athletically inclined and much quicker on his feet than you might suspect. Slow spoken and reflective, he fits in well with the rest of the crew.

3. **Jake** is a native of the "Bronx" in New York. Interrupting his college training to go into the service, he left behind his mother and four sisters. Of a studious nature, Jake takes pride in knowing his job. In addition, he holds up his end, declaiming on the wonders of New York in general and the Bronx in particular. He is typical of those who have New York in their bones, no matter what other localities they see.

4. **Nick** is our farmer from Wyanet, Illinois, where his mother, dad and brothers reside. He made the transition from tractor to plane gracefully and understands the technicalities of each. He takes the kidding about "Why-not" Illinois and dishes out plenty in return. Tall and lanky, he seems mostly hands and feet, but luckily for us, he has plenty between the ears. Easy going and good natured, he takes things in stride.

5. **Al** impresses us from the first with his knowledge of the radio end. Alert and quick, though small of stature, he enjoys the good natured argumentative banter within the crew which started when he announced that he was from "Monessen", PA, a town that was new to many of us. Married, Al has a small daughter. His wife and family await him back in Monessen.

6. **Harold V. Jone**s becomes known to us as "Jonesy" to differentiate from Hal Griesemer. Though the youngest of the crew, nineteen years old, he is serious, quiet spoken and confident, dependable far beyond his years. Jonesy married shortly after our training began, and we all extended our good wishes. He, too, is athletic and well built, participating earnestly in our crew basketball games. He went right into the service from high school.

7. **Dick** comes from Cleveland and his job was with the Federal Reserve Bank before entering the service. His two brothers joined the service about the same time, leaving his parents at home alone. Extremely slender and slight, it

looks like a good gust of wind might blow Dick away. He can eat and sleep all day, he says, and not put on weight. Eager to do his job and conscientious, Dick is a help building up teamwork within the crew.

8. **Charlie Blatt** comes from Pennsylvania, too, from Berks County. Charlie is a lot heavier than Dick, and better than medium height. Before the war, he worked as a steel tester in a factory. Now twenty-two years old and married, he is quiet and dependable. Frequently getting sick when first we flew, he gamely tries to overcome it and after a number of painful experiences he has finally overcome the problem.

9. **George Helland** from Drochester, Mass., with a Boston accent, was the butt of many of the crew jokes, but seemed to enjoy and welcome it. He usually gets in the last word. With blond hair and a fair complexion, he was above medium height and slightly on the heavy side. Getting into the tail position was something of a squeeze for him. Before the war he was an arc welder. Once in the service, he seems to have a knack for lifting the morale of those around him.

10. **John F. Gabriszeski** is the shortest man of the crew, though he tried hard to outstretch Al Horvath in height. Stockily built and well built, he embodies the pugnacious nature of little men who bow to no one. His nickname is a natural, both because of his name and vociferous manner. Married, with a two and a half year old son and another child on the way, Gabby was proud to be the most successful father in his crew. We enjoy his enthusiasm and pep, and are glad to see that he puts all that energy into really learning his job.

11. At the very outset of the program, I determined to be a good "Airplane Commander". As I saw it, and the Training Manuals outlined it, this meant being a good pilot and crew leader. As the manual puts it, "The airplane commander is in a command position. He has the lives of eleven men and a million dollars of equipment in the palm of his hand." So I took the advice and instruction of the Army publications to heart. My realization of the heavy responsibility would permit me no less. I determined to be a good commanding officer and a good guy through the common sense practices of square dealing -- honesty, sincerity, and fairness. By getting to know the men personally, building crew spirit and pride, by having fun out of the job together wherever possible -- I hoped to make a good team. The foremost goal, however, at all times would be learning our jobs, each man as a specialist, and the crew as a unit. By pursuing these policies, I figured that discipline and respect would take care of themselves. There would be no discrimination or flaunting of authority, just as there would be no doubting of any man's word and ability until and if he provoked it.

Memorizing these maxims propounded by the Army, that matched my own beliefs, I determined to spare no effort to do the job right, as the manual said, and to "go to bat" for the men whenever necessary, as their representative. My early concern over getting a good crew dissipated as we worked together. As the men cheerfully cooperated and worked hard together, my job became easy. So far as the crew harmony and effort were concerned, it was a pleasure to be with them. We became friends in addition to being business associates with a grim job ahead. So far as our crew ability is concerned, we are ready to face the test.

The sixteen crews of each squadron are trained and eager to go overseas, so the Group prepares to move to the "Staging Base" where the final preparations will be made.

Chapter 4 The Trip Over

Shortly after returning from our last short vacations at home the crew is sent to Kearney, Nebraska, which is to be our staging base. Some of the crews already have their planes, but most of us get our planes at Kearney along with our last paper work, flying equipment, musette bags and air corps luggage. Finally we are assigned a plane, a brand new Bell manufactured B-29, clean and shiny inside and out, No. 550. How proud and thrilled we are to have that plane as our own. Now we write a will and power of attorney, catalogue all our personal papers, pack our personal belongings and professional equipment, and carry the .45 automatic in the shoulder holster and web belt around the waist. Our frame of mind is right and we are ready to go, inside and out. We have a singleness of purpose which we feel when we finally say our last goodbyes to loved ones and head out toward the airbase on January 10th, 1945. This last day proves to be a busy one with full crew and two cocker spaniels participating. Our dogs "Gyro" and "Turbo", we are told, are strictly against regulations, but Hal and Jake, the guardians, do not believe these rumors.

Instead of immediate activity and departure, we are delayed at the field. The plane needs further modification, additional baggage must be loaded, and all paper work must be assembled. These include all the personal files of the men. We are to keep these with us under constant guard. You can imagine how we shudder at the thought of losing army paper work, like our "shot record" which would require duplication, if lost. The Army can't move without the appropriate paper work.

The weather is questionable ahead of us -- we are heading for Hill Field, Ogden, Utah. There we will take another look at the weather further on. We pass the Rocky Mountains and fly too far north to see Pike's Peak. We are now well above the rugged country. The plane runs sweetly with the engines just purring. We left Kearney around noon and now shortly after 1600 we are flying over a high ridge and there beyond is the Great Salt Lake. On the edge of the lake is Ogden and just south of Ogden, next to some huge warehouses of army and navy equipment is Hill Field. We come in to land just behind P. E. Jones, circling once more to clear him before following him in. As we taxi in it is apparent that a lot of other B-29s are on the way, too. There must be 20 other planes.

After landing and taking care of No. 550, we see that the crew members have quarters, work out the guard details and get our quarters assigned. W. E. (Pat) Patterson, our crew chief, is flying over with us and he supervises the maintenance of the plane. Bill, Hal, Jake and I are assigned to the upper floor of the barracks and we hang up our musette bags. We keep few clothes with us since we want to be footloose. No one can tell us about the plans for the future, but we know that someone there knows of us and will notify us of anything we should know, still we are uneasy and eager to move. Higher headquarters will notify the Hill officials when we are clear to move, weather being the main factor. The west coast has been "socked" in for quite some time.

The morning of the 11th, after dickering with operations, we line up the washing facilities so that we can clean up the plane, but before we can get to it we are given orders at 1130 to be on our way by 1400, no later. So we round up the crew from quarters and mess hall. We also have some lunch at the attractive officers mess and pick up our gear.

At 1345, we are on our way again after filing the proper clearances, thereby satisfying the army paper work. Anyhow we clear for Mather Field outside of Sacramento, California, the field which will serve as our P. O. A. E. (Port of Aerial Embarkation). We arrive later the same day, January 11, 1945, at 1730. A low layer of clouds covers much of the area, but we find a hole to the north and let down through it to a thousand feet, and home in on Mather. There is lots of traffic in this area. A C-47 cuts us out after we have our gear down, but we land and practically roll up the 47's back as he placidly taxis along instead of clearing the runway.

It is quite a sight to see the dozens of B-29s lined up row on row, all on their way overseas. After we land, many more keep the air and runway filled as they come in and form new rows. We wait outside our plane along with all our equipment until a P. O. E. officer comes along and tells us where to put our belongings and where to get quarters. About this time "Gyro" and "Turbo" who, with the exception of the smell inside the plane, have been model passengers, begin to need some attention and the authorities seem ready to give them attention since they say that no dogs or pets can go overseas. Finally, a truck comes along and we check our guns and valuable equipment so that others can't help themselves. It seems that at a P. O. E. everyone takes everything they can get their hands on, thinking it will be useful overseas and that this is the last chance to get it.

We soon get quarters and store our luggage and begin accumulating more since the P. X. is well stocked, particularly with stationary. For the next several days the mechanics and maintenance officials check the plane over in every way -- engines, radio, radar, emergency equipment and other departments; it must be just so, and since we cannot be of help we go to movies or the P. X. to have some lemonade and chit-chat.

We find out that the supposed secrecy surrounding our movements is a farce. Repeatedly we are cautioned not to say a word concerning our whereabouts through mail or phone, yet when we put through our authorized calls home the operator announced to them, "Sacramento calling". Or again, despite repeated Army lectures that our movements are secret, we find that at Mather Field those who have relatives nearby can have them on the post or visit them. The rest of us cannot leave the field, so we realize once again the Army gets its wires crossed frequently. We shouldn't be surprised, but somehow all of us have dreamed that in the importance of going overseas the many Army errors would smooth out. All of us follow the censorship regulations to the letter and then see the Army flagrantly violate them.

By this time we are eager to be on the move, but eagerness doesn't help. We are on the alert and have to report to meetings twice a day to learn if the time has come, but it is not until the 15th that we are told we will leave that night.

Long distance calls ease our minds when we learn that our wives and children have reached home safely, driving cross-country in mid-winter.

So we are ready to go. All our affairs have been checked and re-checked. The plane is about worn out with inspections. Frequently, we see cases of unnecessary inspections made and others overlooked, depending on whether Army regulations demand that it be done. Fortunately, our equipment is new and assumed to be in good shape so we do not feel particularly uneasy. We are much more concerned about the thought of approaching overseas duty and what the future holds in store. If anything, we forgive the sloppiness of the work because we are eager to be gone.

In the early evening of the 15th we check in our bedding, pack our luggage, get the food containers, and go to the briefing building. Along the way we have a hearty meal at the mess. At the briefing the route, weather and various flight considerations are well covered for the C-47s, B-25s, and B-29s going to Hawaii, which is to be our first stop on our Pacific trip. After the briefing, we go to the plane and sweat out the last preparations of the plane, last fuel, life rafts returned, and gear stored in the bomb bay.

Finally, at 0100 we are on our way. By the time we take off, change power settings several times, check cylinder head temps, climb and level out on course, we are over San Francisco. There under our left wing pass the many city lights and also, easily identified, are the yellow fog lights of the Golden Gate Bridge. It is a good send-off, but not so good as if we were leaving by day. We cross two airway lanes and radio ranges and home on a fan marker beacon by that time, and are on course for Oahu, Hawaii. The men must have mixed emotions by this time. They jokingly tell each other to take a good look, that it may be a long time until they see it again.

At 8000 it is clear and smooth and the engines purr right along. Only our fluorescent lights in the cockpit compete with the stars above and on the horizon. Below and ahead all is dark -- no land, no ships, no other planes. So we go along well over 200 m.p.h., hour after hour. It is a hop of some 2300 nautical miles.

As we fly along with the plane on the autopilot, I half dream, slumped in my seat, of wife and home, and the dark skies ahead. What lies ahead? We have never been overseas. None of us has ever been in combat. None has ever been that far from home. Every man in the plane, except perhaps the busy navigator, Harold, must be thinking the same thoughts. When would we be back? What lies ahead? How much are we going to miss our loved ones, our homes, and the conveniences of home? But none of these thoughts can challenge our gladness to be going, to be approaching the chance to do a job.

Twelve hours later, long past daylight, we are in the vicinity of the Islands. In fact we see Maui off to our left. We are a few miles off course left, so we correct toward Oahu. Then we let down through the thick cumulus clouds. There ahead lies Oahu. As we circle the coast as planned, fighter planes look us over. Now in the distance we see the extinct volcano, Diamond Head, a famous landmark. Just beyond lies the Beach of Waikiki and the city of Honolulu. To the left and beyond are the two air-fields, John Rodgers and the once-bombed Hickam field, also Pearl Harbor. We circle and land at John Rodgers.

On the ground the same old routine follows -- we take care of the plane, get quarters, food, and sleep. We are told we will not leave the next day. Our landing is much earlier than I expected because we turned back the clock so much going west -- three hours this time. So we eat, check in and sleep.

Some time later we find "Gyro" and "Turbo" (still untouched by Army regulations) dragging a parking chock around the parked plane making friends with everyone who stops. They are enjoying the trip, smelly plane and all. The rest of the crew have put down their collective feet and insisted that they be confined to the unpressurized rear section, outside the closed sections where the air is so close.

Army regulations here firmly state that we are not to leave the area of our quarters. After inquiring around, we find that the usual situation prevails -- cut and dried orders specifying one thing, while conditions and customs disregard them for other procedures more practical. So, with the assurance of local authorities that we are not scheduled to go for a day or two, we enjoy a bit of sight-seeing. We go over to Hickam field and eat at the Officer's Club, a good meal, too. The Club is attractive, with large rooms and comfy furniture, each room opening on the next with so little partition that it is like one large room -- the lounge, bar, dining room/ballroom all in one. Outside, the grass and lawn chairs overlook the river where many navy ships pass into Pearl Harbor. The grounds and buildings of Hickam look to be of the permanent sort, with paved roads, grass between the lanes, sidewalks, just like a town.

After our visit here, we take a bus and go to the Naval section. The Navy quarters are lovely, much nicer than the Army. The Navy seems to take better care of the men when ashore. The grounds are neat, well landscaped with plenty of recreational facilities unlike the Army. There are even tennis courts. But we are most interested in the Harbor itself, where the Japs had such a field day. We do not see the effects of the bombing, apparently all the ships have been rebuilt or salvaged and the buildings repaired, but there are lots of ships to see. Several battleships are in, including the Alabama. Destroyers, subs, escort ships, cruisers -- there are many there. Many little cutters and launches carry officers and men ashore or from ship to ship. On each ship hundreds of workers are refitting, painting, and moving about the decks -- it is a scene of action. Now the shift changes and thousands of civilian workers pour from the buildings along the docks.

Just outside the Harbor area toward town are thousands of buildings to house the workers. Some are of the smaller type, apartments for five, ten or fifteen. Then there is the large, long type of three floors and twenty rooms per floor. They are light and airy with large windows. The furniture can be seen as quite attractive and suitable. Most of the smaller type buildings are surrounded by lawns and shrubs. These can be seen extending street on street for blocks in all directions. Housing is a problem in Hawaii, particularly in Honolulu where there is still quite a shortage.

The evening of the 17th several of us take a trip to Honolulu. We take the bus out on the main road outside of our back entrance, through which we slip with no undue notice. The bus is filled so we stand, facing all the usual bus ads for Spearmint, shoes, hair-oil and the like. The natives on the bus attract us. There are several old crones with wrinkled, seamed faces and scraggly grey hair. We can't understand their tongue, but they are a sight to see as they puff on home-made cigarettes and talk things over. From our poor vantage point we cannot see much on the way in except the stream of government vehicles, mainly Jeeps. Everyone seems to have one.

Getting off in the heart of town, we are confronted with servicemen on all sides. You can't look in any direction without seeing them, nor walk without dodging them, so it's hard to tell whether we are seeing anything remotely related to the native city of Honolulu.

Tiring of this hubbub we decide to go out to Waikiki. Catching the overcrowded bus we finally arrive at the suburban area of town where Waikiki is located. It seems to be a semi-residential section with hotels, shops, street cars, buses, civilians, and soldiers, sailors, and marines all mixed up with a great hodgepodge. We are disappointed. Probably the war, with the great influx of service personnel, caused by the deterioration of this great resort city. It is like a second-hand Coney Island, even with rifle ranges and ice cream parlors, but we do enjoy the ice cream, and HOW! The natives of the city seem to be on the dark side. They have tanned skin, but are not like the Mexicans. The Hawaiian people have a clearer skin and are better looking -- at least those that we see.

But our stay here is brief. On our return to the base before the curfew, we ride in a bus load of sailors. One lone marine is holding forth, however. He has a good voice and being likkered up, is singing to anyone and everyone. He keeps talking all by himself to everyone, trying to get them to sing with him. He asks questions and without waiting, answers them. He is quite a show, and we all enjoy him. He is a good natured fellow, probably with quite a combat record back of him. Back at the base, we get a good night's sleep prior to departing the next day. McElroy, Preston and Jordan left today. We are one day behind them.

The morning of the 18th we attend the briefing. Pictures are shown of many of the islands south-west and we are warned about mistaking cloud shadows for islands in the distance. We are told to look for tell-tale breakers or reef lines that indicate land, not to get "Islanditis" from cloud shadows.

When we were three hours out, after leaving the States, I opened the secret orders and found that our destination was the Mariana Islands with no particular one specified. Now we are briefed to go to Saipan -- five of us -- while the other ten of our squadron are to go to Tinian. All of us are to go by way of Kwajalein in the Marshall Islands.

We take off and have a last look at John Rodgers and Hickam and Pearl Harbor before heading south out over the Fleet in the bay. It is about 0645 when we take off. After an hour or so we pass right over Johnston Island, a tiny bit of land that is all runway. It is our last landfall until we come to the Marshalls in mid-afternoon. We dodge Wotje Island, since there are still Japs there under aerial attack by the Marines on Kwajalein. Before long, after the dog-leg, we see Kwajalein in the distance, looking at first just like the shadow of a cloud, then we see the breakers.

Almost all of the islands in this area are called "atolls". An atoll is what appears to be the crater of an extinct volcano that has sunk so that water has filled in the middle, leaving only the edges protruding. These edges are what comprise the land. In appearance the atoll is a string of bits of land sticking up here and there in a semi-circular string. Kwajalein is the same, and on the southernmost bit of land is the island which saw so much Jap fighting. It is fair size, about one by one and one-half miles in size. There is just one runway, as is so often the case on these islands, and it faces into the wind. The buildings and tents are ranged along the runway. The living quarters are on the lagoon side of the island. In the lagoon are numerous Navy craft, since the extinct crater makes a good harbor.

After landing and the usual round of activities, we learn that at this point we are to load our guns for the rest of the trip. We are glad of this since we have never test-fired our guns, but it means a lot of work for the gunners who have to wipe off the grease, take off the wrappings, and then load the ammunition. They are busy until after dark. The officers go over to the Area and are assigned quarters, then have dinner and chat awhile at the Club. Donnell, Mutch and I go on a tour of the island before dusk -- we turned the clock back two hours on this trip.

The signs of battle remain all over the island. There are no trees left, all that remains of them are half dozen battered trunks with the foliage shot off and the trunks nicked. On the west side of the island the wrecked equipment is piled all together. There are Jap tanks, planes, guns, even the personal equipment of soldiers in a pile which covers several acres. There are quantities of American goods there too. The American cemetery is located elsewhere on another bit of land, but numerous mounds testify that the Japs were also buried here.

The island itself is not very pretty. There is no shrubbery or grass or trees, only the barren sand which the wind blows to cover everyone and everything, but the damaged spots have been repaired and the place is quite livable. Varied entertainment by the Navy, Marines and soldiers helps out the long evenings. There are a dozen shows on the island with a picture each and every night. The pictures are usually old, sometimes though there are new ones. The monotony there is terribly hard on the fellows. The island is small and there is nowhere to go -- it is just like being caged. The air we breathe is hot and scorching during the day, though sleep is possible at night.

We are rained out of a show and end up with several Navy officers and a coke each. We talk and they tell us we are going to some mighty nice islands, but after seeing Kwajalein we are not too hopeful -- we expect much the same thing.

The next morning we are up before the dawn again, have breakfast and go down to the planes. When the fellows begin to pull the props through -- we always do this before starting the engines to be sure they turn over all right -- we find a "liquid lock" in No. 3 engine, so under Pat's supervision the cowling is removed and the spark plugs taken out to drain out the trapped oil. Oddly enough there is none there, yet we could not turn the prop over. However we lose only forty-five minutes. Hal and Jake round up the dogs who were enjoying themselves and we get aboard. The engines turn over all right and we make ready to taxi out. Now Major Donnell returns with some engine trouble so we leave them behind for repairs.

We now have our final orders and they are to report to Tinian. This we are glad to hear since we thought we were losing our plane by taking it to Saipan, but now it appears that we are going to Tinian with the original ten and we will keep our plane. At about 1000 we take off and head west again. This time we caution the gunners to be on the alert. Naturally we think this leg dangerous since we are getting closer to the forward combat area. The guns are tested and found to fire O.K., so we stow them and the gunners stand by. During the flight Pat, Nick, Bill and I talk over sealing the engines by use of the cowl flaps and we agree that to close them is best even if the temperature goes up a little, since open flaps take more power, which in turn generates more heat which requires more flaps -- a vicious circle. Further, unbalanced flap openings upset the trim of the plane, making it harder to handle and again requiring more power to overcome the increased drag.

Pat at this time and throughout the trip gets a wonderful view of the flight part of the Air Corps, particularly the B-29, in which he has not flown so much. He also becomes well acquainted with the crew and they with him, so we are building up a fine spirit between flight and ground personnel.

After a number of hours flying west and turning back the clock (we have also crossed the International Date Line and have changed a day, too) it is mid-afternoon and land is sighted to the west. For some time we have been hearing the Saipan and Tinian planes by radio and now we see the land ahead. As usual we are right on course for Hal always does himself proud. To the right ahead, we make out the 1500-foot altitude of Saipan extending some eight miles in length, while just south of it is our new home. Only three miles of water separates the two. Tinian is flatter with an altitude of some 600 feet. It appears longer tho' actually it is much shorter than Saipan.

As we approach we can hardly believe our eyes. The islands are green as though with trees and shrubs -- sure enough, that's what it is. The fields are laid out regularly and trees mark the boundaries. Numerous roads wind about the island. By this time, we are over the northern part of Tinian where the field is located. It is apparently in the midst of construction, which we think is strange because we have heard that Tinian is all set up and running missions to Japan. We don't know yet that the Seabees work right along, building the field around the planes while the planes are using it. We learn from the tower that traffic is right-handed, because of the Saipan traffic on the southern tip of the island, and by flying right we avoid overlapping traffic. We circle right and land to the east. Once on the ground we lose our perspective and so begin a long, winding taxi through the maze of taxi-ways until we are on the south side of the runway, parked in our group's area. There are apparently 75 planes already on the island in other groups.

So here we are on Tinian, some 9000 miles from home. In twenty-six hours of flying we have come a third of the way around the world. Instead of the brown, sandy, barren bleakness of the atolls, we find that our base is comfortable and not so hot and sticky as Kwajalein. Even the dogs seem to sense the difference and promptly run off to explore the many friends with outstretched hands. We feel that a new era is beginning. We are at our "forward base".

Chapter 5 Combat

It is noontime in the Marianas, hot and humid with very little breeze stirring to clear the air of today's oppressive heat. But there is no lack of attention as those present listen to the news from home, each immersed in his own thoughts. We are in the squadron "Intelligence" room, some sitting on the wooden benches placed back to back and some sprawled on the tables. Some listen while looking beyond the aged "funny papers" they are holding, elbows on knees.

Now the news is given about the last two raids we made on the "Mainland" to Tokyo, destroying by fire a large part of that city. "Foxie" and his crew did not return from the last one. The raid before that Joe Snyder, John Boynton, and crews did not return. John's crew is the second of the original squadron missing. After a year's fellowship in training and combat, it is a blow to lose those men.

Against my own rambling thoughts and feelings of these raids, I hear the Stateside announcer give his summary. It calls to mind the difference there is between hearing the news and participating in it. Perhaps the folks back home have difficulty bridging the gap between the news and the jobs that their boys are actually doing. Perhaps they worry about us -- worry and wish they knew just what we are doing. I realize the men, themselves, are not very informative, seldom expressing themselves because of censorship, natural taciturnity, or from the feeling of inability that results from trying to reproduce experiences into words on paper.

Occasionally, news correspondents do the best they can, when flying on missions, to give the people back home first-hand news, but this does not happen very often. Beyond learning facts, dates and numbers, I suspect that those back home do not know the inside story; what the men are doing, how they feel, how they do their jobs over the target, or what they think. How, for example (as Cooney, one of the crew leaders puts it when thinking of sweating over the target) "I try to pray and talk to the crew at the same time".

Looking around the room at the quiet, attentive men, all highly competent in a death-dodging job, I am struck by the contrast between their present occupation and what they were doing before the war. There's Nick, the farmer's son from Illinois; George, the former welder and student from Massachusetts, and the others from many States and occupations. They are all young, in their 'teens or twenties', and not so far removed (in years and in their parent's eyes) from the day they joined the other fellows in neighborhood games. Then, later when they went to High School and College, they were still the kids up and down the block, each of a particular family in a particular locality -- boys whom those around them felt that they understood and so took them for granted.

Then came the war and these boys went into the service. Even this, in a way, the unhappy families understood, since they saw the soldiers in their uniforms at the various camps and on the streets of the local towns and cities. But somewhere along the line, after their sons, husbands and brothers had been in the service for a while, the members of these families probably realized that something had happened, and all they now know of the activities of those so dear to them was gleaned from pictures, periodicals, newspapers, and the radio programs.

The kids, the boys who were familiar sights about town, were using unusual equipment -- planes, boats, tanks, ships, subs, artillery, and doing all kinds of strange jobs, -- strange to those at home because they were so different from the previous work-a-day tasks their families remembered them doing. As in our outfit, Nick, instead of riding the tractor, cultivating the corn, flew over home in the largest four-engined bomber as the engineer of the biggest combat plane. There is not much similarity between tractor and plane, and it must be hard for Nick's dad to visualize what his son is doing.

So my wandering thoughts conclude in wondering if the people back home might not appreciate a timely synopsis of the B-29s they hear of daily and the combat crews who fly them. Our crew, so far as we know, is typical since it is composed of normal American boys who, in joining the armed forces preferred the flying and now they are touring the Japanese Empire on long, over-water round trips of 3000 miles in order to do their bit in hastening the end of the war. All they want, beyond this, is to go home.

The job of bombing cities is grim, but it's necessary, we know. It is not the most difficult or the toughest combat job but it is different, and it's a difference, I suspect, that the people back home, have difficulty visualizing, nor do news descriptions help. It might become apparent if you pressed the questions, "Just what does your son do as an engineer (or bombardier, navigator, radio operator, gunner, radar operator, pilot), how does he do it and how does he feel about it"?

During our missions, as a form of hobby, I have kept an account of our activities while in the air -- jotted down while flying. Keeping a small notebook to my left on the throttle quadrant, I periodically described the activities of the members of the crew and their chatter, or listed facts concerning times, distances, speed, weights, bombs, enemy activities or just my own thoughts. As soon as practicable after a "hot" time over the target, I would also jot down the events and activities of the members of the crew. From the beginning, I kept a record for no particular reason, only as a pastime, since I am not a professional writer, nor ever tried to be. Then the crew members asked for copies, to my surprise, and I took more pains to expand it as we went along, thinking it would be a crew book, a permanent record for us alone.

Our crew, Crew 2409, is in the midst of things right now. We have flown nineteen missions for a total of 272 combat hours, most of them being in our assigned plane, No. 11, which by name is "Miss America – '62". We have a good idea of what the job is, who the enemy is and that he doesn't like us and will try to get us if we don't get him. Our chances are as good as any crew's, we feel, to come out of this alive, God willing.

If this account would be of interest to the public, they are welcome to it. At least it is authentic.

Chapter 6 Truk

February 8, 1945 - No. 1

"Dress Rehearsal"

At last! The day has come. We are to fly on the first Combat Sortie. Variety will be added to our days of furniture building and practice missions. We feel trained to a point where the stuff is running out of our ears. We came overseas to battle with a common foe and do nothing but fly to Maug Island, several hundred miles north on a routine dog-leg, drop the bombs, fly close formation at altitude and return. It's a scant five hours work but it seems more like a full day, so dull has it become.

But now "The best trained G-- D--- Group ever to come overseas," as the Colonel modestly addresses us, is going on an accredited combat sortie, the first one for the Group. Lloyd Rinne, navigator on Preston's crew, casually gives us the information in a "by the way" fashion, but he doesn't fool us. He's as excited as the rest and the hubbub is spreading through the tent area where the combat crews reside. Other crews are checking the bulletin board to see if they are among those scheduled. Temporarily at least, the nonchalance and indifference are dropped -- replaced by eagerness to get started on the main feature. The men have trained as crews for seven months and as individuals for as long as three or four years for this tour of duty. Actually we all know that going to Truk, which is our destination this time, is but a side-bout to the main attraction, Japan, but just now, after bombing the Marianas, it looks big.

After dinner in the evening we troop over to the Briefing Building where the crews sit on the benches marked with the crew commander's name. Shortly thereafter the briefing begins with the Colonel giving the introductory talk. The briefing officers each explain the prearranged details of their respective departments which will affect us during the flight. The Group Intelligence Officer follows the Operations Officer who in turn is followed by representatives of Navigation, Bombing, Radio, Radar, and Air-Sea Rescue. Though nervous, the Briefing Officers do creditably, considering their newness.

The overall plan, as outlined to us, consists of a Group formation of the three squadrons. The 3rd Squadron will lead and fly high. Ours will come next, separated by five hundred feet vertically and several hundred yards horizontally from the 3rd. Last, and separated by the same distances, will come the 2nd. The Squadrons are to form over Tinian and then head out on course, climbing. Over the target flak is expected to be light and fighter interception possible. The total bomb load will be 13,000 lb., the heaviest yet carried by the B-29 on a mission. It will consist of 26 500 lb. G.P. (general purpose high explosive) bombs. The total gross weight of the planes will average 131,000 lb. (already we are over the 128,000 lb. gross weight the B-29 was designed to carry). The target will be the airstrip on Kuop Island of the Truk Group.

Additional information is given us several times over by those presiding, who appear to be a little nervous in this big dress rehearsal, but all of us feel that way. The flak analysis and discussion of possible fighter attacks adds the real flavoring, something not considered before on the training flights. We learn that we are to fly on Jordan's wing and that he will lead the "C" Flight element in the 24th Squadron, left wing at that. So this will put us on the end of the "crack the whip", since Jordan, in turn, will be maintaining a position with respect to the lead flight. So, with this meeting as a "night-cap", we return to our respective tents for a quiet sleep before the early arising.

In the early dawn the C. O. from the Squadron comes around to announce it's time to get up for early breakfast, so we all roll out, put on flight overalls and start collecting all the gear that we will take along with us. After chow, which consists of "C" rations, we start putting on the sundry items. Hal is collecting his charts while Bill looks around for his canteen. All of us very seriously check over our .45 automatics, the clips of shells, our knives, first aid equipment, web belt, and assorted weapons until we look like a bunch of commandos. There is no lack of interest in preparedness this time.

The fellows are collecting now in front of the squadron where the trucks are drawn up to take us to the flight line. We each find the truck assigned to us by crews. Everyone is feeling mighty chipper. Gabby asks George "who got your seat?" and we notice that for the first time in our trips to the flight line, someone beat George to the seat in the cab beside the drive, the "copilot" spot. George, with proper Massachusetts accent, sets Gabby straight with some comment about not caring to ride up there anyway. This gives him the last word, but no one believes him.

Down at the line we find the ground crew putting the last minute touches on the plane. At present we are flying plane No. 868 or Victor 7 (the Group number) and have "Mac" MacLaughlin as the crew chief with a fine set of helpers. Mac is not our crew chief, since Pat Patterson is our pride and joy, but we know him for a mighty good man, and have no qualms taking his plane. Like our own crew chief, we know that if he says it's ready, it's ready. Each crew member fans out to do his particular tasks. Such teamwork means that nothing will be overlooked and all accomplished in the time allotted. We don't have very long before we are to run 'em up and taxi out. "Higgy" and I do the general overseeing and check with each man on the readiness of his own position. Jonesy, representing the gunnery end declares that all is O.K. Gabby says the radar is working satisfactorily. Hal and Jake each reports that the navigation and bombing equipment, respectively, are all set. Bill, meanwhile, is making out the weight and balance, checking to see that the plane is properly loaded for takeoff and safe cruising, while I make a general inspection of the plane. How we miss 550, the plane we brought over. We were among those few whose planes were taken away on arrival and given to another crew.

It's a real pleasure to see ground and air crew working together hard, conscientiously assuring themselves and each other that the equipment is ready to go. After our own crew inspection we pile in a little ahead of time to adjust ourselves, each one in his own position. The personal gear must be stowed and the Mae West put on over the emergency rations jacket. There's no doubt about it's being exciting, though everyone maintains a calm and business-like exterior. This time it seems different than the practice missions. It's a good thing that we allowed ourselves plenty of time in the plane to get settled before starting the engines.

Bill, meanwhile, is checking the flight controls with the "scanners" Dick and Charlie, who each chime in stating the position of the elevator, aileron, and rudder as Bill moves them with the controls. Then on to the rest of the check list for pilot and copilot. Actually, each crew member must satisfy himself that his position is in good shape by using a check list applicable to him. Then each man checks in that everything is Jake! In our crew it serves as a double check since this is the first thing that each man does on getting to the plane, and the last thing before we taxi. Since all the details are on the check list, it assures us that we're as ready as we'll ever be after we finish the list.

We taxi out, after Nick starts up the engines and warms them, in our proper position after Jordan. Take-off time is 1000 and we make it right on the nose. Take-off is made at 30-second intervals between planes on two runways. Jordan is well down the runway before we start our roll. It seems a little too soon to me, but we give her the gun and the engines take hold smoothly. They sound good and the instruments look good -- so Higgy says -- as we gather speed. The scanners meanwhile report that the engines' exhaust looks good. Nick calls out the cylinder head temperatures. It's apparent that everything is O.K. Once off the ground Bill lifts the gear, then the flaps, and Nick closes the cowl flaps to the right setting as we high-tail it after Jordan.

As Jordan begins to turn we turn just inside of him in order to keep cutting down the distance and end up right beside him. It's a pretty sight to see the planes ahead, strung out in a row, ponderous yet graceful, each homing on the plane ahead, gradually cutting down the distance. The lead flight is assembled as we pass the southern tip of Tinian, heading west, having completed a half-circle since take-off. We keep cutting down the power as we approach our proper position until we find the setting needed to keep up with our leader and yet economize on fuel. That's the whole problem in a nut-shell. It isn't too tough to fly formation in the B-29, but to fly "cruise-control formation" -- that's the rub. We keep trying to refine the RPM of our props and the manifold pressure to save all the fuel possible, and yet stay right in there tight.

Still in the large right-hand circle, we are heading back toward the field on the take-off heading and the flights are jockeying into position. We try to look good as we approach the island, but our leader keeps jockeying and Bill and I are in a sweat to keep right in there. The B-29, compared to a light plane, is like a truck compared to a Jeep. We must anticipate the power changes required since it takes only a few seconds for any change to be noticeable in the position of the plane. It looks like a guessing game. We are trying to anticipate the changes that our leader will make before he makes them, but there's a limit -- bulldozers can't be handled like scooters.

After a good bit of unnecessary jockeying we settle down on course for our objective on a heading of 120 degrees. Since this is to be a formation flight, the lead plane of each Squadron will do the navigating and the other planes fly along with their navigators doing "follow the pilot" navigating, as it's called. Hal keeps noting our heading and speeds and plots our position as we go along.

Bill and I are in a sweat after that assembly -- clothes soaking. The plane is not too hot, but the exertion is great, both physical and mental, and either one is sufficient cause to sweat. Wrestling the controls is like trying to throw a steer. Now that we are on course we settle down taking turns and relaxing. Bill turns on the Radio Compass so we have the dance music broadcast from Saipan. The relaxation is pleasant. Both of us wanted to look over Tinian and Saipan as we assembled, but could not, except for what we could see unroll beyond the lead plane upon whom we were flying. The old brain was whirling at a terrific rate -- little time then to record the thoughts. Now, as I relax, the question again returns. "Can I actually do it?" Though we have flown countless formations in the past and made many join-ups I can't help wondering when we approach the plane we're guiding on, trying to adjust our position to his, "will we be able to hold it in there!" It just doesn't seem possible that these huge planes can be made to fly close formation, something like the thought that the bumble-bee cannot fly, considering its dimensions and wing-area. Yet we do, and, sweating, we manhandle the "big bird" into place and hold it there. Maybe it's a phobia I acquired somewhere, but it's there -- the thought that we just can't hold this big plane in close with safety for all.

Our rest is short-lived. It seems there is some kind of race on. The Squadron was together, but now some are dropping back, and so are we, even though we are carrying more power -- much more -- than we were briefed would be used. So we shove on the coal and recompute how much fuel we have for this merry chase. Instead of 200, we are now doing an indicated 230 m.p.h., still climbing and not catching up. Somebody's got their wires crossed up front, or else they're forgetting about the "tail-end Charlies" who always have a hard time saving fuel and jockeying to keep up with the complacent leaders. Instead of the briefed 2100 R.P.M. 31 inches of Mercury Manifold Pressure we are using 2400 43.

Nick reports that the cylinder head temperatures, the old bug-a-bee of the B-29, are climbing. No wonder, at this power setting. We're either going to be forced to drop back or endanger our engines. We look over at "Litch's" plane. He's having the same trouble. Finally each of us takes turn catching up and dropping back. The engines are running too hot. It seems our squadron leader has given up the idea of catching the lead squadron which is now out of sight. We have out-distanced the 2nd, too. Ray Ramsey, leading ours, apparently knows someone will run out of gas if we don't. The high power requires more fuel proportionately for the distance covered.

After approximately two and a half hours of these difficulties we arrive near the target area. The gunners are at their target guns and the turrets are energized, ready for action. Hal has set in the necessary data into the hand set, which does the computing for the remote turrets automatically. Jake is on the bombsight and the front gun sight controlling the upper forward turret. We will drop our bombs on the lead plane as briefed instead of Jake using the bombsight himself. However, he keeps it ready, just in case. There appears to be almost solid cloud cover over the Truk Island area and we were to do visual bombing. The briefing officer and weather men did not anticipate this possibility. But it's our baby, so Ray goes about trying to find the target and the Squadron gathers in close for mutual protection. Where are those fighters -- and the flak? Are we going to get by without opposition? Over on the right, ahead, there appears to be a hole in the lower clouds and our formation heads over that way. Apparently Ray has found the right hole over the right island. If so, we're mighty lucky.

The bomb doors of Jordan's plane drop open, apparently the lead plane has opened his, so we follow suit and shift the power up to hold position. Bill takes care of the power, flicking the toggle switches that control the propeller pitch on each engine. I keep the throttles and the wheel. It looks like a wrestling match again and I feel the sweat trickle down my sides under the coveralls and my collar is too tight. Over the interphone Higgy is checking with Jonesy and the gunners, but no fighters, evidently. Jake crouches behind his nose sight and holds the bomb toggle release in his hand. He keeps his eye on Jordan, waiting for the bombs to fall as his signal. It must be turbulent today over the target, judging from the way Jordan's plane bounces around -- or is he just jockeying? I'll see him if he is when we get back, for I don't enjoy these arm and shoulder calisthenics. His plane is tossing like a cork. Beyond I can see the other planes holding in close, so we edge in. It's easy to see the side of Jordan's helmet now and the blister gunner can be seen.

There go the bombs from Ramsey in the lead. Now Jordan lets his go and Jake presses the toggle. The plane leaps up and I shove the nose down to counteract. Bill closes the bomb bay doors and the formation turns right off the target. Everyone is in tight now. I can see the turrets turning in the other planes, combing the skies. The gunners are disappointed not to see enemy planes -- not a shot yet -- but I'm glad. Yet I'm glad the gunners have the competitive spirit. Maybe we'll need it someday -- who knows? I wiggle the wheel -- "you got it". Bill takes the controls and sticks in on Jordan's wing as we continue the breakaway from the target. Apparently we found a hole in the clouds after making a radar run and the bombs were dropped visually. Dick and Charlie report seeing the airstrip down on the island, just like the picture shown in the briefing. Anyway, we'll know after return since many of our planes are carrying strike cameras which take pictures automatically of the area below, beginning with the release of the bombs.

Looking over to the right where Jake indicates, we see that Donnell's plane cannot close the bomb doors. They've had trouble with those air operated doors every time they've flown. The rest of the planes have electrically operated doors which take a long time to open, whereas the air operated doors open instantly, thus not tipping off the enemy ahead of time when the bombs will be dropped -- a good feature, but not so good if they won't close. By this time many of us are low on fuel, having less than we expected at this point, according to the briefing data, and the open doors will serve as an increased drag, requiring more power and more fuel to be used. J. P. Jones leaves the others and tags on to Donnell to "buddy" him home, just in case. The rest of us proceed home in flights. Jordan, Litchfield, and our plane stay together for the balance of the trip home. It's a lot of formation practice, but the work is enjoyable. It's fun to fly formation, even with this big old truck. Bill and I alternate in taking the controls. The weather remains good all the way home and at 1600 we see Tinian dead ahead through a break in the clouds.

The planes each, in turn, peel off and go in to land. We are last, being on the left. Litchfield peels off to the right, entering the right hand traffic pattern, then Jordan a few seconds later, then ourselves. Tinian looks good to us. We see it in terms of chow, rest, and the first mission completed successfully. George has replaced Charlie at the right blister, and we again have the benefit of the Dorchester, Massachusetts, accent over the interphone. Nick, from the engineer's position, says "George, tell me something. If they pronounce Worchester "Wooster", why don't you call Dorchester "Dooster"? And George disgustedly comes back with "a farmer from Illinois wouldn't understand anyway. What difference does it make to you, and you from "Why Not", Illinois! You should talk." Nick says "Well I'll see you later 'bout that." and returns to his chores on the panel, checking his instruments and ascertaining that all is in readiness to land. The "put-put" is on, the gear is down, flaps coming down, and everything set. The landing is uneventful at 1630.

Shortly after we have returned to the parking area we see Donnell pass over the field accompanied by Jones, so we know that everyone is back, without a shot fired. We feel that we're in the swing now, more than before. Now we can build furniture meaningfully. We'll need comfortable quarters to rest in between the missions, for we mean to live a long life on this island, enemy not withstanding.

To make the day complete we learn from the developed pictures that our Squadron's bombs hit squarely on the target. We easily forgive the jokers ahead, whoever they were, who made the mission a race in violation of the briefed plan. In the critique we'll iron it out so that it won't happen again. Unfortunately our flight dropped the bombs too late. The delay between the bombs of the squadron leader and Jordan was just enough to throw our flight's bombs beyond, into the water. The Japs will probably be eating fish tonight.

All planes returned safely with no casualties. Let's hope our luck holds out. Now for the MAINLAND. 1 down ? to go.

Chapter 7 Search Mission

February 11, 1945 – No. 2

"First Enemy Fire"

It is February tenth, the day of the big mission on Japan for the two Groups of our Wing who arrived first on Tinian, well ahead of the rest of our group. We are all reminded that this is serious business. A plane exploded on take-off, leaving only small pieces of scrap metal behind. Next we learn that two planes collided over the target, several were shot down by enemy fighters, and four "ditched" on the way home.

In the evening Crew 2409 is among those summoned to the Briefing Building. There we find eleven other crews from the group, three of these being from our Squadron. The briefing is held amid a certain amount of secrecy. In attendance are a number of Naval officers, all pilots. It seems that we are to participate in a "Search" mission. Lt. (S. C.) Czobek is to be our observer. The purpose of this mission is twofold: first, to locate the enemy so that our Navy can clear the sea of Jap shipping, and second (and at the same time), to find and report those Jap picket boats which serve to warn the Japs that our planes are coming to bomb them long before their arrival at the Empire. In this way the Japs cannot prepare for our arrival and the raids will be more effective and at a lower loss rate for us.

The briefed plan is for the planes to report to the Wing Ground Station back here any enemy shipping sighted, also to send the same message in the clear (without code) on 4475, the frequency which U. S. naval vessels guard. The Navy can then proceed to eliminate some of the reported vessels by proceeding to the locality indicated by the planes. The area to be searched extends over 770 miles long (east and west) and some 200 miles wide (north and south). This area lies to the north of the Bonin Islands -- Sofu Rock will be found in the middle of it. To cover this area the planes are to fly in loose formation up on a northwest heading toward the Japanese Islands, then to turn on a due north heading, still in formation. While on this heading the planes are to "peel off" at regular intervals, taking up an east heading. In this way the planes will be covering parallel stretches of water several miles on either side of the path of the planes. Our Naval strength in the area consists of three submarines which will be on the lookout for any messages, and will proceed to carry out the liquidation of the enemy. With our plans all ready, the briefing breaks up and we return to our tents and to bed. We are aware of the responsibility of this mission and are eager for our first sight of the Japs. It would be a pleasure to locate and help eliminate some of the enemy in this fashion. Apparently the Army and Navy are teaming up -- most surprising, but gratifying!

After "sacking up" to try and get some rest despite noisy neighbors, the rain begins. All night we hear it beat against the canvas and in my corner I keep hoping the seams will hold. The foot of the bed gets wet, but comfort is retained by gradually drawing up the extremities just ahead of the inflow. At 0300 we are awakened and unhappily leave our warm, if damp, beds. What an hour to be up!

Our tent mates Preston, Goodwin, Rinne, and Hett (the officers of Preston's crew) go on sleeping. Bill and I watch a pair of clogs float down the center of the tent. "Do you think these guys will float away if we don't wake them?" Bill says -- it's all we can do to keep from warning them of their danger "for their own good, of course". We envy their sleeping -- not much! Water is coursing all around the raised floor pieces which we each have beside our beds. It looks like a good chance that they'll be washed away, bed and all. Probably wouldn't waken them, either. Jake looks unhappily at his bed and shakes his head while girding on all the divers bits of equipment.

At 0400 we have breakfast and then to a refresher briefing at 0445. There we pick up our Naval observers and truck for the flight line. Lt. Czobek had not yet ridden in a B-29, so he is looking forward to it. Our increasing wakefulness is deepened by the downpour. Water leaks in the truck until we're all wet. It trickles down into the shoes, down the collar and in through the seams of the G-I coats – _some_ raincoats!

Dirty shoes and wet clothes soil the plane when we get inside. We dislike to get our airborne home dirty, but once inside, it's dry. We don't waste any time and after preflight inspection and check lists we taxi out, barely able to see a hundred yards through the rain. The Tower doesn't help us in relaying instructions, since radio silence is maintained by all out-going planes -- no use telling the Japs we're coming ahead of time, they seem to know it soon enough as it is -- so we proceed to taxi out to the runway, led by a Jeep containing supervisory personnel, who apparently think that we'll be able to go. Lt. Czobek, behind a wry face, inspects the dismal prospects and says "I'm hungry", at which we laugh and point out that "We haven't even started yet". It's four hours now since we ate, and we must go at least another eleven or twelve, and all we have are a few rather still and tasteless sandwiches.

The rain continues and we sit, waiting for that open spot. This can't be possible according to the weather man, but we wait on. The briefing staff didn't foresee the possibility of this kind of weather. At 0900 the rain becomes lighter and visibility increases until we're able to see almost to the end of the runway, which is about a mile, so it appears safe to go and now the "expediter" drives up and says that we're clear to go. We start the engines, run them up and check them and take off with very little fuss. We follow behind Jake Schad who is to lead the Squadron planes, and he turns immediately on the course for Japan, or the "Empire" as it's called. It's the first time that we've headed directly up to the northeast. We're getting mighty close to the big league and we're ready. Today we may catch our first sight of the Japs. Lt. Czobek is prepared to identify the Jap vessels, if and when they are sighted. At present we help to locate him comfortably on the flight deck, which is the area between the pilot and copilot, extending along beside the engineer. There he stretches out on some heavy clothes. Bill and I stretch and dispose of the feet and legs while the autopilot does the work.

Glancing ahead we see a plane turn back, apparently aborting. One propeller is windmilling and then is feathered. It's Pete Fortune. Evidently it's engine trouble, but not serious. So we close up the gap and leave Pete to return to Base. Up until now we have seen only four of the twelve planes scheduled, despite the fact that Schad has slowed up to let those behind catch up. We begin to wonder, as I'm sure Schad is wondering, whether the bad weather prevented the others from leaving and the flight was postponed until better weather. So we are not surprised to hear a message from Schad to the effect that we'd better change the peel-off interval from three to twelve minutes and in that way cover the area specified, even though skimpily. Since we are on the right, we'll be the first to peel off.

During this time we are all on the look-out, since we are hoping to sight some of our survivors from the Empire raid. The ditched planes are not all accounted for as yet, and the Army and Navy planes are searching for the survivors where they were last reported. So in addition to our plans to find some Japs we are hoping to sight some ditched aircrew members. Dick, Charlie, and Jonesy are rotating in the waist blisters so that two are on duty at all times. George watches out of the tail for awhile and then comes forward to help in the blisters. Gabby meanwhile has the radar set in operation, first testing its operation and then looking for shipping and survivors. He hopes to find some of the new reflectors that have been put in life-rafts, which are supposed to show up on the radar scope. We keep sweeping our eyes back and forth until the strain grows into full-fledged eye-and-headaches. Several times there's a flare-up of hope, but it's only a coral reef near the surface or a stretch of choppy water. We keep the radio compass on 500 kilocycles which is the frequency used by the emergency sets, the "Gibson Girl", included in each set of ditching equipment.

During this time we keep the plane on C-1 autopilot and fly a loose formation on Schad, governing our position by climbing or diving enough to get more on "the step" or slightly off of it. The "step" in the B-29 is a peculiar characteristic. It is the altitude of the plane giving the maximum speed and range out of the power being used. It might be compared to the like quality found in the motorboat which gets on the "step" after reaching a certain speed, and then gets in its best performance. In the B-29 it's like going downhill on the level, since it is reached by diving the plane enough to get the tail high and then leveling off but still retaining the increased forward speed. So Bill and I experiment with the autopilot, holding our position without use of the throttles, once we have them set.

Schad turns onto the north leg of the trip. We are almost there. At 0330 Schad signals and we turn on the east course by ourselves. Now we're really on the search. The crew is advised and Gabby sets up his radar to get the best possible returns at distance. Lt. Czobek in the nose is scanning ahead, while Jake, Bill and I are looking out the sides and ahead. For over two hours we hold the heading and it begins to look like no go. The headaches have been forgotten, but are now remembered with the disappointment of no Japs. There is a haze over the water which renders visibility fuzzy. In addition there are fluffy, clearly defined cumulous clouds obscuring the horizon.

Bill and I exhort the crew not to give up, but it does look fruitless. Boy, what a lot of water! Hour after hour not a bit of land, just unending water. In some spots it ripples, in others there are long swells, and still others have a limpid, quiet look, very placid, but always more water. Dusk is creeping up on us making us squint a little more. Gabby calls, "There's some shipping dead ahead." Instantly the crew becomes more alert. Jonesy and the gunners check their sighting stations for the umpteenth time, and we strain our eyes ahead. "Appears to be several vessels" Gabby continues, "About ten miles away." We hold our course and see ahead in the distance the rough outline of some objects on the water. No doubt about it, there are ships there. Lt. Czobek looks intently a minute -- "Jap ships: he informs us, and immediately begins to try and identify the type ship so that Al on the radio can send the information. It must be sent as soon as possible and must be right. Just as we determine that the ships are proceeding on a southerly heading, they sight us. Apparently there are escort vessels there. The ships begin to re-arrange themselves, some going to the perimeter of the area in which the ships are located.

Utterly absorbed in recognizing the ships and getting a good look at them, we come up a little too close. Our altitude is now 1300 feet and we are within easy range on their guns. This we learn when we see several black puffs to one side of us. Jonesy, Dick, and Charlie in the blisters, and George in the tail, call out the location of the puffs, each in turn, and it's apparent that they are tracking us. We veer to the left and start a right-hand turn about the ships. The flak creeps gradually closer until it's apparent that we should do evasive action. We make several turns to throw them off but still hold to our large circle. Looking at the escort ships we are surprised to see large flashes of flame from the decks. Lt. Czobek says "They're firing 3 inch shells at us now." Their chances are as good as if they were hunting jack rabbits with a .22, but we can see they are in earnest. They would probably throw belaying pins at us if we came closer. What a tempting dish for our gunners, and we could probably hit them and hurt badly, but thinking of the possible fighter interception around Chichi-jima I ask Jonesy to hold fire. Our main job is to report these ships and let the Navy dispatch them. Meanwhile, we still must get ourselves home. We regret this. What a target! And they certainly don't seem friendly. When the first shells were fired, George in the tail, in a tone of utter amusement said, "Hey, they're firing on us." Someone else added, "They don't like us." And so we receive our first enemy fire.

Meanwhile, Al has sent the information back to the ground station and received an acknowledgment, and now he sends it in the clear on the Navy frequency. We receive no acknowledgment of this since our Naval vessels do not care to reveal their position. We have been told they will hear us, still it's uncertain. As we are preparing to leave the area, with the Jap ships watching us, no doubt with dread, Gabby comes in on the interphone again with, "There are some other ships twenty miles to the northeast, apparently heading to join the others." So we go up to investigate. Sure enough, there are some more Jap ships, and they start to scatter when they see us. What they gain by scattering is beyond me. In union there's strength, whereas alone, we could maul them pretty badly. Lt. Czobek identifies the type ship and Al radios it in. Among the ten ships it seems there are four cargo vessels, two transports and four escorts. Their heading indicates they are going to the Bonin Islands, probably to Chichi-jima or Haha-jima.

By this time it is almost dark. The last three boats were more like shadows on the water, so with satisfaction we turn toward home, happy in having had success. What a tonic it is to know that a job has been done and that you have participated. On the way home we continue to look for American survivors of the last Mainland raid, but no luck. Occasionally, we think we are seeing a blinking light but it turns out to be a star low on the horizon. On a black night without a moon, such as tonight, it is hard to tell where the water ends and the sky begins. In fact, when the horizon is obscured by nightfall, the only way in which to know your plane is level is by looking at the instruments. If the artificial horizon says you're level, you're level.

Remaining alert with the gunners at the guns, we pass the Jap-held islands with no enemy contact, and continue south into the blackness. Except for the dried sandwiches with practically no filling, two to a man, we haven't eaten all day, a period from 0300 this morning to now at 2200. Jake, Bill, and Nick have headaches and so have I. In fact, everyone is feeling mighty poor. Too bad the food situation must be like this.

At last, tired but grateful, we arrive back at Tinian where clear weather prevails. For the first time, we use the night-time search-lights which are for the purpose of helping the returning planes to land. The search-light extends west from the field, making a path beside which we fly in lining up for landing on the runway. It guides us and yet does not blind -- very ingenious. In addition, there are search-lights pointing directly upward marking three of the four corners of the traffic pattern over Tinian, around which we fly.

After landing, we fill out a questionnaire and learn that the Ground Station garbled our message. We check this and find out that the mistake is theirs. Our logs and their acknowledgments of the messages are incontrovertible. Finally, they reluctantly agree, and we feel disgusted over their sloppiness. At least we know that our message went directly to the U.S. Naval units in the area, who will take care of the Japs. We now regret not having fired on them.

So we go to "sack up" with No. 2 behind us. We are now the first crew to encounter the Japs, the first to be fired on, and the first with a flak hole in our plane. We enjoy the distinction 'though we are sure it means little to anyone else.'

What's next?

Chapter 8 Tokyo

March 4, 1945 – No. 3

"The First Big One"

The war effort seems to be redoubling itself throughout the entire area now. It seems very personal to us. February 12th and 13th the Navy and Marines practiced invasion tactics on the west coast of Tinian, just opposite our area, so we had a ring-side seat. The Navy planes simulated bombing and strafing the beach while the landing barges came in under a protective Navy barrage to land the Marines. On February 16th we heard the news that the full scale attack was made in earnest on Iwo Jima and that the Marines were fighting a terrible battle with great losses. At the same time we saw the result of our search missions which cleared the sea of Jap shipping. A large Naval Task Force moved into this area and launched a big attack on Japan herself with Carriers and Navy planes participating. The Navy sent thanks and a commendation to the Army Groups which had participated in the search, clearing out Jap shipping.

With all of these events transpiring about us, crew members were eager to go when the February 25th raid on Tokyo was announced. To our disappointment we were not included, so we helped out as "expediters" in getting the other planes off. Our crew has been made a "flight leader" in the meantime, which only served to increase our interest in the events that followed.

The mission on February 25th turned out to be the biggest B-29 raid yet -- almost 200 planes. Two planes of the 73rd Wing on Saipan collided over the target and a "superdumbo" ditched, of all things. (A superdumbo is a B-29 used as a rescue facility for those who have ditched. It sends messages, gives positions and drops supplies.) But these were the only losses. It was a hair-raising mission, so we heard, since the clouds were thick over the target and all the planes were milling around in them, flying blind and dropping their bombs individually at all altitudes.

Internal dissension reared its head when our Group Commanding Officer publicly declared that he was going to evaluate and take the rating away from a fellow pilot of ours. The Airplane Commanders, as representatives of the crews, rallied around and protested to the Wing Commanding Officer in an effort to clear the unjustly accused officer, and by way of explanation lodged a complaint against the supervisory personnel of our Group and Squadron. The very trouble we had so vainly tried to correct while still in the States had caught up with us, so we decided to fight it out. In the States we had tried, without success, to remove a superior officer (who was only one of the many in command who were incompetent as we saw it). We knew then, as we know now, the danger of trying to buck the Army system or the people in it, but incompetence in units going overseas -- our units -- was so serious that we decided to try to do something about it. We failed then, even though all the combat airplane commanders stood together and submitted appropriate paperwork. Now, when the old trouble had come to a head in the threatened "evaluation" of one of us, we again stood together. It seems almost unbelievable that, in the United States Army, one man can unjustly charge another with incompetency and have that man demoted. So, fully knowing how little chance we have, we decide to try to clear this pilot, to whom this unfair thing is happening as it might to any of us.

Another event bears mentioning. On February 28th our crew led a practice formation to Guguan Island with the Deputy Group Leader as passenger. We flew the usual formation and he thought it swell. We also got some pictures of good formation flying. We were very pleased to have his commendation and though we were surprised, since the Army we knew never praised and only censured, we felt that our effort to do the job right was bearing fruit.

March 1st we were saddened to see E. E. McElroy, our ranking Airplane Commander, leave the Squadron. Mac is one of the surviving pilots of the Doolittle raid against Japan. A bad back, resulting from his parachute jump on that occasion, has continually pained him on our flights which require so many hours in the same seat, so now he is going to give it some attention. While in our Group and Squadron he has been a spark plug, both in his job as Flight Leader and as one of the boys who always manages to find something to laugh about when the going's rough. He's shared our tough times when we have complained about the quality of our supervisory personnel, and done all he could to help change things. Extremely competent and willing to work, we find it difficult to understand how the Army could neglect a man who has done so much. Mac has been in grade for over two years, while his copilot on the Doolittle raid has been a Major for a long time. It is certainly a reflection on General Doolittle and the Army, and in addition, our Commanding Officer who hasn't seen fit to promote Mac. Now we wish him good luck and wave as he leaves in the ambulance for the hospital.

In the midst of these events we see our crew listed on the mission board, scheduled for the Tokyo mission, undated as yet. We all check our gear to be sure we have everything necessary for the "big league" and go to the briefing on March 3rd. The Group has been sobered by its first loss, of a crew in the 2nd Squadron in a mysterious mid-air explosion just before striking the water after going out of control. This crew was going out on a search mission. All were killed instantly. Now we find the crews going out on this mission are Holton, Jordan, Alger, Schad, Jones, Sonwager and Boynton.

The mission is going to be maximum effort, which means that every plane capable of flying will be sent, so we know it's a big one. We're glad to be getting a hand in now, no sense letting the Navy do all the work. The target is the Nakajima Aircraft Engine factory on the western outskirts of Tokyo. The secondary target, in case the primary target is "socked in" by weather, is the residential-industrial area zone No. 1 of Tokyo. The bomb load will consist of 500 lb. G.P. with a total gross weight of 134,000 lb. Our position, flying plane No. 2 this time, is to be No. 2 of the lead flight of the Squadron, that is, the Deputy Leader. The 1st Squadron will be the lead Squadron of the Group. Bombing altitude for our Wing will be 28000 feet. The flight out will be made on the deck, with the climb made just before arrival at Hamamatsu, the rendezvous point, so that bombing altitude might be reached just in time for the assembly.

Hamamatsu is the town which is located on the southern coast of Honshu, in a southeasterly direction from Tokyo. All our guns will be loaded with 750 rounds of ammunition each, so we are going fully armed. Both flak and fighters are presented to us as being very heavy in this area. We have no illusions about having an easy time of it.

But we are ready, willing and eager to get going. After the briefing the men get up, hike up their pants, and go to get some chow, trying to appear calm and unexcited. We're ready. The cool air outside the briefing building is most welcome. The heart is beating mighty strong -- like the old days before a football game. I know the others around are feeling the exciting stimulation. It's odd, for we know the dangers -- whether this trip has our number on it or not, but everyone is eager to go. After a certain amount of practicing for it (and all we've done is practice, even to dress rehearsals!) nothing will satisfy but the real thing. At this particular time we feel a very real part of the war. Having come fairly recently from the States and been absorbed into the combat area, we have perspective and know the part we play, and now we're scheduled to take that part.

In the mess hall everyone falls on the food, liberal helpings of "C" rations with coffee on the side, and diced fruit for dessert, canned delicacies. Bill and Hall fill their canteens with cold water. Jake and I get some hard candy from the Mess Sgt. and we return to the tent. On the way we stop to pat "Gyro" and "Turbo" who worry our pants legs. The long leash permits their bothering everyone within two tent distance and still not get away to roam the Island. The two Cockers are well known in the area. They like everyone but the "Gooks", the native Islanders, who are part Jap, Okinawan, and Korean, and they bark furiously at them.

Our tent mates went on the last mission to Tokyo and have told us wild stories of their milling around in the "soup" over the target with some 200 other planes. We had a good laugh at the story they told. It seems that a camera man for the "Air Force" magazine went along with Preston. He was assured that the weather would be ideal and that he would get excellent chances for pictures over Tokyo. As it turned out, all he saw over the target was the inside of a cloud. It's a wonder, we agreed, that someone didn't drop bombs on someone else -- or did they? Now, as old veterans of one mission, knowing this is our first raid on the "Mainland", they begin to heckle us: "Don't forget your weapons." "Too bad, this is going to be a rough one" (with shaking of heads) "Say, who's going to get your bed?" "Have you willed your furniture to anyone?" We all enjoy the banter, even with its significance, and pass back appropriate rejoinders. Bill says, "You fellows would enjoy cleaning up the tent and the area in the morning, wouldn't you? -- Don't work too hard." We enjoy these few minutes before going to the trucks, by mentally appraising the items on hand and whether we have forgotten anything. We enjoy the banter; we know they wish they were going, too, but it's our turn and there aren't enough planes in commission for them to go. I even feel a little sorry for them, knowing they'll be thinking of the ones gone, wishing they were adding another one toward their quota.

We enjoy our tent mates. In each tent two crews are quartered: in this area, the officers; across the road, the enlisted men. We get to know each other very well. The officers of Preston's crew are Clark Preston, the pilot and proud father of a three year old daughter; Don Goodwin, Michigan copilot, humorously argumentative; Lloyd Rinne, navigator, youthful Nebraska philosopher, who believes in spending most of his spare time in the "sack"; Al Hett, Bombardier, New Yorker in love, who writes her all the time. The eight of us get along fine. About this time, since no conversation in our tent goes long without mention of it, someone says "Who's got some food?" "Food," Clark echoes and we all join in caressing the word. "Did you say you had some food?" "Why yes, I'll be glad to help you eat some food." By this time, everyone having joined in the oft repeated routine, we shout farewells and troop out of the tent headed for the trucks which wait in front of Operations.

Still not having a plane of our own, we are scheduled to fly No. 4, the old reliable. Even at this time, this plane has stood up very well and gone on almost every flight, but we'd still like to have our own plane. Actually no plane will ever mean so much to us as 550, the plane that we flew overseas. It was a blow to lose it. Five of the fifteen originals were ordered sent to Saipan as replacements. Unfortunately, the Engineering Officer picked ours as one of the five. But someone had to lose their plane -- it might as well be us, so we rationalize without feeling bitter. Who knows, maybe we'll get the first brand new plane to come as a replacement later to our squadron.

After picking up our A-3 bags with flight equipment in them, we direct the truck to the hardstand where No. 4 is parked. The usual preflight inspection is begun, and combat stations checked. The crew chief gives us a resume of the plane's recent performance, which apparently has been good. No major repairs of any kind necessary, and it weathered the recent Tokyo raid quite well. The Form 1, which is the written history of the plane, bears out the Sgt.'s remarks. Well, if you must fly a strange ship, it's encouraging to get one that isn't a Jonah. We tell the crew chief we'll take good care of her.

Nick dip-sticks the fuel tanks to check if they're full. Bill is figuring the weight and balance. Jake is checking the bombs and racks, while Hal stows his navigational gear. Both of them talked to the members of other crews about their specialties to find if this plane has any peculiarities. Last minute assignment of this plane to us prevented our personally checking it over this afternoon. We don't like this and wish we could be given more notice so we could get to know the plane better. Al checks the radio and Gabby the radar. Jonesy, Dick, Charlie and George give the guns a last minute check-over to see if the ammunition is in the tins properly and ready to fire. It is, so now we are very careful since the guns are "hot". The ammunition includes incendiary and armor-piercing shells, the former serving as "tracer" bullets, showing the path taken by the rounds as they're fired.

All goes well, so we get aboard and taxi out. There's no denying it's exciting this time -- the first time for Japan, and it's impressive in the dead of the night to see these planes roll out one by one, each squat and massive, yet graceful. An eerie appearance is given the scene by the wing, formation, and recognition lights.

Each left wing-tip has a red light while the right has a green light. Along the top of the wings are blue formation lights, three along each wing. Under the belly are the red, amber, white and green recognition lights. These and the white light on top are generally left off on the ground to prevent overheating the plastic covering. The reds, greens, and blues, marking the extremities of the planes, including the red tail lights, give an artistic, colorful setting, hardly in keeping with the job, yet awe-inspiring. It beats anything I've ever seen in teamwork or precision performance -- and I've seen the Aquacades, Ice Ballets -- even the Rockettes! Ahead of our plane, along the straight taxi-way, are ten or twelve other planes maintaining the same interval between planes, almost nose to tail. Ahead of them around the bend in the taxi-way are another dozen. Only the slight coral dust stirred up by the props dims our view of the colorful wing lights. Everything else is black.

Finally we roll out onto the runway that we are motioned to take by the flagman and we begin to run up the engines preparatory to releasing the brakes. The flagman's light goes out, the brakes are released and we're off. Each crew member is at his post, securely tied down and with all emergency gear properly worn. The engines sound good and Bill shouts out the speed and states that everything looks O.K. After reaching the point of "no-turning-back" on the runway, we concentrate on getting off the ground. The haze combined with the blackness of the night make it advisable to make the take-off on instruments, which we do. In a plane as stable and solid as the B-29 the instruments are doubly reliable. The take-off is accomplished successfully, despite the heavy load, and we fly the prearranged headings and times until we are safely out of the vicinity of Tinian and Saipan. From now on it's one-way traffic, except for the occasional plane in trouble that is turning back or being abandoned. We are within sight of Holton, the lead plane of the Squadron, so we decide to keep him in sight. If we can stick with him until time for assembly it will be effected much easier, since the other planes can spot two together easily. For two or three hours it is easy, but bad weather cuts visibility until we have only occasional glimpses of the other plane, then we lose sight altogether as we proceed into solid clouds that obscure all but our own lights. We're in a world of our own, but we don't feel lonely for we are all too aware of the other ships on all sides of us. Every light is turned on to the bright position, and we hope that what we don't see will see us -- if someone else is going to start crowding. The Homing Signal sent out by the lead plane cannot be heard at all because of the static electricity in the clouds. Perhaps later we'll hear the long dashes and see the radio compass needle swing in the direction of the leader. However, we are several hours out. Maybe the weather will clear up and we can join up in the clear.

By daylight the clouds have lowered further. Our 1000 feet is still in most of the thick clouds whose tops we can't estimate. Sounds of life start to come from back in the blister section and the radar room. Since about 0200 each man in turn has caught naps. Jonesy, Dick, Charlie, and George have alternated two at a time in the blister seats while the other two slept. Al has put his head on the radio table to get a little shut-eye. Jake, in the nose, is sound asleep. Nick is even dosing a little in his engineer's seat. Only Hal works unceasingly over his chart --

"We're an hour and forty-five minutes out from the assembly area." Nick hears Hal on the interphone and stirs -- "I'll start transferring the fuel, O.K.?" he inquires, and with the answer "O.K." he warns everyone throughout the plane to douse the cigarettes, and the acknowledgments come in. Bill works with the radio compass, trying again to get the homing signal from Holton. "There it is," he shouts. I turn over to the compass position on the jackbox and hear the series of long dashes followed by the identification letter. "That's him." So we turn off the radios to lessen the danger of any possible trouble with electricity and the gas fumes that might accompany the transfer of fuel. Since we are flying low the pumps are making the transfer rapidly (altitude cuts their efficiency), so it isn't long until all the fuel is out of the center wing tank into the wings. In this way no fuel will be trapped where it cannot be of any use, for in the center wing section the fuel cannot be used. After enough is used out of the wings to permit more to be pumped in there, we do so, so that over the target we'll not be handicapped if the fuel transfer system is damaged by enemy action -- every gallon counts.

"Is that Holton out there level at 11 o'clock?" asks Jake, who has come to life. Bill and I look and see in the distance a plane passing through the lighter clouds that now surround us. Our radio compass swings until it points toward this plane at the same time that the long dashes come over, so we're fairly sure it is. But it's time to climb and we can't catch them just now, so we hold our course and begin to climb. We are to rendezvous at an altitude of 28,000 feet and that will take some time to reach. Meanwhile the crew members are advised to put on flak vests and all gear. Nick leaves his position to help Bill and me into our equipment. Jake makes out all right with an occasional helping hand. First the heavy jacket, then the emergency rations jacket, and over this the Mae West attached properly to the dinghy (one-man life raft) whose container rests under us on the seat and is fastened to the parachute. The parachute comes next and over this comes the flak-vest. By this time we have a beer-barrel appearance. My gear almost touches the control column. On the head goes the helmet with ear phones to which is attached they oxygen mask containing a microphone. Over this head gear is placed the metal flak helmet, something like the infantry helmet. The flak vest is shaped like a catcher's vest in baseball, it is a series of over-lapping metal plates covering the body fore and aft. In addition we have the bullet plate glass in front of the pilot and copilot and the metal armor plate directly behind their seats, and each crew member has metal flak curtains on the floor and side of his position.

It has turned quite cold this far north. Actually it's as though we had traveled from Florida to Maine, so no wonder it's chilly -- and it's still winter. As we pass the 8000 foot mark Nick puts on the pressurizing equipment. This permits air to be blown into the cabin from the inboard engines, thus compressing the air in the cabin, so no matter to what altitude we go, the air inside remains at a constant pressure. We usually set the regulator to maintain the equivalent of an 8000-foot altitude. At this point we find that the air conditioner doesn't work, so there'll be no heat. It's quite chilly. The crew is notified that there will be no heat, and everyone accepts it as one of those things that happens unexpectedly in flying. Something always happens that even the best-laid plans don't anticipate.

Ahead of us we spot a number of other planes climbing on the same heading that we are holding, and all a good bit higher than we are. Evidently we should have started climbing a little sooner. Now Jake and Bill are trying hard to keep the windows from frosting up and it seems as though the more they rub the more frosted they become. Now we can't see out of the front section of the nose, but Bill and I can still see out of the sides. Bill checks with Jonesy and states that the guns are all set, the turrets energized and everyone at his post. Gabby gives us a radar position report which corroborates the position that Hal had just given from his chart. We only have a few more miles to go. The clouds have been left far below and it is clear above 20,000 feet. We can't pick out Holton, so we proceed toward the group of planes that are circling in a left-hand circle, race-track fashion. It appears to be our Squadron.

The entire nose section of our plane has frosted now. We can't see ahead. Bill's side has frosted about the edges of each glass until only a foot remains in the two back windows. My side is frosted now, except for the double glass at my left shoulder. Evidently the dead air between the panes of glass cuts the frosting. It's apparent that we can't fly the originally scheduled position, so if we're going to join this formation at all it will have to be on the right-hand side so that we can take advantage of the only clear window in the cabin. Up until now the windows posed no problem, but it looks as if we're going to get into this swarm of birds without any eyes. Well, there's no choice, so here goes. The gunners are asked to help out even more than usual by reporting all planes in our vicinity so that we can avoid any collision courses. Meantime we circle wide, staying to the right of the planes circling left. In this way we keep the planes in sight, always on the side of our good window, but we're on the outside of this circle and can hardly keep up for we won't even try to get a position inside the formation. We'll have to tag along on the outside in the No. 2 position of the right-hand flight -- "B" flight. Being assured that there is no one outside of us, bearing on our blind side, we start to close in. There is the big R in a circle which signifies our Group. Now we can read the individual numbers and there appears to be a few outsiders in with our Squadron. Well, that's all right -- the more the merrier -- it means more guns to fire at the fighters.

But where are the fighters? The gunners are combing the skies, particularly on our right side, since we'll be defending the right rear of the formation. It's good to see all the support the close-flying planes give each other. The gunners are at their posts. I see the blister gunners of the B-flight leader, on whose wing we are flying. They are looking around, keeping their hands moving.

Apparently the flight leader is green at this job. One minute he's going forward, the next minute he's dropping back. We try to stick with him and one moment our throttles are forward 'til the engines roar, the next we are depressurizing because it's necessary to pull off the power so as not to pass him. At least 23 inches of mercury must be carried on the inboard throttles in order to keep the air coming into the cabin from the superchargers. What a sloppy way to fly. The plane doesn't like it, either. Up here where the air is thin the superchargers overspeed one minute with power surges, the next they are almost turned off. The sweat is pouring off me, running down inside. I want to tear off the oxygen mask and helmet that seems to bite into my chin. I silently swear, pray, and feel disgust at the character that is making us play crack-the-whip with him. And on top of it all I can't see -- only one window. The gunners are now starting to call attention to other planes in the area, but each time they turn out to be other lone B-29s, trying to find a formation to join. They'd be sitting pigeons for fighters to jump, flying alone like that, so we've been told.

Jake is on the front gunsight. Bill holds the bomb release in his hand and is ready to lean over and open the bomb doors with the toggle switch when the leader opens his doors. In the midst of all this I am aware of the old brain going at a terrific rate. So this is what it's like! I don't like the discomfort. Supposing someone gives us a hard time when I can't even see out. At least I want to see, but this mask, the heavy equipment, the sweat. My shoulders and arms ache -- how much longer is this going to go on? We are on the bomb run now and the formation settles down and it looks like it's going to be easier to hold in there tight without so much wrestling. Wrong again -- we're turning, first one way and then the other. What in the hell is going on? Then Jonesy comes in with "Flak, low at 5 o'clock." George repeats the same and then each begins calling out new bursts, and Dick and Charlie join in. Now they are getting closer with the flak bursts -- there's one in the middle of the formation -- "Flak at 10 o'clock high, 9 level, 8 low." "Any fighter's, Jonesy?" "No, can't see any, no sign yet." "George, how are things back there?" Bill keeps a running check on the crew, and I hear the conversation feed over through my defective jackbox. Though I'm on interphone communication on a very high frequency set, still faintly I can hear the crew talking and it's comforting. Jonesy calls our attention to the flight leader's upper aft turret, which is pointing squarely at our plane. I see their gunner. There's nothing we can do but hope he doesn't massage the button with his thumb. We don't want any U.S. shells for company. Must remember to talk to that A.C. but good!

Then the discomfort sets in again, and I mentally curse. Why can't this mission be as it's supposed to be -- our windows clear, the heat on, this mask off, and a tight, snappy formation without all this jockeying? The leader's bomb doors come open and Bill starts ours open. Al leaves his radio station and informs us that they are opening all right. Dick does the same for the aft bomb bay. We jack up our power to keep our speed despite the drag from the open doors. Still no fighters. Jake is still trying to clean the front window; now he's scraping it off, but it fogs over again -- nothing to do but keep trying. "Jonesy, see anything?" "No, nothing in sight yet." Where are the fighters? But the flak is here. It's hard to be disgusted, prayerful, hopeful and fearful all at once, but a bit of each is with us. I keep thinking that we've got to get through this one so we can return, knowing what it's like and overcome all these obstacles that are fouling us up now -- all of them unexpected. Next time there'll be heat, and a flight leader who doesn't fly all over the sky.

"There they go!", and the bombs are falling from the other planes. Bill pushes the toggle, but no response. The plane doesn't jump as it should when released from a load. Al and Dick check and report that the bombs are still in the bomb bay. "Gotta get rid of them, right now." "Go get 'em Jake." Jake is already fumbling with the release which Bill had turned over to him. Apparently the button is defective. In desperation he hits it against the floor, thereby getting more push behind it than by pressing it with the thumb. "There they go!" chorus Al and Dick. Jake looks up, "Figure, we dropped beyond the secondary." The heavy clouds under us, which obscured the Nakajima Aircraft Works, convinced Jordan, who is leading, that it would be wiser to go on to the secondary target. By this time we are turning right off the target, no doubt passing over Tokyo Bay before getting to the open sea. I try to mentally compute where our bombs must have hit, dropped 1 minute and 20 seconds late, as they were. We were indicating 200 miles per hour, with a tail wind of 80 knots, and the altitude increases the speed across the ground by almost 50%, so our speed is close to 400 miles per hour. Therefore, the bomb must have fallen about 10 miles beyond the No. 1 zone of Tokyo, or somewhere in the dock area while we made the turn to the right. At least they would do damage there, even though not in the briefed area. Who knows, maybe we got some docks or ships. At least it's reasonable to suppose that they did some damage.

Our path since the rendezvous at Hamamatsu has been north to Kofu, the Initial Point for the bomb run, and then almost due east to Tokyo, passing over the heart of the city. The withdrawal is apparently now taking us over the Bay. We are diving slightly now, picking up speed, but not so fast that we lose the planes -- two of them -- that are having bomb door trouble. It seems the doors will not close and at this altitude they must depressurize before any crew member can get into the bomb bay, and that's cold work, too. It's minus 20 on the Centigrade scale outside air thermometer, or about 5 to 10 degrees Fahrenheit -- too cold for comfort. Further, the air pressure for those air-operated doors won't build up rapidly at high altitude.

Still no fighters. We're in luck again, but the gunners do not relax their vigilance until we are well out to sea. Now the planes are splitting up into twos and threes for the long return, each flying as best befits the performance of the particular plane with a certain weight and the computed amount of fuel remaining. Nick finally completes his figuring, based on the power settings against time, that have been used thus far. "We have 2500 gallons left, according to my figures." Bill gets out of his position, takes off his gear, and goes over the figures with Nick for a double check. Meanwhile, still on interplane frequency, I listen to the planes with open bomb doors call to the leader. Landing at Iwo is almost out of the question since the battle is raging there, though it might be chanced in an emergency. The fighters are based there now. So it looks like the planes with open doors are in a tough spot. The increased drag set up by the doors as the plane passes through the air at high speed takes a good deal more power to maintain economical cruising airspeed. The pilots are conversing back and forth, suggesting various emergency methods to attempt in correcting the difficulty. It will be nip and tuck whether they can make it back to Base. Other planes have joined those in trouble to "buddy" them home. No one needs us, so we continue on by ourselves. It seems best to fly our own cruise control problem instead of accompanying another plane and adjusting our speed to theirs. We reduce power as low as possible and still maintain airspeed of 185, which is the speed recommended for maximum range cruising at our present weight.

"Is everyone O.K.? Check in." I ask the crew, and from tail to nose, as is our custom, each man chimes in. "Tail, O.K." "Right Blister O.K." "Left Blister O.K." "C.F.C. O.K." Then the front cabin members join in -- Radio, Navigator, Engineer, but we can see each other up here. The checking in is one of the formal parts of our procedure, a part of what the top brass call "Air Discipline". No one needs to sell us on the importance of a set procedure and now we realize it's all the more important when under stress. And I feel a great pride -- maybe the others are thinking this too, as they listen to the check-in -- "Here's a going concern, for these men know their business." There's no fooling around when we are at our jobs -- that is, when on the bomb run, under attack or working a navigational or gunnery problem. Each man is quick to cooperate in the accomplishment of the other man's job as well as his own. We know now, even more than before, that this is the way to do it, and I know that our training is standing us in good stead. Yet, it's more than the training -- it's the type of men we have on this crew. They understand.

Having established the fact that everyone is all right and the plane is undamaged, we go on about the other chores. Hal and Jake are conferring on the bombing data: "Bombs were away at 0959." "The heading was 120 degrees." Bill and Nick are still checking their fuel consumption in order to get as accurate an estimate as possible on the amount remaining. We are far enough out from Japan to be beyond fighter interception, so we have George come up to the blister section from the tail. Nick depressurizes so the bulkhead doors may be opened, and our ears pop. A minute later Gabby comes on the interphone with "George is in, ready to pressurize." Nick builds up the cabin air pressure with the air valves, while we all remove our oxygen masks, which are necessary when we are depressurized. We are well above 20,000 feet and a human being cannot live long without additional oxygen at this altitude.

Meanwhile everyone is removing flak vests and helmets, and sharing the same wonderful sense of relief. Up front everyone has a grin or is jawing about inconsequentials. We've done it! -- been over Japan, flown right over the heart of the city of Tokyo, and we are returning without a scratch. What a break -- it seems almost miraculous. Why, it can be done after all. In fact, everyone except the two with open bomb bay doors are apparently all right. While these thoughts are running through my mind I hear Charlie, Dick and Gabby passing a few remarks, then George starts heckling Nick again. Al and Hal are exploring the food situation. Jake hands back his helmet and vest and shakes his head with a grin, "Well, there's No. 1." I know he feels glad to have it behind him. The bombs hanging up on us is a strain on him, since he feels the responsibility, for the bombs are his department. It will be necessary to report and repair the bomb release button on returning and to see that it doesn't fail again. The whole trip hangs on that button, which can make it a success or failure.

Jake moves aft and helps Nick break out the meager rations. Bill is wearing a relieved smile as he looks over. "Glad that's over," and I whole-heartedly agree. We set up the autopilot and then sag back in our seats. "Tired?" Bill inquires.

"And how -- how about you?" "Not too tired." So we prop up our feet on the rudder-bar and lean our heads back on the head rest. It seems years since we first started on that bomb run. At least a full day's work was done in those few minutes. We know now that we were under a terrible tension. Jake hands us some sandwiches and we open a can of V-8 fruit juice. The canteens are good and cold from standing on the metal floor of the cabin. So we start on the grub and comment on the bomb run in general. Back in the blisters much the same activity is going on. Hal reaches up from his table and gets some sandwiches for Al, who is standing by on the radio. Just at this time it is important for him to monitor the Laison radio. He hears the strike reports and is ready to intercept any emergency messages. We might be able to help out another plane in distress. At the same time I am still on the VHF set on the "C" channel, which is the interplane wave length also, so we have a double check on the other planes in the target area and on the way home. All is quiet at present and Al is able to put away a couple of sandwiches.

Though he eats, Hal stays at work on his chart, plotting our position and checking our course, to see that we fly directly home, in the interest of saving fuel. We are to have tail-winds for several hours. Based on the winds at the various altitudes that the weather department has given us in advance, as the estimated conditions, we decide that the best plan for return is a gradual let-down, for this will enable us to make use of the tail winds that will prevail at various altitudes and also put us under the bad weather several hundred miles to the south -- otherwise we would encounter severe icing in the clouds that would slow us down considerably and take more fuel.

In the blister section the gunners are rotating two at a time on duty and the others making ready to nap. Gabby is on the radar set, keeping an eye out for surface craft, islands ahead, and planes in the vicinity. Bill agrees to keep an eye on things, so I close my eyes for a nap. What a relief to have it over. Thinking back I recall that I saw my first Jap countryside just south of Kofu. It appeared to be a small mountain country with snow. There were trees along the hills and in the many sharp ravines. But part of this was supposition, since our altitude was too great to discern clearly what sort of country it was. Yet I recalled that it looked the way the Ozarks would look in winter with snow, except that the Jap hills had sharp razor backs to the hill tops while the Ozarks are rolling, but the hills were many and small like the Ozarks. The clouds prevented our seeing more of the country, including Fujiyama and Tokyo. Gabby confirmed with the radar that we flew right near Fuji and directly over Tokyo.

At this point I recall the comments of Jonesy and Dick concerning the plane upon whose wing we flew. The upper rear turret was kept pointing at us for quite a period of time, which was thoughtlessness on the part of the gunner on the sight, but still of consequence to us. Must remember to remind that pilot to check up on his gunners. We do not like to have any guns pointing at us, even friendly ones. Just a slip of the finger and we might be stopping some lead. A couple of accidents on the flight line, in which guns were fired, have taught us that American bullets are mighty potent. The flak on this trip was fairly thick, but most of it was low. Some burst in the middle of the formation and might have caused some trouble, but so far as we could see no one was hurt.

The difference between training flights and the real thing in one respect, it appears, is the occurrence of the unexpected, and the necessary steps that must be taken immediately to overcome whatever the obstacle may be. I recall the running sweat in the cold, the iced windows because of faulty heating, the sloppy flight leadership. These things are unnecessary and unexpected, but there they were and they had to be overcome. We expect conditions to be a certain way, then find they are completely different no matter how long the training and preparation. Well, we'll just see to it that we are maneuverable enough to handle all these troubles as they arise. We'll anticipate the unexpected. That's a lesson today.

The miles of water roll by, sometimes obscured by the soupy clouds. Nick sticks with the cruise control and gives us periodic reports on the fuel remaining, As we pass Iwo Jima, obscured by clouds, we have 1600 gallons, which should be ample. We hear no emergency calls, so we assume all planes are all right. Hal and Gabby team up on the navigation in locating and identifying the Upper Marianas. Jake gives periodic drift readings to Hal. The bombsight is accurate in computing the drift and through this the direction and velocity of the wind, and is a great help to Hal. Most of us have gotten a nap at one time or another, but Hal works on. His work is not in vain. Dead ahead we see Tinian with Saipan to the left and slightly closer to us. In the harbor we see the dots that represent American shipping and Navy. The crew members all are glad to see this sight again, and express themselves variously over the interphone. "I can almost see that sack now," Charlie comments. "You mean you're not going to get that beer?" Nick asks him. Gabby then remarks that we should all see the Doc after landing to get the two shots of whiskey apiece "strictly for medicinal purposes", that is awarded at the end of a mission. "That's all right, give me a thick slice of ham with two beautiful eggs, not powdered," Jake adds.

We head over the channel between Saipan and Tinian so that we can enter the traffic pattern north of the field. Nick and Bill go through the landing check, the others are cautioned to "prepare for landing". We all fasten our safety belts and the crew members are warned to fasten the parachute dinghy strap to their Mae West. These precautions seem unnecessary now over our camp site, but we are glad to take that last safety measure. The gear comes down, and the flaps, the Tower acknowledges our approach and we line up and land on "B" Baker runway, which is runway No. 2. We are home again. That big No. 1 is behind us. At 1700 we cut the switches in the hardstand and wave out the window to the ground crew. They are glad to have their baby home, and I trust us, too.

At the critique of the mission we learn that the outcome is good. The bombs damaged the secondary target. All of our planes returned safely, although a radio man in one crew was severely wounded by a flak burst. We have a flak hole in our plane, we learn later. Some of the planes had difficulty with turbulence and ice in the clouds on the return. We learn, too, that the 73rd Wing on Saipan lost two planes which were forced to "ditch" on the way home. Another plane landed at Iwo -- there's one plane saved that might have been lost otherwise. Iwo will be a life-saver when it can be used safely by returning planes.

In the Area we find that our Squadron's first replacement crew has arrived. To my surprise the crew leader is an old Training Command friend, Rick Cooney. We meet Rick and his crew members -- a good gang. Cooney and copilot, Myer, are 6 feet, 3 inches each and add a distinctive touch to our camp scenery.

Chapter 9 Tokyo

March 9-10, 1945 – No. 4

Low Altitude "Blitz" Begins

At chow on the 9th we hear rumors that a mission is going out and that everyone is going. That is impossible, of course, since there aren't enough planes for everyone to go, but rumors transcend the possible. Bill and I check the mission board and see that we are scheduled, sure enough. Nobody knows much about it, but we find that at 0900 we are to go to a target identification class, and we will no doubt learn the destination at that time.

We pass the word around and return to the tent to check our equipment. Our tents are tailored to comfort now with coral floors and wooden platforms next to each bed. Every man has his packing-box furniture arranged to suit his taste and needs. This means that most everything can be reached from the bed. Wardrobes, desks, tables, chairs -- all made form scrap lumber, boxes and effort. By this time many of us had home-made beds copied from the Seabees, consisting of strips of old inner-tube stretched over a home-made bedstead. In my case, heavy, termite-eaten Jap railroad ties were used to serve as the framework. The rubber, stretched two ways, makes a nice spring for the air mattress and bed roll. Add to this the electric lights, semi-indoor showers, mess hall, and fields cleared of cane and you can see we were living in luxury -- mighty fine for a forward combat area.

At the rear of each tent there is a massive bomb shelter, laboriously built by the inmates of the tent. (Some will almost be disappointed if there are no raids, after all the work and groans that went into the construction of these shelters, and we are almost hoping there will be a raid so all this work will be to some purpose.) The PX is operating with practically no stock except toothpaste, shaving cream, and the other items of which the Army insisted we bring a year's supply, so it serves little purpose. Rationed beer has appeared several times and caused great celebration, but the Seabees have visited the combat crews enough so that all whiskey brought from the States is gone, replaced by radios, necklaces, Coca-Cola, Jap souvenirs and the other goods they had to exchange. Whiskey is the coin of exchange, it appears. The communal life has returned to rudimentary economics -- a question of supply and demand. Money, as such, means little. It is no longer the coin of the realm. No one carries a wallet, probably for the first time in their lives. What a difference from the States, but perfectly natural here. The principal pastimes are cards, reading, exploring, and "bulling" with anyone who drops in. Life is not complicated.

Meanwhile, the morale of the Squadron is up considerably. Owing to our complaints, the pilot accused by the Group Commanding Officer has been completely cleared by the Board of Inquiry -- an obvious reproval of our C.O., and the Commanding Officers of two other Groups welcomed the accused pilot to join either of their outfits. It seems that the Board felt as did we in defending him, that he was unjustly accused. Our C.O. maintained that the accused officer had flown improperly in leading a formation, an observation that he made while riding along with this pilot. "Fully a minute before the wing ship joined the lead plane (which the accused flew and in which I was riding) I could see that there would be an accident if no one gave way." His entire argument centered about this consideration. The defense counsel then simply pointed out to the Board the obvious flight fact that, when planes are joining formation at 200 miles an hour, a minute represents three miles distance, and no one can say that a plane three miles away will collide with another when the object is to assemble into close formation all planes, to within a few feet of each other. After the acquittal the Airplane Commanders of our entire Squadron were publicly reprimanded for having taken a stand (even though our C.O. was adjudged wrong), and to make it more ironical, our C.O. was the man who reprimanded us. However, none of us felt bad, because we had seen our companion safely through. Further, two other officers, whom we had likewise accused of incompetence along with our C.O. in the letter defending the pilot, were removed. One of these men was the man who had so alarmed us with his bungling and mismanagement. He was our Squadron C.O. As a pilot he couldn't fly and scared us repeatedly with his attempts. For one thing he didn't know the equipment. As an example, he put the radio jackbox on "compass" position to call a ground station using the radio compass, when this governs reception only and not transmission. We got some good laughs out of his errors when we finally compared notes, first suspecting and then realizing that he was grossly incompetent. Then it was that we realized that he was also dishonest, actually lying to us, giving each man a different story on how "fly-way" airplanes were assigned, or again telling each that his crew was No. 1 priority. He failed to understand the men or how to manage them.

We all felt happy over the outcome, though fully realizing that men in our position never win out bucking the Army. The entire matter was highly unusual, but we were desperate. The danger to our crews and ourselves through incompetence and mismanagement was all too real, and touched a tender spot with us. Unfortunately, we still have the same Commanding Officer, a ticklish situation for us all. The very best that can be said for the man is that he is a poor judge of the men in authority with whom he surrounds himself. Possibly this in itself is an indication of a far greater shortcoming, but he is our Commanding Officer and whether we like it or not, whether we respect or dislike him, we must do as he says and put up with him the best we can.

None of us suspected that difficulties like this would be encountered overseas. Somehow we felt that the business at hand was too serious for incompetence, and the bickering within the ranks that resulted. Half the total effort went to this internal dissension, the rest to the Japs. Now maybe conditions will improve. Meanwhile we'll all do the things that are in the best interests of our crews, who are doing the job, and taking the consequences, if such there may be. There just won't be any promotions for the offending persons, but there haven't been in the past, despite many having two years in grade and a good record. Higher headquarters only permits a 1st Lt. as Airplane Commander on the B-29 in the Tech orders. It seems mighty strange to us, and to our crews. Fortunately, many of the other members of the crew are allowed promotion so long as they are not as high as the Tech order indicates for their job. Apparently it makes no difference how well or how poorly a man does his job. Merit is not considered, or length of service, either. We wonder what is considered, and this makes for a continual dismay, which we try to disregard.

Target Identification, we find at 0900, is of a very general nature, covering the Tokyo area with an approach from the east. So we're going to the big city again! We don't mind, but we know that it is a hot spot, and this time they'll probably be able to see us with no clouds. This is to be a maximum effort with every plane that can fly scheduled. The crews scheduled are Ramsey, Parks, Mutch, Fortune, Maki, Litchfield, Preston, Jordan, Dawson, and Alger. We are to fly plane No. 13, for we still don't have our own -- No. 13 is Schad's.

The briefing hall is jammed with the largest group of crews yet assembled for a mission. We can hardly believe our ears -- nor are we disappointed -- when the Intelligence Officer, carefully weighing his words, intones "This mission is the first in a series of low altitude incendiary raids against the key cities of Japan. Your target is Tokyo, and you will bomb at night at an altitude of 7400 feet." We almost fall out of our seats. More weighty words are uttered in a significant manner, but we are impressed without the reminding. All of our training and thinking in terms of the B-29 is high altitude, above 25,000 feet and perhaps into the 30 thousands. Now, all of a sudden, we are to be sent in at low altitude above the most heavily defended city in the Empire. Even the boys with beebee guns will have a chance at us.

Quite apparently these thoughts are running through the heads of the other crew members present, for a few low whistles and a loud buzzing begins as the fellows give vent to their feelings in the matter. The briefing officer goes on and there's no trouble holding the men's attention. Bill mutters "They're going to gamble the whole Air Force on this," and I nod. It looks like a bold stroke. As a voice behind us puts it, "Someone's being awful brave for me." As the various officers speak to us we learn that each plane is to fly and bomb individually. There'll be no formation over the target. All Wings will participate and each Wing will be at a different altitude, yet all very low. Our particular approach for the bombing will be from the east. Each Wing will arrive at a different time over the target, each will have a different axis of attack, and each a different altitude. The flight altitude to the target for us will be 1500 feet. The bomb load will consist of incendiary clusters M-46 type, 500 lbs. each, and 28 per plane. Gross weight will be close to 140,000 lbs. This looks like an all-out effort all right. Air-sea rescue this time will consist of 3 subs, 2 dumbos (B-24s), and 2 superdumbos (B-29s), also a surface craft in the area of Pagan Island. The subs will be stationed just south of the mainland. We are further informed that we will carry no ammunition for our guns, in order to save as much weight as possible. We are surprised and skeptical at the thought of going over enemy soil on such a mission without any defensive weapons except our speed, but this is only another startling circumstance in a series of revolutionary pronouncements, so we accept it silently.

As we get up to go to the trucks, the more enthusiastic men are clapping each other on the back, while others, more subdued, smile and shake their heads -- "Amazing, isn't it?" "Amazing!" The men are generally enthusiastic as they discuss the mission while riding down in the trucks. We certainly are an eager bunch and there's no doubt in anyone's mind now that we're part of the main event. There doesn't seem to be anything that can stop us. We've had no losses.

We jolly Dan Cady at the Personal Equipment tent. This is his hectic time, with the crews all coming in together to pick up their gear en route to the planes. We find all our bags intact, so we go on over to No. 13 and begin the usual preflight inspection, each man going about his own. It appears that the plane and combat stations are all right, so we climb aboard and get settled.

There appear to be enough flak curtains shielding the individual positions. The curtains are light metal, to be sure, but they are better than nothing -- it might just be enough to stop a spent flak fragment. So we each get settled, putting in our canteens, cushions and other gear that is not carried on our persons. We are eager to get gone. The period between the briefing and the take-off is always a hard one. We want to get going instead of doing all the chores preparatory to departing, but we do not neglect them. Their positions are checked by Jonesy, Dick, Charlie and George. Gabby checks the radar, and Jake the bombing equipment. Hal sees that the navigational aids are operative. Al preflights the radios. Nick checks the plane mechanically. Bill computes the weight and balance and finds our take-off index number, which tells us whether we are safely loaded or not. By the time we have accomplished all these things, along with talking to the various officials who drive by, we feel like we're half finished, and yet we haven't started.

Now, all settled inside, we give the signal to Nick and he starts the engines. They all fire properly and sound good. The engine check substantiates their condition. The crew members are ready so we release the brakes, check the emergency brakes and coast onto the taxiway. We're right on time to the minute and in our correct position according to the taxi and take-off list.

Two of the four parallel runways are being used. A plane goes off each one every minute, which puts them 30 seconds apart in the air. We wait our turn and roll onto the runway, the Flagman gives the signal and Jake calls out the time as 0715. Since we are using a timed procedure during and after take-off, Jake keeps the time and tells us when to turn after take-off. Bill meanwhile attends to the power, the gear, flaps and general airplane condition. The scanners check in with him. Nick calls out the cylinder head temperatures. Apparently everything is all right and we pass over Lalo point, near the southern tip of Tinian, skirting Tinian until we're on course and at our cruising altitude of 1500 feet. The air is alive with planes, so we are all alert, watching those nearby.

It is dark now, though there is still a faint western light. The brighter stars are visible in the blue-black darkness. Against the fixed stars near the horizon, plane wing-lights are visible, moving quickly across the sky. The reds and greens, and sometimes the top white light, can be seen, mysteriously carried through the darkness. The planes themselves are invisible. When closer, sometimes the blue formation lights atop the wings can be seen. It is peaceful and still. Inside the cabin the engines can barely be heard. They are soothing, excellent for accompanying sleep.

The interphone chatter dies down and quietness settles over the plane. The fluorescent lights illuminate the instrument panels and the instruments seem to leap out into the darkness. Nick puts up the cloth partition which keeps light out of the flight deck where the pilot and copilot are located. Jake sits in his nose seat slightly below us and scans the sky ahead. He tries hard to help spot nearby planes, but it's just a question of time until he begins to nod, wake up with a start, and nod again. Bill and I take turns keeping a look-out ahead. It is very dark and the lights of other planes are easily visible. The curtain keeps out the glare and makes it easy to see out of the nose. After we each handle the controls awhile to get the "feel" of this particular plane, we put it on C-1 autopilot and it flies itself. The autopilot makes navigation easier for the navigator, since a machine can hold the plane more steady than a human being can. Should the plane fall off course at all, it is easy to put it back on course with the turn knob. We each take a nap while the other one watches. In the blisters Jonesy, George, Dick and Charlie are rotating two at a time, keeping watch while the other two sleep. Gabby is quiet, perhaps still checking the radar set, or napping. The blisters check in periodically so we know who is on duty. Meanwhile Bill has turned on the Radio Compass to the OWI station on Saipan and everyone awake enjoys the dance music. Bill and I take turns monitoring the VHF set, which is used between planes for emergencies. It is clear outside and Hal takes occasional star shots to determine and cross-check our position with his dead reckoning. Loran fixes are a help to him while this close to Base. Usually the metro winds are incorrect. The navigator is strictly on his own and must determine his position at all times from combining all the navigational aids at his command, and not believing the metro information. The metro (weather information, winds, etc.) is helpful as an indication, and can be used where it is not possible to get a wind from other means such as from the bombsight reading, or a double drift run with the drift meter.

At midnight I leave my seat and go aft. Hal is bending over his chart with the movable light directed on his work. Nick is sleeping at his engineer's position, uncomfortable doubling his long legs under the panel. Hal folds up his table and lets me by -- it's a close squeeze. Directly aft of the upper gun turret is the radio table against the port side. There Al sits, wide-awake, ear-phones on his head and code card at his elbow. Just above the radio sets I see the rest of his family, his wife Mary Alice and daughter Pamela Sue smiling up at us beside a Christmas tree. "Haven't heard much -- someone's in trouble, but I can't make out who." I nod and finish up at the relief tube, located against the bulkhead. "Kind of cramped here, aren't you?" I inquire. "Not too bad," Al answers. "And I can get out in a hurry if I have to." I look where he indicates and see an axe beside the astro-dome. The astro-dome, where the navigator takes his start shots, is made of plastic and would be a convenient exit in case of ditching. Al laughs, "I'm ready to go at any time, but I'd rather not." "Yes, I see what you mean. Let's hope you never need to," I reply. Al is hemmed in here and can't see out since he has no window, but he could probably get out quickly, with the bomb-bay there beside him for parachuting, and the astro-dome for ditching. Looking back through the long tunnel at shoulder level, I can see Jonesy's ring sight seat, but no one is in it. Looks mighty sleepy back there. Hal lets me by and I return to the darkness of the cockpit where Bill keeps watch.

Shortly after midnight Nick wakens and transfers fuel, after warning the crew members to put out all cigarettes. The fuel transfer is made after we have flown long enough to permit the wing tanks, that feed directly into the engines, to take the fuel that's held in the center wing section. We transfer the fuel so that none will be trapped and unusable should the transfer pumps be damaged over the target. Hal gives us a position report and a correction on the course that will put us in line with the briefed landfall at the tip of the eastern peninsula of land, by the name of Chiba. As soon as the transfer is complete we climb to the bombing altitude of 7400 feet. It is getting colder as we go north so Nick puts on some heat. Shortly after 0100 Bill contacts the blisters and suggests that George go back into the tail and we begin to put on our heavy equipment. Jonesy reports that the guns are ready, and the gunners assume their sighting stations with heavy equipment on. Gabby has the radar set operating and is trying to help Hal with the landfall. When we don't approach land on schedule, Hal tells us that he believes the winds have been strong than the metro indicated and that we had better correct more to the left. Not wanting to fly past our target to the east, thereby missing the IP and the briefed axis of attack, we make a large correction to the west, until we are flying almost due west. "Land ahead 35 miles," Gabby reports. And a minute later, "Looks like the tip of the Peninsula where we want to make landfall." "Are you sure, Gabby?" I inquire, thinking of the next peninsula to the west, something like this one in shape and 12,000 feet, Mt. Fuji. "Yes, sir, that's it. I recognize the shape of the tip of land," he retorts. "O.K., Jonesy, keep an eye out -- remember we're surrounded by our own planes, so be careful." "Yes, sir, we're ready!" Bill makes a last minute check of the men to be sure everyone has all equipment on properly. "Navigator to Pilot -- you can turn now and take u a heading of 15 degrees, that will take us to the I.P. in 6 minutes." "O.K. Hal, turning on heading of 15 degrees for I.P."

We are able to see far ahead to the left a dull glow in the sky, with sudden explosive brilliant flashes. "There it is, boys, look sharp." I take a deep breath and think "it won't be long, now", and then think that's a hackneyed expression for a situation like this. We are unable to see any planes around us, yet we know they must be there. All lights are out. It's very dark except for the red glow ahead. We can feel the other planes around us. Occasionally someone reports a quickly moving white light, and we all recall that may mean a Jap fighter. It's a clear night out so they're bound to be waiting for us.

"Navigator to Pilot -- in one minute turn to a heading of 305 degrees, we'll be on course for target." I acknowledge his message and we turn over the I.P. (Initial Point) and head for the target area. There's no mistaking it now, or the fact that someone has been here already. This is a first time for us on a night incendiary raid, yet we recognize many of the sights. About 20 large fires are burning, an area of several blocks apiece. In between small fires are beginning or dying out. Every few seconds there is a flaming glow as another load of bombs break open and ignite. The bombs are fused to break open at 2000 feet and then fall flaming to earth. Large masses of flaming objects marking the bombs are seen falling below us on several sides. Jake is over the bomb-sight, making a visual run, aiming for a dark spot between large fires. This is the heart of the city, apparently. "I've got it," Jake says to Gabby and the latter gives up the radar run together with the Navigator. "Bombs away!" Jake shouts and proceeds to close the bomb doors. Al and Dick report that the bombs have fallen.

The cabin of the plane is lighted by the flickering light from below. There are fires all around -- a regular sea of flames. Flashes appear in the sky at our level and the gunners call out the flak as they see it explode. Automatic weapons with tracer fire are evidently being used. We see criss-crossing streams of tracer shells trying to locate a target above. The flak must be hit-or-miss for there doesn't seem to be any planning to the flak bursts that we see. There are no search-lights as we had expected, neither are there any fighters so far as we can see. The orange glow of the fires lights the inside of the plane and is reflected off our hands and faces. I see Jake ahead, bathed in the bright flickering color. We see no other planes around us, though they must be there. Apparently there is lots of hit-or-miss fire from below, tracers and shells of various sizes. Perhaps they can't figure our altitude and have been taken completely by surprise. We see the criss-crossing streams of tracers periodically. Let's not intercept any of that!

Having dropped the bombs and closed the door, our big concern is to get out of here. Small weapons fire and automatic fire must be after us. The gunners continue to call out the flak and fire and we make a diving turn to the right to pick up speed and shake off any planned firing on us, if such there is. What a place to be forced down. This blacked-out country feels mighty hostile, and this raid is not making us any friends. Wonder what the people re doing down there? They see the fires on one side and start in another direction. Fires break out ahead of them and then on all sides. Where will they go? Bill looks back, "What a furnace!" he shouts. I look over and see the area even more ablaze than before. It looks like the Fourth of July. Tracer shells are criss-crossing in the air. Flak bursts dot the sky, and below nothing but fire. And to think we went right through that! Fortunately the wind is very strong, thus blowing the smoke and heat away from the target over which the planes must fly -- the advantages are certainly on our side tonight.

We continue to fly the headings that Hal gives us. Our withdrawal is by way of the sea to the east -- anything to get away from Jap soil. The water seems mighty friendly to us now. Here's hoping none of the fellows get forced down tonight -- better to ditch or pile up somewhere than to be taken prisoner. The ever increasing orange glow is beginning to recede now as we depart, yet even at a distance the sky is lit up for miles, much greater than as we saw it on approaching. Most of the planes have dropped their bombs by now -- let's hope they get out all right.

We all stick silently to our jobs until we're out to sea and then far to the south of the southern extremities of Japan. We are mighty helpless this trip. We have no ammunition in our guns and the only protection we have is our speed of 230 m.p.h. The top command thinks we'll be lighter this way -- maybe so, but give me the ammunition any day instead of a few pounds less of weight.

Now we all shed the extra clothes and tackle the food. The fellows are more quiet this time. It's hard to believe that what we saw is true -- that we went in and came out of a flaming city, destroyed before our eyes. This is a far cry from life in the United States, as we knew it and I can see that the fellows are sobered. Perhaps, if we weren't so new it would be nerve-wracking, but as it is it's such a new experience that it's hard to believe it's true.

And we survived it! Thank you, Lord. I realized that during the bomb run I was getting quite religious -- wonder if the other fellows were feeling that way. "Just think of it; this thing's in earnest. We're trying to kill them wholesale and destroy all we can. It's unbelievable, but it's war, and we're representing the U.S.A. This thing is real and earnest." I find myself thinking this over and over. This mission over Tokyo can't be compared to sailing over above the clouds as we did the first mission. This time it almost felt as if we were down on the roof tops ourselves; we could feel the heat of the fires and see city blocks ablaze, and it doesn't seem possible that we could sail through all that and come out unscathed, but we did apparently. We were so low I was wondering what I would do if I were down in that city.

Nick and Bill figure the fuel and it appears to be ample to get us home. This type of mission where we fly alone (not in formation) and do not climb to altitude does not take so much gas, so the 6800 gallons we carry is enough. Before we took 7400 gallons. Looks as though this mission has established a new technique with the B-29 -- wonder if these low-level attacks will be the only kind from now on. First thing you know we'll be dive-bombing or hedge-hopping.

Although we are all somewhat awed by the holocaust and thankful to have survived, sleep, listening to music, and chewing the cud takes up most of the trip home, which is uneventful, and we land on good old Tinian at 1145, after a 15-and-a-half hour trip. We are among the last to arrive home. Postflight inspection shows a jagged flak hole on the top side of the left wing, outboard of the No. 1 engine, along the leading edge.

We learn that all of the 6th Group of planes returned safely -- no casualties -- and we are surprised. The Saipan Wing again hit bad luck when two of their planes collided in mid-air and were lost. Further, statistics include three planes ditched and two crews rescued. Two planes landed at Iwo. We get this news at the Interrogation that is held in the area after we return from the flight line. Always just when you think you will get some rest, along comes the interrogator and you must answer many questions pertaining to the mission and the observed circumstances. Later, we learn that General Arnold sent a special commendation for the mission. Photo Recon. showed that 422,000,000 sq. ft. were burned out of the heart of Tokyo. We don't know how much that is, off hand, but it sounds large in footage.

Chapter 10 Kobe

March 16-17, 1945 – No. 5

"The Three-Engine Return"

These are dark days for Crew 2409 -- we still have no plane. As a result we are used as a fill-in, flying others' planes. Even though we are not the only crew in this situation, we don't like it. The "Blitz" attack is on full force now and the center of interest. We combat crews are not content to stay behind and hear about it from others, and this fact is brought forcibly to our attention because our tent-mates are going on each one, becoming veterans you might say, while we sit here and wait for a plane -- someone else's plane at that. So it is, that we miss going on the first Nagoya low level attack on the 11th-12th, and we begrudge the fact that we are not in on it. Now we are scheduled to go on the Osaka mission in Pete Fortune's plane, No. 8. We are glad of the chance to work again, even in someone else's plane.

Meanwhile, during these busy blitz days, there are several interesting events. On the 11th we are alerted for a possible Jap Banzai attack. It seems that this day is a Jap holiday, and the authorities expect the Japs in hiding on Tinian, of which there are many we are told, to come out ready to kill or be killed. In our almost civilized community such a possibility seems remote, however, as ordered, we put on our side-arms and are careful where we go after dark. We are well aware that there are still a lot of Japs running around the Island loose. In fact we strongly suspect that many of the "Gooks" (native villagers) are in reality Japs in disguise, the remnants of the Jap Army on Tinian. At least they look the part, and we are informed that at Camp Chure, where the Gooks live, the authorities are uncovering Japs every day who are posing as natives. We are very much surprised at first to see these strange looking people building walls and walks around the area. Although they are under guard, many times we see a couple or three wandering around the area, hanging around our post office and operations building where the plans are hanging on the walls. The Jap holiday goes by and there is no excitement except for a guard shooting one of our men who was out after dark.

In the evenings we faithfully attend the picture show, only to see a "stinker" of a show, or have the power fail, the projector break, or the film tear. Boy, how the fellows howl then. During the day we try to use the washing machine that Bill, Hal, and Jake made out of spare parts from old, crashed Jap planes. It's a windmill affair and works a plunger up and down while a fire heats the entire solution. It's quite an arrangement and doesn't take more than twice the time it would to wash by hand.

The day of the Osaka mission we attend the briefing, get into our flying duds, assemble our gear, and go to the plane. After the usual preflight we taxi out for the take-off. The planes are lined up, each moving up in turn for the take-off. As we wait Charlie reports "There's a plane on fire." We all look out and see the entire area illuminated by gas and oil flames which are part way down the runway. Our taxi is temporarily halted while traffic is re-routed to the next runway. It is a fearsome sight. Now the bombs begin igniting and the light becomes intense. Periodically flaming pieces fly off in small explosions. We hope the crew got out all right. Evidently it began burning immediately, since we were watching planes take off there just a minute or two ago. Soon our time to taxi and take-off comes, even while the fire still burns on the other runway, which is temporarily closed. We start our take-off roll and prepare to get her off the ground. At 90 miles per hour No. 1 engine is backfiring and "kicking" badly, so before it's too late, I pull off the power and we taxi around to do it again. This time the engine is running so roughly that we can't even give her full power, so we return to the hardstand and tell the troubles to the crew chief. He is chagrined and doesn't know what the matter could be without a thorough inspection of the engine, so we take our equipment out and return to the area. Here we learn that it was Steel's crew whose plane burned, and that somehow they all got out safely, even after the flames began.

It's a big disappointment not to be able to go on this mission. After all the preparation, not to go is quite a let down. However, maybe the mission you can't go on is the one you should not. Who knows, maybe we'll live longer this way (knock on wood).

Anyhow, we feel that our troubles are the out-growth of not having a plane, and we see to it that the authorities know we haven't given up hope of having one. But often times, in unfortunate Army situations that one tries to correct, it's "damned if you do, and damned if you don't". As it applies in this case, the next day after the Osaka attempt we are offered a choice of two planes, neither of which are wanted by others except by the several needy crews that have no planes. Our choice is between No. 1, which was ground-looped and partially cracked up by another crew on take-off, and No. 11. No. 11 has been the "hangar queen" for the last month because of the chronic bomb door trouble. While sitting waiting for the door repairs, other crew chiefs helped themselves to spare parts -- for worthy reasons, no doubt -- but nevertheless injurious to No. 11. For rather complicated considerations the crews that had these planes have been given new ones and now crew 2409 is given the choice of picking a plane from these two as our combat pride and joy. At the time this seems a far cry from our fond Stateside hopes when we brought No. 550 overseas. As a crew we visualized having a plane like that one, new, and all our own, which would make it the best plane that the Air Corps had. Then we lost 550 to Saipan -- unfairly we thought. Now we are given a choice between two second-hand planes -- with a tinge of unfairness again. However, there's no choice but to make a choice, so we see, and that we do. We are leery of No. 1, particularly. We saw it ground-loop and we are afraid that the strain of that accident might have further damaged the wing or gear beyond what might be detected on inspection. In addition we know that it took a lot of fuel, something wrong with the carburetion.

No. 11, on the other hand, other than being picked apart for the month that it remained inactive, only had door trouble. Every flight the doors had stayed open after bombing, and thus cut down gas mileage when fuel was life insurance. We choose No. 11.

The deal is made with an important proviso, and that is that M/Sgt. Wilbur (Pat) Patterson will be our crew chief. Actually, this was decided back in the States, that Pat would be our crew chief, and we all flew overseas together. But we're wary of further disappointments. We know Pat and he knows the crew, and everyone approves of everyone else. Pat, knowing full well the work needed on No. 11, willingly teams up with us again. We appreciate his allegiance all the more because we know that now and in the future he is on a competitive basis with the other crew chiefs, and many of them have the same plane they started with when it was new. Pat must put this one into shape and try to anticipate its troubles, even while it's an unknown quantity to us, and at the same time forge ahead of the other crew chiefs in keeping his plane in the air most. Pat pitches in and brings his helpers, whom we get to know in short order. They are Jim "Red" Grobe, Bill Kramer, Steve Levine, Bill Gross, and Hank Reinholtz, a first class group of men and mechanics.

On March 14th we give No. 11 a test hop with Pat along, and she flies well except for unusually high cylinder-head temperatures. The next day we go again. The temperatures are better after a good bit of work on the engines by Pat and the boys. On the cruise control she seems better than before, too. If she's going to run out of gas, now's the time to find it out. Apparently no one on the scheduling end is concerned over that possibility, and I remind them of it. Result? We are scheduled the next day for Japan, target Kobe! So we cross our fingers and hope that No. 11 will stretch the mileage. We need another test hop for safety's sake, but since the authorities think otherwise there's no choice. We want to get going on another mission ourselves and it's useless to argue, so we keep quiet and prepare for the Kobe trip. From the briefing we learn that the mission is to be another of the "blitz" attacks, a low-level night incendiary attack on the city of Kobe. Since the Tokyo attack, other cities bombed in this manner have been Nagoya and Osaka. And the luck of our Group still holds. No one lost on the five missions to Japan. Our only loss to date was the unexplained mid-air explosion of a crew going out on the second day of the Search missions, and that crew was from another squadron. I knew the pilot, his wife and baby from earlier days in the States.

Like the earlier mission of this kind, this will be an all-out attack, with every plane participating that can fly. The total bomb load will be 14,500 lbs. Bombing altitude will be 7800 feet. The route will be a slight dog-leg, going by way of Iwo. The policy with regard to ammunition has been changed, so now we are to carry 200 rounds in the tail guns. That still leaves us fairly defenseless, except for speed.

The taxi and take-off are uneventful. The take-off time is 2035K (King time equals local time). The trip up to the Empire follows the usual pattern. We are improving our routine procedure until the many duties and chores that each man must do for himself and the others are fitting smoothly into precise teamwork, better than ever. All of us feel better about it now than after the first Tokyo mission, I'm sure. We're established now and a "going" concern.

By the time we approach landfall on Southern Japan, the crew members are all set, with all the equipment on, and those whose duties permit, securely fastened with the safety belt. The gunners are at their stations, but only for observation purposes, since only the tail guns are loaded. George is in the tail, ready for action. "Plane with lights on level at 11," calls out Jonesy. Sure enough, there is a plane that gives every indication of being Jap, lights on, at right angles to our course, and the lights are a different type than a B-29. Fortunately, it continues right on its course. We make landfall on course, a credit to Hal's navigation, and Gabby's scope interpretation of the radar set picking up Jap landscape. We are over the eastern promontory of land extending form Shikoku Island. From here we head for the southern tip of Awaji Island in Harima Sea, just southwest of Kobe. This is our I.P. Hal and Gabby are working together, since this is a radar run, and it will continue so unless visual bombing is possible. Evidently we are among the first here, since the target is not burning enough to light the sky as we expected. We are directly over Awaji Island and as yet have not encountered fighters or flak. Possibly the failure to use searchlights springs from their hope to remain unrevealed, not giving away their position. Now several fires are apparent and we see that heavy smoke has partially obscured the fires and target from our sight as we approach. The City of Kobe, our target, stretches along the north edge of the Bay six or seven miles long, like a long, slightly bent figure. The city is but 2 miles wide at this point. At our speed the bombs must be released at just the right instant in order to hit in the heart of the city. The darkness cuts our vision of the city, with the docks and narrow, closely-packed buildings. "Flashes or explosions at 10 o'clock low," Dick says. "Tracer shells at 5 o'clock," Charlie adds. We know there are fighters in this area, but we don't see any. The black smoke is more apparent now, climbing up above our altitude ahead. Hal is still making this a radar run, and Jake is crouched over the bombsight. It's apparent that we will continue this as a radar approach. Gabby and Hal are passing on the rate information to Jake, who sets it into the sight, then "Bombs away!" Al and Dick confirm the bombs are gone, and we close the bomb door. It's so darn dark. You'd think that only oil dumps are burning, but as Jakes looks down he informs us that there are quite large fires on the other side of the smoke.

We bank the plane to the left, and as briefed, climb upwind to the west in withdrawing. It feels like we're hanging here and it's easy to visualize the flak or fighters as aimed right at us, but we continue without interruption. Looking back I see several other B-29s as they come between the fires and our plane. So we are not alone, dark though it is. We've been mighty lucky. Jake reports that he saw the bombs hit right beside a large fire and then flames leaped up, so it appears the bombs were well placed. Let's hope so.

"Oil pressure's dropping on No. 1 engine," Nick reports. We take stock of the situation. The plane appears to be all right and the engines sound good. "Pressure's down to 40 lb.," Nick continues. It's dropped 30 lb. already. That's not good. "How's the fuel supply, Nick?" "Appears to be all right, enough to get home," he answers. "Well, we'll use the engine as long as we can, let me know as the pressure keeps dropping." Feathering an engine this far from home is a serious business, not that three engines can't do the job, but then if another fails, then you're liable to get wet. The scanners, on inquiry, report that No. 1 looks all right and Nick reports that the oil quantity is all right in that engine. The engine temperature is all right and it lacks other symptoms of trouble. "Pressure is down to 20 lb.," Nick states. If we continue to use the engine and there is something the matter with it, it will ruin the engine. Further, it may become impossible to feather it. Weighing all these possibilities, it appears a good risk and the wisest thing to do is to feather No. 1 and not take a chance of hurting it further, so Bill feathers No. 1. The big prop gradually slows down and then comes to a stand still with its blades' edges pointing into the wind. The two rotating engines on the right side, as against the one on the left, require that we trim up the plane again. To do this we adjust the aileron and rudder trim tabs, which are miniature control surfaces on the larger control surfaces themselves. The rudder and aileron are not now in a streamline position as before and thus this arrangement increases our total drag. Yet other than for this, we know that it will take no more gas to fly on three engines than on four, so we should have ample. Of course the return will be a little slower.

Nick continues computing gas consumption on the three engines and Hal plans the navigation on a slower speed than intended. We are at 10,000 feet, and should have the benefit of a tail wind for quite some time. Bill and I begin alternating at the controls and catching naps in between. The plane is running nicely and we are not straining the engines. Apparently the fuel is holding out well.

Then it is that we get a surprise, just after daybreak. "There's a bomb hanging by one support in the rear bomb bay," Dick Bush reports. Jake goes aft to inspect. Probably the lack of light over the target prevented this bomb from being seen before, particularly since it was in the No. 8 station, which is in the shadow when viewed through the bulkhead door. A few minutes later Jake returns to the nose and explains that the shackle arm of the release mechanism is released, but that the bomb appears to be firmly attached. Moreover, it is not armed, in case there is trouble. Jake thinks it is wisest to leave the bomb alone instead of trying to dislodge it. So we proceed homeward.

South of Iwo Jima we encounter unexpected turbulence as we pass through some harmless looking clouds. "Bill, we're slowing down," I comment, seeing the airspeed fall off 10 miles per hour. At the same time Dick calls from the blister section, "The bomb's fallen out, it's knocked the doors open." We put on more power to hold our air speed. "O.K. Dick, keep an eye on the doors and tell us if they stay closed." We try to raise the doors with the switch which actuates the air pressure. "The doors close but fall open again," Dick reports. Jake goes aft to try to keep them closed in some way. Only the rear doors are open, but it's taking more power to sustain us now, and that means more fuel consumed. Nick begins to refigure our range in the light of the increased power. "It's going to be mighty close, according to my figures," he says. Impatiently we call back to the blister section learn not much headway has been made with the doors. "Higgy, we've got to get those doors closed and soon," I state and Higgy agrees. "I'll go back and see if I can help." "O.K., get some rope and try to tie them closed -- anything to do the trick." Evidently the doors are sprung and the catch is not hooking.

It's beginning to look like nip and tuck whether we make the base. "Al, prepare a message to the Base stating our position and difficulty," I request. In a minute Al checks back saying "I sent the message stating our engine feathered, low on gas, bomb doors open, altitude, course and speed, and got an acknowledgment from the Base -- I'll keep in touch with them." "Good," I reply and thank our luck that we have a sharp radio operator. Al knows his job and this time it may mean a lot to us -- more than usual. This plane being strange to us adds to the hazard, since we don't know how much fuel there is in the tanks. Ordinarily the tanks of the planes are all calibrated so that the engineer knows how much gas remains, allowing for the error in the reading of the particular gauge. In this plane we do not know the error, nor are we familiar with the residual content in the tanks. The residual content is that fuel remaining in each tank when the respective engine quits for lack of gas. It may be as high as 50 to 75 gallons per each of the four tanks, or three tanks in this case.

Jonesy is helping Jake and Bill. They are using, so Gabby reports, the rope out of the emergency kit and some other cable located in the rear of the plane. Finally they get the doors closed while we are still 200 miles from Base. We are able to cut back on the power and conserve a little more of the precious gasoline. Looks like we have an even chance now. Al continues to contact the ground station. Other planes in the area know of our situation, but we see no one around to buddy us into Tinian. Now we are flying over an air-sea rescue destroyer who knows we are in trouble and is standing by to help if we ditch. We have the choice of making a controlled ditching now or of gambling on getting back to the Base, and if we run out of gas, of doing whatever remains to be done, which probably means a ditching as best we can under the circumstances. We are down to a thousand feet now and our tanks are indicating somewhere around 100 gallons apiece, so it appears wisest to go on and try to make the base. The crew members are warned of the situation and have their emergency equipment on and are brushing up on their ditching duties. Fortunately, each man is well informed in these duties -- thanks to being conscientious in the past.

Al continues to radio the Base so they know of our intention to try to make it. Thanks to Hal we are right on course, and now we see Tinian in the distance, dead ahead. Nick has balanced the fuel remaining evenly between the three tanks, according to the gauges. Things look mighty grim, and we can see the water not far below. The small waves are of a choppy nature at this time and don't look soft, but all we can do is sit here and listen to the engines. We hit a little turbulence and Bill looks up quickly. I know he's thinking "Did that engine cough, and the plane yaw from loss of power?" So I say, "Did it?" He listens intently, "Guess not -- I hope!" The faulty engine, bomb rack, and questionable fuel gauges are abnormal difficulties (though we suspect fuel trouble). Has No. 11 got any more hidden malfunctions to spring on us? All we can do is sit and wait.

Calling the Tower ahead of time we get permission to make a straight in approach which we begin executing while a long way out. Nick calls George, who starts the put-put. Our concern now is to make a wide, flat turn so that the gas in the tanks will not be tipped away from the fuel lines while turning. After rolling out of the turn we keep our altitude, and at the last minute put down the gear and flaps. If need be we can glide in, once we start our descent. The engines keep turning over and we come in on "A" Able runway without a bit of trouble.

We all breathe a lot easier and the tension gives way to a tired let-down. Our tanks register empty, but we're home, on dry ground. At the hardstand we get out and look at the bomb bay door. Oddly enough, there is a gaping hole in the door on the outside, even though the bomb hit the door from the inside. On both sides of the door the skin is wrinkled and warped. There is no apparent damage to the No. 1 engine. And there's no doubt about there being very little fuel left, but the crew chief remarked, "Oh, I don't know, you had enough for me to fill my cigarette lighter."

In retrospect, this mission built up the crew spirit even more than the easier trips of the past. Hal did an excellent job of navigation so that we didn't waste a mile, but came straight in to Tinian. He claims it isn't possible to be that accurate in navigation, but he was and is, and I'll not argue with him. Al, with the radio messages, earned some fine compliments from the Wing ground station as well as Commander Congden of the Air-Sea rescue. And after we landed I learned that Jonesy deserved a lot of credit for working in the open bomb bay without a chute on, in the effort to get the doors closed, and getting them closed saved just enough gas to get us home.

The Intelligence department summary states that two aircraft were presumed lost and one ditched with none rescued. Over the target a B-29 was reported seen in a flat spin. Further, it seems there were fighters after all. Seventy-three enemy fighters were sighted and thirty-four attacks reported. But our Group came out lucky again.

Well, that's five behind us now, and we have our own plane, such as it is. We are in hopes that Victor II won't give us such a thrill next time.

Chapter 11 Nagoya

March 18-19, 1945 – No. 6

"Our Own Dive-Bombing"

A few hours after arriving from Kobe we learn that we are scheduled to go on the mission to Nagoya tomorrow. What a tonic! We forget that we are tired from the Kobe adventure and eagerly plan for Nagoya. All the crew members share our enthusiasm when they are told. It's an odd thing, but dangers or not the combat crew members are happiest when doing their jobs in the air, or preparing for them. And a sad spectacle is the crew that is left behind on a big mission when all the fellows are gone. They may not admit it openly, but they try hard to be scheduled and are disappointed when not. Perhaps it's because we are fresh and rested. Perhaps we are eager because we've not had heavy losses, and the original outfit is still intact. Whatever the reason, it's always an uplift to know that we're going on the next.

"Will the plane be ready?" Bill inquires when he hears that we are going. "Don't know -- let's see if we can't hustle it along," I reply. Both of us are wondering if No. 11 has the bugs ironed out by now, after its long period of inactivity. We were practically forced to choose her as the lesser of two evils. Better to have a questionable plane than no plane, we figure. This may not be the safest course to take, but we must risk it. All of us were tired of shifting from one plane to another on each mission, for under those conditions there's no chance to get acquainted with the plane, and each plane has its own peculiarities -- the way it handles, the power required to get certain indicated speeds, the amount of fuel it uses, the inaccuracies of each fuel tank gauge, these are a few of the things in which planes differ. We argue loudly that they also affect safety. This we truly believe. But we raise our voices even louder, I am sure, because a crew likes the sentimental attachment for a plane, keeping the same one and getting to know it like a friend. To put a name on it and a figurehead, to put the crew members' names on it along with your wife, sweetie, or kid -- these things mean a lot to the crew members and can be done only with their own plane. It helps to "remove Army anonymity and restore individuality", so the papers back home state when treating the subject. Whatever the reasoning, we like to fly the same plane, to be surrounded by the feeling of confidence and comfort in our own plane. The men even do a better job. It adds to the pride they take in their professional skills. They even enjoy working on it and doing whatever is necessary to keep it in first class condition. Thus the mechanics have an easier time of it, the plane stays in better condition, and as a final result, stays more in the air -- the latter is considered the acid test of a plane and its maintenance. It is wonderful to see the teamwork and unselfish cooperation of the air crew and the ground crew members in the care they lavish on their plane. Perhaps this isn't the whole explanation, but it's part of it. These are a few of the thoughts built up about a plane, although other crew members may look at it differently, yet we are glad to have a plane that is our own. And so we intend to make it the best.

By noon of the 18th, with only a few hours to go, there is still no right rear bomb bay door on the plane. It seems that the crew chief is even now out "procuring" one. The Operations Officer says not to worry about where the chief is getting the door. We know there are no spare doors available on the Island, so that leaves us puzzling over where it will be obtained. But we agree that we don't care, just so the door appears in time for us to make the mission.

Back in the area I find Jonesy, Dick, Charlie, and George preparing to go down to the plane to load the ammunition. At last, the big "wheels" up top are going to permit us to have ammunition with which to defend ourselves, tho' it's only 100 rounds per gun. Somehow they have "seen the light" and know that we need ammunition to defend ourselves, just as we know it. We can't help wondering why we were not allowed to take ammunition on missions over well defended Jap cities. Perhaps the 70 Jap fighters reported over Kobe last time has reminded them of the well-known fact that there are plenty of Jap planes left who'd love to find B-29s without ammunition. Two B-29s were presumed lost over the target last time. There would be none of that "you-have-no-ammunition-old-chap-so-I'll-not-fire-on-you" business if they did catch up with us. With only 200 rounds of ammo in the tail guns one of our planes got the first Jap fighter of our Group over Kobe. Without ammo the plane is lighter by a few pounds (1000 rounds weigh 300 lbs.) but any one of us would be glad to have the extra weight and be able to defend ourselves. But we're not supposed to question, nor do we accomplish anything if we do. Anyhow, this time, should the night fighters think we're easy marks, they'll be making a mistake. Our crew's been lucky to dodge them thus far.

After a quick nap we wake in time to learn from the gunners that the bomb door has arrived at the plane, but must be mounted. That's encouraging, for knowing how the ground crew works, we know it will be ready. At 1600 Bill, Hal, Jake and I go over to the mess hall and put away a big meal: mutton, potatoes, corn, coffee, bread, jelly, and diced fruit for dessert. Mostly canned, but filling -- a good base for the journey. "Gyro" and "Turbo" both know that something is going on -- they've seen the preparations before -- and they frisk about and demand attention. But it's time to get ready for the briefing and going down to the flight line. We dress and gather the equipment. Since my coveralls are dirty (so dirty they'll almost stand by themselves) I decide to wear khaki. It's necessary to change shirts since this one is short sleeved and we make it a policy never to fly with so much skin exposed. In case of fire, clothing is quite a protection. Under the shirt I slip my own .25 automatic and stiletto, in holsters under each arm. In the web belt about the waist are carried the canteen, first aid kit, clip of .45 ammunition, and bayonet type knife. Our .45 automatic we wear in a shoulder holster. Bill is garbed similarly and he picks up our clip board on which we later put the flight data. Hal looks like a traveling salesman as he carries in addition his sextant and navigational charts. Jake, too, has an armful. At the last minute I remember to leave my wallet and personal papers, which shall never be taken, and which should not be taken, we're told, being dead giveaways as to our identity and military outfit. As prisoners we're supposed to remain mum except for our name and serial number. Last I grab the sponge rubber cushion which helps the posterior during the long hours.

We take our seats marked with the name of the crew on the bench. The hall is about full. A briefing officer is arranging material on the stage. The feeling of expectancy, tho' less now than on previous missions, settles over those assembled. The Colonel comes in and we pop to attention as is customary, then he opens the briefing with a pep talk. He calls us the best G. D. Group in the Pacific (as our Chaplain cringes) and then states that we have the best record of any Group during these "blitz" missions. It seems that we have put more planes over the target during the blitz than any other Group, and at that without loss to ourselves. This last comment increases our usual discomfort when he speaks to us. We all know we're lucky and we don't like to "look the gift horse in the mouth", much less to aggrandize ourselves, so we knock on wood and hope he'll change the subject.

Following the Colonel comes the S-2 Officer who gives an account of Nagoya's location and industrial importance, it's one and a half million people and the route to be flown up and back. The Radar Officer shows several photos of the radar scope as it will look at landfall, at the Initial Point, and over Nagoya. Next comes the flak analysis, then the Communications Officer who gives the radio data and mentions the need for radio silence in order not to tip them off that we are coming. The Air-Sea rescue follows next. Rescue facilities will include 4 subs and 3 B-29s near Japan, and a destroyer and 2 B-24s near Iwo. The secret code names that will be in effect during the trip in connection with radio contacting the rescue facilities are given. The take-off plan will be as follows: "Take-off when given the green light, out 3 minutes east, 2 minutes south, 5 minutes back west, then straight to Nagoya Bay. After bombing, the breakaway will be upwind west for several minutes before returning on course for home.

After the general briefing is over, the crew members break up into specialized briefings where the plans are gone over in more detail, if that's possible. There's a good deal of repetition, but it serves to lay a better foundation for what is to follow. The briefing officers are improving in their technique. They appear quite confident in themselves and the information that they dispense. It's surprising how certain they sound of the events that will transpire, considering they don't go on the missions. Perhaps that is the answer. We have found the missions to be a complicated jumble of unexpected events, yet to hear the briefing there's nothing to it but certain cut and dried maneuvers. Well it's a good thing to start out with a definite plan that everyone understands, then the unexpected can be placed in the previously devised framework. We learned on the first mission the need for "expecting the unexpected".

These thoughts occupy our walk out to the truck. I don't know how the others feel about it, but I dislike all this preliminary business, and the truck ride most of all. As Hal puts it, while we are careening around a corner, "This truck ride's the most dangerous part of the mission." We nod, laughing, and continue to hang on as the unyielding board seat spanks the posterior. "This guy missed his calling," Gabby says. No doubt about it, he must think he's Barney Oldfield. During the ride the fellows chat and joke or sit silent, each according to his mood and disposition. There is no apparent tenseness, but we will feel more comfortably mentally and physically after we are deposited at the plane and get busy with the chores.

En route we stop at the Personal Equipment room, as is our custom, to pick up our Mae West life preservers, oxygen bottle and mask, heavy clothes, sun goggles, first aid kits and the like. The rest, such as parachutes, one-man dinghies, axes, water, food, flak helmets and vest, are at the plane. This equipment is mostly of an emergency nature. After stowing the gear in the plane and checking the plane over generally, we have a good bit of time left, so we sit out front with the ground crew and chat. Pat and the boys have been working mighty hard, but still have some jollity left, and they won't take sympathy. "Pat, you've been working mighty hard," one of the men suggests. "Oh, I don't know -- keeps us out of trouble -- could use a little sleep maybe -- we'll do that after you leave," Pat retorts. "When will you be back?" As is our custom we give him an E. T. A. (estimated time of arrival). "You better not come before that," Pat warns meaningfully. "We'll be in the sack." So we agree to make our E. T. A. good to the minute.

Meanwhile various people drop by in Jeeps. Those who don't go, crew members and ground officers alike, usually drop by to wish the men good luck. We enjoy the repartee with Ben Lay, Doc Schroeder, Jerry Koleson and Mel Sowers. We miss Pat Murphy, the Chaplain. We were hoping that he'd come by and bless the ship. It was a most impressive ceremony when he blessed another ship that we flew, and now we want him to conduct the meeting in front of No. 11, our plane.

Allowing a few minutes for getting settled, we climb aboard, some of us up the nose wheel well ladder, the rest up the ladder in the rear door. No. 11 looks ready, crammed to the last gallon full of fuel, with the bomb bay jammed with bombs. Gross weight, Bill figures, is about 135,000 lbs. and the center of gravity is well forward, within the allowable limits, an important consideration with regard to safety and fuel.

Nick completes the engineer's check list while Higgy and I do the same for the piloting end. Jake is getting himself settled in the nose seat. Over the interphone Bill checks each man and finds everyone in his seat, ready to taxi. We check the fire guard and give Nick the signal to start No. 1, then as it catches and smoothes out, Nos. 2, 3, and 4 in turn. They fire right off, and sound all right. Pat, who has been sitting beside Nick to see if the engines look all right, returns the O.K. sign and climbs down the ladder. He removes the ladder, shouting "Give 'em Hell!", and we close the door. Pete Fortune rolls by and we fall in behind him, our briefed taxi, and take-off position. We're right on time. When it comes our time to roll onto the runway, we have cleared out the engine, lowered the flaps, and stowed the guns -- ready to go.

At 135,000 lbs., very heavy, we pick up speed slowly after releasing the brakes, then faster. The engines sound good and we commit ourselves to taking off. At 125 M.P.H. we go off just short of the end of the runway. Bill lifts the gear and flaps, Jakes times us, and Nick calls out the temperature. The scanners report the engines look all right. A few minutes and we are abreast of Saipan on the course for Nagoya. At 2000 feet the air is quite bumpy, so Higgy and I take turns flying instruments in order to save the autopilot. It is very dark now. The lights of Saipan are receding. All-engulfing darkness lies ahead.

Since we are to pass near Iwo we increase our altitude to 3500 in order to clear 3000 feet Minami Iwo, just south of Iwo. Some time later we look over and see the lights on Iwo and in the harbor. That's where the Marines fought and died. They're a brave bunch of men. It's hard to see why such a small spot of land can be worth so many American lives.

The lights of other planes are out of sight now. We are certainly alone, and it's so confounded dark. "Darker'n the inside of a cow." Higgy mumbles. Out my window I can see the flame shooting out of the inboard exhaust of No. 1 and the red glow of the wing-tip light. The dance music is being overcome by static as we go farther north. On the VHF set all is quiet. The planes are maintaining radio silence. It's hard to believe that within a few miles of us are many other planes. It is peaceful and quiet. I close my eyes to half-dose awhile. Suddenly in my reverie I smell acrid smoke. My sub-conscious alarm rings, and I'm wide awake. A host of thoughts of darkness, ditching, and the awful reality of being in trouble way out here flash through my mind. "Good Heavens, we're on fire," I think. Bill has jerked up straight, Jake is stirring. Bill and I look aft. The lights are out but I see Nick and his movements with the rustle of clothes indicates he's busy. The darkness is filling with smoke. Looking towards Nick's light I see smoke drifting forward from behind us. Instinctively I grab for the interphone button on the wheel and press the throat mike to warn the crew. A few words serve to inform me that the interphone is dead. I switch the jackbox, hit the switch in case it's stuck, check my headset connection, still no sound. "Interphone's dead." I shout to Bill as he moves aft with his flashlight. The automatic pilot, recently set up, is working and the fluorescent lights on the instrument panel still glow. Keeping an eye on the instruments and the controls I shout over my shoulder to Bill "Get the fire extinguisher -- tell the blister section." But Bill is already gone. He reappears with the fire extinguisher. Nick leaves his seat -- "Gotta remove voltage regulators." Bill stands ready with the fire extinguisher and Jake with the light. Apparently the fire is behind the pilot's armor plate in that section directly across from the engineer. Not being able to leave my seat, I listen to the voices in the rear and recognize Dick's. Then Nick emerges from behind the turret, with a brief "Regulators are out." He joins Bill and they peer, coughing, into the smoking section where various electrical units are located. The smoke is letting up and there is no apparent fire now, I gather from their talk. Meanwhile, Jake and I have raised the pilot and copilot windows to clear the air. From the first everything happened at once. Now, piecing together the conversation and adding it to the earlier experiences our outfit has had with the B-29, I realize that we had an electrical fire whose origin was in the faulty voltage regulators. The extent of damage is unknown, as yet, but the smoke is clearing out, there is no visible fire, and the plane is still flying. The crew all know that something's up and are alert to danger -- probably were from the first, since our senses when airborne are mighty sharp.

Nick and Bill are satisfied that the immediate danger is past. Nick, as surprised as we all were, reports his observations: "When I smelled the smoke I checked the volt and ammeters, saw they were high, turned off four generators, then took out the voltage regulators. We'll have to see what all was burning. Don't know what all's damaged, but the juice is off on the bad regulators. We shouldn't have any more trouble. I'd better keep an eye on them." He slips back into his seat, Hal returns to his seat and tells Al, who has stuck at his radio in case of emergency, that the danger is past. Jake lets out a "Whew!" Bill continues to look at the burned equipment. Meanwhile Hal has shouted the news through the tunnel, so the others know the status quo. Dick remains up front to help Nick. Only a short time, possibly two minutes, has passed altogether since we first smelled smoke. Now, with the air clear, normalcy begins to return. Dick takes Nick's seat and Nick, together with Bill, squats down on the flight deck next to my seat to analyze further the trouble. The engines are purring. I look out at the left wing and am reassured just to see it there with the props turning same as ever. At least we're still flying. Evidently our luck is holding out. For a few instants the water felt mighty close. Thinking over the situation I am impressed again by the utter reality of trouble when it happens, accompanied, as it is, by the wishful thought, "It just can't be!" But it is and you've got to do something about it. Any fire in a plane is bad, but to have one in the blackness of night, hundreds of miles from the nearest land and help, at a time when trouble is least expected by the rescue facilities, that's rough. Or is that just another way of saying it's tough to have a fire anytime and that it's very real when it happens to you.

Now we must take stock of the situation. The main thing is to keep ourselves flying, and the engines seem to be turning over all right. First the interphone should be fixed or some form of intercommunication set up between the front and aft sections of the plane. Al comes forward and decides that the only possible system we can have is through use of the VHF radio. This radio is generally used by the pilots to converse with other planes or with ground stations, but the entire crew can hear the pilot talk when they each switch their jackboxes to the VHF position. So Al removes the "A" crystal from the set and we leave the radio switch in that position. When the crystal is out the pilot's messages will not be broadcast outside the plane, yet the crew members can hear. We try it out and find that the pilot, copilot, and bombardier can carry on two-way conversations with each other while the rest of the crew can only hear. They cannot reply. Despite the limitation it is a lot better than nothing, so we carry on with the new arrangement. The crew members are all requested to check their own electrical equipment and to help check the airplane's equipment without turning on the units which draw a lot of juice. We don't have much electricity since five of the engine-driven generators are "off the line" (not being used) because of improper voltage regulation of each.

In this way we take further stock of the situation. The cabin lights are out, and we find that the wing-tip, formation, and recognition lights are out. The other planes are unable to see us. Nick points out that the normal inverter is faulty and the alternate is now being used. It seems that the power surges damaged the inverter, which is used to convert the generator's direct current into alternating current for the units which require it. The location of the fire suggests that the turbo supercharger amplifiers are damaged, and on inspection we find that they are badly burned in spite of protective fuses, and beyond airborne repair.

This means that we are short the additional 50% speed and power that the superchargers give to each engine. Further, that the air drawn into the carburetor cannot be heated in order to prevent icing in the carburetor. The lack of supercharger means no cabin heat or pressurization.

Hal informs us that the flux-gate compass is inoperative and that we will now fly by use of the magnetic compass, and that the drift meter is out. The Loran set, too, is damaged since it appears too "hot" -- far more so than normally. Hal has been hard hit in his department. Gabby reports that so far as he knows the radar set is unhurt -- it may be a little hotter than usual, but it can be counted on, he thinks. In the gunnery department, Jonesy reports that his equipment should be all right, since none of it was operating at the time of the trouble. Jake states that the bombsight and circuits to the releases, shackles, and bomb doors should be all right. Al says that the Laison radio is all right. The radio compass is out, a fact which Bill noticed.

Meanwhile we are still traveling toward Japan with a load of bombs. The plane still flies. We have quite an assortment of damages -- no turbos, no lights, no flux-gate compass, no drift meter, no radio compass, and faulty Loran, interphone, and power supply. We have one-sixth of the normal electricity available, since only one generator of the six engine-driven generators is operative. The target is 350 miles north of us. The possibilities are being considered by each of the fellows, I am sure, but no one mentions turning back. A mission is all a game of chance, anyway -- it's just a question of degree, no doubt, so we hold our heading for Nagoya. Somehow we must get the speed and power over the target that superchargers ordinarily provide, and we must neutralize, so far as possible, the present handicaps, so that we can drop the load and get back out of Nagoya. So, after talking it over, we agree on trying various new procedures, and each man, where concerned, learns his extra duties. Since the aft section cannot talk on the interphone, any important messages will be relayed though the tunnel by Dick, who will shout or carry them, crawling back and forth. To supplement the power supply to provide electricity for necessary equipment, George will turn on the put-put just before reaching the target area, thus giving two effective generators and a storage battery as the source of supply. Navigation will be accomplished by using the magnetic compass to hold a course and star shots to tell us periodically where we are. Since the gunner system takes a lot of electricity, Jonesy, and through him Charlie and George, agree to use only one turret at a time if we are attacked by fighters. Bill and I agree that to get the necessary speed on the bomb run and withdrawal, we will dive in and out. As for the rest, we trust that all will go well. The entire crew understands that we must be more alert than ever before not to endanger other planes by our maneuvers. While Bill holds the plane I go over the briefing data one more time, so that we can fit our flight into the plan in the best way possible. I see again that we are briefed to go up the center of Nagoya Bay, drop our bombs on the city and then withdraw to the west, all at 6400 feet. There are mountains to the west, just west of Ujimada before returning to sea again. We can't withdraw in that direction since we'll be diving -- we'd be too low and too slow. So we'll withdraw to the east and come back out the east edge of the Bay at an altitude well below the planes coming in -- just so they don't drop their bombs on us, but we'll have to take the chance.

With the plans made we go about the usual pre-target time activities. Nick transfers the fuel. Jake checks his bombing equipment. Al prepares tentative emergency messages to send to rescue facilities in case we have trouble over the target. Hal, meanwhile, is taking star shots and correcting our magnetic heading to put us at the entrance to the Bay. We all get into our heavy emergency equipment and flax suits and helmets. If we didn't know we were playing for keeps anyway, this heavy equipment would make the point, without a doubt. No woman in a girdle ever felt more constricted, I'm sure.

Hal shouts, "We're about 60 miles out! I'm not sure whether we're headed right for the Bay or off to one side." Gabby agrees to try to end the uncertainty by locating us with the radar. We strain our eyes to see the usual signs of fire and flak ahead, but everything is dark. Somehow it appears darker ahead to the left. Dick comes up with the message that Gabby has us plotted just left of course, approaching land. That means we're farther out than we thought. We alter course to the right. Jake says, "Land to our left at about 10 o'clock, 2-3 miles." Sure enough, we see a heavy, dark mass and a curving line where it separates from a lighter colored area -- the water. We are traveling up Nagoya Bay now. Hal continues to use the radar. Now we see the target area. The fires are there, all right, though the sky is not very bright at this distance. A billowing smoke cloud extends up to 2000 feet, it appears. Many searchlights are crossing and recrossing the sky, aimlessly wandering, haven't yet caught a plane. Other appear almost stationary or are moving slowly. Flak is exploding and tracers arching up. Explosions can be seen through the smoke or just to one side as other bombs hit. "Fighter firing from fire level." Bill reports. "He's a long way out." Let's hope he stays there, I think.

We are almost at the IP, about to begin the bomb run. We are now at 8000 feet instead of the briefed altitude of 6400. The put-put is on, Dick reports, and everyone all set in the rear. Nick states that the engines are all right and the generators operating OK. "Just so no one uses too much juice, we'll be all right." He adds. At this point we put the plane into our bombing dive. I have the controls, the autopilot is set up ready for use, in case we need it. Bill is holding his controls, too, in case I need help. We agree that if we need to do any unusually strenuous maneuvering that he would control the elevator and I would control the aileron and rudder. To the left we see occasional lights widely separated, but to the right the land is totally dark. Now we can see the dock area of Nagoya. Jake is over the sight. We are going down at the rate of 200 to 300 feet a minute and indicating almost 250 miles per hour. The smoke ahead makes the area hazy, but we make out many blocks of burning buildings. To the left, a B-29 is caught in searchlights and flak begins to explode all about him. "Poor guy." I think. "He gets caught so some of us can slip by -- hope he makes it out all right." All the time we are calling out flak and searchlights to each other as we see them, trying to replace the eyes and help of the scanners who we can't hear. We are on the timed radar run, holding a steady course. The bomb doors come open and we feel the jar through the plane as they snap into position. The smoke is heavy ahead and to the right, but it appears to be blowing in that direction.

Maybe we won't have to go into it. We start the long wait for the bombs to be dropped. We keep hoping they will be dropped, but it isn't time. "Two minutes." shouts Hal. Meanwhile, in a broad area ahead and to both the right and left ahead, we see new explosions in the city amid fires already burning. We can't see the building as such, but we see structures afire. According to Hal we are headed squarely for the center of the city and are now over the Dock area. I look sharply at an angle out of my window. Fires are burning in pronounced areas there, so that must be the docks and wharves with water in between. We're down to 6800 feet now and still diving, holding our 250 miles per hour. "Bombs away!" Jake shouts and we feel the sudden lift to the plane, telling the whole crew the bombs are released. We are almost in the smoke now and we turn hard right. Flak is exploding all about this area and we want to get out of it. The fires light up the cabin.

Suddenly the cabin is brilliantly lit up -- the light is blinding -- searchlights. So they've got us now. They won't keep us, I say and want to believe it. We dive harder to the right, banking the plane sharply with all our combined strength on the controls. The bomb doors are closed and we are going over 300 mph. We are blinded further by new light and we realize that more searchlights have us now, but no flak. So they think we are coming down? Are they unable to figure our speed and altitude? They could use small arms now, if they cared. We keep expecting the flak, and the flak curtains feel mighty thin underneath our seats. This is the original "hot seat". Now the lights go off of us, why we don't know -- but just suddenly they're gone. Now we are beyond the Dock area, back over the Bay, close to the eastern shore. Our altitude is now 5000 feet. We begin to level off. Dick Bush brings the message that 11 bombs are still hanging in the bomb bay, which means that 173 have been dropped. They are the M47A gasoline gel type incendiary of 75 lb. each. .We open the bomb doors again and Jake clicks the bomb toggle release, but no luck. He checks all the switches carefully, but they are all on, just as they were over the target, so Jake goes aft to try to get rid of the bombs. We caution him to be careful, since we are low over Nagoya Bay, a heck of a place for a swim. "Don't fall out." We continue out the Bay and after a few minutes Jake reappears to state that he had to take the wooden bulkhead brace and knock the bombs loose, and that he reduced the number of fish for the Japs with the bombs. He watched them fall until they hit the water -- apparently they were wasted.

After leaving the target Dick stayed in the tunnel to rest, worn out by his crawling shuttle service, back and forth. Al stopped sweating quite so much behind the turret where he can't see a thing and is always thinking of the emergency end. He hears the other planes in trouble over the radio and is prepared to send messages for us at all times. Nick keeps his eye on the electrical situation, after cutting the put-put. We still have a long way to go, but we all relax generally after getting out of the Bay -- all but Hal. Without his flux-gate, Loran, and drift meter he is greatly handicapped. It is hard to hold a steady course on the pilot's magnetic compass, and the navigator doesn't have one. Jake helps him some with the bombsight, which gives accurate drift readings. But our uncertainty doesn't leave, since we have a long flight ahead and there is no heat for the carburetor air. As the air goes into the carburetor through a venturi tube, its temperature drops and the moisture in the air sometimes tends to freeze, thus restricting the opening for the fuel flow. This, in time, will naturally stop the engines for lack of gas. This difficulty is overcome by heating the air before it reaches the carburetor by using the supercharger. This danger occurs even when the outside temperature is above freezing. The danger increases just below freezing, particularly when there is a lot of water in the air, as in cloudy areas. Since we have no supercharger we cannot apply carburetor heat. It is almost -20 degrees centigrade (10 degrees F) outside, and ahead we are certain to encounter clouds. Our hope is that while in clear air, even though the temperature is low, the ice will not form and when we approach the cloudy areas we will be far enough south so that the temperature will be well above freezing. Though intangible, our situation feels none the less precarious.

Meanwhile, we can't neglect the stomachs. Nick passes out sandwiches ("Jelly vapor" the sandwich spread is called for obvious reasons), fruit juice in the can, hard candy, and hot coffee, heated in the cumbersome food warmers, large contraptions the Commanding Officers insist that we carry. We have no room for them, but carry them we must. But we do like to have hot coffee. Nick officiates in such handsome style that Bill strikes the pose (very effective but amazing with the Georgia drawl) "Waiter, some watah!" Nick does himself proud, draping the towel over his arm and sash-shaying about the crowded cabin, dispensing rations.

By this time we are far enough south so that the temperature is up above the point of danger, we hope. At least we assume so, and prepare to nap a bit. The Benzedrine that I took just after take-off has kept me awake nicely, but doesn't hinder present sleeping opportunities. Bill and I alternate "sacking up" though I sleep the most. In the midst of it the autopilot starts acting up and we almost have more electrical trouble. As a result, the autopilot is inoperative and we fly manually the rest of the way, taking turns.

Low clouds force us to fly at 700 feet as we approach Saipan and Tinian. Over the harbor we see the Navy, cargo vessels, and hospital ships. And there is Tinian. What a grand sight! "There's home, boys." says Jake, and we all feel mighty good. Circling to the right we fly over the camp area, see our tent and the dogs out back, and it looks good to us. We land on runway #3. With the put-put and single generator we have no trouble lowering the gear and flaps. We taxi around to the parking area and see that most of the fellows are back ahead of us. We have quite a reception. They seem glad to see us back and they know we're glad to see them again. We fan the breeze with Pat and the boys, telling them about the electrical fire, the resulting malfunctions, and then of the target circumstances. They are chagrined over the difficulties, but realize that we understand they couldn't have prevented this from happening. While they get to work on the plane we load our equipment into the waiting truck and take it to the P.E. (personal equipment) room. Then up to the area. The fellows all feel jolly, even though tired. Our plane, too, has another mission behind it now. We hope that this trouble we had marks the end of the bugs in our plane. And we've had a lot of excitement. Is it always going to be this way?

At interrogation we relive the mission for the "Intelligence" department. They are surprised to learn about all the electrical trouble we had. We describe the extent of the damage seen, the flak, the fighters and searchlights. Although 88 enemy planes were sighted and 13 attacks made, none of our planes went down over Japan. Subsequently two "ditched" with one crew being rescued immediately. There is always hope that the other will be located.

Now, next day, we are happy to hear that Reconnaissance photos of the bombing show that severe damage was inflicted on the Japs. We feel good to know that we helped. A large part of the city was destroyed by fire. We hear a Jap broadcast and they state that the Jap fighters shot down a large number of our planes, and made other exorbitant claims. We get a good laugh over the "eye-wash" they sell their people on the radio. We wonder if their programs, which are beamed at us, are to discourage and scare us. It's amazing how they "miss the boat" in understanding us.

Chapter 12 Shimonoseki Strait Mining

March 27-28, 1945 – No. 7

"We Get Our First Fighter"

No. 11 flew without us, being taken by Ray Ramsey and crew to return to Nagoya March 24th. On this mission they bombed a specific target from medium altitude -- the aircraft plant on the north side of the city. No. 11 behaved herself nicely, so we heard. Pat says that the pilot write-ups of the plane after the mission were that No. 1 fuel boost (additional fuel pump) failed, and that No. 4 back-fired. He found that the back-firing was not a malfunction but the result of too lean a mixture. No. 11 is ready to go again, with the broken radio-compass aerial replaced.

Life on the island goes on much the same. The day we returned from Nagoya the Group had a big "organization day". All the officers and enlisted men went down onto the ball diamonds (made from cleared cane fields) to eat sandwiches and drink beer. Later there were ball games in which many of the big dogs participated. The General and our C.O. played on opposite teams and seemed to have a great time. Most of us were glad to quit early and rest up at the tent. "Turbo" and "Gyro" bounced all around, frantic with attention, and we played with them. Goodwin and Hett borrowed the use of the washer which had been standing idle, and laboriously washed some of their clothes. The fitting climax to this endeavor (and it is customary) is for the clothes to fall off the line while they're still wet. Meanwhile, Bill read his Thorne Smith, laughing to himself and calling our attention to choice passages. Hal entered events in his diary, and Jake luxuriously read magazines and ate candy from home in bed.

On the 23rd we test-hopped No. 11 and participated in a "mine laying" practice mission, which consisted of the usual radar run to which we are accustomed. The scene of the practice was Pagan Island, located between Tinian and Guam. There was no sign of life on the island. The next day we test-hopped the plane again and did some general sight-seeing around the area. It is surprising to see how Tinian has been built up since our arrival. Many of the large cane fields are gone, replaced by new camp areas, roads, and supply dumps.

It is the 26th of March and we are listed as one of the crews to go on the first mine laying missions against the Japs. Before target identification I talk to Pat at the line and he says the plane is ready to go. The mines are already loaded, six of them at 2000 lb. each, three in each bomb bay.

At target identification, held in the briefing building, Jake, Bill, Hal and I get a seat and are joined by Gabby. On the stage is the usual rubber topographical map of Japan, and also charts of the Inland Sea and the Japanese Islands in detail. The Intelligence Officer takes up his pointer, and in his laboriously painstaking, articulate fashion begins: "This is the Inland Sea, and these are the Straits through which all Japanese ships must pass to reach Japanese ports -- that is, to reach their best ports, and through which they must pass to carry provisions and ammunition and supplies of all kinds to China, the Philippines, Formosa, Korea, Manchuria -- anywhere that the soldiers are located. He then goes on to explain further the significance of the Inland Sea. It seems that the best harbors and biggest business centers are located in this area, with the exception of Tokyo. If the area is successfully mined then all shipping must use the poorer northern ports or western ports near the Sasebo and Nagasaki area, with the resulting long overland hauls, or the ships must go around the southern edge of Kyushu where our Navy, including subs, are waiting. In short, this is the spot! Here's where we're going to mine today and later -- for all those reasons.

I check to see if the words of wisdom from the platform are soaking into the right man, and am happy to see Gabby latching onto the radar info, Hal the navigational, and Jake the mining approach, IP, turning point and the like. Bill and I in overall capacity try to get it all. As a result, we hope to remember enough to use the information that each man gets to the best advantage on the trip. Also, we know generally what each man has and has not been told. Each man has a specialist's view of the mission, depending on his particular job. Though Bill and I always consider the trip as a whole, still we know who to ask in checking any particular facts. With a good crew all this is necessary is to give each man all the rope he needs in his job. But even though we consider each man as boss in his job, yet we absorb the information too, on the principle that two heads are better than one.

We leave the meeting with a good general idea, albeit hazy in spots, of the nature of this first mine laying mission. As a matter of fact, at an earlier meeting we were given the particular spot that we were to drop our mines. Now we are ready for the briefing before the flight. The ground work has been laid.

A long line of combat crew members is funneling into the briefing building when we arrive from our tents. The rows of seats each bear the AC's name. We find our crew members already in place -- good men, "on the ball". The fellows look rested and ready. "What's the matter Dick, you look thin," we kid our thinnest member. Dick answers, "Don't know what's the matter, been spending all my time in bed, so I wouldn't overdo myself." Charlie laughs and adds, "That's no change in his activities." The noisy chatter gives way to a quieter hum as preparations on the stage indicate the briefing is about to begin. We all know that the General, our Wing Commander, will be present.

"ATTENTION!" Everyone leaps to his feet with "poop" (paper work) scattering between the rows. The General and Colonel, our C.O., have arrived. After a proper interval of tense rigidity we are told by the General to "Be seated." He is kind enough (unlike our C.O.) to add "gentlemen", easing somewhat the discomfort of the whole thing. Our C.O. begins with the usual very general talk that's meant to add pep and put pride in us, but it always sounds to us a little like "Keep-on-doing-whatever-it-is-that-you-are-doing-to-hang-up-such-a-fine-record-for-my-group-and-I'll-skin-the-man-who-does-otherwise." Then "O.K., let's get on with it." The Operations Officer then calls to the Intelligence Officer and the pointer is whipped out, the microphone tied on, and the charts materialized from the wings by benefit of roller coasters. He gives in more detail the data given at the Target Identification. He knows that each crew has been given a definite track to make good, and a definite dropping point from which to lay the mines in a string. He designates the course, the nature of the land and water cover in flight. Shimonoseki Strait is flanked by a city on each side. Under the water lies a tunnel connecting the two. The channel is narrow. Our job, he explains, is not to mine that channel, which could so easily be mine swept, but rather to mine the water area on each side of the channel. Our job will be to mine the waters west for some eight miles of the strait. Three groups will participate in this, and one on the Island Sea side. Then he calls for the flak analysis by another member of the Intelligence department. After the exchange of pointer and mike, more charts are pulled out with circles in red indicating flak areas of fire. We are shown that our course is planned so that we dodge most of these centers of fire, if we stay on course.

Bob Hall then gives out with the Air-Sea rescue and we are shown and told about the location of three subs, two dumbos, two superdumbos, and a surface craft. In addition there is the Navy located near Iwo-Jima, a large Task force. We are to call "Agate" instead of "Glacier" to call the Navy when in distress. Lt. Sullivan gives us a brief weather cross-section talk. It appears that we'll see plenty. There are two cold fronts to go through and the target will be just south of a high pressure system. Winds will be normal. The Operations Officer takes over to discuss the taxi, takeoff, and course to be flown. All are the usual. We are to have the Deputy Group leader as a passenger, while the General will fly with Bob Rodenhouse. Our course is by way of Iwo and back direct. He also points out the courses and target location for the other Groups.

After this the specialized briefings are held with the crew splitting up into various specialties. Bill and I stay for the pilot's briefing. After this we all go to our assigned trucks. Alger and Lazin are to share No. 4. With a certain amount of confusion we are off for the flight line, 15 minutes late as usual. The procession of trucks makes use of the haul road, a short cut, as it's permitted now. Ordinarily this road is used exclusively by the Seabees, hauling coral for the construction of runways and parkways.

At the personal equipment building each gets his A-3 bag and hikes over to the plane in the neighboring revetment, or hardstand as it is called. Grobe is lodged down to his hips in the No. 4 nacelles! Pat tells us the No. 4 starter burned out prior to his intended check of No. 4. Otherwise the plane is ready to go. Standing under the wing I can see the cowl flaps bend as one section of them opens but not the other (they are overlapping). Pat sees this trouble. Our passenger arrives. The Commanding Officer has brought him up in his personal jeep, and we put his equipment in the plane. With this he says, "Have a good trip, Alger." To which the answer is, "Thank you, sir. We hope to." The maintenance work is explained to the Lt. Colonel, our passenger, and he seems to understand. It's tough on the ground crew to have some work to finish with the air crew standing by to take the plane. It is raining and the men are wet working in the nacelles, mighty uncomfortable work. The drive arm for the cowl flaps is fixed. Meanwhile, Steffler, the mess officer, has brought up our food and we even inveigle an extra set of sandwiches for the Colonel. Before we run up the engines, Bill checks the personal equipment again to see that each man has his, including the Colonel.

Bill and Nick complete their check lists. We all have our gear stowed and are settled in our places ready to roll. Bill checks the controls with the scanners and ascertains that everyone is ready in the rear. George is in the tail position and the scanners are checking the controls, gears, and flaps. There are a few trying moments, but the engines all fire up O.K., and after a few minutes of running we know they're going to be all right. Bill and I check the prop pitch motors and the feathering motors. Nick checks the generators and mags of each engine. With full turbo boost on we give the plane a complete power check and each engine checks out all right. It is a pleasant moment when we wave goodbye to the worried ground crew and they know the plane is all right. As it turns out, we are only 15 minutes late for the take-off, and still with our own Group.

Taxing out it is a question of not running the engines too fast, that is, over 900-1000 RPM, so that the brakes are not used too much, yet not to let the spark plugs load up. It is downhill to the west taxiway at the head of the runway. Anticipating our turn by the plane ahead of us, we stow the turrets which are "hot", pointed up and down for safety when taxing, and clear out our engines. Then the flaps are run down 25 degrees while Nick has a generator on, and we follow the last ship off, rolling onto the runway headed for take-off. The flagman or expediter, as he's called (extra-dity, as Pete Fortune calls him), holds the flag overhead and we increase power, then down goes the flag and we release the brakes, increasing the power by "walking" the throttles up the quadrant. The engines are at full power very quickly this way and we get the most good out of the runway. Though 8000 feet long, they seem short sometimes. The engines accept the power; it appears we'll fly in short order. Bill, as usual, is busy. He catches No. 2 prop with the toggle switch as it overspeeds and brings it back to 2500. Meanwhile he calls out the airspeed. At 120 A.S. we are doing all right two-thirds of the way down the runway. Shortly thereafter, with about 130, I ease back on the wheel and we go off the way we like it, gaining altitude slowly. With throttles partially locked I can adjust the trim tab with the left hand to hold the elevator. We level off at about 200 feet and at 160 Bill starts up the flaps, Dick and Charlie report the gear fully up, which was started immediately after being airborne. It takes several minutes to get the speed up to 195 and then we back off the power to 2400 RPM and the manifold pressure to 43 inches. The flaps are up. Jake is timing the 3 minutes out that is required on the heading under the instrument plan before we make the first turn. From there on, all goes well with Jonesy, Dick, and Charlie really on the ball calling out the other planes. Off at 1625K and passing the field on course 343 degrees at 1636. The 6/10 cumulous clouds seem to be around our flight altitude of 5500 feet, so we climb to 6500 feet and are well in the clear. This is just one of the many small changes that must be made during a flight, that are not as briefed, and we make it. We are happy to see that the Colonel agrees on the wisdom of this move, so we hold that altitude.

We settle down on course. Higgy and I each take a turn at flying instruments and agree that the plane is feeling good. We set up the C-1; it works beautifully, so we lean back and prop the feet up. Numerous planes are reported periodically flying toward the Base. Must be returning planes of the daylight attack, a diversionary raid to the first big mining effort. The Japs won't be expecting us. Jonesy wonders whether we should test-fire our guns as briefed, but on inquiry thinks it best not to, so we don't. Too little ammunition on hand.

The Colonel seems at home. He has several pillows piled on the hatch and appears quite at ease, a pleasant passenger to say the least. We trot out the hard candy and chat for awhile. Hal goes off the interphone; it seems that he must visit the bomb bay. A lengthy mock discussion over the interphone results. Should the relief tube be brought to him or should he just aim at it. He decides to go to the tube, and we all feel that he made the right choice. Nick believes it's a good idea to check the fuel transfer system at this time, so everyone is warned about smoking and turning off various radios and electrical units. Al asks, "Nick, be all right if I chew candy?" Nick makes a retort in weighty manner about it being O.K. if he could chew without sparking, and goes on about checking the transfer. We lean back like privileged passengers on a plane that flies itself, and agree that the sunset is beautiful. The small rolls of clouds are dappled with brilliant red coloring. It is vivid, the color stretching overhead and around the horizon, becoming fainter the farther the distance from the west. At this point I take my first Benzedrine tablet. It settles the stomach nicely and I don't get hungry. As for its sleep-preventative qualities -- seems like it reverses the urge within me. The Doc claims that these potent white aspirin-size pills affect people differently, varying between individuals as to when it takes effect, how long it works, how long it last. Some people sleep well anyway. Dusk is settling around us, gradually dissolving and obliterating the light in the west, working around from the east.

At 2020K we arrive in the vicinity of Iwo-Jima. Gabby reports that the Navy is some 10 miles southeast of Iwo, and becoming more specific, states that there are about six large ships (carriers) and some fifteen smaller craft (escorts). Gabby is mighty sharp on his scope interpretation -- wish we could check his accuracy on this report. I mention this to the Colonel, who appreciates the accuracy of radar work. He says, "Wish we could do something for these radar men." He is referring to the long struggle by us all with the higher authorities to secure a different specialty number, and the corresponding higher rank for the job. I agree with him and think, "Wish we could do something for this one, at least. They can correct the whole situation later on."

Gabby plugged the food warmer in earlier and we know the Colonel is hungry, so we decide to eat. Nick opens the sandwiches and hot coffee is sent up from the rear, together with cream and sugar. Boy, it hits the spot. Our lunch was not too good, and the exertion has hungered us. Odd how sitting in one small spot can be such work at times, and now I've done that for over 2000 hours. Armchair athlete for sure. The food cheers up the atmosphere and the Colonel joins us in a bull session about various subjects. We discuss, first, the cruise-control problem of the B-29 as we face it every flight. We are never sure of the fuel used. The gauges are not accurate either in the plane or gas truck -- they are not right generally. As a result we never know how much fuel we have in the plane at any time, or the amount that is put in to replenish that used. With all our flying revolving about the fuel remaining -- whether or not we get home in the plane -- you'd think there would be more accuracy involved. An extremely expensive machine with the finest engineering behind it, and yet it uses a faulty liquidometer, which endangers the craft and those flying it. But that's just one of those things, no doubt. The Colonel agrees and adds bits here and there. I kid him finally, saying "It's good to be able to tell you these things -- to deposit our troubles with you." (To let them gain your attention, hoping you can improve the situation, I add to myself.) He laughs and seems to enjoy the thought.

After a silence the Colonel say, "Just think of what you were doing five years ago." I do, and answer, "Hadn't even flown in an airplane in my life." "Strange, eh?" I appreciate the philosophical touch just then. It is odd -- here we are, eleven men of a combat crew and a "wheel" from the staff, all together, all strangers a few years or months before, yet we are engaging in a life or death matter, doing a job completely strange to us before this period of our lives. I haven't by a long way lost the wonder of flying, or of me flying, and with a potent weapon about me so far from home. We might all say, "Strange job -- strange place to be -- strange people." But forgetting the contrast to the past the word "strange" applies no more, not now nor in the future. Now, going to the target, in our plane, with my crew, it seems the most natural thing in the world. Somehow, over a long war-time program we are thrown together, each with his particular civilian and Army background, and now we are a combat team flying a plane, the like of which the world has never seen before. It is a potent weapon, a fitting representation of a mighty nation, and of the brain-work, skill and labor of an intelligent people. It's tough that it must be an offspring of war. And we, in the plane, are doing jobs we would never have done in our lives had there not been a war. Maybe we will never do them again after the war. Right now the risk is great, going to the target, but we wouldn't turn back. Maybe it's good we don't know what is ahead, but I am glad to have a good crew for company, and a good plane around us. May it stay that way, win or lose.

About this time, with the sunset just gone on one side and a beautiful full moon on the other, we decide to dedicate this mission to the girls and wives back home. Probably we always do, but this time we agree over the interphone -- we bring it out in the open -- with a joking remark about that full moon. We kid the single guys for not having a wife at home waiting. We feel sorry for them -- we benedicts.

A strange, unexpected weather phenomenon occurs. The clouds below us rise up in a 50-mile hump, through which we fly on instruments. Above this is a high top layer, then all clear again.

At 2100K Nick reports, after careful figuring, that we are now 80 gallons over the curve (in excess) according to cruise control figures computed on a basis of power settings against time used. Since we have been given an amazing overall reserve of 900 gallons this is negligible and better than we usually do the first five hours of the flight, when we are at our heaviest. Since we figure to save fuel as the plane gets lighter (as compared to the chart figures) we will be below the line before we get home, if all goes well. Al calls to say that the radio compass lead in wire just broke. That makes the record perfect. Every time the plane flies this wire breaks and the compass goes out of commission. We keep thinking the radio department will fix it so that it will stay fixed. Taking a general check I see Jake napping, Bill day-dreaming and Nick on his fuel figuring. The Colonel is sleeping, as is George, so Charlie says. He and Dick are scanning. Jonesy is in the radar room with Gabby, who is using the radar. Al is listening for calls on the radio, and Hal navigating for all he's worth, taking shots, Loran lines, and refiguring the dead reckoning continually based on new information.

Nick, Hal, Al, Gabby, and Bill take some Benzedrine to stave off fatigue. We climb a little and Hal takes a shot or two before the cloud tops envelope us and we bounce around in the turbulence. Hal's ETA for the turning point is 0015, the heading is 311 degrees. By 2300 everyone who can is sleeping. The Benzedrine or something is keeping me awake, maybe it's premonitions. Nick is transferring the fuel, and it "feels" late, the way it used to feel long ago, past midnight, at home with the streets deserted. It's beautiful outside. The moon is high and full, giving a silvery tinge to the horizon and clouds around us, a silvery veil all around with occasional thicker wisps sliding quickly over our wing. I can see the exhaust glow on the inboard side of No. 1 engine -- the flames leap out several inches. These engines are truly wonderful things -- it's almost unbelievable, almost beyond mechanics, to think that the fuel flows into them, and the oil circulates, and the cylinders drive, and the crankshaft turns over 2000 times a minute, hour after hour. That's all we have supporting us. Nick is now transferring fuel in earnest so that all fuel will be gone from the center wing section into the four engine tanks so if the transfer pump is damaged we'll still have fuel, none trapped. Just one and one-half hours to go.

We begin to put on our heavier equipment so that we'll be ready by time of landfall. First, the heavy jacket for warmth. Then the Colonel helps me put on the flak vest over the parachute, which is buckled about me atop the Mae West. Then on goes the leather lined headgear containing earphones. It's hard to hear conversation after this is on, so we talk little except for the interphone, once we're dressed. Over the headgear goes the flak helmet and the oxygen mask flaps beside my face on the left where it is attached to the headgear. The oxygen hose clothes-clamp permits holding it out of the way unless needed. The oxygen "bail out" bottle, recommended as part of the ditching equipment, is in the seat under me, tied to my thigh. The tube from it is connected to the oxygen mask. The mask has been used in this manner by crew members in ditching, who have been trapped under water for short periods of time. It permits them to breathe for several minutes. I take the controls and Bill puts on his equipment. Jake looks ahead so that we are aware of any other planes that might be nearby. Gabby reports the location of other planes as he sees them on the "scope" of the radar. We extinguish all our lights inside and out and warn the crew members to beware of any revealing lights. Gabby turns out his white light and uses the fluorescent, as we all do. The situation is ticklish. We are 5500 feet and are counting on hitting the mouth of the Bungo Strait, between Kyushu and Skikoku Islands, up which we must fly. There is rugged country on each side with elevations of 6000 feet and more. But our main concern, once we know we are in the strait, is to hit Sada-Misaki Point which lies in the middle of the strait on the end of a long finger of land, extending west. This is the beginning point of our planned course. If we don't hit it we'll have to go out and start over, and flying against traffic is endangering everyone. As luck and good work would have it, Hal hits the strait right in the middle with just about perfect navigation. After 1400 miles he pinpoints us right where we ought to be, Gabby on the radar confirms this location. It is 0010 and Hal and Gabby give new headings to fly to hit the point. We are able to see faintly the land on either side in the distance. Now we come to the point. There it is, dead ahead. We find that what we think is clouds is actually clear sky with the moonlight giving the illusion, making a haze that is deceptive. We are two minutes off on our ETA, not bad, eh? Hal calls out a new heading of 322 degrees on the flux-gate and we fly on in a complete blackout. We approach land and see a light-house on the tip of land. The light is extinguished as we are almost overhead. Kind of late with your black-out, buddy, the warden wouldn't like it. Now we are in the Inland Sea. We feel the very quietness of this darkness, a man-made dark-out. It feels like thin ice we're on. All is quiet on the interphone, and I can feel every man doing his job -- alert, searching the darkness for sign of the enemy. They can't stop us now -- we're off to a good start on the mining problem. Now it's a question of flying several headings for a specified time, and then getting out. That's how they put it in the briefing -- nothing to it.

Gabby calls, "They're a lot of surface crafts at 11 and 1 o'clock, big ones, too. They're beginning to turn in circles -- looks like their fleet, lots of big ones, besides the escorts." Gabby can see them on the radar scope. Evidently the ships are more afraid of revealing their position than they are eager to shoot at us. Maybe they think we're here after them. Actually, we are. After tonight they won't go anywhere than right where they're now sitting without hitting a mine.

Some of the boys report a little flak coming up at us here, but not much nor is it accurate. It is dark, but with a bulky quality that means land under us. At 0038 Hal says "Turn", and we go onto the next heading of 240 degrees. Gabby and Hal are working together to determine when to turn, through the slant range on the radar. Since haziness does not bother the radar's eyes, as it does ours, we feel certain of our position, that this is the turning point. "Searchlights at 11 and 1," Jonesy and Jake are covering us ahead, and report the first lights. Some other planes are up ahead of us, and the Japs have given up trying to hide their land installations -- it's too clear a night.

On this heading the moonlight is in our favor when looking ahead. The gunners will still have difficulty looking aft. Ahead I can see the coastline and then the water. We will mine somewhere in that area and then skidoo home -- I think. We are now on the northeast of Shimonoseki. I ask, "Are there ships ahead of us, Gabby?" "Roger," he answers. So we'll probably get flak from them. But we're on the mining run now and can't alter course. We must plant the mines and know exactly where we put them, so the top command will know. "Airfield below," Jake reports, and I look slightly ahead and to the left. Sure enough there is a Jap field. Why? The lights are marking the runways and a plane taking off, or am I just seeing things? Normally the Japs hide all their military installations with a black-out. Maybe they realize we're after bigger game than just a field this time. Dick and Charlie call out lights below, they've caught sight of the field. "Fighter at 10 low," Jake calls, and we see a lighted fighter go by us in the opposite direction. Man, there's a lot of activity here tonight, like downtown traffic. Ahead we see flak and searchlights making quite a pattern, inquisitive fingers of light reaching up accompanied by bright explosions.

"Tracers at 11 and 1," Jonesy calls out. He's covering the forward area while Jake is over the bombsight on the run. Bill and I keep glancing about, along with checking the flight instruments. We are flying manually in order to be more maneuverable in case trouble occurs. Nick is checking the engine instruments and looking out his window to see some of the show. Tracers, leaving fiery paths, cross the sky. Searchlights catch planes and track them ahead to our left. It feels like a busy place, a regular thoroughfare, not near so lonely as it usually feels. Nick reports some flak out beyond our right wing-tip and I glance over to see the black blobs of smoke. All we can do is sit here and take it. We're over the water now, and it won't be long 'til we get rid of the mines and can maneuver. This straight and level path makes me feel like a shooting gallery pigeon. We're in suspended animation. The flak is heavy just to our left, evidently shore batteries. Nick reports more flak to the right, must be from ships. Hope our number's not there. There are fighters about and occasionally we glimpse one going by. Just keep going brother. "Let 'em go," Hal tells Jake, and Jake pushes the switch. Dick and Al check the bomb bay -- "Only one fell, the others are hung up." "Get rid of them, Jake!" I shout, knowing we must keep them in this area, and Jake hits the salve button. "They're gone," the fellows report. The doors come closed and we are ready to skidoo. We're 12,000 lb. lighter now. Jake says "Fighter low at 11." "Get on him, Dick," Jonesy directs. We are bathed in light. "Radar lights on us," Bill adds. It's bright in the cabin now, can't see much outside either. Feels like we're naked on a stage. "Flak high at 11," Jake says. Suddenly the light is turned off, then Charlie reports, "Fighter at 4." "Get on him, George," Jonesy calls. We've got a fighter on our tail. Bright red tracers flash by the cabin, coming over or through our left wing -- whew, that's close -- must have hit us, I could almost touch them. He's after us and I urge George, "Get him, boy." The plane vibrates with accompanying rumble and we know George is firing. "He's in flames," George and Jonesy chorus. "At a boy, George." It is possible? Did he really get him? The interphone is filled with talk and above the exclamations, almost synonymous with the first announcement, George shouts "I hit him first." We all laugh with relief. In the midst of all this death-dealing activity, George comes out with that! Now we've got a fighter to our credit.

We're busy as ever. Still flying west for the minute after mines release, as briefed, I bank the plane to the left sharply so that we can see the fighter crash, after Jonesy says, "See him burning -- keep watching!" A trail of flame ends with an explosion and the fighter has hit the water. What a sight! But we are still in danger and are keyed up with excitement. Jake and Dick call out flak, the surface ships are firing at us. "Better take evasive action," Bill suggests, and we turn back to the left. "B-29 at 7," Dick says. Jake reports "Two islands directly below." So we mined just short of those islands -- must recall that for the interrogation. "Light at 11 level," Jake reports. "Light and plane at 6 level," George says, and Jonesy counters "On him with both upper turrets." George observes "Seems to be turning in." Dick's in on this, saying "On him -- coming low underneath." "Give him the works," Jonesy calmly directs and we wonder up front just what the heck's going on. Piecing together the snatches of interphone talk is aggravating. If I only had a gun myself and could fire! Higgy, Hal, Nick, and Al feel the same way, no doubt. I feel so helpless, but the boys are doing it for us and doing it well -- better than we, could be a whole lot. So Higgy and I grab the wheel a little harder and wrestle the plane, that helps. "He's on your side, Charlie," Dick says. That fighter is still with us. Evidently these fighters don't know a good crew to leave alone when they see one. "Let's get another, boys," I urge. The Colonel is kneeling on the hatch, holding on to the detachable aisle seat. "Got a fighter," I explain, since he's not on interphone. "Keep your eyes open, George," Jonesy warns, and George comes in with utter disgust in his voice, "They're open!" Higgy looks over and lets out a laugh. George has a way of saying things that gives us a laugh, usually when we need it. "Plane at 3 level," Charlie reports. Jonesy's on him, too, it seems. "He's getting our altitude and speed -- dropping back to tail." These fighters are tough to shake tonight. Dick reports searchlights and we recall that this is a big industrial center. Evidently they have it heavily protected. There appear to be six or eight open-hearth blast furnaces, and we are able to see them from here. A B-29 is caught in the lights, we can see him clearly. From the center of the large ring of lights trained on him there comes a barrage of flak -- we can see the muzzle blasts, then the explosions as the flak burst around the plane. He's in a tough spot. That's a neat set-up the Japs have. Probably many of the lights, or all of them, are radar controlled, and so are the guns. Tonight it's so clear they could control them visually. Either way, it's the wrong night for any of our planes to be caught. It's hard to see how they can miss our planes at this altitude. We're still at 6000 feet. We feel sorry for whoever that is, caught in that interlocking field of fire. Evidently the Japs are using their lights in one case to pinpoint and illumine the planes as a target for the big guns, and in another to pick up B-29s and hold them until a fighter gets on their tail, and then extinguish.

Having turned at Jina Shima, we are holding a southeast heading, hoping to skirt the edge of the Yawata fire and yet not to approach the area to the south at Fukuoka, where we know there are guns. As it is, we are well to the south of the briefed course, but we don't intend to brave that fire near Yawata -- no thanks. Meanwhile we can't hold any speed at all with the briefed power of 1900 RPM, to be used on the withdrawal. We've got to get out of here.

Bill has the controls. "22, 35, Nick," I change the power, hoping to pick up speed. We are only going 190. Jonesy, Dick, Charlie, and George are talking over a fighter that is hanging around the rear, flying from one side to the other. Now he turns off the white light that marked him for us, and it's harder for the gunners to see him, but he's there. Gabby says, "I can see him on the scope." Maybe this is one of those radar night fighters we have been warned about. Gabby suddenly says, "I've got about six fighters on the scope." Maybe that crashed fighter has buddies up here. The gunners peer through the moonlight haze and occasionally report that they think they see a plane, but aren't sure. We exhort them to keep looking and to fire when sure it's a fighter. Knowing that radar fighters must work out a problem based on the speed and course of the plane being attacked, we do some evasive action. Bill makes a turn of about 30 degrees to the left, we are well beyond Yawata now. "Let's climb." And Bill changes some of our speed into a gradual climb. This will serve to throw the fighters off and we'll avoid the high ground ahead. "My scope's jammed by the fighters," Gabby reports. "They've closed in." Bill turns back to the right. "That threw them off," Gabby reports. "Let's turn back on course, Bill," I suggest, and Bill puts us on our original heading. We're still climbing and holding a speed of 220. The power is now at 23 39. Jonesy comes in with "Fighter at 6 high." Evidently Jonesy has spotted one of the closer fighters. "30 degrees right, Bill," George shouts. "Tracers under us," and Jonesy adds, "They're shooting down at us." Evidently this fighter is at a distance and is trying to hit us without closing in. Well, we're not going to sit here and get shot at. "Going up to 24 43, Nick," I inform him, so he can check the time and compute our fuel consumption accurately. "We're shakin' and gittin' now," Bill says. We're doing 240 and climbing. "Hold altitude and start a double drift," I suggest. We'll build up our speed and alter course again to throw off the fighter, yet we'll still be on our same general course by flying timed headings of the double drift. In this we hold two minute legs, flying headings of 45 degrees to the right, 90 to the left, then back on the original heading again. This is more trying for we can't see them. It's a deadly game of tag. The gunners don't have much ammunition left -- all we had at the start of the mission was 100 rounds per gun, with 200 in the tail. That just isn't enough. Next time we'll have more, whether it's authorized or not. Somehow I'll get the extra, even though they think we don't need it. It would be silly to be knocked down now because we can't shoot back. Our speed is up to 260 now at 11,000 feet, where we have leveled off.

It seems like years that we've been dodging these fighters, flying to the southeast. We must be near the coast, and the fighters probably won't follow us out to sea. Hal informs us that we're over the coast of Kyushu, heading out to open sea. Gabby states that he has lost the fighters on the scope. The gunners report that they can't see anything. Jonesy agrees to cover the rear of the plane with his guns while we have George come forward from the tail. When we get him inside we'll close the bulkheads, pressurize, and go upstairs.

Gabby reports that George is with him in the radar room. Nick starts to pressurize, and Bill starts to climb the plane again. In a few minutes we are at 20,000 feet. Hal says, "We're 50 miles out to sea," and we all feel better. After another 15 minutes we feel that the danger is past and Jonesy and the gunners stow the guns. We go into some clouds and Higgy flies on instruments while the rest of us shed our heavy equipment. I feel like I'm stoop-shouldered and that the old back is broken. All we need to combat that heavy gear on us is a cast-iron prop for our backs.

We turn off the IFF and external lights. The Colonel has taken off his gear and he and Nick are talking over the fuel remaining. He doesn't know, as we do from experience, that we have plenty of gas, and he seems quite concerned. Nick shows him the figures together with our briefed reserve of 900 gallons, so he feels better. True, we have used far more than was expected according to the briefing figures -- we have 2500 gallons left now. The Colonel and Bill get out their canteens and take a long drink. They are surprised I don't want any. The Colonel looks at Bill -- "We had to get rid of that big ball of cotton in our mouths, didn't we?" Bill laughs and agrees. Both of us are surprised to think the Colonel was scared, too. He didn't show it, nor did he look out of the cabin much, and he couldn't hear the interphone conversation. No doubt he could feel there was plenty going on. I'd hate to ride along without participating, particularly on such a wild ride, but we think all the more of him for having come.

The plane is light now, about 90,000 lb., so we'll get a lot of mileage out of the remaining fuel, more as we get progressively lighter and keep cutting back the power. The strain is over -- only the long flight remains, though it will be quicker because we are at altitude, going faster across the surface for that reason. Everyone begins to let off steam talking about the flak, the fighter shot down, the other fighters, whether we were hit, wondering if the other planes came through all right. Al comes in with the message of a plane in distress, which he has just intercepted. It seems that Victor 757 is at 8000 feet with an air speed of 210 and has only three hours of fuel left. The question is will he make Iwo with that amount? Hal estimated that he might make it, but it's uncertain, so we've solved nothing. We silently send whoever it is our best wishes. There's nothing we can do for him.

I kid Al about not being able to see anything back at his position during the excitement -- there are no windows there. He corrects me, "Oh, yes, I see everything all right. Don't miss a thing that goes on," with a meaningful tone to his voice. Guess he does, at that. The interphone conversation keeps him posted.

Most of the crew fall asleep, one by one. Nick sticks with the cruise control, Charlie scans, Gabby rests up -- only Hal with the navigation, Al with the radio, Nick, Bill and I stay awake. Nick figures that we are 300 gallons above the curve (on the fuel consumption graph), and this will give us a reserve of 600 gallons -- plenty of fuel. At 0300 we are in the clear and the stars and moon are keeping us company. It is a beautiful night. There is a warm glow of satisfaction that accompanies the aftermath of a mission, a feeling of something accomplished. Too bad it's destructive. We did our job and are going home, that is all at the present we need to feel good, but there are welcome additions. Bill gets the OWI station on Saipan and we have the very best in dance music, one of the very few times that we've ever gotten it on the radio compass, and since we get is so seldom on the ground, it is doubly welcome, (we don't have a radio in our tent) and at this time it is like a breath from home. There are tunes we heard before we left home and our wives, tunes that are a part of many good times, that we'll have again when we get home.

The reverie is interrupted by Charlie who says, "There's a flapping noise under the floor of the compartment here that sounds strange." Well, that leaves us stumped. We had felt flak over the target and were expecting to find trouble with the plane's skin. Nick goes to investigate while the Colonel fills in his place. After a period of time Nick comes back and reports that he heard the same thing with his ear to the floor (bet that was a sight). Someone suggests that it might be the static cords from the mine parachutes, and that makes sense, so we all go back into our private comas and dose. The Benzedrine, or excitement, has me still awake, so I night-dream with my eyes open. Over Iwo, at 0410, I turn on the VHF "O" Channel and hear numerous planes calling into Iwo for landing instructions. Evidently they're short of gas. No. 1 calls and can't get an answer. Knowing that it is Boynton, I call him. He acknowledges and says that he'd be glad if I would call for him. Walnut Tower apparently hears me quite clearly, so I give Boynton's message to them. They acknowledge and sign off. Long afterwards I can hear the other planes calling in for landing instructions. Periodically Bill checks with Nick on fuel remaining so that he can satisfy the "How goes it" fuel form. By this time Bill claims that we're almost making gasoline. That's good to hear, but we feel sure there is no need for further sweating. With all four "fans" working, it seems certain that we're in luck this time, so we remain in our semi-conscious state while the engines purr in the background, a pleasant way to travel, and all the time we are crossing over the earth at over 300 miles an hour.

At 0600 we are an hour out, according to an ETA that Hal gave us, a judicious time to start letting down in order to make use of the altitude, turning it into speed while we reduce the power and gas consumption. At this point the range signals become uncooperative and first I get an A and then an N signal, for no good reason. I begin to wonder if our speed has caused us to pass our island home -- it is possible, since I've learned over the years that strange things can happen in navigation and flying, and that man can never be positive in this business -- just reasonably sure. Since I am not, I call Al and ask him for a QNN, which is the fancy name for the Base giving us the proper heading to fly to reach them -- the dry land of Tinian. It is 171 true, which is what we are flying, so it's still ahead of us. Radar confirms our position. After all this, Hal informs me that he has been doing "follow the pilot" navigation, and he figures we're doing fine -- Hal just won't rest.

At 0705 we sight Tinian off to the left ahead. Bill goes over the landing check list and we circle home and come in on runway #3, side by side with another plane on #1. At 0726 we roll into the hard-stand with the solid earth of home beneath us. The brakes cause the plane to rock like a baby carriage, and for no reason reminds me that I'd like to kiss the plane, the ground, and hug the crew. It's good to be home. We faced our Maker several times tonight and, God willing, returned safely.

Now begins our multitude of postflight activities. I throw out my equipment from my window to Hank Reinholtz and he stacks it on the ground. We are all dirty and it's hot in the plane, which makes us sweat, so we are glad to get out. The fellows look as messy as I do -- we're all a sad looking lot. If the folks back home could see us they'd wonder where all that air corps glamour, that's ballyhooed, is. I look at George and think, there's a good representative of a crew man returned from a mission. His shirt's partly out, wrinkled, sweaty, and stained. His face is tired and dirty. The pants bag are frayed at the bottom (his "Gook" pants, he calls them), his hair's tousled, but he's got a big grin and is telling the ground crew about the mission -- "Nothing to it, slept most of the time." While Bill and I look over the plane the fellows remove their belongings from the plane and tell Pat about the mission. The truck backs up and is ready for us to load on. Bill and I have found the static cords from the mines hanging through the bomb hinge, so that made the flapping noise against the plane. Otherwise the plane appears unhit, though we can't imagine how all those traces enveloped us with no hits, not to mention flak.

At this time Sowers, Donnell, Doc Schroeder, and Koltoon drive up and shake hands, welcoming us home. We tell them the plane is all right. They've heard from others, apparently, that it was a rough mission and they are interested to know how it went. The Colonel, leaving with the C.O., shakes his head and purses his lips when they ask him how it was. Grinning, "Ask them," he says, pointing to the crew. Then he tells me, "Alger, you have a good crew, and that was good work. I enjoyed flying with you." I thank him, knowing the enjoyment must have been on the negative side, but pleased over the compliments.

Nick and Pat are laughing together after going over the plane's performance. The rest of us are on the truck, too tired to comment further. We watch Nick while he approaches. He stops, runs back and pats the plane, then jumps into the truck. No. 11 took good care of us. We're proud of her. She's the best, now that the bugs are ironed out.

After disposing of the equipment and the ride in the truck, we go through the ordeal of interrogation. Somehow the word has gotten around that we got a fighter, the first shot down by our Squadron. Numerous spectators stand around as we relate our experiences to Ben Lay and he records them. In addition to the usual round of information asked, we feel we should add other points. We mention the fleet that we located in the Inland Sea, then the airbase on the coast just above Shimonoseki. This is news because the airfield is not shown on maps. George relates the fighter attack and how it was shot down. Mention was made of Dick Bush putting some bullets into the plane as it broke away, flaming. But now we learn the saddening news that Steel and Grounds and their crews are missing. They haven't been heard from either here or at Iwo. Other crews reported seeing several B-29s going down in flames over the target. All we can do is hope that the boys go out of their planes all right -- that would be right into Jap hands, but maybe that's better than crashing.

By the time we finish the interrogation we find ourselves going over to "breakfast" at 10:30, just ahead of the lunch crowd. We're quite hungry, too. There is some whiskey from the Docs for those who want some. It's always a toss-up after a mission whether feed, shower or bed is the most important thing to tend to, except for Gabby. "Give me food!" he always says. Everyone eats heartily, which is a good sign. We have bacon and eggs -- all we want -- fresh eggs, too. In fact, several almost strangle on their bread when the "chef" asks us how we want them cooked. Before breaking up I want to say something to the crew, though I'm uncertain how to put it, so I finally tell them that I'm proud of the teamwork and the crew. I tell them what the Colonel said about them, and finally end up by saying that if we all work together like that in the future, we're going to get home again some day, safe and sound, God willing, and then I stop for fear of sounding like one of the pompous brass who talk and don't do.

That night there is a resume of the mission at the show, so that the entire ground organization, which is so interested in these missions but can't participate, can hear what occurred. George is called on to give an account of the shooting down of the fighter. He does fine and then brings down the house when he describes the plane's crash with "He burst into flames and dove down to hit the water on the ground." Jim "Red" Grobe, a member of tour ground crew, stands up back in the audience and shouts "That's him, that's my boy!" George gives credit to Dick for putting some lead into the fighter. We all get a big kick out of George.

A further result of the mission is that Mr. Brown of Western Electric shows great interest in the intentional jamming of our radar scope by the Jap fighters. Other radar men, officers and enlisted men, seem interested, too, so we explain it as best we can so the others won't be caught napping by this sometime in the future.

We are glad to have this mission behind us in more ways than one. We feel that we're a better crew for it. Jake and I resolve that before the next mission we'll have words with the armament section and see that the bomb racks, shackles, and circuits are properly inspected and fixed. We've had three malfunctions on the bomb run thus far, and that's too much. We agree to try to have the B-7 type shackle installed, replacing these B-10s which remain and cause so much trouble.

We hear a story about the Wing C.O., which greatly impresses us. It seems that the General gave his flak helmet to a crew member and did without on the bomb run. The plane was subsequently shot up badly by flak, according to Bob Rodenhouse, the pilot. The men admire the General for this.

Chapter 13 Inland Sea Mine Laying

March 30-31, 1945 – No. 8

"Lost Over Enemy Territory"

The first announcement of this mission we find on the "Combat Missions" board in the 24th Squadron Operations. Crew 2409 is scheduled to fly their plane, V-11. Other Squadron crews scheduled to go are Lazin, Litchfield, Boynton, Dawson, Jones, Parks, Mutch, and Schad. We begin our preparations by checking the airplane. Jake, Bill and I go to the line to check the bomb circuits, releases, shackles -- everything that might pertain to the cause for our mines hanging up, as they did on the last mission. When the mines don't fall as scheduled the whole program is dislocated. The armament maintenance men have gone over the system and believe that it's all right now. On our check we find nothing wrong.

The morning of the 30th Jake, Hal, and Gabby have a special radar briefing, and I join them to get a better idea of the mission. Our instructions are that we will fly to Sada Misaki Point again, and then north to O-Shima Island. There we will take up a heading of 5 degrees on which heading we will drop the mines, beginning at the end of 7.6 miles and one each 3.5 seconds thereafter until all are dropped. We will carry 6 mines of 2000 lb. each. The altitude will be 5000 feet, the lowest yet. The turn away will be to the left and the withdrawal axis 244 degrees. The approach and mining run will be radar-directed. With this out of the way we go later to the briefing. At 1400 we take our seats in row 7, right. The Operations Officer talks on the axis of attack and withdrawal. He states that if the turning and initial points are not hit properly it will be necessary to go back and do it over in order to be able to put the mines in the proper place. Then the C.O. holds forth. He claims that the Navy has considered the Yawata mining as very successful, far exceeding expectations, so we feel good about that. He further exhorts us to continue the good work, getting the same fine results. We know that it is a feather in his cap when we do, but we want to do the job to the best of our abilities, so he needn't worry that we won't try. The crew members are very conscious of the fact that he is not going along on these missions, and they don't respect him for it. In fact, we are all suspicious for that reason. He would know a lot more about us and our problems if he did. He professes to know, but we know he can't without flying with us.

It seems that there are other diversionary raids by the 73rd Wing during the day, and the Japs will not expect us. Jones and Parks are going to Sasebo, while the rest of us go into the Inland Sea. The Intelligence Officer goes on to say that there are 115 fighters located in the area of the Kure Naval Base, several miles north of our mining area, while 400-500 are located at Sasebo. Kure is a great Jap naval base, while Sasebo has subs. We must be wary, we are told, of the picket boats in the Inland Sea, since they might fire on us, and their fire is very heavy and accurate.

Brockaway speaks on the flak. There are 170 guns in the Kure-Hiroshima area, while the Sasebo area has 75. He suggests that we desynchronize our props to defeat the sound detectors that may track us in order to learn our position. Bob Hall gives us the "poop" on Air-Sea rescue, in his businesslike manner. There will be 1 dumbo, 2 superdumbos, 1 sub, 1 destroyer, and a surface craft, all this the Navy located around the island of Iwo Jima. To contact the Navy and "Agate" control at Iwo, in case of trouble, 4475 Kilocycles will be used. Kirby gives us some radio briefing. Radio silence will be observed, as usual. "C" channel on the VHF will be used for emergency calls. The Tinian Homer will broadcast on 500 KC, and the localizer will be operating on "Y" channel. There will be a cold front and a trough, Sully states in the weather department, but the weather should be good at Japan. The Operations Officer now gives us the new take-off plan, in which we fly five minutes out and then turn left, passing over Marpi Point on Saipan. A very sensible plan. Much better than the method of circling Tinian before heading out. The C.O. gives us more pep talk and we break up to go to the specialized briefing -- the old routine.

At the pilot's briefing the Operations Officer presides with the C.O. as the ranking pilot present. Neither of them go on the missions enough to know what it's like. Nor did they do any of the flying when we were so arduously training in the States to learn this newest of all planes, and the technique of leading a crew using it. However, they conduct the meeting, explaining the plan, answering the questions. One question results from the C.O. suggesting that if the I.P. is approached incorrectly that the crew go out and come in again. Realizing that this would put planes going in and out at the same altitude, a pilot asks if another altitude should not be assigned for such withdrawal. The C.O., in the role of ranking pilot, replies, "No, I don't think so, just keep your eyes open." On another occasion an airplane commander protests that there is not enough ammunition carried for protection against possible enemy fighter attacks. The C.O. inquires, "Did you run out of ammunition last time?" and the pilot answers, "Yes, sir." He adds that the additional weight will be only 300 lb. for another 1000 rounds. The C.O. seems rather displeased with this factual statement of the situation, as though the pilot lacked the right to meddle with the strategic planning, and dismissed the matter with the comment that it would be necessary to go through Army channels to get permission to load more ammo, and that would take time. The airplane commander sits down with a "what's the use" expression, and the meeting adjourns. No doubt many other crew leaders will do as we have done, will load more ammunition at will, regardless of the specified amount. We are being forced to disobey, in a sense, in order to take care of ourselves. But after our experiences, I'm sure that our gunners won't be caught short of ammunition. It's just the old story, do what you know you must and keep quiet. The ammunition is available so we'll load it, and have it to use if we need it.

After the briefing we get some chow and still have time to ourselves before loading the trucks. We like this arrangement. Back at the tent we kid Preston and his gang about their loafing and never flying with us anymore. It just happens they haven't been scheduled so much as we recently, and they tell us not to be so cocky, that we'll be tired and worn out long before they are.

Everyone is in good spirits, eager to get on this mission. Majors Donnell and Sowers drop by the plane as do Docs Schroeder and Koltoon. Now the usual routine of pulling props begins and we all gather around each engine in turn to pull 14 blades through by hand. This is to insure that the engine is not hurt when we start it, since we can find out if there is a liquid lock by hand without causing damage. It's a job to pull the engine through, but you'd think we are out on a picnic. Pat and the boys join us and we pull one blade at a time with 2 or 3 men pushing. The blade is sharp and we use some cloth to keep it from cutting our hands. "Come on, Alberto," George says. "What do you mean, 'Come on?', I don't see you working," Al retorts. "Quit leaning on the blade, George, try pushing," Gabby adds. And so it goes until all four engines have been pulled through. Everyone is laughing and joking. Now we climb into the plane and prepare to start them up. The engine check goes well and we're ready to taxi, right on time. Looks like they can't stop us this mission, we're raring to go, and No. 11 sounds and looks good, all equipment in good shape. We gross only 133,000 lb., the lightest yet -- at least in recent missions. Again I wonder why we aren't authorized to carry more ammunition. We're even light -- it can't be weight. We have 12,000 lb. of mines, three in each bomb bay.

The take-off is normal. The entire taxi and take-off is a pretty picture of precision, as the planes maintain the same interval. The new instrument route proves successful and we pass by Marpi Point, on course, sooner than in circling Tinian. A short way out a blister voice is heard on the interphone. "Something smells funny back here, is there a fire up front?" We all sit up with this and look around. Everything appears normal. Nick looks worried, he smells the peculiar odor. "I'm going aft to check," he says. In a few seconds he's back. "Hal's lit up his pipe again." We relax and comment on that briar. Very shortly Dick comes forward and helps Nick parallel the generators. Two are reading too high on the voltage. We don't want any trouble this time. Everything is fine -- what a plane! It rolls right along, the engines purring. The moon is out and the night is lovely, with clouds casting their shadows on the water and plane. Charlie and Dick call out the planes about us. The crew clicks like an old-time organization. A good crew. Every mission the fellows become better in their teamwork.

At 2020 the bad news starts. The radio compass antenna breaks again, as it does every mission. Gabby then reports that the radar set is out of operation, and this is to be strictly a radar mission. The whole mission is planned about the use of the radar set to get into the mining area and to make the run. We keep our fingers crossed as Gabby tries to repair the damage. The first problem is to locate the trouble. Gabby says that the crystal current is not showing, so perhaps the tube is burned out. Anyway, it does not light up. Subsequent investigation shows that we have no tube to replace it, neither is there a spare in the repair kit, where there customarily is. Some kind soul has taken it out, Gabby surmises venomously. Al tries to help Gabby find a replacement tube that will do the job, but to no avail -- oh, for a tube!

Now Nick checks the fuel transfer system and finds it O.K. At 2150 we hit Iwo right on the ETA, but we're five miles right, so we correct to home in on the island. The lights are bright on the island and in the harbor. It is a small island, and it looks from here as if every bit was being used except the northern tip. It's fine for us that the island belongs to our side in this war. Since it's been taken it has been a part of every planned mission against Japan, the refuge for those who are battle-damaged or low on fuel during the return flight.

After leaving Iwo, where it is clear, we begin to encounter weather in the form of many clouds at our level, above and below us. Without radar we "sweat" a little, hoping there are no other planes nearby, and praying the target will be clear. It is a long chance. At 2215, it is clear beneath us and overcast above. The Hiroshima radio station is a help to us on "loop" position of the radio compass, and we "home in" on it, but the station goes off very shortly after that. The radio compass shows the direction from which the program comes, so we know right where our target is. Ahead, in the present case. Hiroshima is only slightly to the left of the mining area.

Another B-29, which was well out to one side of us, is now very close just ahead and slightly above. We change our course in order to keep distance between us, but somehow the two planes still converge. After a half hour of this jockeying, we decide to end the dilemma. We make a 360 degree circle, which puts us two minutes behind him and well by ourselves. Usually we don't see many -- if any -- planes en route.

At 2350 we are 30 minutes from our I.P., so we put on all the equipment, turn off the lights, and prepare to pick up the Bay or coastline. Without use of the radar it is a question of Hal's navigation and visual contact. We hope that we're on course from the star shots that Hal took along the way. We have no way of telling whether we're on course, or to the right or left. Jake, Bill and I strain our eyes looking forward. The gunners do the same. The light clouds give way to clear sky, but the moonlight gilds the air silvery and it is difficult to penetrate the haze visually. This mission, as in the case of many others, relies heavily on the radar. The APQ-13 scope shows the contour of land and water, almost as though you were seeing a map unroll before you. It is very accurate, and neither clouds nor weather, unless it's unusually bad, affects it. In this case the radar was to serve a dual purpose. It was to establish a course directly up the bay, first, because at our altitude of 5000 feet we are below the level of land on either side of the bay. Second, it was to be the basis for the placing of the mines in the proper place. We can overcome the lack of radar if: first, we can find the entrance to the Bay instead of driving into a mountain side, and second, if we can find the I.P. visually and drop the mines visually with timed runs holding the proscribed headings. So that is our goal.

Aware that the land to our left is 6500 feet, we are anxious to find that left coastline first and stay to the right of it. The silvery haze persists, but we think that we'll be able to see because it's clear out. While looking about I notice that by looking out to the left and slightly back, the haze is not so bad. In a few minutes of combing the sky ahead, there appears to be land well off to the left, a coastline sure enough. Hal has been taking a star shot and the position he gets coincides with the guess that we are left of course, so we correct to the right. This apparently is correct for as we fly north the coast on the left keeps getting closer. We take the heading of 30 degrees then, to try and pick up Sada Misaki.

After eleven minutes we haven't located it and we must be getting close to high ground on that side of the Bay, so Hal suggests that flying north might do the trick. Thinking it unsafe to only assume that we're over Sada Misaki, I suggest that we fly a controlled zigzag course on headings right and left, working north. Hal agrees that we could do that.

Twice planes passed us, headed north, before we could tack onto them, so we continue trying to find just where we are. After a while we are sure that we're well north of the point. Looking back I see what appears to be water. We are over the Bay. Ahead we see flak. Is that Kure or Hiroshima? We can't go sailing into that area, unsure of ourselves. We mustn't drop these mines unless we're certain that we're over water, no sense mining the countryside. Tracers and flak come up at us from an island underneath. What place is that? Jonesy, Dick and George each report seeing a fighter. Bill and I are so busy trying to find a mining area we overlook the mention of fighters. We've got to get rid of these mines where they'll do some good, and we don't want to drop them on land, nor do we want to get over land at all at this altitude unless we can see better than we can now.

We start a wide circle to the left in the hope that looking down from another angle will permit piercing the haze. "There's some water," I tell Bill and Jake, and Jake leans over to see the water reflected in the path of moonlight. We know there's water there, so we'll fly a reciprocal heading to this spot and go out and then back the same length of time. That will put us right over it with the light right for us to see. Jake O.K.s the plan and we head out at 220 degrees. After a minute on this heading we make a 180 degree turn and head back. "In one minute you'll be over the area, Jake." He nods and waves. "Doors open," Jake shouts and the plane jars a little. Bill and I look hard ahead and to the right and left in an effort to recognize a landmark in this gloom. "How does it look, Jake?" "O.K.!" he replies. "There's water." "Mines away!" Jake calls and they begin to drop, one every three seconds. They're gone. The scanners report seeing the mines fall and the parachutes open. We turn right to leave the area. Bill sees an island to the right and I catch sight of land to the left. Evidently we are in a channel of some sort. Knowing the height of the land to the east, we begin to climb fast, with a lot of power. Dick reports a fighter and lets go a short burst -- he says that the fighter high-tailed it away. Probably Dick is a little nervous, seeing the fighter fly so close, even though he didn't fire on us. Can't blame him.

Hal gives us the heading of 135 to fly going out, and we pass over rugged country, with mountains on our right. Everything is dark on the land -- a complete blackout. The gunners remain alert and we watch out for other B-29s in the area. We're high enough to avoid all land now, so we relax and get comfortable. Breathing easily again, it's apparent that our cruising around strange territory lower than all surrounding land is quite a strain. We also know now how much we count on that radar set to serve as our eyes when we can't see. Knowing Gabby's fiery nature and pride in his work, Bill and I surmise that he is fighting mad at whoever tinkered with the set on the ground, and took the spare parts from the kit. Now everyone takes off his gear and Jonesy directs the stowing of the guns. As it turned out, this mission bore no similarity to the briefed plan. Perhaps we should have turned back, but that thought is repugnant. Guess we'd rather take the chance than to give up.

We start our climb to 20,000 feet and cruise toward Iwo. It is fairly cold in the clouds that we encounter and ice begins to form on the nose. The leading edge of the wing and the hub of the propeller also have thick coats of ice. We aren't slowing down noticeably yet, so we continue on. The nose becomes heavily covered with ice, and a large crack appears in the glass of the nose. That's not so good. George is up with the others in the blister section and all is quiet.

North of Iwo the scanners report heavy anti-aircraft fire or Naval gunfire -- couldn't tell which -- and Hal reports this to be a small island, Jap-held, to the north-west of Iwo. We can't figure how they could have such heavy fire. At 0510 we are abreast of Iwo, and can see it in the distance, about 7 miles away. Jake takes over the navigation as Hal comes up front to join the sleepers. For a change I stay awake and Bill catches a nap. Mighty sleepy out.

The remainder of the trip is uneventful, and we arrive back at Tinian with everything O.K. We are surprised to notice, when we lose the ice off the nose, that the crack was only an illusion and the nose is perfectly all right. Our VHF radio is inoperative by the time we are ready to land, so we go in without instructions, landing on runway No. 3.

After landing and taxiing back to the hardstand we get out on the good earth again. Representatives of the various maintenance departments are present and we tell them the malfunctions. Gabby and I are hard on the radar maintenance man, telling him that we couldn't fix that radar because someone took out the repair equipment. He seems very apologetic, claiming not to have touched any of it himself, and he goes off to find the difficulty, with Gabby accompanying him. Shorty they reappear and Gabby wears a smile. They found that the trouble was not the crystal but the RF unit, which could not have been repaired in flight, so we have done the best we could, after all. Gabby looks relieved. We thank the radar man for his effort and he looks much better. Apparently he is conscientious about his job and our grievance worried him. It's a pleasure to see a man feel such an interest in his work.

After jollying the ground crew we pack up our gear and return to the area. The usual round awaits us -- interrogation, food, shower, and bed. Our plane malfunctions this time, apart from the radar, were not serious, so we feel that No. 11 is ready to go again. We are happy to have another one behind us. None of us care to do any more flying where there is a possibility of being below the level of the ground, as there was on this trip, where we were going up the Bay without seeing. As we learned later, our radar set was the only one to go out of commission. All planes from the Group returned safely. The mining was well done. No. 8 is now behind us.

Chapter 14 Nagoya

April 7, 1945 – No. 9

"First Medium-Altitude Daylight"

March 31st we are resting and heckling Preston and the fellows in the dark room, developing pictures, when a call comes for me from Saipan, a telephone call out in the wilds. Art Bridge is down from Iwo on a rest and mentions coming over to visit. I say, "Come ahead." As luck would have it, the tentative mission is canceled and Bill, Jake, Hal, and I spend most of the day with Art and his friend, Skin Ennis. We have a big Easter celebration, getting our rations of beer and coke to share with our guests. In the evening we have a real meal, which they appreciate. On Iwo they have been cooking out in the open or eating cold food with Iwo dust in it. Either way it is usually Spam, they say. We have an amazing meal, steak and ice cream together. The cooks outdo themselves when they learn the men are from Iwo -- they seem pleased at the opportunity to do something. Everyone admires the men connected with the Iwo campaign.

We enjoy this day of visiting and hate to see them leave. Bill and I go down to the field to see them off in their P-51s. As promised, Art and Skin do a slow roll in formation over the field before heading toward Saipan. What a sight! They seem glued together while they roll. We both feel homesick, Bill and I, as we watch them do something we probably never will. As pilots, we'd love to fly the P-51. At one time we flew the single-engine trainers in acrobatics, but we were assigned to heavy aircraft. Our job somehow doesn't seem like flying -- not like these boys fly!

The entire camp is busy these days, building Quonset huts together with the Seabees. All eight of us in our tent turn out daily to build ours. Pres and Don perch on a metal support, splicing supports together. Hal, Lloyd, and Jake are haggling about the best way to put up the siding. Bill and Al are laying the floor. What a commotion. I am able to see the whole operation from a ladder, while trying to put up some wooden end pieces. Some of the Quonsets will be under the trees. We are out in the open in No. 4. The various crews picked their hut mates, generally the same with whom they were living in tents. We have a lot of fun out of the construction, then the big day comes. In our case it is April 6th, and we move in while the floor is still wet from the coat of oil. We all get together to decide the weighty matter of who will have what locations in the hut. First, by flipping, we decide which side each crew will have. Then we draw slips of paper which specify, within each crew, which positions on either side each man will occupy. I drew the north end, a spot which I consider quite promising. Pres is right across from me, while Hal, Jake, and Bill are ranged along our side with Bill at the far end. We each have over 8 feet of room -- some luxury, and we appreciate it. Pres' crew has the east side, we the west.

April 6th we see our name among the scheduled crews for the next mission. The crews listed are: Dawson, Holton, Ramsey, Maki, Jordan, Alger, Parks, Jones, Schwager, Fortune, Schad, Reider, and Cooney. Evidently this is an all-out effort, and most of our planes are in condition to go.

Target identification is held at 1730. We learn that the target is the Mitsubishi aircraft plant in Nagoya. Three combat squadrons will represent our group. For some reason the squadrons' crews are intermixed, so that we find ourselves scheduled to fly the No. 4 position of the lead flight in the 2nd Squadron formation. Rendezvous will be made at landfall in a cove near the town of Owase, then to the town of Seta, at which point a north heading is taken. From there we will go to Lake Biwa and then due east to the factory, which is 7 ½ miles NNE of the dock area of Nagoya. This course will put us over the Nagoya Castle. The bomb load will be 16 500-lb. bombs, the lightest load yet. The bombs will have 1/100 second nose fuse and instantaneous tail fuses and are general purpose, high explosive. We are surprised at this load, and are informed that we will carry an extra fuel tank in the rear bomb bay. We learn, too, that this time we will have a full ammunition load. This cheers us all. Apparently the proper paper work has come through the chain of command, authorizing the 750 rounds per gun, a total of 9000 rounds.

Reville on the 7th is at 0100 and it's a strain to roll out -- no fit time to be getting up. We repair to the mess hall and have breakfast, at least we figure that must be what it is. It must last for the next three meals and late into the next night. We bid farewell to our hut mates in their new homey surroundings and join the groups heading for the briefing hall.

The Operation Officer calls the roll by crew, as usual. We're all present. The C.O., after the customary grand entrance, goes into the matter of fighter escort, which we will have for the first time. The crews buzz with approval and welcome for this addition to the mission. The fighters will go from Iwo -- we wonder whether Art will be on this one, and if we'll see him. We are reminded of the need of taking care of the fighters at all times on the navigational end. It looks like the fighters may be the saving grace this time, since we are going in at medium altitude of 16,000 feet in broad daylight. Now the briefing follows the customary procedures. The Intelligence Officer speaks next. "The Mitsubishi factories produce 75% of all aircraft engines in Japan, and the two factories will be hit today." Our Wing goes to Nagoya, the 73rd goes to Tokyo. "The route as planned is 2671 Nautical miles (3070 statute miles). Should you encounter any 'balls of fire' that have been reported in the past, you can evade them by changes of altitude. However, they will gain on you in the turns. Further, watch out for coordinated fighter attacks." The mention of the strange "ball of fire" recalls to our minds that George reported seeing one over Nagoya once before. There must be something to it. The flak, we are told, will be heavy and we will be flying right through it. The air-sea rescue is ready with 4 dumbos, 2 superdumbos, 2 surface craft, and 1 sub participating. The reference point names have been changed and now are "Halter Post, Behave Yourself, Field Goal, and Lopsided". They are to be used in emergency ditching messages as representing the southern tip of the Tokyo peninsula, Iwo, Pagan, and Saipan, respectively. The words all have an "L" in them. This letter is difficult for the Japs to pronounce, and would give them away if they attempt to give a message.

The VHF channel frequencies have new names for the old A, B, C, and D. They are King, Nan, Queen, and Item, and now coincide with the Navy terminology. From now on we are to monitor the "King" channel at all times. In case of emergency, give the message on King and then switch to "Queen" to give the emergency message again. superdumbo homing frequency is 514 KC, with the signal SM given during the 3rd, 4th, and 5th minutes of each 15. All planes will carry RCAM (Radar Counter Measures consisting of transmitting sets designed to jam Jap radar receiving frequencies). The IFF must be turned off at 27 degrees North Latitude. The weather will be all right, we are told. The Navigator gives the time "hack" and the watches all click together, on the second. Other instructions given concern the course: we will depart Lalo point, the southern tip of Tinian, and climb to 6500 feet to cruise. The assembly will be made in left-hand circles. At 1210 the first Squadron goes on to the target; at 1222 the 3rd Squadron; and at 1234 the 2nd, our formation, will depart in assembled formation. Further, the bomb run must be steady without change of course. (This, of course, is the flak predictor's dream. We would prefer to see some evasive action included to throw off their guns.)

Now we're off to the line in the convoy of trucks. We pick up the personal equipment and go over to the plane. Pat says it is ready and raring to go. "I hope," he adds, but we know that if he's that sure, that it is O.K. Meanwhile Jonesy asks Lt. Cady, who comes by, to get him a C-1 vest as well as the necessary gear for Lt. Karlson, an RCAM officer, who is going along with us as a passenger to see what it's like. He has just arrived.

After checking the plane, the crew members assemble at the nose of the plane, laughing and joking with Pat, Red, Bill, Steve, and Hank. We hold a quick meeting in which Bill and I explain the need for rearranging the seating for take-off, for it seems that our load condition is too nose heavy -- the index obtained from the figuring of the weight and balance is about 23% of the M.A.C. (mean aerodynamic chord), while our nose heavy weight should not fall below 24%. The allowable limits for safety's sake should be 24% to 32%, but we know that the limits themselves should not be approached because in addition to being a strain on the plane, it uses more gasoline. The fact that the B-29 flies somewhat tail-high permits this extra loading in the nose. Bill, Nick and I are surprised to find the 8000 lb. of bombs all in the front bay and only the 4000 lb. of fuel in the aft bay, the container being one bomb bay tank. It appears very thoughtless of whoever planned such weight distribution, and dangerous so far as we are concerned. However, we must make the best of it, so we ask Hal, Jake, and Al to ride in the rear of the plane, preferably in the rear unpressurized section. Their 600 lb., taken from the nose and put in the tail, will make the take-off balance within the allowable limits. This leaves those three without safety belts or the familiarity of their usual positions, which is important in terms of emergency crew procedure. But we have no alternative, other than refusing to fly, so we pile in. The whole situation seems incongruous. Aside from the danger involved, we are repeatedly instructed to learn to handle ourselves in our particular positions within the plane. We are cautioned never to fly without the proper weight distribution. Then, without warning or explanation, we are ordered to fly with planes improperly loaded, necessitating the shifting of crew members about, and without need for it, since it would be a simple matter to apportion the weight between the two bomb bays, particularly since we are not so heavy as usual. What a business!

Before getting in, Bill gives Major Donnell the weight and balance sheet, and the C.O. wishes us luck. To both of them I point out our unfavorable weight situation. The C.O. answers, "All the planes are that way. You won't have any trouble." He might just as well have said, "So what!" I climb in and we fire up the engines.

After the preflight power check we taxi out one minute late, subsequently we wait an additional 9 minutes before take-off. We hate to wait with the engines running. They heat up and the spark plugs are liable to load up. At 0505 we take off. Bill, Nick and I feeling quite lonely in the cabin by ourselves. We're mighty uneasy, thinking of the others "sweating it out" and not in their own seats. After a circle of Tinian to the right, we are off for the "Empire". Hal, Jake, and Al take their regular positions and we're nose heavy again. We take off the turbos, shoving the throttles full forward to compensate. This eliminates the back pressure the turbos set up, and thus a little more fuel is saved. Power setting is 33 2200, a reduction of 2 inches in the manifold pressure. All goes well and time and water slide by. At 0850 we pass by Iwo and see the little island in between the clouds. It's long past sunrise now, though we couldn't see daybreak in the east because of clouds in our immediate area. On the radio we hear the fighters talking to the tower, but we can't make out if the fighters are those accompanying us or just the local flights. At 1000 Bill and I call Gabby, after a conference, and appoint him trainer for the gunners, suggesting that he "warm up the gunners' thumbs and arms, give them rub-downs and the like." Can't have any charley horses in the "trigger thumbs" today. We all have the feeling that this will be a hot one. Over Nagoya at medium altitude looks like we're inviting them up for a little tag. About this time, with the plane on autopilot and everyone sleepy, I go back to the tube and feel immensely better, needless to say. This plane riding is worse than a bus. Last-minute hydrating before take-off has its draw-backs subsequently, it seems.

It is now 1155K and we are about 35 miles from the assembly point, Hal informs us. Occasionally we see another B-29. We are so far ahead of the 1210 assembly (5 minutes at least) that we must kill time. Rather than get involved in the assembly of the earlier squadrons we make several 360s. Gabby confirms our position as just out to sea from the assembly point. Winds have put us here sooner than expected. Finally we head into the assembly area. Nearing the coast we encounter a strange cloud that at a higher altitude would be a cirrus. At our 18,000 feet it is more of a thick base that at times can't be penetrated visually. We see no other planes. Evidently they are trying to find an altitude that is clear at which to assemble. It is obvious that this scheduled altitude is not a good level. On channel King we hear other planes trying to locate each other and three planes, V35, V8, and V49 give their altitude as 16,000 feet and ask anyone in the vicinity to join them. Apparently everything is fouled up by these clouds. We go down to 16,000 feet and circle, finding no one. Even here it is hazy, and we dislike the uneasy feeling that comes from blindly plunging through the cloud in circles, with others doing the same. It's a game of tag, but the wrong kind. We just hope no one comes out of the vapor ahead on a collision course.

Now we hear another plane at 19,000 feet state that it appears to be clearer up there, so we go up to try to find them, but it's soupier there. The sun is a golden ball without any brilliance, seen through these clouds. We warn the scanners over and over to let us know the minute they see a plane, giving its position, course, and altitude, so we can both dodge it, if necessary, and join up. All the other planes here are no doubt thinking of that warning that we hadn't better try to bomb alone -- it would be suicide. We need the mutual help a formation gives; more guns, more fire-power.

Still at 19,000 feet we hear Victor 8 call again at 16,000 feet. Apparently he has lost the planes that he was trying to join at that altitude before. Knowing this is P. E. Jones I call him and he again states, "I'm at bombing altitude over the assembly point." Gabby answers that we're over the assembly point according to the scope. I call P. E. and state that we're coming down to try and find him. He says O.K., he'll be there. We continue cautiously as possible, letting down and circling, clearing ourselves on all sides. Sometimes it clears up and we can see a short distance -- several times we have seen planes that way -- but they've been going away and at too great a distance to catch, and it's hard to tell another plane where you are, without reference points. As we circle at 16,000 feet we are able to look straight down and see the coast with the rugged land meeting the water. Along the cove there are several houses. Now we notice a lot of smoke from one particular area. We call Jones and give our position as "near the smoke". He answers, "We're about five miles southwest and turning back toward the smoke", so we stay in that vicinity. As we cross over the smoke we give our heading as due west. Jones then comes back with, "O.K., I am with another plane now and we're approaching the smoke on a north heading. We'll continue on north and you can catch us." This seems sensible, providing we both have the same smoke in mind, so we continue our circle and pick up a north heading and continue north. We should be a little to the right of them going over the smoke. We have been milling around this area for almost 90 minutes, so this is our last hope. We've never missed going to the target yet, here's hoping we don't this time. It's certainly confusing to fly aimlessly about in clouds that the weather man says won't be there.

All of us look forward, straining to see. We catch sight of land ahead and then in a break in the clouds we see two other planes on a north heading. We put on the power and overtake them. There's 49, and we see on the pilot's flimsy that it's Koser, and there's 8 -- that's P. E., so now we have a three ship flight. We pull up on the right wing of Koser, who is leading since Jones hasn't the necessary maps. George now calls on the interphone, "There's a plane pulling up from the rear." Another B-29 is trying to join up, and soon we see that it's 35 -- that makes a four ship flight. It's Bunting. He takes the diamond position, slightly high. Jones and I are riding a little high on Koser's wing. Things are looking up. We've used a terrible lot of fuel, but that's immaterial just now. First we've got to hit the target.

Now we are breathing easier. That rendezvous was a strain. It was rather humorous in retrospect, though. Jones and I would call back and forth, "Where are you?" and "I'm at bombing altitude less two, ten miles east of the rendezvous.

Where are you?" No time for humor then, or now either, for that matter. As we approach Biwa Lake we close in until I'm looking right in the blister window of Koser's plane and our wings are almost overlapping. Jones is not so tight, but he will be. It always seems that the other fellow is out farther than you are. We are east of Osaka now and south of Kyoto -- dangerous country. Oddly enough, it is a beautiful day for the Japs to make it hot for us, and we can see there are no clouds in the direction of the target. It's the kind of day when, as Cooney puts it, you ought to "carry a cloud along to duck into".

So this is what it looks like in the day time. The glimpses I catch beyond the lead plane show a countryside that is not so very different from some I've seen in the U.S. The hills are pronounced, yet small, with snow standing in the crevasses and along the edges of the ridges. The flat land in between the mountains looks something like the land in Nebraska -- the same color with towns occasionally, and highway and rail lines intersecting them. It is really very pretty countryside. The visibility must be 50 miles now. We reach the lake on the north heading and Bill warns, "We're about to turn right." I ask, "Is everyone set?" "Everything's set," Bill states. Jake is on the front gunsight. Bill has the bomb release button in easy reach. At the proper time he will open the bomb doors and release the bombs. We turn onto the east heading.

Ahead, out of the corner of my eye as I continue to guide our position on Koser, I see the mountains that stand 6000 feet, on the other side of Nagoya to the east. The land along this path beneath us is flat. The sun is almost overhead. It is a bright, sparkling day. Apparently there are no other planes around. I feel that our small flight of planes is the center of all eyes and attention to those below -- feel mighty naked. Well, at least we'll get all the attention, and none of us like it. I'm sure that no one is feeling heroic right now, but I do feel that any fighters who drop around will have more than they can handle. I'll put our gunners against any of theirs. About 10 miles to go now.

"Flak at 3 low." "Flak at 6." "Flak at 9 high." "9 level." Here it comes. They've already plotted our altitude. "Jap plane at 6 o'clock, out of range," George calls. Perhaps this plane is radioing to the ground station our altitude, speed, and course, a trick of theirs to help the gunners place the flak. "The flak's getting heavy," Jonesy calls -- and how! All the big guns must be trained on us, judging from the size of the flak bursts. The sky is covered in our area with puffs of black smoke. Whew, that's accurate. We see puffs ricochet off the lead plane. He must be hit -- should be peppered with holes. Puffs of smoke glide off the side of Jones' ship, but he doesn't falter. That must have hit him. Where are the fighters? Maybe the Japs are holding off their fighters while they fire at us with the ground guns. Maybe they think they won't need fighters, but will get us with the flak guns. Here we are, loaded to the teeth with ammunition, and we can't shoot back. If only we could take evasive action, but we must hold a steady course in the interest of an accurate run, placing the bombs on the factory. That's sensible, but we're sitting here like pigeons.

The bomb doors on the lead plane come open. Ours jar open. I don't take my eyes off the lead plane -- I can sense the activities around me. Jake is combing the sky, looking for fighters. He and the others have given up trying to call out the flak -- too much. This is heavier than we've ever suspected. The flak seems to be concentrated just in the area occupied by our four planes. We're in close now, all four, presenting as small a target as possible. I see the heads of the gunners in Koser's plane, and see the guns turning as they pivot to look in another direction. No fighters. Bill is ready to drop the bombs at the instant they fall from the lead plane. Puffs of smoke are surrounding P. E. and I wonder how he's getting by. Some slide off the belly of the plane, we hear the explosions one after another, a series of heavy crunching sounds. No. 11 must be peppered all over by this time. The crew members seem to be all right. "There they go," I holler, just to let off steam and be sure that Bill sees the lead plane's bombs, and now our bombs are dropping. Now we close the doors. Dick reports that the other plane to the rear appears all right -- his bombs went away with ours. Evidently everyone is still O.K. All props are turning. No fighters yet, but the flak doesn't let up. The explosions stick right with us and the smoke is all about. Sometimes we fly into large puffs before they dissipate -- this is a long way from home! Will we ever see home again? It doesn't seem possible that we can get out of here safely -- this must be looking the old Reaper right in the face. Every minute I wonder if we can dodge the shells just another minute, and still they explode about us. Jones is in tight, so is Bunting. We must all look like one plane at a distance. We couldn't be much closer, but the scare works wonders. It's a consolation to have others right up here too. The gunners are right with their guns. I see a small plane several thousands of feet below make a diving turn toward Nagoya -- must be one of their fighters going in to land.

The flak is letting up -- is it possible? This is the first time we've heard of flak tracking so accurately while in a turn -- perhaps the guns were radar controlled. It's ironical that all the ammunition in our guns did no good. We have every shell left. Bet the fellows feel like shooting at anything here now in retaliation for that shooting at us -- I do. Looks like we'll make it, now. We're still in close formation, so I don't take my eyes off the lead plane, we are keeping our position a few feet to the right and high. The black puffs are gone. Thank you, Lord. I realize now that a continuous prayer on my part has just been concluded, and within the length of that prayer I committed myself to doing certain things if I were spared this time. It's ironical to think of us praying while we deal death and destruction with bombs, but there's no explaining it. Prayer at these times comes spontaneously. We think we're in the right and that should make our prayers acceptable, but I rather think the Divine Power doesn't see the United States' record as spotless as we like to think.

We are headed toward the coast to the southeast. We pass over several airfields. There seems to be no opposition ahead, so we loosen up the formation a little. Bunting drops back, Jonesy reports, but doesn't seem to be in trouble. This is no time to lag -- we're still over Japan. Dick and Charlie report that they see what appears to be balloons over an inlet near the coast, and Jonesy confirms this with the binoculars. We can't figure out their purpose, but we'll report them. We're over the coast now. An appraisal of the appearance of the other planes shows no visible damage. We're lucky people. I confirm this by talking to

Koser, Jones, and Bunting. Everyone reports their engines are O.K. We turn right about 45 degrees to put some lateral distance between us and the others for the climb through the overcast ahead.

Over the interphone the fellows are discussing where the bombs hit. Dick and Charlie are sure the bombs hit in the target area, so that's good. They are disappointed not to have had any action, but mighty glad, I'm sure to be out of the flak. There's something fatalistic and personal about the flak bursts. You look out and see the bursts so close. Will the next get you or not? At a distance it is highly impersonal, but up close it's meant for us and it has our immediate concern, all the more because there is nothing we can do to avoid it. But the gunners report that there is no visible damage to the plane and everyone is all right. Looks like we got through unscathed, although it's hard to believe. We still haven't seen any of our P-51s.

We climb through the clouds and they break up just beyond. Nick and Bill compute the fuel remaining, and it seems that we have used up most of our large reserve. We remove the heavy gear and get comfortable, with many a "Whew" and "That's that!" My hands and arms are still quivering from the strain of wrestling the plane for so long a period -- 90 minutes assembling, and the long trip overland. The close formation is strenuous, too. My arms and shoulders are tired. We all feel the let-down now, and it's good to lean back with the autopilot doing the work. Gabby and Al, who can't see out from their positions must be even more relieved than we are. We begin our napping and all goes well. The fuel is holding out. Since the bombs were dropped and the fuel transferred the plane's balance has been O.K.

On awakening I hear the lovely strains of "Stardust" being played by many strings -- from Saipan, home, the U.S. again. It's a different world from that over Japan. The music has a wonderful sound, far beyond the mere rendition by a number of violins of a lovely song. Everyone in the plane is very quiet, there is only the synchronized purr of the engines in the background, each is busy with his own thoughts. Twilight settles over us and the clouds gradually turn from white to black on the horizon toward the west. The water loses its reflections and ripples under us and becomes a black void. There are no lights in the sky.

At 1900 we see in the distance the lights of Saipan, and then, slightly to the right, the lights of Tinian -- a welcome sight. We come in over the Saipan harbor, with its many ships alight, and circle the north field of Tinian. Everything goes well on the approach, and our landing lights pivot out to light the runway ahead. We have two rows of lights marking either edge of the runway to line us up. Carrying plenty of speed, we glide in close to the ground and then let the plane "settle in". By carrying the nose wheel slightly high at this point, with power off and good forward speed, the big plane settles onto the ground as gracefully as a big bird. The wheels touch with our hardly knowing it -- unusually smooth -- and there's chatter on the interphone about "what a grease job" -- welcome words to a pilot who is very much concerned over the quality of his landings. A bad landing, that is, rough or with a bounce, makes him unhappy far out of proportion to its significance. It's the test-case of a pilot's ability so far as the passengers are concerned, though many other things are of greater importance in flying (so long as safety is not endangered in the landing).   Like the cook who makes many complicated and tasty dishes, still it's the crust on the pie that's the real test.

We are puzzled by the worried expressions on the ground crew's faces as we stop and holler out when reaching the hardstand. Pat, Grobe, Kramer, Reinholtz and the others explain it finally by saying, "We heard you were missing." We are unusually late, but where they got that idea is beyond us. But they're wrong and that's what counts. We chide them for ever thinking such a thing. "Why, you thought us missing? You know better than that!" But they look serious and shake their heads. I feel a huge rush of gratitude well up inside me. They were really concerned about us, and are glad to have us back. The other fellows are feeling the same, I can see. Pat, Grobe, Kramer, Reinholtz, Levine -- I'd like to hug them right now. Maybe it's just some kind of reaction, but I almost feel like crying. Instead I end up saying, "It's good to see you, Pat." He smiles and returns the same, and I know he means it. Major Donnell and Sowers come up all smiles. All the planes are accounted for now, it seems. Ramsey returned with two serious casualties, the blister gunners, right and left, wounded when flak bursts tore huge gaping holes in their plane. It seems that Ramsey and his whole formation got the works over Nagoya, but hit the target. Bill Phillips, Ray's bombardier, got two Jap fighters. Some of the Japs dived right through the formation during the bomb run. We appreciate, again, our luck in getting through unhurt. Possibly our formation was far enough behind to catch the fighters refueling on the ground. Evidently the Japs fire on the B-29s even with their fighters attacking.

Bill, Nick and I confer on the mechanical end and our only write-up, with the usual shaky hand, is the radio compass, whose aerial broke again. Thanks to Pat and the boys the plane is in A-1 shape. So we go up to the area and go through the interrogation. After this we get the food, and it is welcome! A whole day's fast makes lots of room for what's to come. We eat four eggs covered with large orders of ham. What a meal. Guess the Mess Officer and the cooks know that this one means a lot to us. We all settle down around one table big enough for eight. Rather crowded, but better than splitting up. Elbows are all over the place and a certain amount of sparring is necessary to do the job. What a time! All is jollity now. We even have ice cream for dessert.

By this time it is late, almost midnight. We return to our new home to find Pres and the boys already in bed. The Quonset is surely nice to come home to. No coral floor now, nor water coursing under our beds. We try to be quiet, but Pres is awake and he asks about the mission. Seems that he and the others about the area thought we were missing. Evidently our not being present at the assembly with the others caused the trouble, or maybe they confused us with some plane in distress. We learned at the briefing that many others missed their formation because of the clouds and haze at the assembly point. We learned, too, that many of our ships were damaged by the flak, even though we were not, other than many small punctures of the plane's skin.

We tell Pres what we know about the mission and what we heard at the

Interrogation about others' experiences. It seems that 50 B-29s were damaged by flak, and that 270 enemy planes were sighted, with 159 making attacks, some diving through formations, and we had none! None of our crews saw our own fighters while there. Pres then tells us that he's scheduled to get up at 3 o'clock this morning to bomb an airfield on southern Kyushu, to help out the Navy and the invasion at Okinawa. So we say goodnight and let him get some sleep. We're glad we don't have to get up in the middle of the night, this night.

Chapter 15 Tokyo

April 13-14, 1945 – No. 10

"The Big Thermal"

We have just learned that Preston and his crew ditched after take-off this morning. All were killed but three gunners and the radar operator. We listen silently as the circumstances are told to us. It seems that an engine failed during take-off, just as the plane was airborne. They couldn't stay aloft on the other three engines, handicapped by the extreme nose-heaviness resulting from the bombs remaining in the forward bomb bay. When salvoed, only the rear bay emptied and the improper loading made a bad situation worse. The full weight of a combat loss saddens the entire 1st Squadron. Unbelievingly we try to adjust ourselves to this stunning news, and listen to the subdued comments of various neighbors who drop in. We learn that Pres was not flying his own plane, but No. 7, Fortune's plane, which had just returned several hours before from the last mission. The fellows seem puzzled and I wonder, too, over their being scheduled to fly a plane so recently returned from a mission. It takes time to inspect and recondition a plane for another strenuous mission, and this plane was on the ground only six hours between flights instead of the customary 12 to 24 hours.

Bill, Hal, Jake, and I are the "Summary Court Officers" for Don, Lloyd, Al, and Pres respectively. It is our duty to collect their belongings and personal effects, tabulate them, and take them to the Quartermaster's Corps, which will prepare them for shipment home. Only Lloyd's body was recovered. He evidently escaped from the cabin, or been thrown out. His body will be buried on Saipan. The four who survived, Wipperman, Ford, Douglas, and Birsner, are in the hospital, suffering from shock and force of impact. They are very dazed when we see them, but give us an account of the crash and attendant circumstance. It seems that with the unbalanced power, they caught a wing in the water as the plane ditched, causing it to break in two. Probably the open bomb doors aided the rush of water into the plane, snapping it in two. It sank immediately. They escaped through the break and were later picked up by the rescue boat which cruises the water under the planes as they take off. Pres had called the Tower and said that they were in trouble, but said nothing further.

We feel mighty low, each in his own thoughts. I recall the fun we had sharing the tent with them, then building the Quonset. So many incidents come flooding back -- here and back in the States, down in Cuba, of Pres trying to speak Spanish, his infectious grin, the humor he found in everything, livening things up, his wife and baby girl. I enjoyed knowing them so much, though I knew Pres the best. I look across the room and at the spot where I am accustomed to seeing him among his belongings -- old sox, shorts used when building the Quonset, pictures of his wife -- it's just unbelievable, and to be lost on take-off. So now we've lost a crew, one of the originals. We've looked about us when in class in the States and thought about who might not be with us so many months later, after we're flying missions. Pres is No. 1. The luck of the 24th Squadron is punctured, but why shouldn't it be? We've just been lucky, and we've known it -- the whole Squadron. It's a sobering thought. We know very well now that it doesn't just happen to the other guy. We've heard Pres and the fellows express these thoughts themselves, just as we do now, but we know it better now. Pres, as a pilot, had as much experience as any of us, and more than most. For four years and more he has been flying and before that he worked on planes as an enlisted man. He's come up through the ranks from Private in over 12 years. He was just 30, though he seemed even younger than many of those who were his juniors.

We feel better when others move into the Quonset with us. They are a replacement crew -- Ertresvaag's. There are five officers in this crew, including Karlson, the radar operator, who has ridden with us on a mission, and is a commissioned officer.

Meanwhile we go to ground school. Hal and Jake get the navigation and bombing end, while Bill and I are informed that we may participate in missions in which B-29s will fly in at 100 feet, tree-top level, to bomb and strafe. We whistle with the rest, but aren't too surprised. We're liable to do anything with the B-29. The high command is evidently pleased with its new weapon and wants to experiment some more. We'll be the guinea pigs, as usual. We dislike the experiments since they are foreign to our training, and it's a human quality to resist change, no doubt, but we're aware of the success of the "blitz" low altitude missions and that it is a new wrinkle. We also returned safely from the medium altitude missions in day-light, even when we had been taught to consider the B-29 as a high altitude bomber exclusively. In many ways concerning the actual handling of the plane, such as in the cruise control of our own plane, we are ahead of the planning staff, but possibly this low altitude tree-top work will be in the category that it is workable, too, despite its revolutionary nature. Now we "sweat out" the raid to Koisumi where the Kori-yami Chemical Works is to be bombed. As it turns out, our plane is out of commission, so we don't go.

On April 12th we hear that Iwo was bombed by the Japs -- quite an event. Probably they flew down from Chichi-jima or Haha-jima, where there are still hostile forces. Our fighters made short work of them, we assume.

Finally we are scheduled to go again, this time to Tokyo. On the mission board appear the names: Boynton, Holton, Jordan, Mutch, Fortune, Litchfield, Alger, and Reider. Before the target identification class the whole crew gets into a truck and goes down to the line to see Pat ant to test-fly the plane. Damage to a cowl flap motor after we arrive prevents our going, so we return to the area for the 1100 class. For two days Pat, Kramer, Grobe, Levine, and Reinholtz had worked to change a cylinder in the No. 4 engine. The first night they worked until 0330, the second day from early until 0500 the following day, and then returned at 0700 to work all day again. With work like that our plane will be the best. It's too bad the men do not get the credit we want them to have. We appreciate their efforts, as we do our lives, but their superiors take them for granted, and always try to get the last breath of work out of them after the big job's been done. After getting us off this time they will probably be asked to do some other work, and will get some rest only because they, themselves, point out their need for it. How is it that those in charge do not understand how hard these men work, and what a pride they take in their work? The authorities are quick to speak in generalities about the excellent quality of the mechanics' work, yet when these men could be resting they are required to stand inspections and to police their areas for blowing paper. After three days of almost unceasing toil Pat and the boys are "bushed". I request some time off for them, but it's refused.

Another crew, Parks' crew, test-flies the plane for us while we go to class and Pat goes along. It checks out fine, we are told, a testimony to the excellence of the work. While at the line, Jonesy and the gunners load the guns themselves instead of leaving it to the armament department. They see to it that we get almost 300 rounds per gun instead of the specified 100. Jakes tests the bomb circuits and shackles to be sure they work. He also checks the salvo mechanism, since that is so important on take-off. In an emergency a crew doesn't want a load of bombs aboard.

At Target Identification we pour over the photo mosaics, target charts, and detailed maps of the Tokyo area. Our target is incendiary zone No. 2, wherein are located several strategic targets consisting of ordnance works and depot, a powder factory, and Quartermaster clothing storage for their Army. The entire area is highly inflammable. The bombing run, we learn, is to be radar, with the approach from the east. Goi, on the bay side of the peninsula, is the I.P. The navigator will time the run from this point with a stop watch. The release point is due north of the heart of the city, bounded by two rivers on the north, just where the river makes a southerly loop. The bomb heading will be 308 degrees.

We convene again in the briefing building at 1500, all ears to absorb further "poop". The Operations Officer takes the roll and the C.O. gives us the introductory talk. "Tonight's mission will be a low-level incendiary attack on Tokyo, such as we did so well before. It's right up our alley, so this should be a good one for us. I would like to caution you about the turbulence you may encounter over the target. Thanks to the earlier raid there isn't much left of Tokyo, and the rest of the people should spend their time in the county, anyway, so let's go." The Intelligence Officer covers the importance of the target in this way: "This area is not so highly inflammable as the other section bombed before. However, there are some good targets in this area, including a powder plant, ordnance depot, steam plant, arsenal, and electricity plants. This is a precision target. We must hit in the assigned area. The course is 2671 nautical miles (3200 statute miles). You will go by way of Iwo, thence to Cape Nojima-Zaki, up the east coast, until abreast of the I.P. From there you will cross the peninsula to hit Goi Point on a heading of 300 degrees. You should be over the target at 0215. From the I.P. you will fly over the dock area at the mouth of the Edo River, thence to the target area. After the release you will turn north to Iwatsuki, then 60 degrees to Sagafu Homa, 120 degrees to the coast, then home. In the target area the 314th will be hitting southeast of us, and the 73rd to the south of us, so that the entire area should be well covered. There is no moon tonight, but the fires will illuminate the target. There are 80 fields within a 100 mile radius. In a 50 mile radius there are 48 night fighter planes, and a total of 304 planes in the area. Recently the attacks have been increasingly aggressive. Watch for the 'Balls of Fire' -- use evasive action to avoid them. There are 173 searchlights in this area, but probably only 50 to 60 will be used. Since you will be arriving later than the others, they will be thoroughly warned of your approach."

Brockaway covers the flak: "The east coast has 30 guns (pointing to the chart), and there may be flak boats in the bay. Heavy fire may be expected north of the Palace. There are 14 balloons reported in the area, west of course, also some low ones at 3000 feet to the east of your course. For safety's sake make any errors in course to the left as you withdraw from the target area. Fly straight through barrage-type fire, since you are then exposed a shorter time than when taking evasive action. Avoid the holes in the clouds, if there are clouds, since the guns will be trained through those."

Bob Hall gives the Air-Sea rescue, stating that, "There will be 1 dumbo, 3 superdumbos, 2 surface crafts, and 3 subs to help in an emergency. Calls will be 'Halter Post', 'Field Goal', and 'Lopsided' before 0400, changing to 'Molly's Muff', 'Libel Suit', and 'Floy-floy' after 0400, for the reference points of Hachijo-jima, Iwo, and Pagan. For rescue purposes monitor frequencies 4475, 500, 1108, 1345, and Q channel."

Kirby takes the stage and gives out the radio information: "You will monitor channel Queen at all times in order to intercept emergency messages. Each plane will send a strike report. IFF off at 27 degrees north and on 100 miles out on return. Any sighting (of shipping) north of 28 degrees will be sent after leaving the target. Do not report subs sighted."

Sully, the rapid-fire Irishman, gives us the weather: "There are two cold fronts along the course. Altimeter setting will be 29.97. Return at 15,000 feet to get favorable winds." The Navigator then gives us a time hack.

The Operations Officer takes over again to give the Operational data, which will be covered again in the specialized briefing: "Take-off will be to the east. You will be the second wave to hit the target, 30 minutes behind the first plane of the other Wing. You are loaded with 6800 gallons of fuel, 27,500 lbs. of incendiary bombs, one G.P. bomb (high explosive), and 1000 rounds of ammunition. Total weight will be 136,700 lbs. Be especially careful when firing guns in case of fighter attacks, since there will be many of our own planes in the vicinity. Turn lights out and IFF off. Do not take evasive action on the run. The 73rd Wing will be at 7000 to 7800 feet, the 314th will be at 9000 to 9500 feet, and the 504th at 8000 to 8500 feet."

Now he goes over additional points already made by others over and over, so we won't forget, I guess. These points have been covered three times already. He has apparently forgotten, through lack of participation in the missions themselves, no doubt, that we get these points the first time, and that if we don't, we'll ask. We're vitally concerned, and no one has to drill these lessons into our heads. It's a good thing to get the information, but another to have someone keep repeating it. The men dislike his rather smug presentation of these facts in repetition, as though if we memorize them nothing can happen to us and the mission will be run off perfectly, just as delineated in the briefing. But he does his best -- he sees these missions from his office, based upon the available "paper work". Now the Chaplain leads us in a short prayer.

Specialized briefing is next on the list. The meeting breaks up and the individual crew members go to meetings where the information is covered again, in great detail. We'll be tired out before we get started, at this rate. More do's and don'ts, and the earlier points are re-emphasized. The Operations Officer seems to be enjoying a new confidence in his duties in this capacity -- looks to us like he's overdoing it, but he doesn't know it. We learn, in addition, that all four runways will be used simultaneously tonight for take-off; there will be no emergency runway left open.

Now another comment, showing utter lack of comprehension of our work, is dropped -- this time by our Commanding Officer. He says: "Keep an eye open and check up on planes that drop their bombs at places near the mainland other than the target." Evidently he is referring to a seldom mentioned, unbelieved rumor that some planes are dropping their bombs out at sea instead of going into the target area, thereby sparing their crews from going into the target. He evidently has overlooked the facts, as we know so well from flying the missions, that first, the planes have no lights on them and can't be identified at night (if there are such planes), and secondly, that we are utterly too preoccupied and busy to think of policing duties -- much less to chasing them and finding out who it is -- even were we able to do so. But far more rankling to us than his failure to understand the general nature of our work, is his very mention in this manner of such a shameful practice. In the first place, we don't think that such cowardice is possible, and if it is, the many crews who do the job as ordered would not care to admit that there are some who don't. Further, what of it? Such a matter, if such there is, is between a crew and God and their consciences. They have to live with themselves! The rest of us can bomb the target to submission in time, but those poor devils will know all their lives that they're 'chicken-livered', not like their buddies. The whole matter leaves a bad taste in our mouths as we leave, and we think far less of our C.O. for having mentioned it, particularly in the way in which he did -- very upsetting to say the least. But it's always stabilizing to look around and see the crew. There's something real and meaningful. Hell or high water couldn't keep us from doing our job as we see it our duty to do, so I forget upsetting angles and we go to chow. We have meat loaf, potatoes, bread, butter, and raisin tart -- not bad, but no gravy, and it was advertised on the menu. We protest, but no luck. Imagine, no gravy-bread! We load our canteens with luxurious ice water and get several portions of hard candy.

We share the truck with Captain Reider and his crew, a new and temporary addition to our Squadron and Group. They are members of the 58th Wing and have just come over from their China bases. They will have their own field here after it is finished and the rest of the outfit gets here. Meanwhile he is flying with our Group. He is quite disturbed about going on this mission, since he feels that his plane is not ready to fly, and he seems bitter about the lack of proper maintenance checks on his plane in between the almost daily flights. He claims that this will be the last until the plane gets some attention. He doesn't seem so concerned about putting more planes over the target than any other Group, as is our C.O., and I silently agree. In fact, he seems unhappy with our outfit in general. Somehow the supervisory personnel of our Group manages to step on everybody's toes, judging from the dislike engendered among the other outfits toward our Group. We are not surprised at this, since it substantiates our complaints in the past. Within our Squadron we get along fairly well, and the combat crews think that we have the best set of crews in any outfit, but beyond that we're not so proud of our organization.

The remainder of the bombs are being loaded as we arrive. After completing many of the preflight chores we hold a crew meeting to discuss our duties in relation to this flight. We work out a communication with George in the tail to be used in case the interphone system goes dead. We're always worried over George, who is all alone in the tail. Since our only contact is the interphone, we devise a system to replace it for emergency purposes. To contact George, Jonesy, Dick and Charlie agree to energize the amplidynes for the power turret at George's station. He can hear this, and it is controlled by a switch in the blister section. For communication in the other direction, George will press his action switch on the gunsight, which causes alight to flash in the blister section. About this time old "Whiffinpoof Eli" -- Yale-man Dan Cady -- comes by and we joke with him a bit, after telling him the personal equipment is all right. Major Donnell and the Deputy C.O. drop by and we tell them we'll be ready to go on time, and then we fan the breeze awhile with them. Hal returns from getting some Loran charts left in the area. After this we pull the props, have a crew inspection, and get in the plane. The boys make fun of the prop pulling and do some hollering when Al or Jake pulls a blade alone, looking like the strong men. "Alberrrrto" George shouts, using his Puerto Rican name, as he tries to get Al to do more pushing than himself.

We taxi out after engine check right on time, and head west with the others until we hit the new taxiway at the west end of our new parking area. This cuts down the taxi time and we get off 3 minutes early. Take-off is normal, though we use every bit of the runway because of our weight.

"There's gas siphoning out of the left fuel tank," reports Dick. It stops, however, after several seconds and everything appears to be fine. At 24 43 we climb through the clouds and level off at 8000 feet on time. Not being able to hold our speed with less than 2200 RPM, we stay in auto-rich mixture longer than the briefed time and so use extra fuel.

Dick, Charlie, Jonesy, and George are calling out the other planes in the area. Nick is 'meter-reading', Jake is watching out front, Hal is plotting our position and course, Al is monitoring the radio, and Gabby is on the radar set. Bill and I alternate at the controls, flying instruments as we always do before setting up the autopilot. The ship feels good. Again I have the feeling of a sharp team operating, doing a job that they do well and enjoy. It's easy to see how we've improved as a unit while on these missions. For myself, I have a sudden, rather unusual realization of how I like to do this. It is a distinct pleasure to sit at the controls and feel the plane with all its power and weight respond to pressure on the wheel and throttle. It is a glorified amusement park game of skill, keeping the gyro horizon level by keeping the miniature plane's wings level in the instrument, and cross checking with the altimeter, directional gyro, airspeed, and subconsciously noticing any movements of the rate of climb.

Using the whole panel of instruments is a long way from the cadet instruction of using only the needle, ball, and airspeed. Now all of the instruments relating to the plane's altitude in space are assembled in a large group, in duplicate sets on instrument panels in front of the pilot and copilot. After a few minutes of instrument flying I make smaller and smaller corrections through the controls until the plane is flying itself, with human supervision added only when a wing drops or the nose climbs or dives slightly.

Aside from the professional enjoyment of my job (it doesn't seem like flying by something else, fighter pilots 'fly'), there is the solid satisfaction of being a participant in a crew, and in knowing that the undertaking ahead, whatever happens, does not find us unprepared. The crew is good, each knows his job, and in doing it his efforts dove-tail with the others in the plane. It is a fine example of coordination and team work -- the result of training in the States and some combat missions tucked under our belts. It dates back to the beginning of the army career of each crew member, and all that he has learned since that time. In fact, the teamwork is actually the result of the combining of eleven lifetimes of experience in the U.S. The result is competency in professional duties and a crew spirit that can't be beaten. If all of us can find work to do as civilians which we know as much about as we do our jobs here, we'll be satisfactory citizens. There is much that I do not know, and much more that I learn on every flight we make, concerning the flying and the combat use of the B-29 in all departments. Still, I have the comforting feeling that the job is not beyond my ability, but rather that it is right up my alley, and the endless months of flying behind me are now an invaluable back-log of invisible experience, aiding decisions and judgment. It is too bad that at our most formative years we are learning a job we may never work at as civilians, whereas, if we could step into civilian life doing this type of work we'd be a success right off. In knowing this job of ours, however, we have a yardstick against which we can measure our knowledge of other and different types of work in the future. Each member of the crew, in a sense, is a professional man, a skilled worker, be he a gunner, radar operator, engineer, bombardier, navigator, radio operator, or pilot. If we each had the same level of knowledge of a civilian occupation, we would draw good pay.

Now Bill and I chat about the possibilities of a novel on the life of married couples in the Army, of ourselves and our wives as examples in the B-29 program. Now we think of the narrative accounts of these missions, if they could be printed in the States. Possibly what we take for commonplace on these missions would be of great interest to the folks back home. Ernie Pyle's articles are very interesting to people in the U.S., and yet we feel that they are far from portraying life out here as it really is. In fact, Ernie has never been on a mission out here, and his entire program is dominated by the central theme of flying over Japan. The combat crew members could portray it, but they don't write.

At 2110 Hal gives us an ETA for Iwo of 2215. We see someone jettison their bombs and head back to base -- must have engine trouble. The bombs bursting into flame look like flak exploding at first, but not for long. Now several of the fellows take Benzedrine. I always take mine just after take-off, since in my case it requires a while to operate, and I want it to be in effect at the target, but most importantly, for me, it kills my hunger.

At 2240 we are still in the clouds, though we can occasionally see through them above. It's hard to tell how high they are. The ETA for landfall is now 0135. At this time a trip to the relief tube is really a relief. Squeezing by Hal is always a problem, but I continue to make it even with the C-1 vest and Mae West on. This might serve as a test of waistline through life -- trying to make it through the space between the turret and navigator's table. All I'll need is a B-29 handy in which to make the test periodically. This thought has the same sporting flavor to it as has the current assertion that we go up to Japan just to cool the canteen of water which sits on the cold metal floor -- all for a cold drink of water. After such a statement someone will look strangely at you and say, "You're Island happy," or "Rock happy," as it is called, to which the answer is, "There's nothing wrong with me that a life-time in the States won't cure."

Al intercepts a message stating that we should monitor channel King when within 30 miles of Japan in order to receive messages from 'Dragon', a plane in the target area which will act as 'Master of Ceremonies'. We can't think of a thing that plane can do that the lengthy briefing hasn't already covered. Possibly new altitudes will be given.

At 2400 Nick is finished with the fuel transfer. We alter course so that a plane overtaking us won't run into us -- they must be asleep not to see us. Horns don't help on this highway. The Japs would be surprised to see this great "Sleeping Army" approaching. In its present condition this force would hardly be effective. At 0030 Jonesy and the gunners energize the turrets and George goes back into the tail. We all begin to don the myriad bits of equipment, assuming the beer-barrel shape. It's the first time in my life that I have been able to sit comfortably with my hands folded on my stomach.

Gabby is sharper than a firecracker on the radar and together with Hal he gives a correction that puts us in line with the turning point. We passed right over Cape Nojima and never a light along our flight path. To the left a few miles is Tokyo Bay, and to the right the ocean. A faint glow tinges the sky to the northwest. Here we are again, someone is lighting our objective, and as yet we're over 40 miles from the target. This is a favorite haunt of the fighters who fly out with one plane and then pick up another coming in. Dick, George, Charlie, Jonesy, and Jake are concentrating on scanning the sky for any odd lights or shapes. I advise the crew to fasten all safety belts. Higgy checks the men on their personal equipment. Al has a tentative emergency message to send in that is designed for trouble over the target, a message which is precautionary on our part, in our effort not to overlook a single activity that will protect us further. Hal is working with Gabby on the course as it appears on the radar scope. Our whole problem hinges on hitting the IP on course, heading 308 degrees. Only in that way can an accurate timing be made from there to the release point. Hal has our ground speed figured, from winds which are unknown until we get there, and the time computed that it will take to fly from the IP to the target.

The glow of the fires is becoming brighter in the blackness of the night. "Watch out for fighters from here on in fellows!" Higgy says. Not having heard anything on the King channel, I switch my radio to interphone so that I can be with the crew over the target. Bill checks the crew members once more on their safety belts and that their parachutes are securely fastened. It makes a terrible load on our shoulders to have the chute fastened, but it can't be helped. If we have trouble Bill and I will be the last to leave the plane, and we want the men ready to go so we won't need to wait too long -- certainly not while chutes are being fastened. Our altitude is 7000 feet.

"In 20 seconds make a turn to heading of 308 degrees," Hal calls. I acknowledge and he adds, "Ready, turn!" and we begin the $1/4^{th}$ needle-width turn, which is 45 degrees a minute. We roll out on 308 and Gabby and Hal confer with, "That's it, right on the button." So, we're headed in, and after a period of time on a straight and level course the bombs will be released.

Looking ahead we see a cloud over the target that was not noticeable before this time. "Look at that cloud, Bill." "A cumulo-nimbus," he answers. A thunderhead, usually associated with violent storms. But it can't be a cloud. The night is clear. It appears to be huge, miles wide, and towering many times this altitude above us. Now we realize that it actually is a man-made cloud, part smoke and part water-vapor. It has the anvil top of the conventional thunderhead, which pilots always detour for safety's sake. Lying squarely across our path we can't tell how far it is from us, but it must be over the fires unless the wind is blowing it away from us.

The fires are clearly visible now as big orange patches. We see what must be burning timbers that reveal outlines of blazing structures. Whole blocks seem to be on fire to the south and southwest. But we can't see the fires that lie ahead, making this cloud. They must be terrific to build such a huge thunderhead. The smoke itself stretches high above us. We can't tell where it stops or whether it goes to the top of the cloud with the water vapor. The heat of the fires in rising must cause the moisture in the air to condense into vapor, just like a cloud, and this together with the smoke itself pillars up into the air. We should know about it directly, for apparently we are going right into it.

Ahead we see various cargoes of bombs as they break into flame at 2000 feet, then fall, flaming to the earth. Heavy explosions are noticeable periodically. These must be the high explosive bombs hitting the ground. "Searchlights ahead," Jake reports as we see many lights in areas that are not burning. Now we see searchlights from several areas that are burning -- must be suicide operators. Outlying areas to the south and across the river to the north slant their beams into the path we are taking towards the fires. Evidently they are familiar with our path by now. But where is the flak? Tokyo has more flak than any other city, very heavily defended. The absence seems a sure indication to us that there are fighters about, and the gunners know this.

It's nerve wracking, this waiting, for you know not what will happen. The glow of the fires, now almost under us, gives an eerie cast to the night sky, and distorts the appearance of everything about us. Even the cabin is alight now. Suddenly the cabin lights up more brightly -- searchlights! "We're on exhibition again," I think, hating the exposed and helpless feeling the lights give. We can't do anything but sit. We can't even alter course, since we're on the bomb run. Well, what are the lights for? Where are your fighters? Where's the flak? Dick, Charlie, and Jonesy are calling in the location of the lights that have us. There are 12 lights on us now, from three sides. Only the smoke lies ahead -- no lights. The cabin is brilliant and we dare not take our eyes off the instruments, but can see through our peripheral vision. We should have dark colored glasses on, Bill and I. Dick and Charlie fire on several of the lights. Maybe that will teach them the error of spotting us. The cabin light lessons and the scanners report "Two lights off." "Three more off." Then they're all off; why we don't know. "Four minutes to go," Hal calls, and we know we're a long way off from the dropping point.

"Bill, look." I indicate the cloud, and see him studying it. The cloud is in convulsions, apparently, violently rolling and spiraling and boiling upward. What a sight! It now stretches to either side of us, endlessly it seems. It towers above us and reaches out to envelop us. I think to myself, it is like a bad dream to even look at it, and now we're going into it. "Three degrees right," Gabby says, and we correct just as the outlying wisps of smoke glide over the nose of the plane. Now we're in it. It's dark as pitch. It becomes rough, like a bumpy road. We're riding on square wheels. It's really getting rough -- not air-cushioned bumps like the usual turbulence, but jarring solid jolts like hitting something continually.

"One and one-half minutes to go," Hal announces. Bill is holding tight to his controls, as I hold mine, trying to keep the plane level and to hold the altitude. We'll wrestle, if that's what it takes, but we find that these forces are far greater than ours. Here's the thermal -- the hottest part of the cloud, formed by the rising air from the fires beneath. Still level by the instruments, we're going up 2000 to 3000 feet a minute, the airspeed jumps from 200 to 290. I chop the throttles almost off, but we're helpless to combat this. At least we're level. Dear God, are you with us? With a violent lunge the plane drops -- it's a change of air. We are hanging on by our belts and they cut into the legs. The dinghy under me slides about until I'm on the edge of it. Cans of juice are waist-high in the air. Jake's loose papers are up about his head, but I can't see much for I'm watching the instruments, or trying to. The gyro is acting crazy -- maybe it's going to jump out of its case.

My head is dazed -- my metal helmet hits something. That, and being thrown forward, has addled the brain, and the instruments are cock-eyed. No, it's just the gyros that are off. Bill has his helmet over his eyes and is trying to get back into his seat properly. The plane can't stand it, I'm sure. "Are the wings intact?" I wonder. A plane just can't take this, not built for it, and with all the bombs still inside, but we're going on, or are we going down? If this is the end of the road, anyway we tried. Countless thoughts parade by. But we're still aloft. I look at the altimeter; we're down to 9000 feet and the airspeed is about 250 now. Maybe we're still flying! Instinctively we keep holding the plane level as though nothing had happened. Bill is with me. Gabby breaks the dead silence -- "Can't find my pencil." What a joke! He's worrying about a pencil. Now I realize that we're still on the bomb run, and the fellows are still plotting the run. "Now," Hal shouts and Jake, like a veteran, hits the release switch. The plane bucks and then settles down as usual after losing a load. The plane is acting all right. Maybe we're still all right. Well, might as well get the bad news. "Everyone, O.K.?" I inquire apprehensively. "Blisters O.K." "Radar O.K." "Tail Roger," the answers come in. "How about Al?" I inquire. "He's O.K." Hal informs us. "He was knocked around quite a bit but he seems all right."

Hal tells us he dropped the bombs a few seconds ahead of time since we were high and fast compared to expectations, and thus compensated to put the bombs where they were intended. "Good," I say mechanically, and think that even that thermal didn't upset the boys. The plane feels all right and the instruments are normal now, except for the gyro. Maybe everything's going to be all right. The sudden events seem less like a bad dream. The men are all right, the wings are still on, the cabin, Jake's back, the scattered papers -- they all look normal. Reality seems restored and the mind tries to catch up with the habitual routine the hands, eyes, and senses have been pursuing during all the excitement.

We turn right onto the north heading. We are out of the smoke entirely now. The gunners are at their guns. Searchlights pick us up -- from the frying pan into the fire! But we got through the thermal, we ought to make this all right. From the brief comments that begin over the interphone I gather that the others are not fully recovered from the shaking yet. "My teeth are jarred loose," Higgy states. Where do these lights north of Tokyo come from? They were not mentioned by the all-knowing briefing officers. Still no fighters; this is mighty fishy. Well, we're running the gauntlet and searchlights should be accompanied by something. We boost the power and start evasive action.

As we leave the Tokyo area the lights leave us one by one and we find ourselves alone. "Is everything all right, Nick?" I ask. "Looks like it. Don't see how a plane could take it." When we reach the place where we think Iwatsuki is located we take up the 60 degree heading and leave the brilliant fires further behind. "The cloud's even higher now," Charlie marvels aloud, and Bill looks back. "There really are some fires there. Can't see how anything remains." Bill's still rubbing his leg. It seems that a can of juice bounced into his shin either on the way up or down. We caution the gunners to look alive for the fighters. It's unnecessary to warn them, but it makes us feel better up front. Well do we know they are looking as hard as they can with an itchy trigger finger.

We swing onto the 120 degree heading and shortly are out over the water. We stay in our equipment, expecting trouble, until we are almost 100 miles south of the tip of the peninsula. Then, amid quite a hub-bub, we shed the gear and relax. To my inquiry concerning the condition of the plane, Gabby relates again that his floor is all over the place, and that his pencil is still missing. Everyone was badly shaken, and scared even worse, yet here we are still flying, and with enough fuel to reach home, we think. In our let-down of relief we get some good laughs from the various comments. Gabby says, "Radar set's working a lot better now, shaking it up did it good."

Everyone has something to say about pieces of equipment floating through the air when we hit the down draft, but the best joke is at Charlie's expense, and he ruefully joins in. Dick relates the story. It seems that after the thermal, while getting adjusted in their seats again, Charlie shouts to Dick, "I've been hit." Dick looks at the foot Charlie indicates to see a dark red, moist area above the shoe top. Apparently the foot is virtually oozing gore, and Charlie hesitates to remove the shoe. It looks bad. After a few moments of horrible concern Dick sees the blood splotches are elsewhere in the blister section, but most of all right around the open tomato juice can, which was upset. After earnest entreaty, Charlie finally tastes his soaked sock and sheepishly admits it's a tomato juice mixture.

The flight home is uneventful. I feel so thankful that I sit there and marvel to myself how a plane could go through that and that we are still alive and going back to the base. While Bill sleeps I attempt to draw his picture, sprawled all over his chair. I'll label this "Higgy at work" and send it to his wife to give her an idea of how we spend most of our time in the air.

On arrival we fly the usual pattern and land. It is broad daylight. We taxi into the hardstand at 0915, the exact time that we told Pat we'd be back, of which we remind him rather smugly. The usual gang greets us and knows that the thermal had exceeded all expectations, according to others' reports, but those who didn't go have no idea just how bad it was.

We learn from talking to the interrogators that 8 aircraft were lost on the mission, with all crew members missing. 50 airplanes were damaged as a result of flak and fighters. 80 fighters were sighted and 42 made attacks. 10 'balls of fire' were sighted, some of which apparently had wings, and trailed after the B-29s until finally diving to the ground and crashing -- a mighty strange apparition. Several B-29s were observed going down over the target. Of those who returned, 9 men were wounded. The Japs are putting up an opposition. Others had similar experiences with the thermal and like us are happy to have gotten through it alive. Various anecdotes are told of the violence of the thermal. In one case large pieces of wood from one of the buildings afire were found lodged in the engine's nacelles of a plane.

So we eat, wash, and "hit the sack". 10 behind us now.

Chapter 16 Yokohama-Kawasaki

April 15-16, 1945 – No. 11

"Flak-Alley"

After our return from Tokyo we sleep, rest, and chat with out new hut mates. Dick Willis lives directly across from me now. Somehow I don't feel much like chatting with the newcomers much just now. Pres and the boys are still too present. Hal, Jake, and Bill are resting, and we're at this occupation when Corporal Segaithus from Operations drops by to tell us that we're scheduled to go to Target Identification at 1600. A mission is going out the next day. We dress and check the mission board. There we see the names Boynton, Alger, Cooney, Lazin, Maki, Dawson, Parks, and Schwager as those going on this next one. We're still tired, but we're glad to keep busy with missions -- the more the better -- particularly when we can fly our own plane. That means a lot to us and is a big safety factor, we feel sure, for we know what the plane will do.

At Target Identification we lack the necessary photo mosaics, maps, and target charts of the target, so we don't get much out of the meeting. However, there have been so many changes of the plans for the missions on the last few that we expect a change by the next day. The high command seems to have trouble getting the plans set.

At 1400 on April 16th the crews of the three squadrons that will participate in this mission are assembled in the briefing building. After the roll call the Operations Officer mentions that the plans have been changed from the day before, so our premonition was correct. After the jar of "Attention", we are reseated and the C.O. says a few words: "Yokohama is a difficult target, by the same token it is hard to defend. It has never been hit before. It's importance centers around it's being a large seaport shipping center and Naval base." The Intelligence Officer gives the "intelligence" data, which when condensed is: "Kawasaki is your target, the northern urban area of Yokohama. The course if 2587 Nautical miles (2975 statute miles). The route is to Iwo, to Kozu-shima, skirt the east coast of the peninsula which lies to the southwest of Tokyo Bay, then into the target. The 214th Wing will be with us and the 73rd will go to Tokyo. The IP is Mansuru-misaki. You will pass the small town of Chigasaki. Mt. Fuji will be to your left as you go in. The highest terrain otherwise will be 4700 feet. The target is bounded by the Tama River on the north and the Tsurumi on the south, six miles on a side, while there is a four-mile front along the bay. 25% of Japan's steam and electric power are found in this area. As for fighters: in a 100-mile radius there is a total of 302 planes, 188 single engine and 66 twin, with 48 night fighters. The Yokosuka Naval Works will be to the right of course as you go in. 'Balls of fire' may be in evidence tonight. They are Jap suicide fighters and you can shoot them down, even though they are equipped with armor plate in front of the pilot. The fighters will team up with the lights, and beware of decoy fires." During his talk he illustrates with the large charts of the target area mounted on sliding panels on the stage. Rescue facilities will include 1 dumbo, 3 superdumbos, 2 surface craft, and 3 subs.

On the weather side we learn that there is a "front" lying just south of Iwo at 19 degrees. The wind at the target will be from 290 degrees at 25 knots. Best return will be at 15,000 feet.

Colonel Tucker covers the operational end: "This is a medium effort with over 400 planes participating. Take-off deadline will be 2100. (If we're held up later than that we are not expected to go on the mission.) The total gross will be 134,000 lb., with 6800 gallons of fuel and 1000 rounds of ammunition." (This means that we are allowed 300 lbs. of our total weight in ammunition with which to defend ourselves -- 100 rounds per gun. Eight planes were lost over the target last mission, and many fighter attacks were reported. "Balls of fire" were in evidence, and yet the authorities don't think we need ammunition in quantity. 100 rounds in one of those fifty-caliber machine guns is expended in two or three bursts, and then the gun's out of ammunition.)

"The bomb load will be 184 M47 incendiary bomb clusters. The altitude will be 1000 feet until south of Minawi-Iwo, then to 6000 feet until off the coast, then up to 8000 feet for bombing. The axis of attack will be 50 degrees. After the release the turn away will be to the right in a climb, to Wada, then on to Tinian. The 504th Group will attack on an opposite heading, but will be off the target prior to our run." This is a condensation of a rather lengthy talk.

The C.O. again takes the floor and speaks repetitiously about the "balls of fire", boring in through the smoke over Tokyo, and the like. At the specialized briefing the C.O. again talks on the "balls of fire", suicide attacks, not firing on the lights, tying down everything in the plane, and decoy fires, doing what he can to warn us of the various dangers we are liable to encounter. We wonder how he (who doesn't go along) feels qualified to tell us, who have seen these things. The crews feel that they know better than he the things he is talking about. We are interested in the discussion of the balls of fire, which are now known to be miniature Jap suicide planes. Many of these have been reported -- possibly some of our planes lost over the target had trouble with them.

Now the C.O. makes what we consider a mistake by mentioning Preston and the circumstances of his accident as an illustration to strengthen a point he is making. He states that he is safe-guarding us -- "my pilots and crews" -- by insisting that we have 130 miles per hour before we leave the ground, and that in having this speed we are safe in case an engine fails, and we can take care of ourselves. My whole nature rebels at such flagrant misstatement -- or worse still, such misunderstanding -- of a critical situation. Every time that we take off we are aware that until the gear and flaps are up an engine cutting out would be "it" and that we might as well prepare to ditch, if we have time. Naturally we would drop our bombs and try to get back, but a controlled ditching would probably be the result. The C.O. is telling us that 130 mph at take-off is enough speed to take care of us in case of engine failure. Damn foolishness, and he has used Pres as the case in point, and that recalls the whole sorry situation to my mind, and an earlier talk that I'd had with the Colonel, as Preston's Summary Court Officer.

At that time he had informed me that he was further safe-guarding us by seeing to it that we were taking off as light as possible. My last take-off at that time, of which I reminded him, was at 138,000 lb., 20,000 lb. heavier than the plane was ever intended to weigh, even after the weight allowance was increased. He countered by saying that others were taking off at 140,000. Since I wasn't making any headway in putting over my idea I "yessirred" and departed. Then, to find out how the Air Corps looked at it, I got the pilot's operating handbook of the B-29. There I found the verification that I needed. It pointed out that at take-off, with the flaps extended and an out-board engine failure, it's impossible to control the airplane without decreasing the power proportionally on the opposite side of the plane. This is true because of the terrific propeller blast against the extended flaps by the good engines, tending to lift that wing, and the lack of this effect on the side where the engine fails. Unless the power is balanced the airplane will force itself into the dead engine, and lack of control will result. It is obvious that even with the bomb load jettisoned, a fully loaded B-29 cannot fly on less than three engines under the circumstances of take-off, and the result appears to be a controlled ditching. Possibly by putting the turbo-boost in emergency position the good engines will stand the strain of unusually high power to overcome the balance of power loss, but there is just as good a chance that another engine will quit under the strain.

Now he mentions Pres as the case that proves his point, when actually it proves the opposite, the fact that the take-off speed is not a cure-all for subsequent trouble, and in his inferring that Pres was to blame he estranges the combat crews even further, if possible. We are all aware that Preston was scheduled to take a plane not his own, one that had just returned from Japan, and which, in the several hours intervening, could have hardly been properly inspected and maintananced to prepare it for another full-load mission. Preston and his men gave their lives because an engine failed. It is not a good example for the Colonel to cite to prove his point of safe-guarding our take-offs.

Feeling keenly the responsibility of being Summary Court Officer for Preston I was particularly alarmed to learn that the C.O. thought Pres guilty of pilot error, even though an engine failed and the forward bay bombs would not jettison, facts which I called to his attention. At my insistence over the point, the C.O. admitted that an engine failure is not the fault of the pilot, yet he gave no indication of changing his opinion. It seems a sad commentary on our combat endeavor that a man may give his life trying to do a job and then has the incident written off, for the benefit of the living who are accountable and the dodging of blame, as pilot error. The counter claim might read, "Assigned plane (not his own) just returned from mission, without proper inspection. Engine failure, malfunction of bomb circuit." That would not add up to pilot error.

The briefing concludes and we go out to the trucks. Down at the plane I talk to Pat and he says that a careful inspection of the wing girders fail to show any cracks or signs of strain caused by the thermal on the last mission. We are all the more impressed over the ruggedness of the B-29. Steffler brings by the food. Now we all saunter over to the P.E. room to have a dinner consisting of sandwiches, lemonade, and cake. After the scanty, but tasty grub we get back to the plane. Gabby needs some radar maintenance which he speedily gets and the plane is ready to go. The C.O. drives by and inquires if we'll be ready to go and we reply in the affirmative. Beside him sits Charlie Butterworth, who looks twice as natural and confused as ever he appeared on the screen. The Colonel introduces us, and in the rush I fail to tell him that we appreciate his coming to entertain us.

From here on the old routine holds us, with the props to pull, crew inspection, and getting in the plane. The power check is O.K. after starting the engines at 1648. At 1658 we taxi out and down the west taxiway. We take off in turn at the scheduled time, right on the nose, 1706. The plane takes the power and we are on our way past Marpi Point at 100 feet. Bill puts on the radio compass and the fellows are entertained by the Andrew Sisters, Frank Morgan, and Nelson Eddy -- a good program.

Nick thinks that the cruising balance of the plane would be helped with some more weight in the nose, so Dick and George come up front. The flight goes smoothly, just like the others at this point. The change in balance has helped, and we go into 2150 31 at 1910. Hal gives the ETA to Iwo as 2050. Nick gives the transfer system a tryout and it's O.K. It is very dark by this time, with only a new moon to light up the sky (it is more like a quarter moon). It is very pretty with some clouds scattered below to make lights and shadows very faintly on the water beneath. Gabby calls our attention to a return that his is getting on the radar scope. Its smallness suggests that it might be a radar reflector, such as is a part of the emergency equipment. There might be survivors in this area, of an earlier mission. We turn the radio compass on to 500 KC, the emergency frequency for the Gibson Girl radio, and the needle swings in the direction the radar scope indicates. These might be survivors. Hal notes the time and location in his log. We'll report this, giving the position. The darkness prevents our looking for them -- if they are survivors.

It is 2225 and Nick is in the midst of the fuel transfer. Bill and Jake are asleep. The autopilot is handling the plane. After I have some candy Bill wakes and I go aft to the tube. Looking down beneath us all I can see is absolute darkness. Higher clouds cut off the light of the moon. It looks like a cold and unfriendly world down there, into which to bail out or to ditch. At night it is cold in this latitude, particularly on the water. Cold at night, hot in the daytime.

It is 2330. We approach the point where lights are to be turned off. Sometime before we turned off the radar IFF. Now we put on the heavy equipment and prepare for the bomb run. In the distance we begin to see lights in the sky and what appears to be explosions or photo flash bombs lighting the sky. Evidently many planes are there already. We are abreast of the lower part of the peninsula, and Gabby and Hal decide that we're a little right of course, and give a small course correction to the left. This will put us right on the IP. Gabby reports that he's taking the radar scope picture of the IP. Now on Hal's instruction, we turn on course for the target at Mansuru. Under us all is dark.

Jonesy, Dick, Charlie, and George are at their guns, combing the skies for fighters and strange sights that might appear. We don't want any "ball of fire" to drop in our lap. "Tracers at one," Charlie reports. "Searchlights dead ahead," Jonesy adds. Jake calls attention to some flak at 2 in the distance. Apparently the Jap boats are throwing up some flak from the Harbor at the Yokosuka Naval Base. Our course will be a little to the left of that. The surface craft usually have very heavy fire.

There appears to be plenty of activity ahead. There is the old string of fires scattered throughout a broad area directly ahead. Brilliant flashes light up the sky frequently and we guess that these are the photo flash bombs. There are always so many strange lights and occurrences at night over the target that it's hard to put a name to everything that we see, or think we see. One minute there's a strange light and the next nothing. It might have been a hallucination -- but not those fires. They're there and they cover a wide area. We are approaching the city area of Yokohama.

Since we know that the bombsight is not operating properly, from Jake's preflight inspection, we know that the run must be entirely radar, and that means a high degree of precision, of holding the course no matter what occurs, and of accurate timing on Hal's part. As a cross check Gabby is reading our location on the scope during the entire run, and then will take a picture of the point where the bombs are away. The lights ahead aimlessly criss-cross the sky from left to right and back, directly across our path. It's hard to tell whether these are radar operated or just being moved manually. Maybe there are some green operators down there. Now we are in the area covered by the lights. Several times the lights strike us and slide off without finding us. How can they miss? Here we are at 8000 feet, just the right altitude for them.

The sky is a hazy orange, reflecting the fires scattered throughout the area just ahead. There are no clouds, but we can see the large smoke-cloud building up ahead and slightly to the left. There are plenty of searchlights, even in the area where fires are burning, yet the darkness of the ground apart from the fires and lights makes it appear uninhabited -- a ghost land to us. Where are the fighters and the flak? Tracers flash in different localities about us and there are explosions in the air in the distance. That must be flak. Off to the right a B-29 is caught in the lights and flak explodes about it. Bill keeps busy desynchronizing our props so that possible sound locators will not be a menace, aiding the lights in locating us. They spot us now. Charlie says, "Light at three, now two, on us." Dick adds, "There's one from 9." Three lights hold us as we move along. There is no flak -- that means there must be fighters teaming with the lights. O.K., where are you? But we can't take evasive action. We hold our course. The gunners are alert and combing the sky, looking for possible trouble.

Gabby gives a three degree correction to the right, and a short time later a few degrees back to the left, but the course is basically the same, right down the alley without deflection. This should be a good run. "Flak at 2." "Flak at 10." But they don't seem to be shooting at us. It's hard to tell sometimes. Bill reports the thermal and smoke ahead and to the left, and checks the crew against the possibility of our going into the thermal. Gabby gives a correction slightly to the left, and we head toward the edge of the smoke. "Fighter far out at 7," George comes in. "Fighter at 9," Dick adds. "Is that a fighter at 5?" Charlie inquires, and he and Jonesy take a look at that side. "Looks like it." So we have fighters on either side to the rear. What are they waiting for? "Charlie, watch that one." "Roger." Evidently there are fighters visible against the glow of the fires now.

"Five seconds to go," Hal warns us. "Time!" and Jake hits the switch, starting the large 500 lb. bundles of many small incendiary sticks. The plane bucks -- they're going away, that's good. "Here he comes -- watch it, he's firing," Dick tells Jonesy. Red hot tracers go by the left side of the plane. Evidently Jonesy's firing at him with our upper rear turret, one of those guns is inoperative. Give it to him, Jonesy, I think to myself. Better that one of him goes than all of us. From snatches of talk, it's a Hamp and it is making a breakaway now, going up on a wing. We hear and feel Jonesy's gun chatter again with that faint vibration that goes down to the bone with anticipation and hope. Get him! "He's flaming, Lt.!" Jonesy exclaims, and Dick adds, "He's in a steep dive, his engine's flaming!" "Good work, Jonesy. Did the flames look pretty bad?" "Well, he broke away, hoping to dodge the smoke, and when he was up on his wing, almost stationary, I got him square. He burst out in flames, but then we went into the smoke, we couldn't follow him."

Meanwhile we are to the right of the turbulent cloud, and though it's rough, it's not bad. We continue the turn right, climbing to get away from the target area. The bombs were dropped at 1227 and the fighter downed at 1228. (Hal comes in now to insist that one-half minute be added to each of those times in interest of accuracy.)

As we are leaving we hear P-51s calling in -- so they're here, too. Evidently they want the company of B-29s on the way home. That's a long trip for a fighter, and they do not have the accurate navigational results in weather flying. The instrument weather is a trial in itself for them, since the planes bounce around quite a bit, and the instruments with them. Probably they are homing on their assigned escort B-29s in the vicinity, who are waiting to take them home.

All goes well on the breakaway. We return from the target area with as little commotion as possible. It's all right with us if we can sneak out unnoticed. Thirty minutes from the coast we have George come forward, the lights are put on, and Jonesy turns off the turrets. The gunners stow their guns, and relax preparatory to the big sleep. Now all is dark to our rear, but after a while we are able to see the fires and glow in the sky 125 miles out from the target. Meanwhile I have been monitoring the VHF set and hear another B-29 having a hot time with a "ball of fire". Somehow their interphone talk is being broadcast and I hear the gunners chatter as they work over and down a "ball of fire". They're having a big time of it.

As we approach Iwo we can hear the Naval aircraft monopolizing the VHF Queen channel for routing messages. Can't see how an emergency message could get through, if one had to be sent. This isn't the first time we've heard the emergency channel absolutely blocked with triviality. It seems this time that "Laughing Boy Snooper No. 6" is trying to contact "Agate 15", and, of course, bad reception makes it necessary for him to repeat his message over and over. He says, "Oranges are sour over the target area." We enjoy their fancy code. The Navy, as well as the Army, has a lot of clever code words. We remember the time we first landed at Kwajalein, when the tower talked to us. "Dreamboat clear the runway, chickens coming in to pancake." This is just abbreviated talk, not code, but some of the words were used similarly. Now a B-29 in distress is a "monster". An unidentified plane is a "Bogey". It would take a catalogue to list them all.

At 15,000 feet we move right along, thanks to an increased true air speed (tail wind plus altitude causing this). Our speed increases 2% for each thousand feet of altitude that we have. This means that the ground speed is greater, and that is what takes us home. So, at 15,000 feet we are actually going 30% faster than our air speed meter reads, and we have a favorable tail wind now.

It's odd how the climate changes as we go north to the target, and then back again as we return. In some 15 hours it's as though we control the seasons -- we change them from summer to winter and then back again. Over the target we leave the air cool inside the plane, so we won't sweat too much from the strain and exertion. This time I even had a sniffle, as though the cold weather had brought on a cold. As we reach further south, and the plane's temperature becomes warmer, both from cabin heat and from the air outside, my health improves. There's no doubt that this climate is good for us. The sore throat and sniffle have gone.

The C-1 autopilot continues to do its fine job and Higgy and I are free to rest, listen to the compass when not monitoring the VHF, and think about home, or more immediately, the food, sleep, and shower back at the base. Between the radio compass and the autopilot, there is not much work for the pilot. In fact, if the two were combined, they could almost do without the pilots in the plane. Someday there will be a series of buttons for someone on the ground to operate and we can all stay home while the planes go by themselves. As it is, briefing officers give us the impression occasionally that we're hardly needed after they have given us the "poop", as if they have done it all for us.

Daylight comes and we have hot coffee, a nice combination, topped off by a nap. It's a far cry from the drives to Ohio with Dad, the two of us staying awake and taking turns with coffee mixed in at the roadside stands. Life has become highly complicated. The comparison stands out now between those jobs the crew members do now as compared to those before the war. Ours is a highly skilled job -- the gunners, radio operator, bombardier, navigator, radar operator, and pilots. Most of us knew nothing of all this before our lengthy training and subsequent use and growth of our knowledge. How can we explain it to parents and family, whose knowledge is just what ours used to be? We've outgrown it and acquired a whole new branch of information about a new job in which our parents and families have no part. When we go home there will be the gap between the two, and they will never be able to bridge it. No wonder folks back home look at the papers and marvel at what their boys are doing. It's something that they know nothing about, a very complicated, exacting business which they know the boys understand and can do, and, since the price of ignorance and mistakes is very high, they must know it to be able to continue to do their jobs. We've taken to the air while they've stayed on the ground. Now it's a question of how the boys can convert what they know to post-war advantage and make a living out of it. There are some jobs which will be difficult to convert, such as the armament, ordnance, and bombardment. The piloting, navigation, radio, and radar can be put to use in some other direction after the war, if the men choose to do so.

While these thoughts run through my mind I am interrupted by Al, who reports that a plane has ditched in this area at 0609. We keep our eyes open for a ditched crew and plane. Al heard the last message and then the transmitting signal from the key screwed down, and finally the gurgle as the radio went under water. The message was loud and clear, so it must be in this area somewhere, but though everyone keeps a sharp watch, we see nothing.

At last we sight Tinian and come in for a normal landing. We are off on the ETA given the ground crew by two minutes, and they rib us about such a large discrepancy. We got to the area for the usual interrogation by "Uncle Ben" Lay, breakfast, shower, and bed. Al immediately reports to Air-Sea rescue division the intercepted ditching message and learns that help is already on its way to this crew. We learn that five aircraft were lost with 55 men missing. Among the observations reported are accounts of B-29s which seemed to crash into the target, going down flaming into the bay, and exploding from fighter rocket attacks -- the first time that rockets have been used so far as we know. The fighter we shot down another crew saw and confirmed as one of the four "kills". Three "balls of fire" were shot down. 173 enemy fighters were sighted and 30 made attacks. Fourteen B-29s were seriously damaged and three landed at Iwo, one crash landing.

Now (the next day) we are mustered out of bed to attend the critique. The radar pictures have been plotted and are on the map, shown as the various courses that were flown. The Briefing Officer says, "Alger's crew had the best course, so far as we can see." Our course falls right along the briefed path, as proven by the radar pictures. However, as we find out later, the Wing photo lab labeled them, and have our bombs plotted short of where we actually dropped them, so the entire course plotting is inaccurate.

The mission critique ends on a sour note again when the Operations Officer, evaluating further the bomb runs (as determined by the radar pictures) arbitrarily accuses the crew present of unnecessary evasive action while on the run. After we tried so hard to make the run just right, not varying an inch from the proscribed path, he comes out with a statement like that! By the expressions and murmurings it's plain that the others are incensed. He didn't even go himself, yet reserves the right to criticize, without thought that he might be wrong. The men stay silent until getting outside, when once again he is the butt of everyone's humorous disgust. The men are pretty sharp and see through the blunderings, more so now that they have a few stiff missions under their belts. When, as volunteers for this duty, their professional pride is hurt, they take a mighty dislike to the offender. Doesn't the Operations Officer realize that such erroneous accusations may be a reflection of his own character?

Now we have eleven behind us. No. 11 is still ready to fly. A few scattered flak holes are of no consequence.

```
                    Parsons
                       ·
              Cooney  ·   Dawson
                 ·    ·      ·
                 ·           ·
                 ·           ·
         Alger                    Meadows
           ·                         ·
Boynton    ·    Maki
   ·       ·     ·       ·           ·        ·
   ·             ·       ·           ·        ·
   ·             ·       ·           ·

                       Koser
                         ·
                 ·       ·       ·
                 ·       ·       ·
                 ·               ·
```

Chapter 17 Kanoya Aairfield East

April 17-18, 1945 – No. 12

"First Okinawan Help"

We are on the right side of a good night's sleep when we hear of the next mission. We are not scheduled. The others go to Target Identification and then join us at chow. Only three crews are scheduled from the Squadron; Holton, Litchfield, and Lazin. Two crews are out now on a mission to Kanoya East airfield; Jordan and Schad. Major Donnell drops down onto the bench beside us and we pass him the food. For awhile the conversation is on generalities of "shoptalk", then he inquires, "How'd you like to go on a mission tonight?" Since we are one mission ahead of the other crews I am surprised. "Sure, we'll go if the crew is ready, and I think they are," I reply, thinking they may not be on hand, or may be indisposed. The Major adds that he's been thinking of scheduling crews to fly when their planes can fly, and when the planes are out, letting them rest. This is a good idea. Under the existing system the crews are kept abreast of each other regardless of what plane they can fly. Their time is kept equal. None of the men like the resulting constant change of planes -- they'd rather fly their own.

As we leave the mess hall we encounter Dick Bush, who appears to be headed toward the chow. "Say, Dick, looks like we've got a mission to fly," I announce. He astonishes us with, "Yes, I know about it. The fellows were telling me." We are amazed, but we laugh. Well, that dumbfounds the Major, since he had only made up his mind several minutes before. "I've mentioned this to no one," he says aside, and the idea of letting a crew fly when ahead of the others on flight time is a radical departure. With shaking of heads we part, with comments on how amazingly fast Army information gets around. To learn the Army plans we ask the Seabees, or even our own mess hall G.I.'s. They always seem to know ahead of time, even when the "Big Wheels" are trying to find out whether we'll fly, they know -- only no one will listen to them because they are not supposed to know.

Bill and I go to the flight line to see Pat. He is just about to preflight the engines and he thinks that the plane will be all right. We stay for the run-up and the engines sound good and look good on the instruments. The bombs must still be loaded, and that's more than a five-hour job to load fragmentation bombs, but that's up to ordinance.

At 2200 the briefing begins, and I see all the familiar faces present, despite such short notice. What an eager bunch we are! The planes are loaded with G.P. bombs, we are told, since there was not time enough for loading any others. According to the diagram we see on the stage, we are scheduled to fly No. 3 position of "C" flight, the toughest position of them all. The C.O. now gives the introductory talk, which is, in brief: "The target is the same target bombed yesterday. This airfield has been a menace to the Okinawan campaign because its planes have damaged our vessels in the Okinawa area. This is an emergency mission. There are two fields side by side and we must bomb them both. There must be tight formation to get a good bomb pattern, and also for safety from fighters. Frank will be leading and will give instructions on VHF." So we are to help out the Navy, and become part of the Okinawan campaign. Looks like the old B-29 is a Jack-of-all-trades.

Major Speers gives his usual talk about course, target, and return. Sully gives the weather, which appears to be all right. The formation will assemble at the Island of Jurajima, just to the east. This is not to be mistaken for Yakujima, which has an elevation of 6000 feet, while Jurajima is only 3000 feet and much smaller. They are quite close together. The target is the center field of three fields strung in a line on the southern part of Kyushu, east to west. The 314th will hit the Kanoya field and our Wing the east field, Kanoya East. In the event of no visual contact, the radar target will be the Kokubu Airfield to the north of the bay.

Kirby gives the radio information, saying to monitor Queen channel for emergency messages of other planes. If the lead plane for any reason must abort, he will send the signal R-1 so the other planes in the formation will know and the deputy leader can take over. The homing signal in the lead plane consists of 20 second dashes and then the letter "U" (dot dot dash). Bob Hall states that Air-Sea rescue will consist of 2 surface craft, 3 subs, 2 superdumbos, and 2 dumbos. Keep an eye out for survivors! If you sight any, drop your bombs and stick with them. Then he mentions that the radar reflector of survivors was seen by Alger's crew on the last mission (our report had coincided with the spot where the survivors were last seen). Now we are further informed that the fuel load will be 6900 gallons, and the bomb load 13,000 lbs., consisting of 26 500-lb. bombs. We are to have a strike camera and will take pictures of the bombs leaving the plane and their pattern as they hit the ground. Further, the altitude out will be 6000 feet, while the assembly will be at 16,000 feet, turning to the right. The 504th will be assembling 1000 feet above, making a turn to the left. The leader of the formation will release red smoke, send the homing signal, and use the aldis lamp as aids to getting the planes together. The leader will open his bomb doors six minutes from the release, while the others will open on the deputy leader three minutes later. If the radar or C-1 fail on the lead plane, the deputy leader will take over.

The C.O. now gives us a talk, on what appears to be an irrelevant topic, as to the way we feel about these missions. "There is no such thing as a milk run to the Empire. The Japs are still mad at us." Does he think this is the way we feel? If he went on some of these missions he'd know more about how we feel. We know they're not milk runs.

Take-off deadline will be 1140. Departure from the assembly for the target will be at 0825. Single planes may bomb the target, since the opposition is not expected to be heavy.

Down to the line we go with Holton's crew. At the plane we find the armament section still working with the guns. Fortune had aborted on our plane earlier in the day because of three turrets inoperative, now they're all right. It seems that someone stepped on a common plug located near the upper forward turret, and this did all the damage. They couldn't help it, no doubt, but it's symbolic of the trouble that comes from other people flying your plane.

Our total gross weight is 136,700 lbs., Bill reports, and keeps the weight and balance sheet to give to Operations before we leave. Steffler brings the food while we are chatting with Pat and the boys. Now Doc Schroeder drops by to extend good wishes, along with Koltoon and Ben Lay. Major Donnell and Sowers come by and we give them the weight and balance. We philosophize about how strange it is that some people, such as our C.O. and Operations Officer, when given authority, make so many needless mistakes because of smugness, the over-eagerness of ambition, and lack of knowledge. Listening and doing, instead of continual talking might be of help to them. In our business mistakes mean lives, hence their significance and our concern. But it's dangerous to criticize one's superiors, no matter how true, so we laugh and shrug it off. I suggest that those of us who fly become quite humble about our ability and what we know, and that we feel as we learn more, and grow older, that actually "we know less and less about more and more". Others, however, not facing the endless uncertainties of these missions, give the impression that they "know more and more about less and less". We agree that when the crews feel they know "nothing about everything" and certain higher officers know "everything about nothing", that it will be time to go home, if anyone remains. After the Majors have left and we are getting ready to board the plane, the C.O. comes by in his decorative jeep and asks, "Do you go on every mission?" I reply, "We try to." He nods and drives off after I've stated that we're ready to go. Wonder if his conscience ever bothers him.

Once aboard we pull the power check on the engines. Engines were started at 0053 on schedule. At 0103 we taxi out for the take-off. Litch is just ahead, behind are Holton in 9 and Lazin in 14. We have agreed to get together to protect the weak spot where we might have some turrets inoperative, if ours cause trouble again. The take-off is uneventful except for our delay in getting the flaps up because of the prop wash from the other planes ahead. We know the ground crew is watching so they can see the take-off from a nearby hill, and Bill blinks our lights. We told them we will be back at 1538. Now we're actually on the way, and it's just six hours ago that we first learned we were going -- something of a record.

Once airborne, and on course for the target, everyone is feeling mighty chipper and there's a lot of banter on the interphone. Bill, Jake, Nick, Hal, and Al conspire to surprise Charlie Blatt. At the signal we all sing "Happy Birthday" on the interphone. He is surprised that we remembered, and we're all surprised that the singing turned out so good. We have a lot of April birthdays: Charlie, George, and Gabby, and all the same age, born in 1921, and unlike myself, all after the last war.

At 0210 the C-1 is on and Hal takes shots. I recall with pleasure that Bob Hall, in briefing, mentioned our crew for the good work in locating the radar reflector of the survivors on the last mission. Gabby did a good job, in addition to being alert, and it's a reflection on the whole crew. While things are quiet I re-read the pilot's flimsy and note the range frequency of Iwo is 210, Saipan 260, and Guam 345 KC. It's good to memorize these. The B-29 is referred to as "Dragon", while ditched it becomes a "monster". The 6th Group radio identification and call name is Daredevil, the 504th is Albatross, the 505th is Squeesix, and the 9th is Domino. Before we reach the target we always have the additional pertinent information memorized so it is not necessary to look at the flimsies.

At 0320 another B-29 flies beside us on the left and I look out and see it so close it's almost in formation with us, apparently without their seeing us. It's a jolt to see an unannounced airplane that close, and I call Dick's attention to it. It's hard to be alert for such long periods of time, but it's life insurance. Our blisters must strive to be vigilant. We can stand improvement in that direction, as in all ways. We ease away from our unaware companion plane and look for more elbow room.

We turn off our lights as daylight comes, and Nick begins transferring fuel. At 0730 we climb and energize the turrets in case of trouble. Jonesy test-fired the guns earlier at daylight. All guns were operating, and with additional ammunition in the "Tins" (feed boxes). Thanks to the good teamwork of Hal and Gabby in the navigation and radar, we arrive at the assembly area at 0815, on time. We begin our turn to the right. There is the little island of Jura and the larger Yaku; the latter is rugged, almost entirely mountains and valleys. We see a small town in a cove -- very pretty -- that would be a resort spot, like Catalina Island, in the U.S. Here it's probably a modest fishing village. Apparently these islands are not fortified.

"Ship releasing red smoke at 1 o'clock," Jonesy calls out. We have made a 270 degree turn by ourselves, now we see several other planes in the direction of the Marianas. Sure enough, there's red smoke. We cut the corner on the ship ahead, which is likewise turning right. Now there appear to be quite a few planes, at varying altitudes, circling either way, each seeking its own formation -- very confusing at a glance. Cutting inside the other planes sharply, we pull up quickly. It's Frank, all right. Frank was an old class mate at Kelley field when we began our cadet days in the end of '41. Since then he has put in a full tour of duty in England, flying B-17s -- good man. We pass underneath Frank and pull up into position on the left. Holton, in 9, comes in quickly to slip ahead of us beside Frank, taking the No. 3 position of the lead flight. We are not sure whether he intends to fly there or to lead "C" flight, as briefed. When a plane comes up on our left wing we know that we are leading the flight. Lazin is on our left and Litch pulls up to take our right wing. The lead flight is formed, too, and a plane comes up on the right in the "B" flight position. We are still short some planes but it's 0830, so we depart for the IP, which is on the peninsula to the west of the bay, which we must cross to reach Kanoya.

We gradually pull up on the lead flight, so we are well forward, and yet leave enough vertical separation so that Litch, who lies high on our wing, is below the lead flight's prop wash. When a B-29 hits prop wash, the turbulent air just stirred up by a proceeding plane, it becomes like managing a row-boat in the surf, or an ornery bronc. In formation when we are close it is bad. It can be controlled, generally, by wrestling the controls, but at best it's a terrible workout, and no pilot care to work that hard. The planes are in nice and tight now, and the gunners are at their stations. We'll be a tough nut to crack if any fighter cares to try. The company of other planes is mighty welcome.

In our present position, flying low on the lead flight while B flight rides high, it is necessary for me to look at an angle through the cockpit and out the top of the nose glass section. "We're about to turn," Higgy informs me and I nod, appreciative of the warning, since we'll be forced to apply extra power on the outside of the turn in order to hold our position, and we must keep the wingmen in mind all the time. We make the 90 degree turn until we're heading east, right into the sun. This isn't good. The air, though clear, appears to be very hazy when looking into the sun, and it makes it almost impossible for a bombardier to see the target through the bombsight. Here's hoping Frank's bombardier can spot the field. Looking through the formation and ahead, as we do while watching the lead flight, we all see a small plane come and go, flying in the opposite direction. "What was that, Jonesy?" and Jonesy reports that it was a Tony, a single engine Jap fighter. Not a plane fired on him, nor did he make a pass. He must have seen us. Perhaps he's reporting our altitude.

The lead plane opens its doors, and we continue to hold the flight in tight. The bombs must be dropped in a concentrated pattern and the closer the planes are in formation the better will be such a pattern and the more damage will be inflicted. Now the deputy leader's doors come open and Bill opens ours. We put on enough power to compensate for the increased drag. Bill has the release toggle in his hand and is watching the lead plane for sight of the bombs. "There they go," I shout, but Bill has already pushed the toggle. The plane bucks, but we hold her in tight. "Flak in the formation," Jonesy calls, and we see puffs of smoke beyond B flight. The smoke quickly dissipates after the flak bursts -- must be a good wind up here. The flak is inaccurate, however, and meager. The bomb doors come closed and the formation picks up speed. We're out to sea already and turning right toward home. Everyone is all right. We loosen up and prepare for the long flight home. Nick figures the fuel. We'll back off on the power to conserve fuel. Our wing ships are spreading out, too, settling down for individual navigation. We had it mighty easy over the target that time. Evidently the C.O. knew about the earlier missions having it fairly easy here. At any rate, we get off mighty easy.

At 1205 we arrive in the vicinity of Iwo and see the island with no clouds to obscure. It's a good day to get a picture, but we have no camera. At 1225, just south of Iwo, we are still at 15,000 feet when Nick reports some dye marker in the water. We circle the spot. Sure enough, it stands out quite clearly, a much lighter shade of green, very bright and noticeable, even at this altitude. We are always hesitant to give up our altitude without turning it into mileage because it is such a basic part of our fuel computation, but this time we pull off the power and circle down as quickly as we can. It takes quite a while since the B-29 doesn't lose altitude quickly in this way. At 1000 feet we level off and continue our circle until we are well away and then we pass back over the spot. The water is definitely a different color. The choppy waves with countless reflections make it difficult for us to determine whether there is anything there or not. After a number of passes we decide it must be a coral reef a short distance under the water that causes the color. By this time we are low on fuel in relation to our expectation. Looks like it will be a close one.

We head for home. All goes well. At 1603 we sight land ahead at 11, and then to the right the additional land which marks Tinian, to the right of Saipan. Nick estimates that we have 400 gallons left, so instead of circling the field we make a straight-in approach. As we pull into the hardstand we find the crew and others "sweating" us out. We are over 40 minutes over the ETA I had given them. The other planes are all back. We explain our delay and fan the breeze awhile with the ground crew.

We unload the plane, go up to the area, and, hot and dusty, go in to be interrogated by Ben Lay. We report the mission as we saw it. We, in turn, learn that there were 42 enemy aircraft attacks on the other formations. All our planes returned. We report having investigated the area north of Minami Iwo, thinking we saw a dye marker, and learn that this color is the result of a coral reef beneath the surface, as we'd suspected. Now we have some lemonade, eat, shower, and bed. No. 12 is behind us. Our plane is still raring to go.

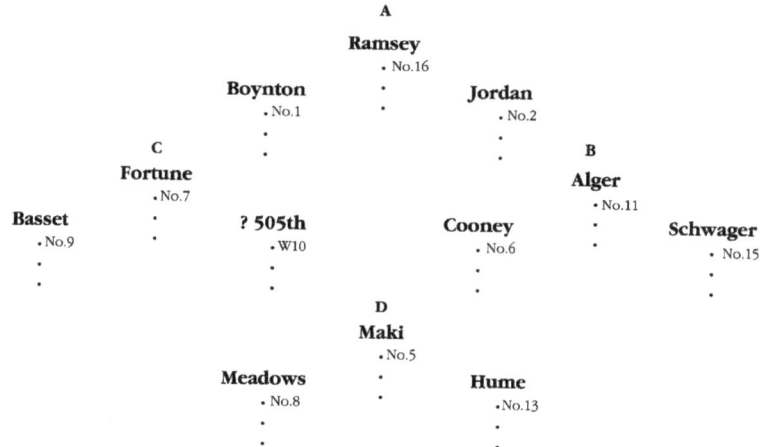

at their stations. We'll be a tough nut to crack if any fighter cares to try. The company of other planes is mighty welcome.

In our present position, flying low on the lead flight while B flight rides high, it is necessary for me to look at an angle through the cockpit and out the top of the nose glass section. "We're about to turn," Higgy informs me and I nod, appreciative of the warning, since we'll be forced to apply extra power on the outside of the turn in order to hold our position, and we must keep the wingmen in mind all the time. We make the 90 degree turn until we're heading east, right into the sun. This isn't good. The air, though clear, appears to be very hazy when looking into the sun, and it makes it almost impossible for a bombardier to see the target through the bombsight. Here's hoping Frank's bombardier can spot the field. Looking through the formation and ahead, as we do while watching the lead flight, we all see a small plane come and go, flying in the opposite direction. "What was that, Jonesy?" and Jonesy reports that it was a Tony, a single engine Jap fighter. Not a plane fired on him, nor did he make a pass. He must have seen us. Perhaps he's reporting our altitude.

The lead plane opens its doors, and we continue to hold the flight in tight. The bombs must be dropped in a concentrated pattern and the closer the planes are in formation the better will be such a pattern and the more damage will be inflicted. Now the deputy leader's doors come open and Bill opens ours. We put on enough power to compensate for the increased drag. Bill has the release toggle in his hand and is watching the lead plane for sight of the bombs. "There they go," I shout, but Bill has already pushed the toggle. The plane bucks, but we hold her in tight. "Flak in the formation," Jonesy calls, and we see puffs of smoke beyond B flight. The smoke quickly dissipates after the flak bursts -- must be a good wind up here. The flak is inaccurate, however, and meager. The bomb doors come closed and the formation picks up speed. We're out to sea already and turning right toward home. Everyone is all right. We loosen up and prepare for the long flight home. Nick figures the fuel. We'll back off on the power to conserve fuel. Our wing ships are spreading out, too, settling down for individual navigation. We had it mighty easy over the target that time. Evidently the C.O. knew about the earlier missions having it fairly easy here. At any rate, we get off mighty easy.

At 1205 we arrive in the vicinity of Iwo and see the island with no clouds to obscure. It's a good day to get a picture, but we have no camera. At 1225, just south of Iwo, we are still at 15,000 feet when Nick reports some dye marker in the water. We circle the spot. Sure enough, it stands out quite clearly, a much lighter shade of green, very bright and noticeable, even at this altitude. We are always hesitant to give up our altitude without turning it into mileage because it is such a basic part of our fuel computation, but this time we pull off the power and circle down as quickly as we can. It takes quite a while since the B-29 doesn't lose altitude quickly in this way. At 1000 feet we level off and continue our circle until we are well away and then we pass back over the spot. The water is definitely a different color. The choppy waves with countless reflections make it difficult for us to determine whether there is anything there or not. After a number of passes we decide it must be a coral reef a short distance under the water that causes the color. By this time we are low on fuel in relation to our expectation. Looks like it will be a close one.

We head for home. All goes well. At 1603 we sight land ahead at 11, and then to the right the additional land which marks Tinian, to the right of Saipan. Nick estimates that we have 400 gallons left, so instead of circling the field we make a straight-in approach. As we pull into the hardstand we find the crew and others "sweating" us out. We are over 40 minutes over the ETA I had given them. The other planes are all back. We explain our delay and fan the breeze awhile with the ground crew.

We unload the plane, go up to the area, and, hot and dusty, go in to be interrogated by Ben Lay. We report the mission as we saw it. We, in turn, learn that there were 42 enemy aircraft attacks on the other formations. All our planes returned. We report having investigated the area north of Minami Iwo, thinking we saw a dye marker, and learn that this color is the result of a coral reef beneath the surface, as we'd suspected. Now we have some lemonade, eat, shower, and bed. No. 12 is behind us. Our plane is still raring to go.

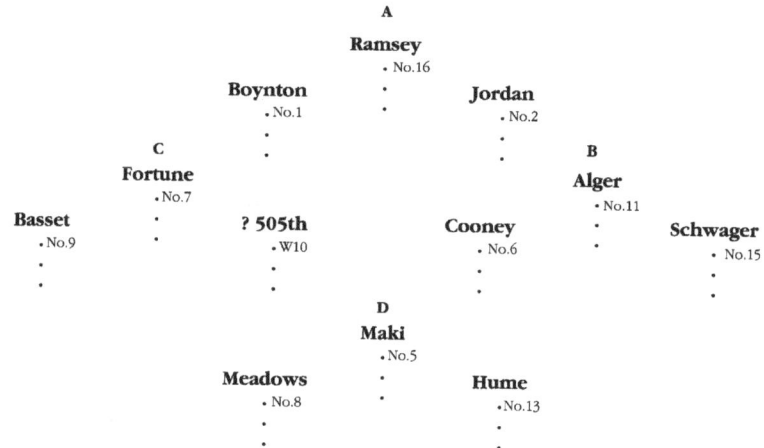

Chapter 18 Kanoya Airfield West

April 21-22, 1945 – No. 13

"Near Perfect Assembly and Bombing"

We are all surprised to find that we've completed three missions in five days, from April 13th to the 18th. It looks as though we'll have some time off now. Hal is now a first lieutenant! We are glad to learn this -- and high time. In fact, Bill, Jake, and the whole crew have served the time and done a job to warrant a promotion. But such things just don't happen very much around here, despite length or quality of service, except in the higher brackets. "Tough!" is the expression.

On the 21st we all go swimming at the South Beach, taking Gyro along. On our return we are notified that a mission is going out tonight, so we begin to get ready. In the eyes of our new hut mates we are an old, experienced crew, and they seem respectful of our frequent missions. A large part of our conversation has been "hello" and "goodbye" since they moved in. They'd like to be going, but they're flying training missions to acquaint themselves with this area. Occasionally they go along individually, as passengers, on missions with the old crews.

We have learned that our formation hit the wrong airfield on the last mission, and we are quite disappointed. However, we feel that the formation leader did his best. Flying into the sun is not easy. As matter of fact, this criticism was made at the critique. But it's anyone's guess whether the high command will see fit to change the axis of attack. It's an old, established fact that bombing is at a handicap when conducted into the sun, and usually missions are not planned that way.

Many planes in the Squadron have names now, given them by their crews. There's "Fortune's Follies", "Holton's Hellions", "Patty Sue" (Lazin's crew), "Snooky", "War Bride" (Litchfield), "Ernie Pyle's Milkwagon" (Parks), and others. Our entire crew for some time has been trying to give a name to the plane. We want to name our plane. The custom in the past has been for the airplane commander to name his plane, but I feel too conscious of our crew as a unit to give it a name myself, so I ask the others to suggest names. After days of thought a short list is submitted by the men, but even among themselves they seem divided. After a period of waiting I finally broach a suggestion. I've had a name in mind, but have hesitated to mention it since it's on the personal side. It came about through the crew members themselves, at the time of their giving Peel and me a present for our newly arrived daughter before coming overseas. A lovely blanket was accompanied by a card which said, "To Miss America of 1962, from her ten Godfathers". We were very much impressed by their thoughtfulness, and the way in which they had expressed themselves. A baby is a symbol of the future to all of us, possibly even to the hope that our children may have a peaceful world, and that we're fighting for them. It means that to me, and to Al Horvath who has a baby daughter, too. Judging from her picture, she may be "Miss America '62". Gabby has a son, and is prospective again. Charlie and Jonesy and Bill are married, too, and the others are on the verge, we suspect. The thought seems pertinent to all of us, and ties us to home and the future. There are no dissenting voices when I suggest the name, though I can't tell whether the fellows are just sparing my feelings, and so she is named "Miss America -- '62", our pride and joy, a plane that deserves a name and the best that we can give her, judging from the care she has taken of us. We are eager to paint the name on her, and for all the crew members to have their names on the plane, but there's a shortage of paint and painters, and we are on the go. We'll get it done soon, somehow.

Too bad the plane wasn't painted at the time we went to Kawasaki. On that take-off a photographer got a perfect picture just as we were off the ground. The props were almost stopped, though they were turning at 2800 RPM, the wheels were stopped, and the heads of the crew members were visible within the plane. It's an excellent action shot. It looks as if the "big bird" is suspended by invisible supports, not like a 70 ton mass going 150 miles per hour.

Target Identification for this mission is held at 1700 on the 21st in the briefing room. The usual information is handed out concerning the route along the well beaten path, then the approach on the target from the east, and the breakaway north and east. Obviously they've seen the mistake of going into the sun. The briefing is held at 2100 for our No. 13. All crew members are present and smiling. We are anything but a dapper bunch, but the spirit is good. Each man is wearing what he considers his most comfortable outfit, and it brings out some unusual flight clothes. George has on his "Gook" pants, as baggy as they are long. What a sight. The bottom is frayed without a hem, and George calls that his "lace work, real fancy".

After the roll call and the flimsies are passed out, the C.O. describes the mission as very similar to the others on the Kyushu airfields, with the bomb pattern being the important thing, so the formation must be right. The Operations Officer, in his ignorantly confident manner, relays further factors. The target is to be the West Kanoya field, a radar secondary target of Kokubu airfield, at the north end of Kagoshima-Wan (Bay). Coordinated attacks are being made on these fields by all wings, the 73rd, 314th, 505th, and the 313th. The load consists of 7400 gallons, ammo is 500 rounds per gun (6000 rounds), making a total gross weight of 137,000 lbs. (this including eighteen 500 lb. bombs). With the fuel tank in the rear, as before, it looks as though the plane will be unbalanced again. We are to have a strike camera. We will use "B" and "C" runways. The course will be 5000 feet to 20 degrees north latitude, then climb to 7000 feet, flying on to Iwo, then toward the mainland. Twenty minutes out from the assembly we will climb to bombing altitude of 15,000 feet. At the assembly point, which we are to make by 0725 (the lead plane having arrived at 0705), we are to circle to the left at 15,000 feet and depart at 0800.

The first Squadron to go, which is ours (composed of our group) will be followed by a composite squadron which will bomb from an altitude of 15,500 after assembling at 16,000. The first squadron is entirely our Group. Anderson will lead and we will fly the right wing of the B flight, which will be led by

Fortune. That means we will be outside wing again, a tough place to fly, with all the sky to our right guard. But we can fly formation and the gunners can cover the sky, so we're ready and willing. Mutch is to fly the left wing of the flight, opposite us. Donnell will be his copilot. Fox and Maki will be replacements. The axis of attack will be 279 degrees and the bombs will be dropped on the leader or deputy leader, whichever drops first. Airspeed will be 195. The formation should be held 100 miles out from the coast. Any field will do as a target of last resort.

The Intelligence Officer tells us that the Navy has acknowledged our raids, saying that they are helping noticeably. He further illuminates the matter by pointing out that the IP is to be Ko-Saki, 14 miles from the target. There are three other fields in this area, all to the right, but "don't mistake them for your target". The breakaway is to Sakura Jima (Island) then to the east before taking a course for Base. As for flak, we are warned to steer clear of all surface craft in the area. Then, in a significant tone, Speers gives us the first direct information about the new Jap jet plane, which we have known as a "ball of fire" up to now. The exhaust, or jet flame, seen at night gave it its name. The official name now is "Baca". It has a 16-foot wingspan and is carried until launching by a twin engine Betty. It is a suicide plane. The pilot has a lot of armor in front of him to ward off the gunners' fire. The Warhead in the nose of the Baca is a large explosive charge. 89 U.S. Vessels at this date have been destroyed at Okinawa by the Japs with the help of this new weapon, and perhaps some of the missing B-29s.

Bob Hall states that the Air-Sea rescue will consist of 3 superdumbos, 2 dumbos, 1 surface craft, and 2 life-guard subs. There is a plane reported down just 10 miles off the coast of the Empire, near Kyushu. Also, a raft has been sighted just south of Minami Iwo, so be on the lookout. It seems coincidental that we investigated the reef just north of Minami Iwo, since there's now a raft sighted to the south, but we have been told that this coloring of the water is due to the reef that is known to exist there.

Kirby informs us that Okinawa is open for emergency traffic, but that lacking service facilities, we would be unable to get any help on our plane. Sully takes over to say that a tropical storm to the southeast of Tinian will not bother us, as it is moving due north. There is also a front between us and Iwo. The C.O. gives us cautionary pointers: don't shoot down our own planes, and do not go into Okinawa unless in trouble, but then it will be alright. We understand.

Down to the line we go. Pete Fortune's crew shares a truck. Pete's crew is a jolly gang and together with ours makes itself heard above the truck and bumpiness. We enjoy their infectious good humor, a trade mark of Pete. We find our plane ready to go and the fellows give us a good welcome. It's a wonderful experience to have a ground crew like that -- a mighty fine group of men. We think the world of them -- all of us. We miss Bill Kramer, who is now assigned to PLM, but he still seems one of the gang.

The "Big Wheels" and "Cogs" ("Cogs" are the low-ranking workers without much future in the outfit, but with a lot of good humor to pass on) come by. They include the C.O., Kenzie, Major Sowers, Ben Lay, Bob Hall, Docs Schroeder and Koltoon. We really should have a reception line (the Docs get a laugh out of this), and we enjoy the fun we have batting the breeze with those coming by. P. E. Jones, Lyle Hurd, Ellis, and Heming now come along. It is the last mission they'll see off, and goodbyes are said. They'll be leaving for the States and "lead crew school" tomorrow. We're sorry to lose them, but they'll be back before more than two months are gone by, we understand.

In accordance with the C.O.'s wishes, we leave our personal equipment on the ground until just before getting into the plane, so that the crew inspection will be the last activity before departure. This new announcement causes us to change our routine. In the past we have had the crew inspection just before preflighting the plane so that all gear may be stowed inside the plane and ready to go. Now, in order to comply and still look good we agree to pile our equipment in a row at right angles to the nose wheel of the plane. It rushes us to sandwich the inspection between pulling props (which must be done not more than 20 minutes before starting the engines) and firing up. However, "orders are orders". We have a snappy inspection that permits us to see that our Mae Wests and parachutes are in good condition, then scamper up the ladders to get settled before time to start the engines. After the hilarity of pulling props and the seriousness of inspection we feel ready to go -- all details have been attended to.

The engines check O.K., so we taxi out at 2351, on time, though hurried. In order to make the weight and balance more satisfactory, we shift Al and Hal to the rear, against our wishes, and take-off at 0001. Everything is all right and we fly instruments a while to get the feel of the plane. Hal and Al are now back in place and the crew is functioning smoothly. It's a pleasure to hear their prompt answer to questions about the appearance of the engines, gear, flaps, and the other planes in the vicinity. It's a beautiful night and we try out the new blinking recognition light atop the plane, connected to the deicer pump, which causes the alternating on and off. They work fine. This is the first time our branch of flying has had blinking lights on our planes. No doubt we attract more attention this way, and we are easier to see, which is a safety factor. Further, the light no longer blinds Jonesy in his upper blister, as it did when a steady light. Between alternations he can look around for other planes.

As we fly into the small cumulous clouds that are often found near Saipan, I feel the smooth speed as they slip by. When other objects are at a distance the feeling of speed is missing for a basis of comparison is lacking, but up close the clouds go by so quickly that our speed becomes quite apparent. These clouds cause little turbulence, since the updrafts that formed them have dissipated, yet the cloud still hangs together. Outside of the cloud it is clearly defined, but on entering it the edges become frayed and indefinite, grayish-white fogginess replaces the unrestricted visibility. It's like some dreamland that opens and swallows us up. There's no impact when we hit the cloud, it swirls about us and seems like an illusion. Tonight the wing lights cast a glow on the surrounding mist. It is a lovely night. The moon is bright outside the clouds, which are small. A lighted pathway extends from underneath the moon on the horizon to us. From this height the water is not shimmering, but calm and smooth and the path follows us right along. Only the brightest stars are competing with the moonlight tonight -- it looks cool, damp, and very remote about us. Inside, the plane holds the warm Tinian air of our southerly latitude. It will cool as we go further north. Nick gives us a little cool air with the turbos.

Bill and I take the Benzedrine. Jake doesn't need it. He has given up staying awake and his head continues to bounce backward as the muscles give up every several seconds in favor of relaxing, then he subconsciously exerts them again. We enjoy watching the "ball and socket with back drop" movement.

We arrive at Iwo at 0330. There's the old familiar shape. It's hard to believe that with all those lights belonging to our forces, there are still Japs on the Island hiding out, but that's true of all the Marianas. The entire harbor and island are alight, only the far northeast and northwest fringes, that blend with the water, are dark. Art and Skin are down there, resting up from fighter sweeps of Japan, no doubt. That's a rough job, flying alone for seven hours or more over such long stretches of water.

The dance music from the OWI station, the moonlight making a silvery filigree to the cloud edges, the soothing, quiet drone of the engines -- all make it a good time to drowse and daydream. The plane is quiet, that is, the interphone is quiet. Only the music is heard from way out over the endless stretch of water. So I think of Peel and that reunion ahead, and the fun of the past. It's the next thing to religion to think of these things and what they mean. Somehow, the meaning of life is tangled up in all this. Now back to the job. At the next critique I think I'll suggest that from now on we should not have definite formation positions assigned to fly, but take whatever position is open when we arrive, filling up from the front to the rear. That's how it actually works out, anyway.

At 0245 we climb to 7000 feet, then cut back to 2100 RPM. The music is now "One Night Stand" from the Chicago Black Hawk Restaurant and it weaves its own spell. Are we actually flying over the far distant southwest Pacific en route to Japan, war, and sudden excitement? The music is the same we've heard in party spots or on our radios and vics in the States. That could be U.S. soil under us, as it has been for countless hours in the past. For a moment it seems unreal that we are actually doing this, yet here we are, surrounded by the equipment and instruments of our trade. I can feel the pressure and warmth caused by the .45 in my C-2 life vest. The emergency water tins and rations press into my back, those are for use in ditching or bailing out. Even the water cans in the dinghy underneath me, that are so hard on the posterior -- the sensations are pertinent to the job at hand, but the body and thoughts are the same as I had in the States with the security of home about me. Now 11 Victor is our home.

We have a heavy load of gas, plenty of ammunition in .50 caliber guns, and a load of bombs -- mighty business-like tools. Yet in the midst of this death dealing equipment we are sitting in various positions -- 11 of us -- not wanting war, only wanting to get home to peace and security. It doesn't seem possible that with our minds and bodies we can do this, but even more staggering is the thought that the minds and bodies of people back home designed and manufactured this 70 tons of flying technical equipment. Theirs was a wonderful achievement. Now, if we but follow the rules of the equipment we are using we'll do the job and, God willing, return to Tinian. Little do the folks back home know how much their routine, perhaps humdrum, work on this plane means to us. It means, in a nutshell, our lives. We don't want to die. This equipment, if working properly and operated properly, will bring us home after a 3000 mile trip (as far as across the U.S.), having accomplished a job they want done. If the equipment is poorly made by someone back home, no matter how well we operate it, our lives might be the cost. The cost might be the same, too, if we don't operate the equipment properly, no matter how well it is made, so we strive to learn the intricacies, all of the fine points, so we may use it as it was designed to be used. Sometimes we even try to widen the breadth of its use. It's too bad that the folks back home may never know, in particular instances, how we count on that equipment working, and how it doesn't fail us. Few of the crew members will think to tell them. We take American excellence of equipment for granted. Only during strikes have the people let us down, and indirectly that means lives lost, and the lives lost might be those near and dear to the people who are on strike.

Since midnight it's been Gabby's birthday. He is 24 years old -- some way to spend the day celebrating! The endless thread of thought wanders on and I think of how we've come to enjoy flying over the water. It is secure in a way, you know where the water is. It is not like the land where the terrain elevation changes, making low flying hazardous. Barring pressure changes affecting our altimeter, we know exactly how far the water is beneath us, and no mountains to hit. We laugh now over the time we flew to Orlando, when we flew over water, cutting across the northern tip of the Gulf in the old B-17. We shied away immediately and insisted that Hal take us back over land. We were actually afraid of the water. As we laughingly said at the time, knowing the age of our plane, "We know we're over water, and we're afraid the plane may know it." We didn't know that planes take to flying over water quite well, even when the crews don't. That reminds me of the old thought in reasoning out the difference and choosing between the Army and Navy flying. The deciding factor was that I did not want to fly over water, but rather over land. Now look at us! And we prefer it to land (except the land that means U.S.A.).

Again the beauty of the night attracts my attention. The moon is setting and as it does it changes color. It was white -- very bright -- now it's yellow changing to orange. As I watch it's color deepens and now is almost red as it slips behind a thin cloud on the horizon. As Charlie Blatt shouted when he saw his first moon on the horizon, partly obscured, "Look, there's a fire out at 3 o'clock." We all got a kick out of that. He knows now what the moon looks like on the Pacific horizon.

After transferring the fuel we climb toward the assembly point. Nick helps Bill and me into our equipment and then puts on his own. Jake does the same and we check with the rest of the crew to see that they are ready. George is in the tail and the guns are energized, ready for any unfriendly fighters. Seems like several lifetimes we've been doing this. At 0705 we are at the assembly point and spot three other planes circling the same way, obviously our planes. We join up and see that Anderson is in the lead, as briefed. On inquiry he answers that we should hold our B flight position to see if the No. 2 man of the lead flight will appear. After a half minute he arrives, then Pete appears and comes inside to pull ahead in the B flight lead.

At 0800 we have an 11 plane formation, though Maki has the left wing of our flight, replacing Mutch. Fox is in the diamond of our flight. It is a good formation, Pete holds the flight in fairly close and we get right up to the tail, then forward until we can look into the blister. We are the high flight. It's obviously a good formation, looking like a demonstration from the rule book. I can look down a stepping stairs of four planes diagonally to our left, all in a straight line. On paper that's just how it should be.

As we make landfall there is a light scattering of flak, but it does not bother us, since it is not inside the formation. Now there's flak straight ahead of our plane -- little black puffs. We fly right through the smoke. The adage is that if you fly where there has just been flak you're safe, so I guess we have nothing to fear. Now we're turning to the west, which is to be our axis of attack. The formation is nice and tight. I am proud of the boys. My crew comments on the tightness of the formation. That's good flying, and safe. No one can make any sudden maneuvers without endangering others, but at the same time we have terrific fire power, since the fields of fire of the guns overlap so much. Actually, when it's this close, it's more like having one vehicle for all those guns. In the closely packed planes there are 132 .50 caliber rapid-fire machine guns. Of course there is the danger of an inaccurate gunner, but that's the chance we must take. They must remember, as they swing the turret by their computing sights, that the turrets precede the point where they are actually looking. Being so close, however, the gunners are very conscious of the presence of other planes. We have the outside position on the right of the formation, so our gunnery is important. Ours is a large field of fire that we must cover because many of the other planes' guns are obstructed by our plane.

As usual, the bomb doors coming open on the lead plane give us warning, since it's six minutes before the bombs are to be dropped. We open on the deputy lead and Pete, which is three minutes later. Bill throws on additional power with 2300 RPM at the same time he opens the doors, so we can stay up. The pilot can shove the throttles forward, but he should not exceed the maximum power for each propeller setting in RPMs, so we must change the RPMs of the prop along with the throttle. There must be no dropping back now. We are in tight, expecting trouble. Now the flak starts to come up and it's apparent they have our altitude and course, so we sit and take it, always a helpless feeling, there being little to alleviate the situation. "Bombs away!" shouts Bill, as he presses the release. Hal, Jake, and I chorus the warning when the bombs are seen to leave the leader, but Bill has already started the bombs away. It's 0805. Now the scanners report that the bombs hit squarely on the hanger line. That's good bombing and makes us feel good. It's apparent from here on it's to be the fighters' try.

We are turning right off the target and will be over land for quite a while, on the north and east headings. We stay in close on Pete -- he's holding the flight forward on the lead flight, that's good. "There they are." "Fighters at 5 low." the gunners chorus. "They seem to be coming up." "They're circling to come in." Looks almost like a prearranged meeting. Beyond the formation I can see little black dots moving quickly across the sky. It's apparent that there are fighters, they're all about the formation. Looks like bees buzzing around.

Busy with flying, I miss some of the antics of the fighters, particularly since I'm on the VHF radio. Bill takes care of the interphone side. I miss much, but I do see the first fighter boring in with a head-on attack. "Here he comes," I think to myself, and I see the upper four gun turrets of four other planes swing around to the front and I know ours is doing the same. "C" flight has guns on him, too. That means a terrific hail of lead for him to wade through. The fighter starts from well out ahead of us and then dives very slightly, coming straight for us -- no, he's aiming at "C" flight. Now, with a rush, he's over us and gone. I see the big red circles, "meatballs", on the wings, as he barely missed the "C" flight planes. Our four-gun turret stops jarring and the cabin stops shaking. The fighter, according to the gunners who take other shots at him, drops down and away from the formation in the rear. Evidently he wasn't hit. He's mighty lucky.

"Fighters are out there, a lot of them. They're Zekes," Bill gestures out of his window. They are in a closely packed string and one by one they "peel off" and come in from 3 o'clock, making the conventional pursuit curve attacks -- this should be easy for the boys. The plane shakes as the turrets are fired. The noise is great and nerve-wracking inside the cabin when the forward turrets fire, so we know that plenty is going on. I catch sight of the fighters as they flash by to the left of the formation, making their breakaways. No one is hitting the fighters, though it's evident that everyone is taking a crack at them. We begin the turn to the east now, and the fighters cut inside of us in order to be waiting as we come out of the turn. This seems like a game instead of for "keeps".

There are four fighters not coming in, just hanging at 3 o'clock high, as though waiting. It's easy to see their game. They're waiting for someone to lag, to drop back behind the other planes, so they can work him over without having to brave the hail of lead. They no doubt see the five planes whose bomb doors aren't closed yet. And Sharp has feathered an engine. He's in "C" flight and he might have been hit by the first fighter. The Squadron and Flight leaders are checking to see if anyone is in trouble. All reports indicate that everyone can keep up. Sharp is the only plane with obvious mechanical trouble.

Hal, Dick, Charlie, and George report as many as nine fighters in the area, and then estimate that there are twice this number. It's the most we've seen in daylight like this before. Hal took 25 pictures of the formation, flak, fighters, and the like. Dick reports that we've still got one hung bomb and so we open the doors to prevent the bomb from falling on the closed doors in the event that it is loose. Jake goes to the rear to check the bomb, after hitting his release switch. The bomb falls but the doors won't come closed. Probably our air pressure is down and we must wait until it builds up again. Sooner than we expect, the pressure builds up and the doors come closed when the switch is actuated.

Jonesy is at a loss to account for our not hitting the fighters, and we kid him and Dick, Charlie, and George about it. He suggests that the "Jam handy" would be a good thing in the event that they are actually short on gunnery practice, and need practice on the tracking and framing. Maybe so. But there seems to be something to the idea, too, that we check the gunnery system with an eye to the harmonization of the guns with the gunsights. Jonesy suggests that we get the help of a gunnery specialist from the factory, a G. E. man, and I agree. Anything he wants to do is all right with me. Jonesy and the men have shown a commendable spirit when it comes to maintaining the guns or doing extra work. He also demonstrated that he knows the system, which is the important matter.

After spreading out and leaving the Jap coast behind, we lose sight of Pete and the other planes as each does his own navigation home. We get the OWI and some good music. Sammy Kaye entertains us with some of his nostalgic music and sing-song titles. The autopilot is doing the work, and I recall that Doc Schroeder made some comments on how the missions are a strain on the men and that they take something out of them, which, if overdone, may damage them for life. Except for the tired, let-down feeling after leaving the target, I never feel too bad. Is it really a strain? Oddly enough, I can't judge at this time. While I want to go home as soon as the next man, I must admit that so far I feel O.K. This is only our 13th. I cut another notch on the control wheel for crew 2409 and No. 11. Thirteen of them in a row, now.

The debate among the Docs is over how many a crew can fly before going to a rest camp. There's a difference, of course, between going to a rest camp and home, since the latter is a much greater rest and the final goal. Anyhow, the question is how many can a crew take, and Doc claimed that the Group was trying to set 20-25 as the total number before going home (which I can't believe as coming from our Group), but that Bomber Command was favoring more, possibly 35, with a rest in the middle of it, but this will all take care of itself, no doubt. You might say, in a sense, that this is not a dangerous war for some -- not for those who get through all the required raids. The black puffs just pass you by, instead of hitting you. But for others -- those who are killed -- the war couldn't be any more dangerous. It's all right for those on the ground to point out the losses percentage-wise, but to those who are lost, the war is mighty real and final. For those who get through it is more like training missions, the elements are somewhat the same, yet there is added the flavor of the terrible uncertainty -- the heavy take-offs, the time under fire over the target, the fighters, the welfare of a crew. It helps to believe that a higher power has the situation under His control, that He leaves certain latitude wherein a man must take care of himself and exercise his abilities.

About the time we approach Iwo it becomes apparent that the Queen channel, which is reserved for emergency use, is filled with the Navy giving routine messages. We wouldn't have a chance of getting through if in trouble. They have been assigned this channel, too, and I make a note to mention this to Kirby for whatever good it will do. It's no new situation. The Navy must have channels for communication, too. Emergency should have a separate channel.

Now the thought occurs of what will happen in our post-war days, and the possibility that I may not be flying. I'll miss it, certainly, just how much, I'll find out when the time comes. Now, sometimes, I think it will be as easy to give it up as it was to begin, but that may not be true -- we'll see. I imagine that we'll look back on these days and marvel that we did all this. In the line of emergency drills, the memory of the "dinghy" drill comes back to me, and the afternoon we spent in the Tinian Harbor in one-man and five-man rubber rafts. That was a good experience and we learned a lot. Cady goes out of his way, as the P.E. Officer, to see that the men know how to use the equipment. We'll all have a fighting chance to survive a ditching experience, if and when.

This life of ours is an odd one for a group of energetic young men -- armchair athletes, that's us! Our hardest combat duty is served sitting down. Heads, eyes, and minds get tired from the exertion with so little muscular energy required, and we must rest up between missions, which means sleep, not the devigorating exercise in the hot sun. We need sleep and relaxation, but this is an abnormal situation for all of us, for we need physical exercise. Looking at some of the rather heavy individuals, it's easy to see that it's taking effect. For myself, I am not inclined toward stoutness, but I am aware of the 25 lbs. lost during the time in the services, which exercise might replace, that does not speak well for inactivity.

With the steady stream of daydreams parading through my mind, the time has passed so quickly that I find we are in sight of Tinian, the most welcome sight of the mission -- home! We go through the landing check and land on "C", Charlie, runway. We greet the ground crew and chat a minute about the mission, since it means something to them to share the experiences. Then Pat informs us that the Dean Mutch "cracked up" at West field, aborting from the mission. They don't know the details beyond the fact that two engines failed on the same side and the aileron control cable snapped while landing. Their plane hit two others and broke into three pieces, then burned. We learn to our joy that the entire crew got out of it, and are all right, recuperating at the Navy hospital. It's remarkable that they got out of it -- that's stretching the luck of the 24th pretty thin. Dean remained conscious and pulled Donnell and Juskiewicz out of the plane.

We go through the interrogation and then to bed. Oh yes, the ground crew insisted on taking our picture at the end of the "13th mission". They thought that very significant.

Chapter 19 Matsuyama Airfield

Imabari – April 26, 1945 – No. 14

"Rendezvous In the Clouds"

Several days of Tinian life have transpired since our return from Kanoya West, and we see another list posted on the Mission Board to be going out a midnight tonight. Ramsey, Jordan, Boynton, Alger, and Parks are the crews scheduled. The diagram has us flying the outside wing of "B" flight. The crews are glad to be going again, but are somewhat surprised to find there is to be a mission tonight. All day we've been attending various meetings and ground school -- not much rest. We'd appreciate having more notice, but perhaps it's just as well, since we're not going anywhere -- our social schedule is not so well filled this season.

On the 23rd the Group had its first presentation of medals, our first affair of this sort. The General (the Wing Commander), a tall, fine looking man, was present and made the awards himself. The combat crew members all received the Air medal (being eligible, so we heard, because of having flown eight required missions). We find the orders are written alike for all participants, the only difference being in the dates given as the period in which the flights occurred. "For notorious achievement while participating in aerial flight as combat crew members in successful combat missions from a base in the Marianas Islands against the Japanese Empire. All missions were flown without fighter escort under rapidly changing and oftentimes adverse weather conditions. The flights were subjected to enemy anti-aircraft fire and fighter opposition. There were constantly present difficult navigational problems, danger of engine failure and consequent ditching many miles at sea. Under prolonged periods of physical and mental strain, and undaunted by the many hazards faced regularly and continuously, each crew member displayed such courage and skill in the performance of his duty as to reflect great credit on himself and the Army Air Forces." In the case of our crew the dates within which the flying occurred were given as February 8th to March 23rd, 1945. Evidently many crews are eligible for another by this time. Eight crews of our Squadron were decorated a second time for having participated in four of the five "Blitz" incendiary mission within the set period from March 10th to March 19th. Those awarded were: Mutch, Preston, Parks, Fortune, Litchfield, Jordan, Dawson, and Holton. For Preston it's posthumous, and Dean Mutch and crew are still hospitalized. We were not included, since we had only gone on three, the fourth (for us) having been the night we couldn't go to Osaka because of the plane's engine trouble at the time of take-off. We were, and are disappointed far beyond the importance of the matter, but that's how it is. The crowning blow to all of us there assembled was the awarding to our Commanding Officer of the Distinguished Flying Cross for his having gone on one mission, and at that, as a passenger. The citation accompanying the award, read aloud to the dumbfounded crew members, made a piker out of Superman. That rankled in the men and was the object of their consternation and disgust after the ceremony, but we are still learning the ways of the Army. The Colonel hit rock bottom in the men's eyes. I felt ashamed for him, but I am sure he didn't share my feeling -- he took it as his due.

As a follow-up on the gunner inaccuracy of the last mission, the afternoon of the 25th Jonesy, the gunners, and the G. E. specialist from the factory, assembled at the plane to give the gunnery system a good check. Thereupon were discovered some large discrepancies in the harmonization of the guns, that is, concerning whether the guns are pointing in the direction they should be in relation to the gunsight. By using the "boresight" (we do not have electrical harmonization equipment on Tinian as they do on Guam), errors were uncovered which showed that the guns were not parallel to each other, and were not pointing in the direction established by the gunsight. 8 and 12 mils error were found in the guns individually. In addition, the top forward turret guns had an important mounting belt loose.

Mr. Freeland then summed up with the information that guns are knocked out of harmonization by the roughness of landing, from being fired, and from various other causes. He said he knew this all along and that he stood ready to help those who requested his services, and he agreed that the guns needed attention continuously in harmonization. Further, he agreed with our observations that the other planes are in the same condition. We had noticed on the flights that the fighters were not being hit. Thinking this matter important, I mentioned it to the Commanding Officer and he requested that I put in letter form. This I did, with the gunners help, and we got action. We now have the entire gunnery department leery of working for us because they know we'll turn them in if the work is bad. Good way to have it, we think, though we are unhappy to have any friction with ground maintenance men. But this is the first time, and even our own ground crew agreed with us on the wisdom of our stand. Too bad there isn't the same understanding relationship between flight crews and the specialized maintenance departments (Armament, Radio, and Radar) that there is between the flight and ground crews -- the latter maintaining the engines specifically and the plane generally.

At 2130 we assemble at the briefing building. Tucker, Gibson, Speers, Kirby, Hall, Sullivan, and the Chaplain participate in the usual routine. We are surprised to learn that we are to have as a passenger Major Speers, the Intelligence Officer of the Group. This should be a good experience for him, since he is among those who so authoritatively present the briefings without actually knowing what it's all about, not having flown on the missions. However, he is not morally bound to fly as are "rated" officers, like our C.O. and the Operations Officer, who hold pilot ratings. These men must fly, if for no other reason than to put in the necessary time (4 hours per month) to collect their flight pay. It is their shame that they have trouble acquiring this time unless it's in local formation practice, while others of us get 100 hours a month.

This mission is similar to many of those which were earlier conducted against the airfields to prevent the hammering of the Okinawan participants. The target is the Matsuyama Airfield, the center of three, located on the west coast of Shikoku Island. Other Groups and Wings are hitting the other fields. The load is to be 136,000 lbs. Runways "B" and "C" will be used. Trucks at 0020, first take-off at 0205, target at 0948, and land at 1604. The assembly is scheduled to take place at 14,000 feet, circling to the right over the southern tip of Shikoku. 11 Victor, our plane, will fly the No. 2 spot of "B" flight. At 0905 the lead planes will arrive, other ships should arrive no sooner than 0910. Red smoke will be released at 0915 along with green flares, and departure for the target will be at 0930. The second Squadron will assemble at 15,000 feet with left turns. From the assembly we go 50 miles to the IP, the town of Kaminado, then 27 miles on the bomb run. Air speed will be 195 mph with no evasive action, then a descending turn to the right at 500 feet, down at 200 mph air speed, turn at 15,000 feet, hold formation until 100 miles out and return in flights of three. The entire run will be 2687 nautical miles (3100 statute miles). P-51s and P-38s from Okinawa may be present. The secondary target is Imabari, to be bombed by radar, if used. Air-Sea rescue is adequate and the weather is O.K. except for a warm front near Iwo. This, in a nutshell, is the briefing information.

Down at the plane all goes well except for the weight and balance situation. Again we have a critical situation. The bombs and extra fuel tank are so placed that we have 9000 lbs. in the forward bomb bay and 4500 lbs. in the aft bay. When the loading is a matter of choice we dislike this weight distribution for our plane. On earlier missions we have had trouble with our cruise control and used additional fuel unnecessarily. We've had to shift the crew members around, endangering those who are moved during the always precarious take-off (they have no safety belt when not in their seats). This might mean the difference between life and death, all the more so because they are not so familiar with emergency procedures as they are at their own stations. But we've borne it with good grace, thinking it necessary, but now we are well aware that the loading can be rearranged, and should be for our plane, since ours has a basic index that is slightly more nose heavy than the other planes. The C.O. comes up prior to take-off, as is his custom, and I mention this to him -- that our weight and balance is too nose-heavy -- but he passes it off lightly and suggests moving the crew to the rear to change the C.G. (center of gravity). I don't like it, but what can I say? It's time to get going. Hal and Al agree to move to the rear. Bill, Nick, and I must make the take-off, and it helps to have Jake with us for timing and additional eyes. Major Speers, our passenger, is less familiar with the B-29 than the rest of us, so we keep him up front where we can watch out for him.

Our take-off is the slowest yet, and we're "sweating it out" the last half of the runway when we see the speed building up slower than usual. At 130 mph we are at the end of the runway and are airborne. Most planes take off short of the end of the runway and by the time they have reached it have additional speed. The controls are sloppy at this speed and we strive to keep the wings perfectly level. This is the slowest we've ever made a take-off fully loaded. Finally we reach 160 mph and Bill starts the flaps up, we back off on the power and the engines begin to cool at the proper rate. Everything's O.K. We breathe easier and have Hal and Al come forward.

But apparently the nose-heavy center of gravity is going to keep bothering us. We are unable to pull off the power to save gas as the briefed plans direct. We keep the power at 2200 RPM in order to maintain the necessary 195 mph, which keeps the airplane "on the step", with the tail high. For two and a half hours we use 600 gallons an hour at 2200 RPM, an hour and a half longer than briefed, when we should have been at 2150 RPM. Now we manage to hold 2100 RPM to keep 195 mph, as the load gets lighter from using up the heavy fuel. We hold 2150 the entire way to the assembly area, using 500 gallons an hour, when for two and one half hours of this time we should have been using 2050 RPM with consumption of 400 gallons per hour. Nick waits until the last minute to transfer the fuel out of the additional fuel tank, since this throws the center of gravity even further forward. We have a briefed reserve of 1000 gallons of fuel, and as we approach the assembly point Nick estimates that by assembly time, if no further complications arise, "we will be 500 gallons over the curve" (500 gallons more used than is indicated by graph curve based on fuel against time). Major Speers seems surprised. I can almost hear him saying to himself, "Why, this can't be. This isn't as briefed. This isn't the way it's supposed to be." He seems sympathetic to our situation, as though he understands, however. He is a pleasant passenger thus far, interested, inquisitive, and a good listener to the answers to his questions.

We get on our equipment and prepare for the rendezvous with the others. "Are we about there?" the Major inquires after we settle down from dressing. "Be there is 25 minutes," Bill replies, giving Hal's latest estimate. "Right on time, eh" -- he looks at his wrist watch and seems pleased. We tell him that our navigator is never far off, and he shows a renewed interest in Hal, who is busy over his chart and log. We are climbing now and see clouds ahead. "Here's hoping they break up and aren't thick," Jake says, turning around and indicating the sky ahead, and we agree. "All set, Jake?" I inquire, and he nods his head. Bill checks the crew and tells us that everyone's ready with equipment on and in position.

Into the clouds we go at 14,000 feet, and reach the assembly point encased in the grey-white mistiness of cloud which, apparently, is not cumulous, since there is little of the turbulence which is associated with the cumulous type cloud and bad weather. Mighty strange. So we start climbing and at 21,000 feet we begin to hit the frayed top, while still circling the rendezvous point. I call Victor 16, the leader Ramsey, and tell him our status. He says to continue on to "Heaven (20,000 feet) plus two" (22,000 feet) and meet him. So we continue to climb. Now we spot several planes a few miles off, flying in different directions. It is evident that Ramsey is there, but it's hard to tell which he is. He tries to describe his position and we tag onto a No. 16 and say, "Coming up on your right wing." We get an answer, "There's no one coming up on _my_ right wing." We counter with "Well, we're on the right wing of No. 16," and he laughs and says "Then there must be two. But stay there -- I see two planes, I'm coming over."

Major Speers still seems surprised that there are clouds here and that conditions are so uncertain. There's no doubt, this is hardly the mission as it was planned and presented to us in the briefing, and I realize now, all the more clearly, the difference between the planned conception of the mission and the way it's flown. This present situation is surprising only to him -- we accept it as just one of the unexpected things that always occurs on a mission, the sort of circumstance that can change, instantly, the entire nature of the mission. Major Speers is probably thinking, "But the weather is supposed to be good, to be clear over the target. We didn't expect this possibility and only mentioned in passing that the secondary target would be Imabari." He seems quite interested in what we are going to do now, and he is probably surprised at our lack of concern over finding this situation and the obvious need for changing plans, like horses, in midstream. Our years of flying have taught us to be certain only of the uncertainty of the chain of airborne events.

A plane flies by to the outside of us and we see a large 16 on the side, together with the stripes of a lead plane around the fuselage near the tail. "There he is," Jake points. "Coming over, Ray," I say into the mike with the radio on VHF. "Take deputy, Bruce," he replies. We drop down and to the right of our companion plane before crossing to the left and taking Ramsey's right wing. The present circumstances coincide with the briefed plan in this, our position. Now several other planes angle over toward our two ship formation and in a few minutes we have six planes. Major Speers appears reconciled to the strange turn of events by now. "We're going to Imabari," I tell him, and he nods. Our altitude now is 24,000 feet, and even so we skim through the top of the frayed clouds. The air is cold and smooth up here -- the sun bright. The reflection of the sun on the silvery skins of the planes is very bright and hard on the eyes. Bill and I have on our sun glasses. The gunners are at their guns, but it looks quite lonely and remote up here -- no fighters around us, no water, no land -- just sun, clear sky, and planes above the cloud carpet.

In the usual sequence we open the bomb doors three minutes after Ray does, the other planes open with us, and then three minutes later, "There they go!" and Bill releases ours while Jake mans the gunsight. Behind us and slightly right is another formation of five planes. Apparently quite a few planes are bombing alone or in smaller formations, judging from our absentees. The Major's getting a big dose of changed plans this trip. We're bombing a different target, at a different altitude, with a different type formation of planes, without reference to the ground, and all the result of a last minute decision; none of the briefed plan being used. We close the doors and stick in close on Ray's wing. The formation is flying good and tight. But there's no flak and we've seen no fighters. We stick together and maintain our altitude on the withdrawal so that we won't be going into clouds as a formation. Flying formation with limited visibility is dangerous business. These clouds do not appear to be the type that will cut off the view of the next plane, but evidently Ray's not taking any chances.

We have a "hung" bomb, Al informs us, so Jake and Bill go aft to look it over. They take their oxygen masks plugged into a "walk around bottle", a portable oxygen supply apart from the plane's built in supply. Nick depressurizes and the crew all put on masks, which is necessary before depressurizing the cabin. Now the bomb bay bulkhead can be opened and the men can get into the bomb bay to dislodge the bomb. We want to get rid of the bomb over Japan where it will do some damage, instead of waiting until we're at lower altitude out at sea. The boys have succeeded in releasing the bomb and we close the bulkheads.

While depressurizing and pressurizing Nick checks to see that everyone's ears are all right, since this mechanical change of altitude is very sudden. Nick customarily releases the air, when we depressurize, at a rate of 2000 feet a minute. The relationship between the air pressure inside the plane and that of the free air outside is the subject of the pressurizing problem. Whenever we fly at altitudes above 8000 feet the equipment is regulated to keep the cabin at 8000 feet, which the authorities believe to be sufficient air pressure for human beings' maximum performance. Sometimes when below 8000 feet the pressurizing is used as a means of air conditioning only, keeping a flow of air through the interior. It is also a means of heating, since the air flowing in can be warmed or left the same temperature as outside. In order to get the hung bomb, it was necessary to equalize the inside and outside pressure.

In this case, the cabin air pressure was released and the air pressure went from pressurized 8000 feet to 24,000 feet, which was our actual altitude, and the bulkhead door could be opened, since the pressure was the same on both sides. After the bomb was released, the bulkhead door was closed, and we pressurized until the cabin was again at a pressure of 8000 feet altitude. We usually change pressure at a rate in excess of 2000 feet per minute and (accompanying it with a series of swallows) are in no discomfort. The entire procedure is unique in that while the plane is flying at a constant altitude, the crew inside is experiencing air pressure changes equivalent to violent dives and climbs. When we pressurize it's the same as diving, and when depressurizing, it's the same as climbing. Contrary to earlier scientific and public knowledge, the human ear can withstand terrific sudden changes of air pressure. In fact, the pressurizing has taught us that we can instantaneously change altitudes of 20,000 feet or more, which is the situation when a B-29 blister "blows". That is, when a weak blister plastic window explodes from the great pressure within the plane.

We remove our equipment after having spread out from formation. The clouds are behind us now, and we are letting down with the formation. We decide to keep the others in sight, but not to fly back in flights. Ramsey must go down immediately in order to get his air doors closed -- the air pressure will not build up sufficiently at this altitude, so he leaves us, diving below and ahead. We soon pass him since we are making a greater speed at this altitude than he can at a lower one.

Nick now confirms our suspicion that we can't make it back home. The additional gas required to climb to 24,000 feet for assembly, plus our earlier excess used from incorrect balance, leaves only 2000 gallons now, and that will not get us home, even with the 1000 gallons reserve. We are aware that Iwo may be closed to traffic because of bad weather, for Sully briefed us, saying that a warm front lay in that vicinity. That means an entire clouds system and low ceilings, perhaps closing the field to traffic, but we can hope. Sully was wrong on the weather over the target, perhaps he's wrong on the weather that will prevail at Iwo. Either way, our only choice now is to stretch the fuel as far as it will go. We begin to use the lowest possible power settings.

With the bombs gone, our center of gravity is at the normal place and we are holding a good speed with only 1800 RPM, using 330 gallons per hour. We decide to start letting down to 15,000 feet, using the altitude as forward speed, thereby cutting back our power even further. We end up with a setting of 1650 RPM at 28 inches of Manifold Pressure. Our consumption now is only 292 gallons an hour. We are indicating 190 miles per hour, which at this altitude -- figuring 2% per thousand airspeed increase -- is over 265 mph across the surface. In addition, we have an estimated 25-knot wind, which means that all our speed is better than 300 miles per hour. In other words, we are using one gallon per mile, or ¼ gallon per engine per mile, which is the most economical cruising we've ever done. If we could continue this situation we could make the base on 1500 gallons -- but we can't, for we are letting down, thereby slowing up all the time. The tail wind will soon give out and be replaced by a cross wind and later by a head wind. Although we are getting lighter all the time we are going more than proportionately slower, so by the time we reach Iwo we will have neither the speed nor the fuel to make the Base.

Nick keeps figuring and refiguring the remaining fuel, and the distance to go in terms of the hours ahead, which Hal gives him. Bill works with him after Nick does the figuring, and then I confer. They check and recheck and the answer remains the same. Nick summarizes, "We should have 1500 gallons left when we get to Iwo in order to make base with a margin. As it is, we'll have slightly more than a thousand -- it's just not enough." Nick's figuring is substantiated by the time we approach the vicinity of Iwo. We have only 1100 gallons, several hundred short of the amount needed to get us to Tinian. The situation gives the Major cause to sweat since he knows, too, that the weather is supposed to be bad at Iwo, so now he is in the peculiar situation of not only realizing the briefed information can be wrong -- as it was at the target -- but of actually hoping it will be incorrect, so that we'll have good enough weather at Iwo to permit us to land.

Lady Luck stays with us and when we arrive at Iwo we find only the usual moderate scattering of medium altitude cumulous clouds. What a break! It is clear, thank goodness, and the Major shares our relief, since he is aware that the earnest computations which have been going on are important to all of us.

"Walnut Tower, this is 11 Victor 758 (we use our victor call sign instead of the "Daredevil" Group name) over your field at 15,000 feet, low on fuel. Request landing information." The tower answers asking our condition, whether we have any battle damage, and further informs us that fighters are expected to land shortly, so that we must circle, awaiting further instructions. We are content to wait because the fighters will be lower on fuel than we are, but after an hour we get restless. There is no sign of the fighters. Our No. 1 fuel pump is inoperative, though the booster pump is supplying fuel to the engine. Now our No. 2 propeller governor goes out. We decide it's time to do something, so, with an eye out for the fighters up until the last minute, we prepare to land and go in. The tower doesn't clear us, but they don't say "no", so we land and taxi off the runway.

Evidently the tower has thought better of the situation, for several of the other planes which have been circling land after us. After parking and cutting the engines, the Major accompanies me to the bomber command headquarters and we file our trouble, lack of fuel, fuel pump, and governor head. I try to contact Art at his squadron, but no luck, so I leave word there. Probably Art is on the mission himself. Major Speers and I tread the volcanic ash over to the P-I and get some candy bars. Judging from the magazines and candy, Iwo has priority on merchandise for the men, and rightly so. We hear planes overhead and step out to see the fighters sweep over. Back at the plane we are surprised to see "Skin" Denis drive up, and he suggests that we drive over and see Art. Leaving Bill and Nick to manage the maintenance, I gladly jump at the chance.

The volcanic soil is very dusty, it appears, and the dust combined with the sticky heat makes it very uncomfortable. Skin says it's cold at night. Sure enough, Art is dressing, having just come back from the fighter strike on Kyushu, the first mission we've both flown at the same time. They went in low, he tells me, to strafe airfields. "That's mighty low for comfort," I observe. "Too darn low," he adds with emphasis. Apparently that's quite an understatement. Art returns to the plane with me. "What good does it do to take a shower with this dust around you?" "It doesn't -- just makes you feel better for a time." We talk over our respective living conditions and flying. He urges me to stay overnight -- we have a lot of catching up to do. He seems curious about just what the B-29 will do, having been surprised at our high speed, maintained during a climb. We continue to talk shop and arrive at the plane much too soon. I turn down his invitation, much as I'd like to stay, but the plane will be ready and the crew has no desire to lay-over on Iwo when they could be back on Tinian -- that I well know. Art says that Skin is going back home, as all the older pilots are doing. As Squadron leader, Art hopes to be next -- the last of the old gang -- and has been promised his Majority. It's time that he went home, after three years and more in the forward areas of combat zones. He shouldn't be flying these missions now. He's had enough and his luck is being stretched too far just now. He agrees, but is too conscientious to quit -- a good man.

Finally we head for Tinian. We tell Art that we'll show him a short take-off, since the runway is bumpy. With such a light plane it is easy to pick up speed quickly, and we're off and gathering speed at a great rate, so we bank it up and make a pursuit climb. We're climbing over 1000 feet a minute with gear and flaps up. It's like a different plane when unloaded -- all the power in the world.

At Minami Iwo, just to the southeast, Jonesy, Dick, Charlie, and George fire on the island to get rid of some of the ammunition and to have some target practice. We circle the small volcanic island with its abrupt slopes, and they pepper various recognizable landmarks with shells. The tracers show where the shells are hitting. Jonesy points out that the error seems to be consistently behind the point where the guns are aimed, so we decide to make a check of the gun computer on return.

The ground crew gives us the old welcome when we land at 2100. They knew we were at Iwo, having been told of Al's message back to base. Major Speers is all flowers for the way the crew did their jobs, and seemed to enjoy the whole Cook's tour. He was a good passenger and we enjoyed having him along.

Perhaps he feels better acquainted with the "real thing" now. More of the ground staff should go on these missions, but whether they do or not, the men in command -- who are rated pilots -- should fly and find out what it's all about, but they won't. They evidently think they don't need to do so to understand.

Back in the area we are interrogated by Ben Lay. Then we get some chow, wash up, and "hit the sack". Another one behind us.

The next day we are all summoned to a critique. The Operations Officer is conducting it. There is little of interest, since everyone had our unsatisfactory experience of assembling in the cloud area and bombing the secondary target. There seems little reason for the meeting. We are not learning anything. In fact, Colonel Tucker gives us a synopsis of the mission. It seems strange that he goes through the mission, that we flew on, giving us the information that we know so well, as though he were informing us of data that is new to us, as it is to him.

During the critique the subject of loading the airplane is mentioned. In the interest of my crew, and whomever else it may concern, I explain the dangerous situation resulting from the nose-heavy condition of our plane, causing the use of excessive fuel with the result of our having to land at Iwo, which might have been difficult if good fortune had not been with us and the weather had not been good. Further, I mention our slow speed at take-off and the crew members not being at their stations because they had to be moved about to balance the plane when, actually, this should have been accomplished by proper placement of the bombs and fuel, which is quite possible. Having had to brave this situation several times, I frankly state that we can't take that chance again, unnecessary as it is.

This bold statement from a combat crew member provoked his angered answer, "There's a war on and you'll do as you're told!" The seriousness of my position as leader of a crew, for which I am responsible, does not permit accepting this viewpoint, which I am sure he suspects. Striving hard to control myself, I resume the floor and with carefully chosen words explain again why it is dangerous for us and that so long as I am an Airplane Commander, I will not do it that way again. He cools down and tells me to come to see him after the meeting is over so that he can give me a lecture on cruise control. There are subdued, concealed chuckles around the room greeting this, which displeases him further. After the meeting he walks by me as I stand waiting, without giving me the lecture. Possibly he knows that it would border on the ridiculous. Those of us who fly these missions live by our cruise control, and we're now experienced over hundreds of hours of B-29 flight. The other fellows who fly feel as I do. Further, the Group Flight Engineer confirms my position, though he, like many of the others, is afraid to speak up when he sees that something is wrong.

The engineering section on the line now finds that the situation with regard to our plane is indeed serious. Four cylinders in our No. 4 engine are faulty and losing power, aggravating an already bad situation. On the take-offs, with improper loading and lost power which resulted from such loadings, we were in a dangerous situation, and in addition, the crew members who were moved to the rear to help out with the balance were at a dangerous disadvantage. So I feel vindicated.

Once again Lady Luck has gotten us out of a bad situation. We knew something was wrong, but did not realize that in addition to the incorrect loading, we were also losing power. We have been very fortunate to get through those take-offs safely, and we know it, and we're thankful. We realize more than ever that we must take care of ourselves in the Army, and that in this case I must watch out for the plane and crew, regardless of the censure of higher authority. We can't help wondering if the Operations Officer realizes that he was a little hasty. Judging from the past, he probably doesn't, but rather thinks it is strictly coincidental that I complained of the situation just when the plane was losing power and was loaded poorly.

We are informed that "Miss America '62" will be out for a 300 hour inspection and that we'll not be flying for a few days, waiting until it's ready to go again. Possibly it's a good thing to have a rest now -- both for us and the plane.

		Holton				
		• No.4				
Litchfield		•	**Jordan**			
• No.2		•	• No.12			
	•		•			
	Dawson					
	• No.6			**Alger**		
	•			• No.11		
	•	**Lazin**	•	**Schwager**		
		• No.14	•	• No.15		
		•	**Maki**	•		
			• No.5			
			•			

Chapter 20 Kanoya Airfield

May 7, 1945 – No. 15

"Phosphorus Bombs"

On May 6th we see our name included among those scheduled for a daylight mission the next day. Those going are Holton, Alger, Parks, Jordan, Schad, Schwager, and Fortune. Nine crews are still out on a mining mission at this time, and several of them are among those scheduled here -- Parks, Schwager, and Schad. Feast and famine -- that's how it goes. We've had several days without a mission, others have gone on the mission to Kyushu and Shikoku airfields, and on the two latest mining missions. Looking at that part of the combat board which shows the crews, their total number of missions, and total combat flight time, we are pleased to note that we are the first crew to pass the 200 hour mark with over 205 hours. Others are crowding us close however. New crews have arrived to swell our numbers, the most recent being Ertresvaag and Meadows. They've served their apprenticeship and are on a crew combat flight status. They're eager to catch up with us and will fly all missions on which they can persuade the authorities to schedule them.

At an officers' call on May 2nd Colonel G. informed us, as representatives of our crews, that we will fly 30 to 35 missions with no rest leave except a three-day pass on Tinian (empty meaning). As part of the rest we will be given a Jeep, a quart of whiskey for the officers, and a case of beer for the men. Looking over the flights we've made to reach the 15 mark we think the goal is a long way off, but we feel all right, and we'll go on flying all they schedule us on. The lack of rest leave surprises us, however, since it disagrees so radically with what the flight surgeons think we need, as they've told us in the past, but we feel all right.

We have chores to do these days. Most important is the final disposition of the belongings of Pres and his officers. The survivors of the crash, Wipperman, Douglas, Ford, and Birsner, dropped in to see us and we gave them the toilet articles, food, stationary, and trinkets remaining -- the things that are not important enough to send home to the parents of the deceased. The four seem to be all right. They are quiet and serious. Douglas bears a scar on his forehead, the only visible mark the foursome show from their accident.

We carry the belongings of the four officers to the Quartermaster. There they seem to know just what to do with them, and they assure us that the articles will be boxed and sent home. It's a depressing and sad job, disposing of a friend's belongings. We miss Pres, Don, Al, and Lloyd every day, less now than before, yet they are a long ways form being forgotten. It doesn't seem possible that they aren't around the corner somewhere, about to step into the room and kid us as they used to do. Pres in his dark room or stirring around among his photos, Don in his homemade shorts with ragged edges, trying to convince you with his idea about something, Lloyd smiling defensively and good-naturedly answering accusations about his "sacking up" all the time, and Al -- looking off into space, pen tapping teeth, writing a letter to his girl -- the many memory-pictures of them surround us in those places where we were so accustomed to seeing them. Their sudden departure makes it all the more vivid. They went as we could go. We all do the same job; have the same chance here -- all of us who fly.

Hal was the first of the officers to work on the "rock pile", as we call the coral floors that are being laid just down-wind of the latrines. It seems that the Colonel wants us to have a "Beer Garden" whether we want it or not, so each day a group of officers is detailed to work on the "rock pile".

On the 29th the whole crew turned out to clean the airplane while it remained in PLM (production line maintenance). We get gasoline and rags and clean the thick coat of dust on the skin. It was a good chance to visit with Pat, Rod, Hank, and Steve. This we enjoyed as an important follow-up to the cleaning, and while the plane stayed in PLM we have it painted. Does it look good? And How! It looks like it definitely belongs to somebody. To us it looks even better than that, but no one sees it as we do -- our plane. All Sixth Group planes have a Pirate's Head on the nose, painted on either side. Now in the long white streamer that extends aft from the Pirate we have "MISS AMERICA '62" in bold red letters, easily visible at a distance. And outside his position, each crew member has various names. On the pilot's side is the name of the pilot and the crew chief. On the copilot's side are the names of the copilot and engineer. Bill also has "Marie" beside his window, just as I have "Peel", thus including our better halves in our chariot. Jake has "Gyro" and "Turbo" painted on the nose before his position for our two well-known and beloved cockers. By the window at the engineer's position is "Nick." Beside Hal's position under his window is "Hal and Thelma". Outside Al's radio position are the names "Mary Alice and Bub" and under that, "Pamela Sue", so his whole family is represented. Further back, under the blister windows we have "Dick and Evelyn" and on Charlie's side, "Hilda -- Charlie", with a heart in between. Jonesy, beside his upper blister, has "Hal and Betty", representing a different combination from Hal Griesener's, however. Somehow we have always called Harold V. Jones "Jonesy", while Harold A. Griesemer has been "Hal" to us. Gabby has, opposite the radar room, "Cassie and Gabby", then under this his son "Johnny", while under the third is a "?", representing the baby that he and Cassie are expecting. This family remembrance is arranged about the Air Corps insignia of the rear door. Finally, at the tail position, there is a painted "George" and "LaVera". So we are all represented on our plane and it looks mighty good to us.

That night we had a good entertainment when Claude Thornhill's show played in our theater -- a Navy show. It was good! Claude Thornhill played some of his own compositions. In addition, Dennis Day sang, and Bobby Riggs presented his Betty Lou, then Jackie Cooper played the drums. The whole camp turned out since there wasn't a mission going out. After chow and the early evening gab on the front porches of the Quonset the groups began to collect and stroll down the hill toward the theater, raincoats over the arms, old hats on the back of the heads, with cigars or the old pipes between the teeth. Laughter and joking remarks floated up the hill on the breeze. The nicest time of day, when the most charm of what little there is on Tinian is present.

The fellows fill up the seats of the theater with lots of joshing and repartee from row to row. "Say Tom, I hear you're going back home soon." We hear this comment and the reply, "Sure, within the next year at least." "Who, me? I don't want to go home -- I like it here." Then from another quarter, "Examine that man -- he's rock happy." The fellows relax and enjoy each other's company, for there are a lot of long lasting friendships here, and good-will built up through the mutual effort, joys, and disappointments. The time after dinner, while the twilight fades, is the high spot of many an evening during these days off, and back of it all is the solid feeling of a tough job well done, with another to do sometime in the near future. It is a definite enjoyment of the present moment -- let the past and the future take care of themselves.

On May 3rd a rumor swept the camp that a Jap envoy of peace had passed through Guam on the way to the United States, and we wondered if something was doing, but doubted it. May 5th dawned and we learned that the Germans had surrendered and the fighting is over in Europe. From now on all the allied strength will be concentrated out here and we'll get it over and go home, but there is little feeling that all this news really affects us -- we are in a world apart. Logically, reading the news releases or magazines when they come in -- always late -- we can rationalize our position in the conflict, and just what the B-29 is doing. But actually all we know for sure is this area of living quarters, the Japanese Island, and the long pathway between the two. The perspective we had at first has dwindled -- possibly because we've gotten too close to the events themselves. We just go on checking the scheduling board, putting on our equipment, flying, and resting, knocking the missions off one by one and hour by hour. Strikes, housing problems, reconversion -- these belong to a world apart, along with the other news from home that seems so insignificant out here. We'll go on flying -- who knows how long!

On the 6th Bill and I and the men go to Guam to take Russell and his crew who were to fly back another ship. Now for the first time we land on Guam and see the advanced civilization of this island as compared to Tinian. We are surprised to find the difference in climate, since it is only a distance of 125 miles further south. There are palm trees. It is tropical here and the air is sultry and warm. It looks something like Florida from the air, so far as the vegetation goes. The flight to Guam serves to put the slow time on "Miss A." that was necessary after an engine change and 300 hour inspection. The No. 4 engine was replaced. This trip should make the plane ready to go on the next mission, but we are disappointed in our plans for flying our plane. Somehow, through a mix-up between the Maintenance Control, which controls the maintenance work and repairs on the plane in PLM, and the Operations, which schedules the planes, we end up scheduled to fly No. 5, Maki's plane. I protest to Major Sowers, our Squadron C.O. and Major Donnell, the Squadron Operations Officer, and they take up the matter, trying to correct it through Group Engineering and Maintenance Control, but to no avail. We are still scheduled to fly No. 5, though our plane is ready to go. So we prepare to fly No. 5, swallowing our disappointment and frustration. These men made headaches!

The briefing is held at 2130, the evening of the 7th. The crew is all present, indicating so with a wave or a smile when I count noses. Everyone's in good spirits, evidently, and that's good. We are to have a passenger from the newly arrived combat crew. Lt. Bob Hume, the Airplane Commander, will fly with us. After "Attention" and reseating the C.O. give us a short talk on the strategic significance of eliminating the airfields on Kyushu in order to help the Okinawa campaign. The Operations Officer takes over and describes the planned attacks. There are to be two attacks, one by each of two squadrons. One force will strike the Ibusuki Naval Base and the other, which is the one in which we'll fly, will hit the Kanoya field again.

Force No. 1 has 2000 lb. and we have 1000 lb. bombs -- eleven of them. The flight out will be at 7000 feet, or 500 feet above the overcast, should there be unexpected clouds. We will arrive at the assembly point at 0825 and leave for the IP at 0850. The assembly will be made over the Island, south of Kyushu, at 15,000 feet, circling to the right. Green flares will aid identification of the leader. Radio silence will be maintained and not used in assembly, as previously, so that we will not notify the Japs that we are coming (as if they didn't know). The guns will be test-fired at daylight. The base speed on the bomb run will be 220. We are instructed not to bomb lower than 10,000 feet or higher than 20,000 feet. Apparently we are being given leeway on paper to plan the mission after we get there, a radical change from the cut-and-dried instructions up to this time. Should there be radar tracking it will be disrupted by the "rope" that will be thrown out of the planes. "Rope" is the name given to the rolls of tinfoil which, when thrown into the air, upsets the radar picture received by the Japs. It is a part of the RCM (Radar Counter Measures) department.

The remainder of the briefing follows the usual pattern, and is concluded by the Chaplain who gives a prayer, in which we all silently join. We have dinner at 2230 and then to the trucks at 2300. Here we go, taking our lives in our hands, on the hair-raising truck ride. "Air travel is safer than this," Bill comments.

Down at the line we untangle our personal equipment and go to plane No. 5. Here we locate the ground crew and find them to be a pleasant foursome. "Big Joe", the crew chief (with an unpronounceable last name), reminds me of a man I know in Ohio, slow talking, hardworking, serious, but with a wide grin -- a dependable man. Various people come by. Docs Schroeder and Koltoon drive up and get out and I wait, expectant for their confidential and boisterous farewell. With a rather impressive flourish and erect stance Koltoon presents me with a large nail, or a small spike -- I can't make out which. It has been painted a purple color. Puzzling over it, but expecting something screwy, I am given a short speech of a man-to-man nature: "Alger, it gives us a great deal of pleasure to present you with the shaft -- the purple shaft -- which we feel you will treasure and appreciate." Without faltering I thank them and express deep gratitude. They say they are pleased to present me with this shaft, and I, in turn, say that I have never been shafted so nicely. We bow and they get back in their Jeep, wave, and sail off for the next plane, leaving me with the "shaft." What screw-balls! The significance is humorous. The shaft is an expression which we use when we feel that we've been given a "dirty deal", we've been "shafted". Their visit makes me feel mighty good. They're a lot of fun.

The Deputy C.O. drops by and we tell him that everything looks all right, but that we miss our plane. He sympathizes, says "Good Luck" and drives off. We have learned in the Army not to miss a chance to air grievances. After a certain number of complaints about the same thing something <u>might</u> finally be done. At least it's better than just lying down and taking it. But it's surprising how the Army scares men until they won't speak up. Instead many just think, "Oh, what's the use."

We all get aboard and Bill goes through the check list, checking the crew and controls while Nick gives the engine instruments the once-over and then declares that he's ready to start them. George, in the meantime, has started the put-put in the rear section to supply juice to the starters for starting the engines. The engines appear to be O.K., so we turn around and fall in line with the other taxiing planes out to the head of the runway. How graceful, though ponderous, the B-29s look as they roll along the runway and turn the corner of the taxiway. Finally our time comes and we head down the runway, await the flagman's signal, and "give her the gun" by pushing forward on the throttles.

Bill watches the tacks (tachometers which indicate the propeller RPMs) and manifold pressure gauges (showing the pressure of fuel-air mixture forced into the engine), and regulates the prop pitch if the tacks indicate that there is any overspeeding. We gather speed and Bill states that everything's all right. "O.K., Nick?" "O.K." he answers and we commit ourselves to take-off. The airspeed builds up faster now until at 130 mph we go off. Bill raises the gear, then the flaps. Nick calls out the temperature and the scanners report the condition of the engines, flaps, and gear, and also the planes in the area. We're off again!

After setting up the autopilot and seeing that the plane is normal, we settle back to catch a nap or two. We have a little trouble "trimming" up the plane -- the left wing wants to drop. We recall that we have one extra bomb on the left side -- six against five on the right. When we correct the problem by raising the left wing with the trim tab and readjusting the rudder it feels to Bill and me as though we're flying out of line, like a dog running down the street. This plane has just had a new tail put on it to replace the one shot up. That, too, might have something to do with the problem, however, she's running fine otherwise, and we catch some naps.

At Iwo Hall informs us that we're 20 minutes behind time. That isn't good. Our take-off was late, too, and yet we must make good the assembly time, so it's necessary to increase the power more than that briefed, thereby using more fuel. We go above the curve again on the fuel, to Nick's consternation.

Off and on Bill, Hume, and I fan the breeze about conditions here and in the States, from where Hume has just come. He spoke of the 2nd Air Force and I thought how glad we are to be out of that organization. He has had a hard time of it in the Army, too, so we laugh and tell him that he is a good member of our Group. Hume tells us that in the States they heard about how easy it was out here, flying these missions, and we listen, taking it all in. Needless to say, we are surprised. Our losses have been less on a percentage basis, we understand, but we didn't know that that made it so easy, but we keep quiet and hear the viewpoint of a newcomer from the States.

Nick transfers the fuel, and Jonesy stands by to test-fire the guns. This is delayed because of the low level of cloud cover below. We climbed to 15,000 feet after leaving Iwo to get the advantage of the increased true air speed, the only way we could make the assembly on time. By the time land is spotted about 50 miles ahead we are in our equipment, fuel transferred, and the guns tested. We see the assembly point and head for it, dodging the larger Island, Tanega-shima, which has flak guns located on it. "There's a formation," Jake points ahead to the left. We are just in time, only five minutes until the formations depart for the IPs. We pick out the formation that should be ours and head for it. That's it, with Jordan leading, and Pete leading the "C" flight. We see that his right wing is not covered, so we come in high from the left and slip into position over the top of his plane, something of a squeeze, since we try to stay low enough not to get any prop wash from the lead fight ("C" flight is the low flight). Shortly after taking our place, surrounded by a pretty formation, we head for the IP. Bill cautions the gunners to keep an eye on Parks in the No. 4 spot (the diamond) of the lead flight. If he doesn't stay well forward he will be slipping back into the line of fire.

We see the other Squadron leave for its target, Ibusuki, and we in turn are diverging from them toward our IP. We are going into the target from the east with an IP of Kosaki, the track of our earlier flight. This is the first time we've flown over the same path for the second time. We have no trouble staying up, being on the inside of the turn. Jake comes in, "Fighters ahead over land," and we see quickly moving specks circling ahead. We roll out of the turn. "On course for the target now," Hal reports. Bill asks, "All set, gunners?" and Jonesy, Charlie, Dick, and George come in to answer: "Ring-sight set." "Right blister, Roger." "Left blister all set." "Tail, everything's O.K." It's comforting to know that they're on their sights with guns ready to fire, alert and capable. It's like an extension of ourselves, I think to myself, those of us who don't have weapons. Jake checks the bomb circuit switches and his gunsight again, and puts both hands on either side of the gunsight with the sighting window in front of his eyes. "All set here," he says. Bill has arranged the bomb release switch on the extension cord so that it's beside the bomb door switch. Nick is intent on the engine instruments, as if to assure himself for the thousandth time that the engines are all right.

Flying on the inside of the low flight we are aware of the turbulent prop wash overhead to the right from the lead flight. Pete does pretty well to keep us low enough so that we don't catch any of it. The formation is good and tight, except for Parks, who keeps dropping back in the diamond spot on the lead flight -- a precarious place for him to be. A certain amount of unnecessary jockeying occurs and we're frequently forced to change power and wrestle the plane into position -- can't relax for an instant.

"We're almost over land," Bill says, and then Jonesy comes in, "Here they come." Two fighters come in from the front on converging courses. I see the spent shell cases dropping from the B-29s to our left -- they're firing. Now I feel the chatter of our aft guns as Jonesy and Charlie take shots at the fighter going into his breakaway. The other fighter veers off to the left after a short run. Now we see what he was doing. A phosphorus bomb slowly blossoms ahead and grows, with the white streamers radiating from the center. It settles slowly. We're going to pass right under it, but it isn't falling very fast. We fly under it now, dropping down to clear it with room to spare. We've heard of these phosphorous bombs dropped from above. They'll burn right through a plane, should they hit one, possibly causing an explosion.

The guns of our plane chatter again and I know the gunners are firing to the rear. We must be careful with our fire to the right because of our own planes, and directly to the left for the same reason. Ahead is the lead flight, so we're cut down there. It's clear to the rear and in certain places high to the left, and low to the right under the "B" flight. Charlie takes a shot to the right, then Dick takes the turret for a shot at a fighter's breakaway to the left. Jonesy tells Bill, "There must be 12 fighters making passes now." Switching back to the VHF from interphone I miss some of the conversation of the gunners, but see more shells fall from the plane on Pete's left wing, the plane protecting the outside of the formation. The plane jars and I know the bomb doors are open. The fighters increase their attacks, coming in closer. Evidently they mean to destroy our aim and make us throw the bombs out from our target. No doubt they know we're going for their field. Switching back onto the interphone for the bomb run I hear Jonesy and Charlie call out several more phosphorous bombs, all slightly wide of the formation. I'm thankful for that.

"There they go." Bill releases the bombs and the plane bucks. We stick together and the formation begins the turn to the right. Evidently the fighters are going along with us. "Fighter at 3 coming in." I feel the chatter of our aft turrets, now the upper turret fires, with Jake hunched over the sight gradually turning as he tracks the fighter who is coming in overhead, but he's gone almost immediately. The big four-gun turret shakes the whole cabin and our ears hurt. The smell of Cordite is strong.

Now I realize that Pete is switching the flight across to the right, going under the lead flight as we turn right. At the same time the "B" flight, on the right side of the lead, is crossing to the left, above the lead flight. It's a pretty maneuver and well executed. This keeps the flights staggered into the sun, so that on the new heading we present our greatest fire power in the direction of the sun. During the turn our guns are blanked out by our own planes, but fortunately we have no attacks. "Planes at 1 coming in," Jonesy calls. Now we are on the outside of the formation, protecting the right flank. Watching Pete, I can't see the fighter. The cabin shakes with the nerve-wracking rattling explosion of the four guns firing together. I hold the plane closely on Pete's wing, and now I see the upper aft turret of his plane swing in an arc, with smoke drifting from the muzzle; they're firing, too.

"Plane at 11 high -- here he comes," Jonesy calls. I can see the plane above the lead flight dropping down on a collision course with the center of the formation. His size increases rapidly, he's really coming. He turns to the left and then, in a roll, comes in between the lead flight and ours. Whew! That's close!

He may not shoot anybody, but at that rate he'll run into one of us. He was so close that I saw the dirt on the unpainted fuselage of the plane and the large, red, solid circles on the wings. Couldn't have been any closer without hitting us. The fighters break away and make several attacks from the left rear, and we don't get very good shots at them. Now suddenly they are gone, and we are left intact, so far as we know. That was mighty hot while it lasted -- a lot of lead was flying around!

Looking at the formation we see all the planes in place. On the VHF this is verified by the flight leaders as they call the lead plane, reporting that their planes are all right. Jonesy estimates that we had 20 fighter attacks, over half of which we couldn't get a good shot at. Dick, Charlie, and Jonesy agree on having seen seven phosphorous bombs being close to the formation under which we flew. Several times the fighters dove through the formation. I shan't forget the fighter who swooped down between the flights. Those are skillful pilots. Flak was meager and inaccurate, probably because of their fighters being present.

Nick checks the fuel and Bill checks with him. The plane feels better with the load gone. The extra bomb hindered the trim of the plane. Now we should do a lot better on fuel. We have already used 400 gallons beyond the curve. Nick figures that we have enough to get home and Bill agrees. In our favor, too, is a good tail-wind, making our speed over the surface 260 mph. Since we haven't much fuel to spare, we leave the others and do our own navigation. Nick breaks out the meager rations and we have "chow" and chatter. Hume observes, "Pretty easy, isn't it?" He seems pleased that it has turned out to be what he expected -- nothing to it! We agree, and wonder if he'll get his pants scared off him, as we have in the past, and as I always have over the target. I'm scared from the first attack, or burst of flak, until we leave the target well behind. I don't recall ever being completely unafraid, even the first time, but maybe he's tougher that way than I am.

The trip is routine, and we make it with fuel to spare, according to our figures. George puts on the put-put, Bill puts the gear down and the flaps, and I call the Tower, saying we're turning on the Base leg, and we line up for landing. The big bird is light and manageable without a load. We come towards the field high, cut our power, and enter a sharp glide, carrying plenty of speed. We land well down the runway. Nick cuts the generators, the gunners unstow the turrets, Bill raises the flaps with a generator on, and we taxi back to the hardstand. We go to the Interrogation, back in the area. There we learn that all Sixth Group planes are all right, and that both targets were hit squarely -- a nice job. Of the 42 planes in our Wing that participated we learn that two were shot down by fighters and one ditched, but nine of the crew were rescued. Eight B-29s were badly damaged by fighters. It seems that our Group formations were very lucky.

Now it is the next day and at the critique both our Commanding Officer and Operations Officer are highly critical of the way in which we flew the mission. At first, in the summary of the flight, we thought that we would be commended for the excellent bombing results, which mean so much to us, but instead we are criticized for the manner in which we fly the cruise control. Tying up the whole reprimand about Jordan's flight, because "Porky" saw fit to fly it other than as briefed (he stayed at 20,000 feet all the way home) more obviously than the rest of us. The C.O. points out that Jordan used more fuel than the rest of us to accomplish the flight, even though he arrived home long before the rest of us. When Jordan could finally get in a word, he informed the Operations Officer that they had flown beyond Tinian by mistake and then doubled back, flying many miles further and thus using up the fuel. Having proved his point, that he got better mileage per gallon, Jordan, still restraining his anger, quietly sat down. That should have stopped the Operations Officer, and it did slow him down, but he changed the subject and called our attention to discrepancies in other matters, too trivial to recall. This ignorant attempted supervision we encounter all the time is discouraging. We are hitting the target and returning because of the skill of the individual crews and with God's aid -- not solely because of the briefing officers' dogma, that we know.

We are pleased to learn later that all bombs for both formations hit within 1,000 feet of the predecided aiming point. That means that the formation was in close, making a good bomb pattern. The ordinary formation is figured close to 1,500 feet wide. For this mission we all receive a commendation from the General of Wing headquarters. His praise counteracts the crews' disgust by lauding the skill of the crews which participated. Rather ironically, it seems to us, our Commanding Officer then extends his approval, but he has no choice, and we don't believe what he says. The morale of the crews, because of the Group leadership, is getting low. In our crew I ask the officers not to discuss our disappointment with the enlisted men. We don't want any part in lowering other officers in their eyes. Even with the officers on the crew I don't discuss these difficulties or disappointments unless they directly concern them.

It's a bitter disappointment to us, who came overseas with high hopes, not to have the kind of leaders whom we can admire and respect. It affects everything we do. In contrast, we hear of C.O.s in other Wings, even in the companion Groups of our Wing, whom the men respect and admire. They fly on many missions and treat the men considerately, and as a result their men really like them. We still think it's possible for a man to be a good Commanding Officer and a good guy at the same time.

Chapter 21 USA

MAY 10, 1945 – No. 16

"No Gas Reserve"

The mission scheduled for the 8th is canceled. Tinian rumors are about a Jap peace "in the works". It's V.E. day in Europe. Now -- the next day -- the peace rumor is not repeated, but replaced by talk of V.E. day in the States. Bet the home folks are celebrating. It looks like a long war in the Pacific, rumors notwithstanding. The mission board lists crews for the mission going out -- Boynton, Cooney, Meadows, Dawson, Lazin, Maki, and Alger. The target -- USA. That has us puzzled. We're not aware that any target has this name or such an abbreviation. "So now we're going to bomb USA!" comments Hal as we stand in front of the board in Squadron Operations.

The crews settle into place, the Operations Officer takes the roll, and we get ready to absorb all the information we can on the mission as planned. There are some distinguished visitors from the Navy to be present, we are informed. Several Admirals with their staffs, accompanied by our Wing Commanding Officer. The tip-off is presented to us as though we are errant school boys being told to behave. I look about me at the mature faces and think what a shame it is that the Operations Officer fails so consistently in understanding us. The men will be themselves, and that will be sufficient.

We get to our feet while the "brass" come in, and are reseated at their request. A fine looking group of men they are. Their neat uniforms are quite a contrast to the flight coveralls and fatigue suits of the combat crews. Colonel Gibson opens the briefing with a few general words, in his most business-like manner. Higgy nudges me, "Take a look at that." I look up from the varied assortment of papers describing the mission, which we are issued before each flight. The Commanding Officer is wearing coveralls, like the rest of us -- is it possible that he is going along on this one? We wonder whether he expects another decoration for this trip. Perhaps the visiting dignitaries will think we have the kind of C.O. who flies with his men. If so, that's like locking the barn after the horse is gone.

The bomb load will not be so heavy this time, only 10,000 lbs. -- 10 1,000 pounder-ers, high explosives. The fuel load will be 6800 gallons and total gross of 133,000 lbs. -- unusually light. Our curiosity about the target USA is now satisfied, for we learn that it is to be an airfield near the small town of USA (Yoosa), which the Japs so named in order that their manufactured goods could be marked "Made in USA". This, no doubt, for the benefit of us gullible Americans.

We see from the flimsy that we will have a K-20 strike camera. The C.O. is listed as a passenger in the formation leader's plane. Now we are presented with the facts which, when condensed, are as follows: The take-off will be to the east, using the runways "A" and "C" at the same time. There will be two squadrons. The lead squadron will take off on "A" runway and the second squadron (of which we are a member) will use "C" runway. Altitude out will be 7000 feet all the way, by way of Iwo. Our assembly point will be the area 35 miles due south of Okino-shima, over open water, an area lying between Kyushu and Shikoku Islands. The first squadron will circle right at 18,000 feet, while ours will circle left at 20,000 feet. The first will use red flares and ours green. The two squadrons will make the run together with a separation of 1000 feet vertically and 500 feet horizontally. If the assembly is not completed by departure time, the other planes will tap on while on the way to the IP, and from there to the target on a heading of 291 degrees. "Miss America" will lead "C" flight, holding the flight low, while "B" flight flies high on the lead flight. During the approach to the IP we will let down 2000 feet to 18,000 feet bombing altitude. The breakaway will be to the right, descending at 200 mph. Return to base by flights. There is the possibility of fighter attacks for 30 minutes in and out, since this is the area where one of the Tinian Groups lost several planes on the raid a few days ago. The secondary target is Oita. The flak may be heavy -- stay away from Tokuyama, a Naval Base, and beware of surface craft. Fuel reserve will be 250 for the Wichita planes and 150 for Renton.

"What's that -- did he say '250?'" I wonder. Usually we have 500 to 1000 gallons reserve and then we sometimes run out of fuel. Witness the ditchings when almost home, or the frequent stops at Iwo. But perhaps we misunderstood or he read the figures incorrectly. Many of us are looking at their neighbors -- why that's the same as saying we'll be exactly out of gas on return -- no reserve at all, since the residual content of the tanks is that much. As for the Renton -- I look toward Fortune's crew, they have a Renton. Pete was looking at his engineer who was shaking his head. Bet they think they misunderstood what was said. Maybe we did.

The briefing continues. Air-Sea rescue facilities, presented by Hall, will be more than before: there will be 3 dumbos, 5 superdumbos, 1 destroyer, 5 subs, and 1 seaplane tender. Sully now takes over to present the weather. The weather will be good at the target, according to the latest information, but there is a front lying south of Iwo which may mean bad weather at Iwo, perhaps the field closed. Jake, the bombardier, will take pictures of the weather, with a camera provided, on the way up and back. This is a new wrinkle. The General, the Wing Commanding Officer, now takes over and says a few words about the Okinawan campaign and the significance of our present bombing. I am impressed by his frankness in the presence of the Naval representatives. He states that our program has been interrupted by the Navy, and that we are helping them out temporarily until their own fighters take over to bomb and strafe the fields of Kyushu, and that this is out of our line. It sounds as though he wants this to go on record while the Navy is there to listen, and we appreciate being addressed as he talks to us. He is serious, direct and manly, with respect for our interest and intelligence in the matter. The men hang on his words.

The crew members go to the specialized briefings. In the pilots' meeting the first question asked of the Operations Officer is, "What is the fuel reserve?" He repeats the earlier figures and we realize that we heard correctly -- there was no mistake. The reserve for Wichita is 250 and for Renton 150. The other pilots about us look nonplussed. They still seem to wonder if they have heard right. The heads of the pilots and copilots bend toward each other and I am aware that the other crews, too, are trying to translate this startling fuel situation into terms of their own planes. We are aware that even the 250 figure is less than half of any reserve we've previously had, and then, on occasion, we've had trouble. Several times we've had as high as 1000 gallons for the unexpected. Fortune, with his Renton 150 gallon reserve, can't theoretically make it, according to past consumption and residual content, so it may mean refueling of else? on the return home. Moreover, because of bad weather there is the strong possibility that Iwo may be closed to traffic or greatly reduced. What's the answer? The authorities are not going to risk it, surely! Then there are the other conditioning factors. The total weight, which is lighter than usual this time, the types of wind, always unpredictable, the plane's center of gravity, and the many unexpected events that dog us, as in the past.

The Operations Officer, in his juvenile manner and high pitched voice, makes light of the fuel situation and our concern, dismissing it with the statement that a bomb was removed earlier from the load, and that our briefed weight is lighter than it might have been. We think one bomb is hardly a deciding factor. However it is apparent that we cannot change things. Evidently the High Command planned this. It's hard to believe, but if that's the way they want it, we'll do our best. It's either that or get "wet". As Pete puts it when we get outside, "Oh, well, see you in a boat!" throwing up his hands. "Dinghy, dinghy, who's got the dinghy?" adds Johnson, his navigator, and they've got a Renton. "Iwo, here we come!" "If it's open!" Jake exclaims.

Down at the line we are happy over the appearance of the plane. The new paint job looks good. The lucky penny, mysteriously stuck on the under side of the nose, facing forward, is still there. We hadn't noticed it for quite a while after we got the plane. Abe Lincoln is getting quite a ride -- one he may never have anticipated. I get Pat aside and explain the mission to him, saying that we'll "sweat" the gas this time. Pat thinks that the new engine will not burn an excessive amount of fuel, so I feel a little better about our chances. Our plane has always taken more fuel than many others. As usual, I give him the ETA, this time of 1500, so he'll know when to expect us. I point out the possibility of our going into Iwo on the way home or, if Iwo's closed, of being later yet -- but not to worry.

Looking about at the activity I miss Gabby, who is sick from four serum "shots" given to him by the Doc. This is the first time that any crew member has missed a scheduled flight, and his absence has been quite noticeable, but he'll be with us next time. The gunners are checking the guns, the engineer is making out the weight and balance, the bombardier is checking the bombs and shackles, the navigator is getting his equipment in and ready for work, the copilot is making out the loading list and checking the food, while I talk to the various parties who come by the plane. It's a pleasure to have a crew like this.

Al stops a minute and informs me that the radios are all right, and our new radar operator reports that his oxygen is low, but otherwise his position is ready. I tell Pat, who then goes to contact the oxygen department through the line chief, who drives by. With men like this who are dependable, conscientious, and hardworking, we stand a good chance of coming through, and I'll do everything in my power to see that they get a square deal, collectively and individually. Maybe that's why these briefing difficulties bother me so much -- the responsibility for the crew rests on me and I can't stand back, remaining silent, when I see something that appears to be wrong or dangerous. Mistakes, if such there are, made by those above us in rank (and we are all human), must not be enacted by those of us who fly. At our level a mistake may be fatal. At a desk a man planning these missions can make a mistake and not be conscious of it, I'm sure. But sending the planes upwind over the target, bombing into the sun, reducing ammunition for the guns in order to save negligible weight, improperly loading the plane, cutting the fuel reserve too short -- all could mean death to the crews and loss of equipment and are inexcusable. We hope that these things are not done intentionally. It isn't good planning, even if the combat crews are considered expendable. Further, we have seen the mistakes made by the authorities in our Group and we are suspicious, because we are the ones who pay. Those above us seldom fly, if they do at all.

Not only do the crew members have commendable personal traits of character, but they try hard to be skillful at their jobs, to learn more about them. Al Horvath knows his radio job even to having memorized the frequencies and emergency messages. Hal knows the navigational end, both the equipment and how it should be properly used. Gabby knows the radar end, studying on the side so that he can do certain airborne maintenance to keep the set operating and he has studied navigation on his own accord many times in order to understand his job even better. He can pick up and distinguish surface crafts, airplanes, and land. Jonesy knows his CFC system. He works willingly and skillfully on the guns and is accurate in telling us the status of the guns at all times, so we know where we stand. If he says they work, they work. Nick Mount goes about his engineering job diligently, taking it to heart, and working harmoniously with the crew chief, Patterson, so that the plane is always in the best shape possible. Bill Higgison is responsible, dependable, and hard working -- all qualities that make him one fine pilot and copilot and that make it easier for me, and safer for us all. Dick, Charlie, and George are always there to help Jonesy with the guns. They have a pride in their jobs and are becoming better scanners every flight. It's good to hear their voices on the interphone, brief and business-like, calling out other planes in the vicinity and the condition of the engines. Jake Kagan is a good bombardier and is getting better, as he sees mission by mission the importance of hung bombs, knowing his job, and preflight inspection of the equipment. Our whole mission is centered around his department and he is trying hard to do the job.

It's no wonder that, as I check the last pre-mission details, I feel a pride in the way the men go about their work to get the plane ready for the big job ahead. As a result of our work we're never late for take-off. The ground crew matches the work and concern of the air crew in conditioning the plane -- it is an unbeatable combination. For hard work and skill our ground crew is hard to beat. I'm lucky to be associated with men like these.

Various visitors come by. Ben Lay wishes us luck. He has that "chaw of tobaccy" which he hates, but somehow he thinks it brings us all luck, and even though "green around the gills", he carries on while seeing the crews off. The Docs come by and shake hands. Koltoon gives me another shaft, which I receive gratefully and with the proper ceremonious thanks. The Deputy C.O. comes by and inquires, "How's everything?" I tell him frankly that I don't think we'll have enough gas, since the plane used well above the fuel consumption curve on the last several missions. He seems surprised and I tell him the particulars, adding that our briefed reserve is very little this time, which he knows. He answers that I should use my head and go into Iwo if necessary. I don't remind him that Iwo is supposed to have bad weather -- what's the use?

We taxi out after the engine check. The plane sounds good, including the new engine, No. 4. The takeoff goes uneventfully and we roll out in turn. Take-off time is 0031. After take-off we climb immediately at 24 43 to 7000 feet and level off. Actually we climb to 7600 and then let down in order to cool the engines. We use the new power settings (which permits a higher manifold pressure for the RPMs) and find that we can hold 2150 with 34 and ½ inches. We have been assured that the high power for the RPM will not harm the engines. We're not convinced, since we were schooled to think otherwise and dislike seeing the engines heat up. With 2150 we can keep the engines in the auto-lean position (above 200 we use auto-rich) and thus save gas. It looks like we may save a little gas this way. We're holding an air speed of 202, which is very good. "How's the temperature, Nick?" I ask. "They're high, about 220, but not going up," he answers. Well, that's hotter than we like to run the engines, but they've said this won't hurt them and we do need the fuel.

We pass Iwo in good shape without encountering more than 30 minutes of clouds, and they are not excessively turbulent. We take up the next heading. All goes quietly with Bill and me alternating sleeping. The crew disposes themselves according to their duties, and the engines grind out the miles.

Two hours from the assembly Hal informs us that we must change our air speed to 240 in order to make good the assembly time, which is a must. Evidently our winds were other than briefed and now we must alter our flight plan. At this altitude Hal figures that we must hold 240 from here on in in order to make good the assembly time, but we can't afford to use that high a power setting with the resulting exorbitant amount of fuel. The only alternative is a questionable one -- that of climbing to 20,000 feet now instead of waiting, to get the benefit of the increased ground speed which altitude gives more proportionately from the fuel required than to get that speed at lower altitudes. Hal believes that there will be head winds at that altitude, and that will slow us down. The advantage seems to be on the side of the altitude, however, so we begin to climb. We level off at 20,000 feet and continue on. After a while Hal reports that we have a head-wind slowing us, but that we're still making a speed across the surface of the earth which will put us there on time. It's taking more gas, Nick states, but maybe we can make it up somewhere else. There's just "so much gas" in these tanks to do the trick.

At 0740 we arrive in the assembly area with Hal and radar man Whiney guiding us. Here we see several other planes in the area, but no twosomes. It's evident that this is liable to be another one of those endless circles with each plane trying to catch someone else, and everyone using too much gas before recognizing and joining the leader. So, instead of first inspecting those present before joining anyone, we head for the nearest plane. It's Maki, our wingman, and we're on his inside so that puts him right where he should be, on our right wing. He sees this and tags on immediately. Another plane comes over to the two-ship element and it's Boynton. He takes his place on the left wing. By this time I've called Parsons, the leader in 51, and told him we have a formation started. He answers, "I see you, be right over." Meanwhile Fox has joined us, taking the diamond spot of our flight. Parsons, with whom the C.O. is riding, comes up inside and crosses over. Now Parsons calls the other and says we're heading for the IP, and they can join us en route. Dawson arrives on Parsons' right wing and Cooney squeezes through to take the left. Now we've got something. At this time Bill takes the controls, since the leader is on his side, and I check with the crew and look over the formation. Meadows has just taken the "B" flight position with a strange plane on his wing -- it is from another Group, the 9th.

We approach the IP and I see, out to our left, a single flight of three B-29s, flying a parallel course by themselves. While Bill flies I keep the RPMs at the right setting to give us maximum fuel mileage, yet not strain the engines. As a flight leader we must jockey our position on the lead flight, maintaining a constant position, and yet not varying our position to the extent that our wing planes must constantly be changing power to stay in position. The wing planes and "tail end Charlies" are the ones who use the most fuel. The formation leader uses the same steady power setting and thus gets maximum gas mileage. The flight leaders combine this with jockeying, and the wing planes must keep changing power, wasting fuel, in order to stay up with the rest. Today that's a dangerous factor, so we do all we can to hold our position steady in the interest of saving fuel for them and ourselves.

On this heading we are angling toward the Shikoku coast three or four miles to our left. It is a bright, sunshiny day, the sky is blue with no clouds in our vicinity. Bill is keeping our flight low enough to miss the prop wash, but close so the planes give the maximum fire support. There are the fighters! Jake edges forward on his seat to look through the gunnery sight. Our field of fire extends ahead and to the forward left. Our wings and rear are covered by the overlapping fire of the wing ships. They also cover part of the area ahead, limited only by the amount of our plane blanks out their fire. Jake says, "I have it!" to Jonesy, referring to the upper forward turrets. "Roger," Jonesy replies briefly. Jonesy has the upper aft and Dick and Charlie each using his own sight variously control the lower aft, depending on which side the enemy plane is, through pre-arranged coordination. They will be able to fire below us, as high as the bottom of the wing planes. Jake can fire the lower forward, and Jonesy can take the upper forward, too, if they so desire. Ahead of us the tiny moving dots become recognizable. They're twin engines, "Irvings", Jonesy exclaims. "Wing span 50 feet," he continues. The gunners set the wing span into their computing sights. Anticipation is worse that the real thing, I've heard, and here the real thing is about to begin. There's no doubting their intention and without the controls to handle I feel even more exposed.

"Here they come, 12 o'clock," says Jonesy, tense but quiet. Looking ahead, for an instant I get the impression of an endless line of Irvings as far as I can see, with variously cocked wings, diving and turning, yet all coming right for the formation. The upper forward turret chatters and shakes us. We hear the empty shells rattling inside the turret as Jakes gets in a burst at the first one, which is in a bank at 11 o'clock high. It drops something then rolls back toward us and fires, it's guns twinkling as the flames leap out of the barrels. Involuntarily I duck, though there's no place to duck behind, then I catch myself and look at Bill. He's cringing, too, since he sees that fighter while he flies the plane. The upper turret shakes -- Jake's on him again. The turrets of the lead flight swing in an arc, smoke comes out of their barrels, empty cartridges drop from the planes. The first fighter goes by with a rush -- where did his shells go? The flight's in tight, Bill closes in closer on the lead flight.

Here's another one. Jake fires and the cabin shakes. We smell the smoke from the guns. "You got him," Jake says as the second fighter zooms past, diving. "I've got him," Dick echoes and we hear an aft turret chatter. Jake passes them to Dick and Jonesy. The fighters keep boring in from ahead. "12 low," Jake calls, and we see him lean forward over the sight, firing the lower forward guns at a low nose attack. The fighter climbs up level with us well ahead, then dives down, only to pull back up, his guns firing. Jake shoots again. The fighter turns and dives sharply to our left. Jake calls out two other fighters coming from the other side low -- he can't get a shot at them. They breakaway on the other side.

The formation's in good and tight. Looking out to the left I see the lone flight of B-29s. The fighters that just attacked us are heading over toward them. The first one goes in. Tough luck, those boys caught out there alone. A fighter tries the same attack used on us, starting out front he comes in from the nose, climbs, dives, and then goes straight at them, coming up underneath at an angle. The B-29s are firing, I guess. The fighter wings by them in a sharp climb, levels out, just as smoke pours from the cowl. The plane goes into a wide spiral, gaining speed, then it dives steeper finally striking the water. The pilot got out -- Dick and Jonesy report a parachute. "They're coming to join us," someone reports, and we see that the B-29s are coming toward us. Good thing if they do, they need company.

We reach the IP and start a turn to the left. The other flight joins us in the diamond position. They appear to be all right, and we're glad to have their guns. The fighters are climbing back up above us. They'll be back in time, no doubt. We cross the IP and head toward the USA airfield, the target. We hold a steady course -- no flak yet. I stand ready with the bomb doors and the bomb release switch. Bill has the controls. Jake checks his bombing switches. "Everything's set," he states. The bomb doors come open on the deputy leader -- our cue -- and we open our doors. We continue straight on. Watching the lead ship, I wait to see the bombs fall. The fighters are still out of gunshot. "Bombs away!" I push the release button and the plane climbs. Al and Dick check the bomb bays. "They're gone." Jonesy and Charlie report that the other planes dropped theirs together with us. I note that Bill has the flight in mighty tight. The scanners report they are watching the bombs fall. Dick and Charlie state that the bombs hit squarely on the hangar line, the briefed aiming point. Our twelve-ship formation has overlapping wings. The bomb pattern appeared to be very small, the gunners say, and that means a good formation and accurate bombing. We close the doors and turn right onto the breakaway. The fighters have left us to attack several smaller formations in the area. Evidently our twelve-ship formation, with all of its fire power scared them off after the one pass. So many four-gun turrets must be fearsome looking to those fighters.

Bill holds the formation in tight for quite a while. We pass over the Inland Sea on the breakaway. Out of my window I see another airfield, not shown on the map, and fighters taking off. We'll be up to get you next. Numerous surface craft are quite apparent, mainly in the coves and along the shoreline. Farther away we see eight ships in wide-spread formation on the water -- might be their navy. There must be mines in that area to worry them, whether they know it or not. Our flight looks all right, and the other planes appear not to be damaged. We loosen up and shortly after break away from the formation, taking stock of the situation. Hal reports that the bombs were dropped at 0840.

We head for home with Nick and Bill closely computing the fuel. We get off lucky not to have had flak this time, and the fighters left us alone after the initial procession. After computing the power settings and times flown, Nick believes that we might have 30 minutes to an hour's reserve of fuel, if all goes right, and if his figures are correct. The many power changes needed over the target in formation are hard to keep track of because of the length of time each was used, but it looks like we can make it. As flight leader we used less gas than some of the others, since this position requires less jockeying than an outside position. On inquiry, the crews of all the other planes estimate that it will be nip and tuck on their gas. We're playing it mighty close, but so far the mission has been ideal on fuel. We took very little time to assemble, we flew a good steady formation, and now we are going into individual navigational problems to make the most of our fuel. We can't fly back as flights, as briefed, since adjusting a plane's speed with relation to another plane reduces maximum performance.

The winds are a lot different than as briefed, and hurt us going up to the assembly, and we used more fuel than briefed. Yet conditions have been good so far in making the mission coincide with the briefed plans, more so than usual. We assembled in less time than before and have cut down on the power changes needed to hold position. We've also asked more of the engines by using a higher manifold pressure for each RPM setting. So far we've done everything in favor of saving fuel but to actually "will" that there be more fuel -- maybe the authorities figured that we could acquire a little additional gas that way!

As we approach Iwo we encounter a solid carpet of clouds and then enter the tall masses of cumulous clouds which cut our visibility to zero. It is turbulent and the crew are warned to keep the safety belts fastened. On the VHF we hear planes calling Iwo for landing information. Evidently the field is open. There are numerous calls. There are many who must stop for fuel. Several estimates given on the air of fuel remaining indicate that some are several hundred gallons short. We continue on, figuring and refiguring the gas remaining. Except for No. 4 backfiring we have no engine trouble and the fuel gauges substantiate Nick's figures.

The last several hundred miles are nerve wracking. It looks like a toss up as to whether we can make it. At one time we stand by for a repeat message since we hear someone in trouble who is about to "ditch". We silently send them best wishes. Sitting, hoping, and "sweating", we see land ahead -- the hills of home, Saipan and now Tinian. We are given a royal welcome at the field. Pat and the boys were worried over the fuel situation. As we land, the tanks read 50 gallons or less on each engine, but we know that when that low they are unusually inaccurate -- we might have more or less.

As we touch foot to the ground we feel thankful. The others join me, I know, in thanks to a Higher Power. We realize how fortunate the entire trip was in permitting us to save fuel sufficient to make the last few miles. Many are the ditchings that occur within sight of home base. But we made it! We haven't lost our surprise or consternation at whomever planned this mission in giving us so little fuel. The B-29 can carry up to 10,000 gallons of gas, though each gallon taken reduces the amount of bomb load that can be carried. We know this and want to carry the maximum possible load, but this trip strained the situation. We don't like to feel that expendable! We still feel that there was a mistake somewhere along the line. If Iwo had been closed, as the weather forecast indicated, many would have paid dearly this mission. This trip has drawn heavily on our already reduced bank account of luck. Thank you, Lord, for safe passage. Our feeling of thankfulness is to a Higher Power, no the Operations personnel.

So we conclude the day with the interrogation where we learn, tentatively, that 7 Jap fighters were destroyed and 9 damaged. Three of our aircraft were damaged by the fighters. Don Fox, who flew in our flight, shows us a large piece of metal, a shell apparently. "This Jap cannon shell came out of my wing," he informs us. So that's where those shells that didn't hit us were going! Don was slightly above us to the rear. This particular 20 millimeter cannon shell came into his upper turret, went out the side into the wing, through the nacelles, and lodged in the wing, all without hurting anyone. Several of the other planes were shot up, too. A number of our planes landed at Iwo for refueling, but this news doesn't surprise us.

At the critique we listen to the summary of the mission, given by the Operations Officer, who reads over our interrogation reports. After the summary, during the general discussion, one pilot seriously inquires why the combat crews can't be given a list of possible targets. It seems that he and several others missed the assembly and went over Japan to bomb alone. In such a case as this, or when you're alone and clouds cover the main target, the pilot wondered further if such a list wouldn't be a wise thing. It seems like a good idea and the rest of us know of crews who were unable to go over the target because of mechanical trouble, or lack of guns, or lack of fuel, and dropped their bombs anywhere along the Japanese coast because they didn't know whether there were any targets in the area. The Operations Officer, with a knowing laugh (while we don't see anything to laugh at) replies in his piping voice, "Yes, we thought of that, too, but we think it would do more harm than good -- you might not want to hit the assigned target, eh?" I can feel the waves of resentment about me toward this man who dares to make such a statement to us.

Our Commanding Officer, for some reason, is not present at the critique. We would be interested in hearing his comments on the trip, now that he's made another one. In retrospect, Bill and I get a laugh out of recalling our cringing when that first fighter came in, then catching ourselves and feeling sheepish. In ducking, there's no place to hide behind, no place to go. In fact, by ducking, a pilot's liable to come out from behind his safety glass and expose himself to a nose attack. But there we were, trying to duck, like trying to find a shielded place in a greenhouse. The movement seems instinctive, like "trying to crowd right up into your flak helmet" as Ramsey puts it. Now we have 16 behind us and 229 and ½ hours combat time to our credit.

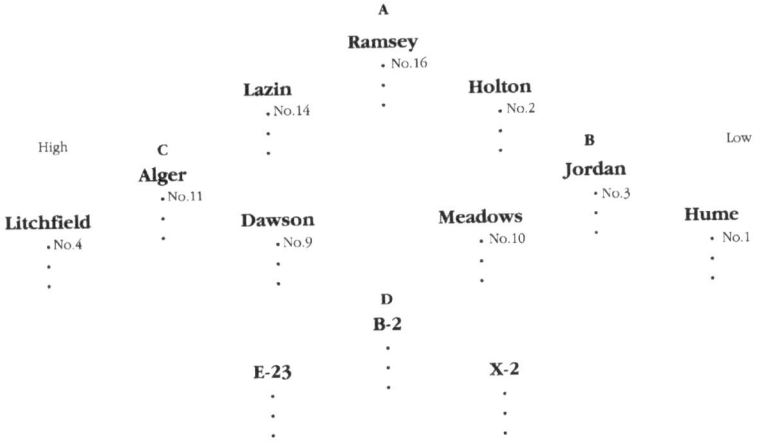

Chapter 22 Airman To Family

"An Open Letter to Parents"

May 12, 1945

Tonight we saw a picture called "Target Tokyo". It was in the nature of a short reel, lasting some twenty minutes. The subject matter consisted of the B-29s and our Bomb Group, showing our training in Nebraska, the flight over, and the first bombing of Japan. No doubt you will see it sometime at home. It is not to be confused with a Hollywood fictional film. This is a film with a narrator -- sort of a travelogue, not an Errol Flynn adventure.

The training in Nebraska and flight to Hawaii were of our group, also the flight from Hawaii to Tinian. Our first raid on Japan did not show our group, actually, but it might as well have been for it is indicative of our work. The picture is exaggerated in a way -- United States style (witness the radio and newspaper commercials). The exaggeration shows up in the tone of wonder and amusement of the narrator -- as though he were describing the miraculous. True it is, in a way, but let's call a rose a rose. The B-29 is a wonderful plane but it need not be described breathlessly in awe-inspiring tones. In short, the picture, by its very nature, seems to be directed to filling the audience with wonder, amazement and awe -- even fear, and it is this of which I write tonight. People are usually afraid of that which they do not understand. Ignorance causes fear while knowledge and understanding dispel it. I believe you know what I mean.

I am writing this to point out to you something of our side of this business -- to dispel, partially at least, the worry and fear that must arise in you over my job -- a feeling which is further strengthened by pictures and raids you may see and hear about in the future. Now that the war is concentrated here the news and ballyhoo will deal with the B-29s and the terrific missions sent to Japan daily.

This picture combines pictures of our training with flight pictures taken later in the Marianas. At one time or another many men appear in the picture, including Bill Southworth and several of our combat crews. It may be shown locally sometime in the future. On seeing it one of the fellows kiddingly remarked to another "My, isn't the B-29 fearsome -- we ought to be too scared to fly it". That is our reaction for the men readily recognized the hokum, but you may not.

Looking at the B-29 from what I believe to be your standpoint, you see a huge plane and you are aware of its great size, its terrific power, weight and speed. You know there must be intricate equipment to run it -- strange instruments and gear. You may have heard of the bomb load, drift-meter, tachometer, manifold pressure, autopilot, bombsight, the carload of gasoline carried, shackles, releases, remote turret fire control, and countless other associated equipment and skills found in it. It's all strange to you, for though you have read and heard stories of the B-29, you are limited in first-hand knowledge. As a result (and this is very understandable) it adds to your worry. When you think of all this strange equipment, the great distances to strange lands, the ever-present fear of enemy fighter planes, flak and bombs -- and us flying through it all -- you get jittery -- is that right? Assuming I have diagnosed your feelings correctly let me go on: In contrast to the way you feel, the B-29 is not strange to us and our feelings are representative of the other combat crews out here. I understand the B-29 better than I ever understood a car, and we all take cars for granted. So you see the worry you may have through lack of knowledge does not exist as far as I am concerned. For three and a half years I have been away from the kind of life you understand -- doing a job at home, working among people we know, living in a routine similar to yours, and on the ground. Then, like others, I began to fly and so entered into a new phase of life which included aerodynamic principals, manifold pressure (force behind fuel, forcing it into cylinders), tachometers (instruments indicating revolutions per minute of propellers), fuel pump, oil pump, importance of air speed, rate of climb and principals of instrument flight.

We learned to fly at night as well as in the daytime, to fly navigational trips over long distances alone, then in formation both day and night, controlling the plane with stick and rudder staying a specified distance from the lead plane. This, too, became easy for me. Then we were taught to fly "blind", that is by instruments, relying only on the instrument panel to tell me where and how (what altitude) my plane was situated in relation to the ground.

At my assigned stations I learned to fly bombardiers and navigators and to drop bombs. I learned all this myself, first going to class and then flying it; the latest equipment was not foreign to me for I made use of it all the time.

Then we went from twin-engine to four engines. The principles were new but not strange, being similar to those encountered in single and twin-engine aircraft, they came naturally, logically. We learned about "feathering" propellers -- that is to stop a propeller so that its edges point straight ahead into the wind so that it would not revolve. This saves the terrific "drag" or slowing down of the plane due to a wind-milling propeller on a dead engine. We also learned the principles of the exhaust-driven superchargers by which the outside air is condensed to be sent to the engines, thus giving power up high where the air is thin. All the time the planes were getting bigger and heavier -- flying at higher altitudes with oxygen was commonplace, so the B-29 was not strange, though new, to us. The biggest change was its three-wheel gear instead of two. The nose wheel caused us to land it differently.

In the B-29 we navigated long distances, flew formation, dropped bombs, doing only what I had done before. The plane was bigger and heavier, that's all.

Now we are right in the midst of raiding Japan but in one sense we are right at home, for we are doing what we have done many times before. Actually, I, for one, am better qualified through knowledge and practice to fly over water than I am to drive in downtown St. Louis, and I believe my chances of coming through safely are as good. In reality I look on my work with the same warmth of familiarity as you do in your kitchen activities, Mother. I climb into our own plane, slide into the old, familiar seat, adjust parachutes, check all the gadgets, turn on the radio and adjust my seat to the right height and tilt. I even use the special sponge cushion I brought along to soften the long hours in one chair.

We can fly the plane, reaching anything or any point in the night's darkness, think of you and home, whistle, and listen to the radio all at the same time. In my car I have to <u>look</u> at the ignition, just one key in one slot, but I can set up the automatic pilot without looking (it's below my right hand at knee level, right beside me) inside 30 or 45 seconds, although it consists of six toggle switches, three large rotating knobs, ten small rotating knobs, and six blinker lights -- these all performing some twelve different functions.

We can do several things, if necessary, besides fly instruments, and the latter consists of continual mental evaluation and reaction to the flight controls -- reading more than ten dials which tell the ship's altitude, speed and general conduct. It's almost like breathing, because for over 2200 hours I've done just that. There's nothing new or strange about it for me.

Here's an example: Depending on the circumstances, over the target we fly by instruments or through judging the distance from the lead plane, in close or loose formation, converse with other planes, talk to the crew of our own plane concerning their gunner, bombing, navigation, or engineer's instruments and have a finger in the pie generally.

I know, too, what each of the other men is doing and what his job is -- this is going into the general appraisal of the situation -- and I find lots of time to sleep. I delegate all the responsibility and authority possible to the individual members of the crew so there is little for me to do -- just oversee the job and relax. And the copilot -- he does much of the flying. We have a good crew.

So you must not worry about us, thinking the B-29 is dangerous because of its bigness and strangeness. <u>Our</u> worries, or rather scares, come from outside our plane. In this connection, the difference between being worried or scared, out here anyway, is this -- there is no element of choice in being scared. The "scares" are in the Good Lord's department, on Whom we lean heavily; The worries, mostly man-made, should be thrown out through understanding and faith. Seeing this picture may cause you to worry, but try not to. I hope this letter will help to allay your fears.

Yes, we do have some trying moments but we are too busy to worry. On taking off we are aware of the danger, over the target we know the possibilities, but we do our job, try not to let our scare hinder our work and place our faith in the hands of one higher than we. We are not atheists, believe me.

Now -- do you feel better? There are losses here, of course, but the percentage is low.

So do not worry -- God has control of that.

Sixteen behind us now. "Miss America – '62" is doing fine.

A
Litchfield
. No.4

Jordan   **Meadows**
. No.3   . No.10

C   **B**
Alger   **Schwager**
. No.11   . No.15

Cooney   **Dawson**   **Maki**   **Rodgers**
. No.14   . No.9   . No.1   . No.17

Chapter 23 Nagoya

May 14, 1945 – No. 17

"Incendiaries Again with 'Ditchings' "

It's time again for briefing. Hal, Bill and Jake give up playing with Gyro and "George", a small pig; they are quite a pair. George wants to be left alone but Gyro wants to play, and he plays rough, and now George gives voice to his indignation. Nor is Gyro very brave. When George starts to squeal it scares Gyro a little and he backs off. Then the cycle starts all over again -- a regular three-ring circus.

We are all feeling fairly chipper from the three day rest since the last mission. Joining the other crews we struggle into the briefing room and find our row. The sagging slats of the benches have become no softer. We see the other crews from the Squadron and Group present. From the Squadron this time there are the crews of Ramsey, Jordan, Fortune, Boynton, Maki, Alger, Schwager, Snyder, Meadows, Bassett, Hume, and Cooney. Our hut mates are flying now, too. In fact, we have several of the new crews with us tonight on a full flight status -- Hume, Snyder, Bassett, and Meadows.

It's 2100, too late for a briefing and too early to go to bed. Since we do not have an alternative, however, there is -- as usual -- no problem. We sit and listen. The room becomes quiet and the roll is taken. The Commanding Officer now appears to give us the "between halves" pep talk, the "go git 'em". He points out that this mission will be the biggest yet for the B-29s. Over 500 planes will participate. It seems we are to go back to the incendiary attacks, and the Colonel lets drop that this is the beginning of a "Blitz" again. We are both glad and sad over this. It's a pleasure to feel that we are getting in the required number of missions, but it's becoming a pleasure -- oddly enough -- when a mission is canceled, as though a big load has just been taken off of us. "Miss America – '62" is ready to go, and if they let us fly we ought to knock off 5 or 6 missions in her in a row. Let's hope so.

The SOP file (flimsies containing information about the flight) has been distributed to the ACs and I turn ours over to Bill. He checks it further and passes the specialized information to the various crew members. The entire planning of the mission is contained on these sheets. Whether we read it now or not, the information is covered by the various briefing officers, who embellish it. They describe it while we listen intently. Tonight is no exception. With all the confidence in the world they present the pertinent data. The briefing goes as usual and we break up for the specialized briefing, where the material is covered again, this time for the pilot's end, in our case. The mission is stripped naked and studied from every angle and all this before we even get into the planes. We try to learn all the points, as usual, so that the mission as it evolves can be fitted into a pattern as close as possible to the original plan. We are to carry 29 incendiary clusters which are fused to break up at 5000 feet and scatter. Our fuel load will be 6800 gallons, plenty, they tell us, and we are glad to see that the reserve is 500 gallons, twice what we were allowed the previous mission. We usually find unexpected gas-consuming factors during the flight that upset the plans, and the reserve represents the unexpected to us. We hate to see the planning staff deny us any reserve, like last time, thus refuting the unexpected, which to us is the one immutable fact.

Now to the trucks. We take No. 4 with Bassett's crew and go bouncing down to the line. After the milling around at the P.E. room, getting in each other's way, we go to the plane. Two crews with all their gear is a terrific crowd in the truck and a strain on everyone. Here's the plane and we unload in a hurry. "Good luck, Bassett!" we holler at the various crew members as they drive off. It's their first mission.

We go through the usual routine checks of the various departments of the plane -- bombing, navigation, radar, radio, engineering, and gunnery. Each man checks in with me stating the condition of his equipment so we know we're ready when it comes time to climb aboard. It's good to have Gabby with us again. As is our custom, we start the engines three minutes before the starting time, this to cover any delays, in case of engine trouble, but all goes well, the engines purr and Pat, satisfied, jumps out of the plane. We taxi out. The planes roll quickly down the taxiway and take positions on the various runways until, in short order, it's our turn. We line up, give her full power, and are airborne at 0143, leaving "A" runway quickly behind us. We wallow a bit but keep control and the wings level. All is well, we're off. The take-off is a precarious situation. Our weight is close to 140,000 and take-off speed is slow. Between flights our plane was weighted and we learned that it was 500 lbs. heavier than expected and that the center of gravity was somewhat forward of the point it should be, which explains past nose-heaviness.

We climb to 7000 feet, our cruising altitude. By using the new power settings of 35 inches of manifold with 2150 RPMs we are able to go into Auto-Lean immediately on leveling out, and this means an appreciable saving of fuel. No one is more concerned about the fuel consumption than the combat crews -- not even the "armchair strategists" who plan the missions. It's we who ditch, not the strategists. No one has to sell us on the idea of accurate computation of the fuel. We've learned the lessons well, and many fine points that the strategists might not even appreciate. Nick keeps the record of power settings and the exact times that the changes are made, and we know the plane -- better than anyone else. We know her from repeated experience and "close calls".

The quiet of the night swallows the mileage, almost magically, since there is so little sensation of movement at altitude, particularly in the darkness of night. The clouds are few. We have no gauge of our speed but the needle of the airspeed meter and Hal's position reports. The warm air of the southern latitudes gradually blends into that of the farther north and the cabin begins to cool. Nick gives us a little cabin heat. Here we are flying north, changing "seasons" again. May weather on Tinian is not similar to that found in Japan, we're sure, judging from the air above these areas. Nick tries out the transfer and it works. Hal lights up his pipe and the unmistakable aroma fills the cabin, but we do not get alarmed and look for fires as once we did.

The old routine fills the hours that pass quickly. Dick, Charlie, Jonesy, and George take turns in the side blisters scanning the area for other planes and keeping an eye on the hind side of the engines. Hal bends over his navigation table, disturbed only by our frequent questions concerning the location, distances, and his recomputed estimated time of arrival as well as by the passing traffic to the tube. It's always a squeeze to get by him when going aft. Actually, for a big plane, there is little room in the B-29 -- it is surprising. It's always with a feeling of relief that I return to my seat, where I feel at ease again. It is a comfy chair (one-man dinghy with a sponge cushion) with many adjustable gadgets, and everything is within reach to hands that know where to find the desired switch, lever, dial, or knob. This is home. I wonder if ever again I'll be so thoroughly familiar with my surroundings as I am in this plane. If life may be considered from the standpoint of moving the body from one resting spot to another I doubt if there will be another spot so well known to me. It's my place of business, and of rest -- even of sleep. In a sense, each of us is a part of the machine itself. We blend into the surroundings in the use, as the guiding mechanism that knows when and which gadgets to operate. Familiarity breeds understanding. Though we spend so many hours in close proximity to this plane, we become increasingly aware that we must be ready and able to exit in the shortest possible time. But sentiment is hard to overcome. I hope that I never have to leave "Miss A -- '62" in such a hurry.

We are briefed to arrive not sooner than 0835 at the assembly point. Other groups, forming earlier, will thus be on their way and we won't confuse them or ourselves when we arrive. Since we are a little early we circle short of the assembly area. There in the distance is the coast of Japan, rugged and irregular as ever, with the many inlets and bays. I can see the earlier formations joining at the specified altitudes. Actually there are three forming at the same time, in the same general area and altitude that each of the succeeding groups will use. We are to assemble at 17,000 feet in a left-hand circle. At 0830 we proceed toward the assembly point 10 miles off the southern tip of Honshu. We are the first of our formation to arrive, but from the south we see more planes coming.

It is a wonderful sight to see the strength of America here, 8000 miles from our country. Those large silver planes, gracefully airborne, each represent the strength of our industry and national purpose. Even for an old hand at this it's hard to realize -- over there in that one, No. 7, is Pete and "Horsecollar" Holtzclaw, and Floyd, and Johnny. And in that one just arriving over there is my old Carlsbad fellow pilot, Rick Cooney, meeting me as scheduled over the coast of Japan. We didn't know about this meeting then. It's hard to picture these ordinary "good ole" American boys flying these complicated machines which a few years ago were unknown. Even the twin-engined airliners looked big to us years ago as we watched them fly overhead wonderingly. They seemed huge. Now we fly the biggest four-engined plane in the world as a routine job, and we're far from our home country in a place in which we never expected to be. But here we are and there they are!

A little dot in the distance to the north is diving and zooming about a formation as it goes in to the target -- looks like he's playing from here, but he's not, and we don't want him around her, at least for a few minutes. While we're assembling we're mighty vulnerable. We haven't any concentrated fire-power. In fact, we might even shoot toward each other if a fighter mixes us up.

More of the Squadron show up. We tack onto No. 7, just so we'll be together when the assembly is made. Pete will lead "C" flight and "Miss A." the "B" flight. Other planes, seeing two planes together, are closing in on us. Bassett takes Pete's left wing and another Group's plane, W10 by number, is on Pete's right wing. Evidently he missed his own formation. "No. 16 pulling up," George calls, and we see Ramsey, the leader, come inside of us with two planes on his right. Pete crosses above him until he's on the left, and we slide between the two planes beside Ramsey. They are Cooney and Schwager. We have a flight together now -- the semblance of a formation.

Jake's on the gunsight and talking to Jonesy about the control of the forward turrets. Dick, Charlie, and George are in their positions. "Here's some trouble," shouts Bill, and we see a fighter coming at our skeleton formation head-on. He must think we're a juicy plum. His guns spit and I can see the little red flames dance on the business end of the guns. The planes close up quickly. Jordan, in No. 2, who bore the brunt of the fighter's attack, comes from behind and below and slides into position beside Ramsey. We bring the flight in close again after sliding out to let Jordan into position and head for the target. Now the lead flight is together with Boynton on Ramsey's left in No. 1. From our rear another three plane flight pulls up to fill in the diamond position. The gunners call out planes Nos. 5, 8, and 13. That's Maki, Meadows, and Hume.

The formation closes together. We're on the right so I fly and Higgy takes care of domestic affairs such as checking the crew and preparing for the bomb run. "We'll turn at Lake Biwa," Bill reminds me, and I nod, always watching the lead flight. "About two minutes," he adds. In order to make it easy for the wing planes of the flight, and Snyder, who is the No. 4 spot now, I hold the flight high enough so that we can over-run the lead flight without danger, and slide wide or close laterally. Instead of changing the power we slide out slightly or climb slightly until we have the power setting that matches the lead plane. This helps the fuel consumption for us all in the flight. In this way we hold constant power and yet stay in close.

By the time we reach Lake Biwa we have settled down with little variation of position. We begin the turn and then head for Nagoya, straight ahead. There's heavy traffic here. Ahead we see two formations at different places on the bomb run. Judging from the smoke that's pyramiding over the target, it's evident that many others have just bombed and departed. The 73rd Wing must be off the target by this time -- the smoke ascends to our altitude. Our aiming point is to the left of the smoke and the aiming points of the earlier formations. There is no flak in evidence as yet. Where are the fighters? Bombing them with incendiaries by daylight should stir them to feverish activity. Bill keeps telling me our approximate position on the run so that I know what to expect and can anticipate the power changes and change of course. Meanwhile he has opened the bomb doors together with the deputy leader. All the planes' doors are open now and they are ready to let loose the load. Still no fighters. "Bombs away!" Jake shouts, seeing the bombs cascading from the other planes. For a few seconds it looks like an endless supply of bombs coming from the twin bays of each plane. This is a bad day for Nagoya.

"Flak at 12," Jake reports, and the gunners begin to call out the flak, but it's meager and inaccurate. Probably the other formations just ahead have stretched the defenses already. The Japs must be very upset to let us come over Nagoya at medium altitude with no more resistance than this. We see fighters buzzing about two other formations but they do not approach us. Maybe the tight pattern we are flying, with our guns overlapping in concentrated fields of fire scares them away. The other formations are not flying so close together. The doors are closed and the power reduced while we withdraw at 200 mph. Down below I see the east coast of the Bay where we had so much excitement the night our electrical equipment fouled up eleven missions ago. There appears to be some reclaimed land in the bay and an airfield on it. There are barrage balloons located there, the gunners report, but we can't see what it is they're protecting. I call the other planes of the flight and learn that everyone is all right. Pete is doing the same. We both tell Ray that everyone appears to be in good condition for the trip home, so far as we know. While Bill takes the controls I write two post cards while sitting over Nagoya Bay, one to the folks and one to Peel. Maybe they'll enjoy the association of ideas. Probably it will scare them more than anything, but censorship won't permit anything of interest.

As we were briefed, we start out by flights, but soon the flights break up. The planes are low on gas and feel their cruise control is more economical on fuel when they do their own navigation instead of conforming with someone else's navigation. We apparently do not get quite the speed the others get on their economical setting, so we drop behind. We are flying below the suggested power in order to make up an earlier loss. We're doing all right, Nick figures, and we'll stay on the cautious side. Oddly enough it's at this point that Squeesix 10, the stranger in the formation, pulls away and leaves everyone behind. He must have a lot of fuel to burn to go that fast on the return, or perhaps he wants to be the first to arrive at Iwo and avoid the long delay while trying to land.

Many are in for a bad surprise we find when we reach the vicinity of Iwo, for Iwo is "socked in" -- clouds right down to the ground with reduced visibility. In fact, to listen to the talk, it must be so bad you can't see your hand in front of your face. That's going to make it tough on some of the boys. "They're using 'darky'," Bill says after listening in on the VHF conversation between the planes and the Tower. That must be a mess down there now, with an unknown number of planes circling the field, unable to see the others about them, and unable to get clearance to land. Some planes are getting in, those with the priority of feathered engines, battle damage, or wounded men aboard. Those landing are using the new GCA, the "Ground Controlled Approach", or "darky", for short. Through the use of radar apparatus that plots the position of the plane on a screen with relation to the runway, the planes are instructed as to what turns to make and are actually guided onto the end of the runway by those on the ground. The instruction consists of course corrections until the plane is lined up with the runway, and then of further instructions that tell the pilot to gain or lose altitude so that he is kept on a glide path coming in -- a path that will put him on the end of the runway where he can see the runway lights. It's a wonderful system. It must be a strain to use it, however, since the pilots and crew coming in cannot see a thing and must rely on ground information, and many of those coming in have plane trouble that make it tougher on them.   500 foot Mt. Suribachi on the southern tip of the island is always a threat, too.

There are a number of planes in the Iwo area now, waiting to land, but the Tower cannot handle them, and they are told to go on to base -- even some of those that are low on fuel. We hear several Squeesix planes call in.   Evidently another Group is having fuel trouble all the way around today.   Nick and Bill check and double-check the fuel and we are on the ragged edge, but decide it's worth the risk to try to make base, and considering the mess at Iwo there's little choice.

So we continue on south.   Hal works on the navigation so that we won't waste any distance by straying from the bee-line course to Tinian. Standing by on VHF I listen to the talk of the planes in the Iwo area and those who expect to have fuel trouble. Someone is going to be ditching -- someone who's taken the gamble on making Saipan or Tinian -- it seems apparent.   South of Iwo we intercept a call from Cooney, Daredevil 6, to any plane in the vicinity. His voice is loud and clear, so he's nearby. We try to locate him. "What's the trouble, Rick?" I inquire. "We're getting pretty low on fuel -- we'd like a buddy," he answers. "We must be near to each other, you're loud and clear. See any other planes near you?" I ask, thinking that the relationship of planes he describes might be the same that we see. "We have a plane at about 7," he explains. "Well, we have a plane at 1, maybe that's you. Wiggle your wings," I suggest. We watch the plane ahead of us, but it remains level. "Well?" "Did you see us roll?" "No, we didn't." So I ask him for his estimated fuel remaining. "We've got enough for another hour and three quarters, we figure," he says. So I check with Hal and inform Rick that according to our navigation we are only 180 miles from Base and that should take him home all right. He signs off with "O.K., see you later."

Now another plane chimes in, Squeesix 10. It seems that he's out of fuel and expects to ditch in 15 minutes.   After several minutes pass we hear his message "97 Floy-floy 211." He repeats this several times. This gives us his position, where he expects to ditch. Floy-floy is the code word for Pagan Island, the reference point, and he is 97 miles from this Island on a heading of 211 degrees. The bearing is given from him to the reference point. Hal does some quick figuring with relation to our position and we let down, proceeding on a heading that is ahead and to the left in order to be present at the scene, if we can. Now we hear the same voice singing the Air Corps song until abruptly ceasing. This is a heck of a time to be singing.   Other, too, are in trouble and need the emergency radio to get their messages through to the rescue agencies.

We circle the area which we believe to be the position given but no sign of a plane in distress. The low clouds that surround us hinder visibility. We proceed on home. We are low on fuel ourselves, and our ditching won't help anyone else. Thirty minutes later we are 25 miles from Base when we see some surface craft ahead. We head for them. "Somebody's ditched," Jake reports, squinting ahead. We see the tail surfaces of a plane sticking at an angle from the water. It's a B-29. The surface craft is headed for it. Now we see two yellow life rafts with men in each. The boat has already gotten some of the survivors. We fly low over the boat and circle the life rafts. The men look up and wave. We count noses but aren't sure how many there are. The front part of the plane has sunk, only the tail is still afloat, and it appears to be settling. By the markings we see that it's a Saipan plane of the 73rd Wing, not the plane we heard. Tough they couldn't have stretched it any further, just 25 miles from their field, after a 3000 mile flight.

We head for home. They're all taken care of. In a short time there is Tinian, dead ahead. Our fuel is near the bottom, but none of the engines has coughed. We make the straight-in approach instead of circling the field, and land uneventfully. The firm coral of Tinian is most welcome, and the ground crew is a sight for sore eyes. We joke and kid with the fellows while we unload our gear and put it in the truck. Then up to the area and to the interrogation. We report the ditching message and the ditched plane, but they have heard of these already. In fact, they told us that Squeesix 10's ditching was not witnessed, and that it was the pilot singing as they ditched, monopolizing the radio when there were others in trouble, too. He's in the dog house, even though he was in trouble. Maybe these men will be located tomorrow and picked up.

It's odd how fate twists circumstances. This mission, with a fuel reserve, Iwo was closed in by bad weather when the forecast said it would be all right, and planes ditched. Last mission, without a fuel reserve, Iwo was open for traffic when the forecast said it would be closed, and the planes got by without ditching. We learn further, at the interrogation, that Jordan's bombardier, Clint Wride, received a hand injury during the fighter attack at the assembly, while Jordan was coming up on our inside to get into position. Again we know that we were extremely lucky.

Of the 524 planes that participated in the raid (79 of our Wing), 10 aircraft were lost and 64 damaged by fighter flak. Of the personnel involved 51 men are missing, 8 known killed and 12 injured.

Thank you, Lord. We appreciate the safe passage and hope to merit continued trips, doing our job as best we know how. I offer a prayer in my own fashion, knowing that others are doing the same. Now we have 17 behind us and 255:30 hours.

Chapter 24 Nagoya

May 16-17, 1945 – No. 18

"What a Send Off"

On May 15th a scheduled mission is canceled and the pace of the second "blitz" slackens. We stroll back to our quarters and continue the reading, writing home, sleeping, and other activities that fill up our spare time. The usual bull sessions gather at the entrance to the Mess Hall before chow time, on the porches of the Quonsets, and around the wooden pyramidal buildings in which the ground officers live.

The evening of the 15th finds many of us chatting behind Ben Lay's quarters, a group including the Docs, Ben, Bob Hall, Srebro, Cooney, Mutch, and others who drift by. Ray Ramsey, seeing the group at a distance, refers laughingly to our group friction -- "O.K., break it up. You're not allowed to gang up -- looks like mutiny." We laugh and talk about the missions, home, war's end, if and when, all acting as amateur news analysts, and all handicapped by being too close to the scene of activities. All we can really see are these drab surroundings, as though our world has narrowed down, condensing us more and more into this small area. We fly thousands of miles, yet rarely stray out of this living area when on the ground. There are the same faces, the general routine, the same corny jokes. "How" is the standard greeting. Comments include: "Let's face it -- the Army won't support you all your life." "You're going to be forced to go home one of these days!" "Me go home? Why, I like it here!" "Who, me?" This accompanied by fits and starts: "There's nothing wrong with me!" "Better see the Doc, you've got it bad."

The same disappointments face all of us concerning certain of our Superiors. But through it all the combat crews and various ground personnel of the Squadron have a terrific team spirit. It opens to include some of the Superiors who are liked. It closes tight against those who are obviously unfair, rank conscious, or making things tougher than they need to be. The team spirit camaraderie, enjoyment of each other's company, seen and felt within the Squadron is a wonderful thing. In our Group it has been intensified, the Squadron members have drawn within themselves because of the dislike for men who have proven themselves unfair, unfriendly, and incompetent while administering their authoritative Group positions. Long before we left the States the same trouble caused us to laughingly call ourselves the "fighting Squadron" as we faced the same disappointments and unfairness at the hands of a few top men in the Group. All of us have tried, then and now, to do what we can to correct the situation for the betterment and safety of the combat crews whose lives are at stake. We have succeeded, somewhat, in having several incompetent men removed and in clearing a fellow pilot of an unjust charge. But where you succeed in this respect, in the Army you fail. We have incurred the enmity of those commanding us and have made it tougher on ourselves in many ways, beyond the personal and public reprimands. But respect for ourselves and our crews would permit no less. We had to take a stand. But so long as the same Commanding Officer remains, things cannot improve since he colors the entire activity and surrounds himself with a certain type of men.

The schedule for the next mission has a large number of crews listed, most of the planes are ready to fly. Ramsey, Jordan, Fortune, Boynton, Maki, Alger, Schwager, Snyder, Meadows, Bassett, Hume, Cooney -- these are the crews going. The briefing begins with the usual pep talk by the Commanding Officer. We are now so suspicious of certain of our "Superiors" that we scrutinize and weigh everything that is told to us. He begins, "We're out to knock the Japs out of the war." (Wasn't that our aim all along?) "This attack will be the largest yet." (Our forces are steadily growing out here.) "We're going to continue to knock out the Jap towns and by this method get the war over with. There will be a thermal, so just barrel right on through. We of the Sixth don't turn back at the target." Does he think we would? Why must he make remarks like these? There are some things in life that need not be mentioned for their very obvious nature. His talk has given us little except to reawaken the resentment.

Now the Operations Officer, in his usual smug, self-important manner, passes along the information that he has read from higher headquarters, that this raid will include all the 21st Bomber Command -- over 500 planes -- all hitting the target within an hour (looks like a possible traffic problem). Pathfinders will be used, sent ahead of the main striking force to light the target, and the other planes will follow flying singly. The pathfinders will hit the target from 0330-0400, while we'll hit from 0410-0440. Additional data is given to us, duplicating what we see on our flimsies.

The Intelligence Officer takes over and says "As a result of this and the other raids on Nagoya this may be the largest city in the world to have been knocked out of the war by bombing in the shortest period of time." He makes the statement with great emphasis and we are impressed. This will be the fourth incendiary raid on Nagoya. Each raid has been designed to hit a particular section and remove that part of the city from any participation in the war. The first two raids burned out the center of the city, the recent raid gutted the north and east. This raid is directed, we see, to the south and east portion of the city. He continues by saying that we must beware of the fighters coming in on our tail. The thermal might release barrage balloons, so keep an eye peeled for them. Also, this is the city of unusual defenses, so be on the lookout for most anything. There are 125 heavy anti-aircraft guns in the area around and in the city. As for the Air-Sea rescue, Hall tells us that there will be 4 subs, 1 destroyer, 1 surface craft, 4 superdumbos, and 2 dumbos. 514 KC will be the frequency for homing on the superdumbos, with call letters SM. Sully, with the weather, points out that Iwo will probably be closed, owing to a cold front that lies just to the north of the island. The planes of the other Groups will each have an assigned altitude, from 10,000 feet to our altitude of 15,000 feet. (We make a note to watch out for those under us.)

We get on the trucks, each carrying an assortment of gear. This time I wear a two-piece G.E. fatigue suit with lots of handy pockets. Equipment carried includes the .45 with a clip on web belt, the .25 automatic, bayonet knife and stiletto, and the sponge cushion from our first plane. The latter goes for reasons of comfort, sentiment, and superstition, but long on the comfort side. At the plane the usual people come by, some wishing us a good trip, and we engage in repartee, but we're fairly busy, not having quite so much time to accomplish the preflight chores. It seems that we have a weight and balance problem again. We are heavier than briefed by almost 2000 lbs., being about 139,000 lbs., but most important, the bombs are again so arranged that we are too nose heavy. There are 19 bombs forward with a weight of 9000 lbs., and 12 aft, weighing 5600 lbs. Well, we've made it before and we'll try it again. Perhaps we should unload several bombs to even it up, but that would mean that many less on the target, and we'd be late for take-off, and even later if they are changed from one bay to the other where they should be. To my complaints in the past the only answer was that all planes are loaded alike and it would take too much time to load them differently. It doesn't do any good to point out that our plane is unusually nose-heavy, and our fuel consumption greater as a result. It's an unnecessary chance that we are compelled to take, but that's just "tough". Our safety, apparently, is not worth the added time (if it would take any extra time, which seems doubtful). That's what they infer, but they don't mean it, I'm sure. There's not time now for any more pros and cons.

Pat says the engines are in A-1 shape and raring to go. We pull the props at 2038, go in the plane at 2045, and start No. 1 engine at 2054. While we are starting No. 2 in our hardstand, facing south, Bill and I look up to see a flame coming from underneath a plane just coming into sight over the hill. "That's not a torching engine," Bill shouts. We lean out of our windows to get a better view, after calling the crew's attention to it. The flame grows. It passes overhead and heads east. Then it begins a left turn with the flame growing and begins to lose altitude. Something's wrong. It continues to turn back toward the field, losing altitude. It looks like it's heading for the control Tower just beyond "A" runway. The dive steepens and it plows into the ground at an angle. Instantly there is a terrific explosion and the plane leaves bright leaping flames as it slide several hundred yards. The flames seem to extend upward 200-300 feet, blending with billowing orange smoke. The entire area is as bright as day. The bombs inside are going off, the orange flame turns to white. The heavy black smoke of the burning oil darkens the sky in contrast to the intense brilliance of the burning bombs and the magnesium in the engine cylinders.

Bill is back in his seat when I slide down from looking through the window. I can see Pat as if it were daylight, standing on the ground. He comes in and we start Nos. 3 and 4. Whose plane was it? Did they get out? What a way to start a mission. The fire is still so bright that we can see inside our cabin easily, even in the darkness of night. We taxi out on time and line up for take-off when our turn comes. Evidently the plane crashed beyond the runways to the north, but it looks very close. We are all shaken, but the old routine stands us in good stead. We go through the various checks and are airborne to the east several minutes later. We turn on the 60 degree heading for the briefed time, then on course for the Empire. Now I switch my Jack-box to VHF and hear Lotus Tower on Tinian, but at first get nothing informative about the crash. As I look back and see Tinian before it disappears behind Saipan, I see a bright series of explosions lighting the sky and clouds. That means another plane is burning and exploding. Meanwhile the Tower is directing other planes to use runway "A". That runway was not to be used this mission, so an accident must have occurred on "C" or "D", the runway that our Group is using now. I offer up a prayer that the fellows get out. The Tower is conversing with a plane in the air, and the plane answers saying, "Yes, there appears to be a plane crashed south of the west field." (The Navy field.) That's on the far side of the Island, not visible from here, so it looks as though a third crashed. A Tower comes in with, "There are survivors in the channel east of the field," and identifies itself as Gardenia Tower (Saipan) talking to Lotus.

What a send-off on a mission, and these are operational losses, before making contact with the enemy. Each of us is engaged with his own thoughts while we go through the routine procedure. We are climbing to the cruising altitude of 10,000 feet. Now we level off and start the gentle dive that cools the engines before we reach and hold 10,000 feet. After a few minutes, in which Bill and I watch closely the airspeed and altitude, it appears that we can't hold the needed 200 mph with the briefed power of 2150 RPM, so we increase the power to 2200. We're digging into our gas reserve already. Bill and Nick are sharing the thought, but there is nothing we can do about it, only to hope that we don't exceed the gas needed to accomplish the trip, or if we do, that Iwo is open for landing. "Going to sweat it out again," Bill says referring to the gas. I nod and we set up the autopilot, having checked the trim.

Recalling the plane we watched crash, the suddenness of those events impresses itself on me. From the first time that we saw the plane with its small flame, until it struck the ground, was less than a minute. Here we are, all of us, theoretically prepared to ditch or bail out at an instant's notice, but we're not. It takes time to recognize trouble, realize whether anything can be done to correct it, if so what, decide whether to abandon ship or not, and then to get out. Most of these things must be done in a few seconds of time, sometimes they can be, but such a series of events ordinarily would come as a surprise, no matter how "ready" we are. Surprise or not, it still takes time to get out, regardless of our careful preparation and drilling in the past, no matter how cleverly it is handled. These accidents, just like all unexpected airborne events, occur despite the best laid plans, and they must be handled by the individuals present. All briefing information in the world won't help when emergencies strike.

We're still using too much fuel. Just one of those bombs would change the balance of the plane, and two would put us close to the best loading condition of the plane, making the aft load 6500 lbs. and the forward 8000 lbs., a spread of only 1500 lbs.

All goes quietly, with catching a nap at one time or another. We arrive at Iwo at 0050. From our altitude we are well above the surface weather that is bothering Iwo. We are able to see the line of clouds, which from above make a sharp line only several miles above Iwo, but which are right on the ground. They extend to the south, a long way beyond Iwo, no doubt. Listening on the VHF a few minutes later I hear Iwo tell a plane that the field is closed. Looks like it's out of the question as an alternate base for us to use.

Leaving Iwo we are aware of a large number of planes about us, more than we've ever seen in the past. Lights dot the sky. When we make a slight change of course it brings lights blinking on several of the nearby planes. We get a kick out of that. It's regular downtown traffic. There's not so much sleeping up here now. Everyone has an eye on his neighbor. Well, that's good. At least they're all awake. Hal gives the crew an ETA for landfall of 0425 and a target time of 0450. After checking the sunset-sunrise chart we see that we'll be there in daylight, not night as briefed, since sunrise is 0450 and daylight begins before the sun appears. Someone planning the mission evidently made a mistake. They wouldn't intentionally put us over the target area in daylight, exposing all the planes flying singly to fighter attacks, surely. Perhaps just a few minutes will make all the difference in getting there ahead of daylight, so we put on extra power to increase our speed, and yet not change the set-up of the mission. We won't arrive ahead of our scheduled time, yet we certainly don't want to arrive during the latter part of it, yet this will cost us extra gas.

The crew members are alerted and we all put on our gear and prepare for enemy territory. Landfall is made at 0417 and we head for Lake Biwa. The gunners are all set, Gabby's on the radar, Al's on the radio and each of us is looking ahead for signs of any activity. Gabby reports that landfall was made at Esu-Saki, as briefed. Our heading is 350 degrees to the Lake. We feel the menace of this land below us, its hostility all in our minds, no doubt. "We're almost over Biwa," Hal reports. "Take a heading of 80 degrees in three minutes." I repeat the figures and at the appointed time turn to the right in a shallow bank until we roll out on the heading for the target. It seems as though we've been over land a long time -- it's a strain to be over this unfriendly territory. We are able to make out the layer of clouds below us, though at what altitude they are we can't determine, nor can we see whether they are solid or broken. Far rather would we be over water with our subs lurking about than over this enemy land. How much longer do we have to go? With a tail wind at this altitude we are actually getting there rather fast, over 330 miles per hour across the ground, but it seems interminable.

Occasional talk on the interphone breaks the silence. "See anything back there?" we inquire from up front. "Not a sign, yet," is the answer. "Searchlights ahead," Jake calls out. We can see the lights hitting the clouds on the underside, but unable to penetrate. The well-defined circle flits about the clouds or remains motionless by turn. There are some more. Looks like polka dots. Farther ahead we see an orange glow in the clouds. Evidently many have been here before us, but most of the smoke apparently is being held low by the clouds.

"Keep a sharp eye to the rear," I caution the gunners. The dawn is breaking and the light in the sky ahead makes the sky behind us look dark and forbidding. I can't help but notice what a setup it would be for a fighter attack. It would be hard for us to see anything to the rear, while we are framed against brightening skies. "See anything, George?" Bill asks. "Not yet," is the answer. We can feel the gunners, quietly alert, as well as Jake in the nose, mothering his sight. There are other B-29s in the area. The gunners call them out occasionally. They know how careful they must be not to fire on any plane until it's positively identified.

"There are no Jap four-engined fighters," as the saying goes. Several times a white light is reported moving through the sky above us, but none comes toward us. Anyone up there could see us with the daylight coming and the exhaust flame belching from the red-hot turbo exhaust. These are easy to see from below. By now our plane should be silhouetted against the eastern sky.

Gabby, on the radar, has located the bridge that is to be our aiming point. Jake checks the bombsight as Hal and Gab by give him the data with which to check it. Gabby and Jake prepare to work together -- this is to be a combined radar-bombsight run. Gabby begins to give Jake "Marks" on the various degrees as sighting angles, beginning with 68, then Gabby strikes a snag. He finds an obviously incorrect figure in the paper work given to him at the briefing that upsets the radar end of the problem, but knowing now that he is only a few seconds from the target and on course, Jake lets them go at the estimated point. The plane climbs, the bombs are away.

It's quite light now. Looking down I can see a break in the clouds. Several buildings or blocks of buildings are blazing and other places are smoldering as though the fire has burned itself out. Evidently some of these were started a long time ago. Dick and Charlie report that they see the light from our bombs as they open and ignite in mid-air. Still no fighters or flak. They just can't find us, and even if their devices are able to locate us, the number of planes over the city at the same time would confuse them. We are able to see other B-29s in the area now, quite clearly. It is light even in the west, daylight certainly is here. Yet we arrived right on time, having to hurry at that in order to make it. Someone was kidding us when they called this a "night" attack.

"Navigator to pilot, turn to a heading of 68 degrees for 4 minutes." I acknowledge by repeating and make our breakaway. We have quite a distance to go to get away from Japan, and the sooner we get out the better. Before long we turn to a southerly heading and are on our way home. Nick is working over the fuel and finally gives his estimate of our remaining gas as 2600 gallons. Bill and he check the figures again and agree that's what the quantity should be. In the light of our past experience, that is enough, so we settle back for a rest. The plane acts like a lady and we arrive in the Iwo area. There we find the weather perfectly clear and no clouds in the vicinity. We are surprised and can't figure what happened to the front with its low clouds -- we'll let the weather man answer that one. Briefing information is anything but infallible.

Hal takes a rest while Jake fills in the navigator's spot. We approach the area where the survivors of the last mission were reported to be. Squeesix 10 survivors have already been rescued, but there were only 6 of the 11 found. We all keep our eyes open, combing the area. We listen to the emergency channel of the VHF and hear occasional routing messages but nothing else. Once we hear the mention of "yellow jackets", which is code for survivors in Mae Wests, but we don't hear the message repeated. In a short time we arrive at Tinian, circle, and come in on "B" runway. As we slow down Jake and Bill point out the ground crew standing on a nearby hill, waving to us. We wave and then taxi to the hardstand.

After a short chat with the boys we load our gear and go to the P.E. room on the way to the area, where we go through the usual routine. After that, sleep before the 1630 critique of the mission. The meeting is disappointing, as usual, with very little learned from the discussion of the Operations Officer. It isn't a discussion -- it's always a lecture. Never learning, I say my piece again, that the plane was improperly loaded and that we had difficulty with our cruise control as a result. The other crew members present agree, but the Operations Officer changes the subject to something else. No doubt the same condition will prevail on the next mission we fly.

After the critique we inquire about the crashes that we saw before leaving on the mission. We learn that the crash on the field was a 58th Wing plane which had just taken off from their field further south on the island, and that the crew members had bailed out. Then our fears are confirmed that another plane had crashed, or ditched rather, out in the Channel. It was not from our Group, and the survivors were rescued, though several men were killed. Another plane, forced to jettison its bombs because of engine trouble, somehow missed the ocean to the west and dropped them on a Seabee camp, but fortunately did not hit anyone -- an amazing coincidence. We learn that of 496 aircraft participating, 18 were forced to go into Iwo for fuel. What would they have done if Iwo had been closed, as the briefed weather information clearly indicated would be the case?

Out of a clear sky, Captain Rudolph, the flight surgeon for the Squadron, tells me that my crew is to go on the three-day rest period. I immediately balk at the short notice, and the lack of consideration shown for our feelings in the matter. The crew members need warning of an impending rest so that they can begin the paper work arrangements that will allow them to visit relatives and friends on the nearby islands, Guam and Saipan, as they'd like to do. And all of us dislike the thought of being cut out of the "blitz" as we were before, and want to stick with our plane, flying it now while it's in good condition. Our Squadron Commanding Officer and Operations Officer, unlike the Group officers, back us up and understand how we feel. We hope that the matter will be taken care of for us, but we're not sure. It seems that we have to fight for anything we get in the Army. However, we have faith in our Squadron officers and think that since it is their affair now, too, we can expect a square deal.

Chapter 25 Hammamatsu (Tokyo)

May 19, 1945 – No. 19

"Secondary Target"

The morning of the 19th we find the list of crews going out on the next mission posted: Holton, Litchfield, Maki, Alger, Lazin, Schwager, Jordan, and Dawson. The target identification is held that afternoon and the briefing at midnight. The briefing begins with two crews jammed together on a single bench, and it's extremely hot. The Commanding Officer gives the usual introductory talk and then the Operations Officer takes over. We listen to the data, evaluating it in terms of our own experience. As we become more skilled through participating in the missions, we see more and more the divergence between many of the things that are told to us and the reality as we experience it. On the first missions we accepted carte blanche the instructions given to us. Now we interpret what is told to us in the light of our experience and hard-gained knowledge.

We have learned within our own Group that what we thought was excusable pride on the part of our Commanding Officer ("we're the best G -- D--- Group ever to come overseas.") is inordinate ambition to make a name for himself. We see this ambition manifest itself. It endangers the crews as the C.O. tries to prove statistically that we have the most outstanding record of any Group. At various times we hear that we've dropped the greatest tonnage of bombs per plane or per Group, kept our planes in the air the most, put in the most combat time per crew, flown the most practice, or lost the fewest men and planes, and so on. Any proven statistical advantage reflects direct credit on the C.O. and that's fine so long as we aren't involved in dangerous situations just to add a few superlatives to the record. The more scared we of the combat crews get, the more humble we feel, and the more we thank the Almighty Power for assistance. We do not feel like boasting of our prowess. We aren't going to quit doing our job because we're scared over the target or on take-off, but we're certainly not going to thumb our nose at our continued good fortune and not render thanks.

Since the Operations Officer patterns himself after the C.O. we have learned to weigh carefully what he says also. In the course of the briefing the C.O. points out, "We must go easy on the ground personnel, they are working hard, so we can't load each plane according to the individual specifications." The various crews take this stoically, but are thinking just as we are. We know the ground crews are busy, but his statement means simply that the combat crew must fly the plane with an unfavorable balance factor and endanger the entire crew and the plane. Perhaps that's what they mean by "expendable." We get the facts and then go to our planes, making jokes of our disgust over parts of the briefing.

Pat and the boys say the plane is ready to go. We make the usual preflight checks. The bombs are loaded, 500-lb. General Purpose bombs, 14 in the forward bay and 4 in the aft. We have a fuel tank in the aft bay in addition. On figuring the weight and balance we find that this time we have a good balance factor. Evidently something caused the change to be made. It's too much to expect that our criticism did any good. Anyhow, we have sensible load condition now.

I'll try to explain the center of gravity and balance of a plane. The plane in flight has the weight distributed evenly, that is, the overall weight may be considered as being equally distributed fore and aft in relation to the wing. The wing does the work of lifting the weight, together with the engines which supply the thrust. Therefore the weight must be considered in relation to the wing. Tests have shown that the best center of gravity of a plane may be found between 18 and 32% of the mean aerodynamic chord (M. A. C.). This time our M. A. C. is 27%, which is better than the usual nose-heavy condition of 24% or less. The M. A. C. may be found halfway out the wing, being an average of all the chords of the wing. The chord itself is represented as the part of the wing extending along a straight line from the leading edge to the aft edge of the wing. In the B-29, we are told, the percentage of the M. A. C. within which the weight must be balanced is 24% to 32%, but actually, when heavily loaded, it is important to strike a better average than the extremes. The extreme of 24% represents nose-heaviness, while 31% is tail heavy.

Another factor enters when considering the B-29 as compared to other aircraft, that is the fact that the B-29 has a "step" characteristic, which means that it flies "tail-high" when getting its best speed for the power being used. This means that a better loading condition is found when the weight is placed further forward than exact center. It aids the plane in maintaining the "step" attitude. But we have found that this is not true to the extent that the Group Officials think. For our particular airplane the optimum load condition is not around 24%, but more nearly 26-27%. We have found this to be true by trial and error. On some missions, when the other planes seemed to make out all right, we had great difficulty trimming the plane and reducing power when the paperwork called for it.

"Trimming" the plane is accomplished by moving the little tabs on the control surfaces. These tabs look like miniature control surfaces on the control on which they are located. We move them by wheels located in the cabin. For example, when we go faster the tail has a tendency to rise, causing the nose to go down, and this requires back pressure on the control pedestal. This would become tiring if there were not some way of removing this pressure, so the tabs are provided as a means of recentering the elevator. Once again the pressure is gone and the tab is trimmed for a level flight. Thus the strain is removed for the pilot.

When the plane is loaded improperly in any one of the two axes, that is on the fore and aft side or on the wing to wing side, the tabs are used to compensate for this condition. If there is more weight on the right, then the aileron tab is used to pick up the right wing, which has the tendency to drop. The rudder being closely related to the wing must be used, too. All this means that if the plane is incorrectly loaded, the tabs must be used excessively to restore the control balance of the plane, and the tabs set greater "drag" in the slipstream of the plane. The plane becomes less streamlined and more power is needed to maintain the flight, so the entire weight and balance problem resolves itself into the amount of fuel used, because of the increased power needed when the weight is improperly placed.

Since our missions are limited in duration by the amount of fuel carried, and each trip is a cruise control problem, the weight and balance becomes very important. So it is that we have become concerned about the weight and balance, for we have found that our plane is more nose-heavy, and heavier overall, than the other planes, and so, when loaded, will not have the same range as the others unless the load is placed to the best advantage in accordance with the characteristics of our individual plane. This mission is the first in which the balance of our plane has been considered. We have only an additional 1000 lbs. in the forward bay as compared to spreads of over 4000 lbs. in the past. Something has caused the authorities to change this loading condition. It might not have been our complaining, but whatever the cause, they obviously have recognized and corrected the mistake after so many repetitions of it in the past.

Before getting into the plane we have the usual visitors. Now we get in, go through our various check lists, and start the engines. We taxi in turn at 0428. At the east end of the runways (we're taking off to the west today) we are flagged onto "A" runway. There are many delays as we move slowly along, waiting our turn. Must be a tie-up. At "A" runway we sit for half an hour before we learn over the radio that a plane has ditched off the end of the runway. It must be a plane from our Group, since they've been taking off, and we figure it must be Jordan.

We are now directed to taxi to "B" runway and wait our turn there. Pete, in No. 7, lines up and is flagged off. We are enveloped in a cloud of coral dust as he starts. As the dust clears away we see that he is turning off the runway. Must have trouble, so we figure that he'll not make it. Boynton takes off and now we get the green light as the all-clear signal comes from the other end. We run up the engines, release the brakes, and apply full power. It's now 0524. No. 1, 2, and 3 engines kick slightly against my hands (the throttles) but I'm sure that it is only the plugs that are a little fouled, but otherwise all right. Long periods of idling on the ground usually cause this in the B-29. The end of the 8000 foot runway is coming all too soon. Going west, we are going slightly down hill. Also, we have a tail-wind. It gives us a good ground speed, but not airspeed, and the latter is what makes the plane fly. Bill keeps calling out the speeds, and when we reach 125 we reach the end of the runway. As Nick puts it, "We didn't take off, we just ran out of runway." The end markers of the runway flash by. The trees and shrubs are almost brushing our wheels as they slowly retract. The engines sound all right and the mushing turns into lift and the plane begins to pick up speed.

Jonesy calls out, "There's a plane hanging off the end of "C" runway." I glance over and see the B-29 with its nose over the cliff and its tail almost vertical in the air. About a quarter of a mile out to sea I look over to the left and see a life-raft, but no one in it. The crew members look for the ditched crew, but don't see them. It's almost dawn now. What a grim send-off.

"Miss A. – '62" is purring along now and we turn on course, climbing. Two planes ahead of us are having trouble. First one and then the other drops its bombs in a long string and turns around toward Base. Now, on the VHF, I hear the Tower call Condor Base, which is the home of Saipan Air-Sea rescue, and inquire about the ditched plane. It seems that no one has spotted the survivors or knows what plane it was. Later an answer comes back that six survivors have been rescued, two very seriously injured. I had previously reported the location of the life raft. Perhaps that helped them locate the survivors. But Condor did not tell Lotus what plane it was, so we figure it was one of ours.

We are to continue to fly 7000 feet to Nishimo-shima, well on the other side of Iwo, and assemble, then continue for the several hundred miles in loose formation to the Mainland. We level off and note that the plane handles better and trims up nicely. The load condition is better. Bill takes a nap while Nick, Hal, Al and I take some Benzedrine. After a while we fly through the front that Sully mentioned. It is only 10 miles through it and it is not very turbulent. The rain in the cloud is very heavy. Abreast of Iwo, at 0828, we hear the fighters taking off, calling to the Tower as "shadows". Our ETA for the assembly is 0930. Having taken off late we are carrying more speed than briefed in order to make the assembly line on time. Our briefed arrival time is 0848 and departure 0922, after several other formations have formed. The others were late in starting, too, so we don't try to make the briefed time good, but let the 0939 time stand.

On arriving, we see four other planes circling. Calling Litchfield in No. 2, whom we hear, we tell him that we'll take the lead of "B" flight. Jordan calls to say that he'll take the deputy. All of us are still a ways out. Within a few minutes, however, we join up and have a formation of six planes. Litch is leading with Jordan on his right wing. We are greatly relieved to find it wasn't Jordan who ditched -- but who was it? We are leading "B" flight, with Lazin and Schwager on the wings and Maki in the diamond. We start for the Beyonaiso rocks, the reassembly point. Putting on the autopilot, we fly very loose -- several hundred yards from Jordan. The other planes spread out likewise. Perhaps those who haven't shown up will join us up at the line as they overtake us. There are no other squadrons in sight, as briefed, but we are not surprised. We were delayed, and they've probably gone one. Just another example of how the missions change from the briefed plan. The crews must make decisions continually, as new circumstances arise. No amount of briefing can do it for us.

Reviewing the flimsies, I see that we are to fly up "Flak Alley", the course on which planes were so badly shot up before. Landfall will be made at Numazu and the course goes straight to the Tachikawa Airplane Factory, the Wright Field of Japan. On the way, Fuji is just to the left and Yokohama to the right. The secondary target is Hamamatsu.

At the Beyonaiso rocks, 200 miles south of Japan, Holton appears and takes the lead, Litchfield dropping back on his left wing. Now we have seven planes. Now Dawson joins us and we head for the target. Despite the briefed weather given to us as being clear at the target, we see clouds ahead. As we approach we see that the clouds extend up above us. Holton starts to climb and we tag along. When we get to the bombing altitude of 18,000 feet we go into the clouds and lose sight of each other. We are in loose formation, so we hold the same heading and speed. For quite some time we lose sight of Jordan, then break into the clear in time to prevent getting too close to him. From here on it appears that we are hitting the tops, though the clouds are thick beneath us and we're still climbing. At 25,000 feet we level off. Al, standing by on the radio, reports that he has just intercepted a message, a strike report of another Squadron, which said that the target was completely "socked in".

    The crew members are in their equipment and at their stations when we start the bomb run, but it becomes apparent that the target is solidly covered with clouds, so we go on to the secondary target and the leader begins the radar run. At this altitude we are having trouble staying with the others without drawing excessively high powers, but we "pour the coal" to her and close in the flight in preparation for a tight bomb pattern. The leader's doors come open. Our wing planes are in close now, so we're all set. Evidently the Jap fighters are engaged elsewhere -- they're not here. We don't see any flak bursts in the area, either. It's almost too good to be true. Below us the impenetrable misty clouds cut off all vision. We are quite alone up here. The deputy's doors come open and we open ours. The planes are ready to unload now. Bill has the release. "There they go!" chorus Jake and I as we lead the flight dropping its bombs. Our plane jumps, released from its load, and we begin the turn toward home. Dick and Al report the bombs are gone. Hal gives bombing time as 1252. George says from the tail, "Looks like nobody home today," and we leave the land of the rising sun.

    The planes widen out one from another. We decide to stay at 22,000 feet and get the benefit from the altitude on our speed. Holton and Schwager are staying at this altitude, too, so we stay within sight of each other. We leave the clouds behind shortly after leaving the coast and it's clear beneath us. Looking down we see a foaming streak in the water. Through the binoculars we see it's a surfaced sub, heading full speed to the ENE. It's evident that it's going at a great speed, judging from the broad, foaming wake. We know it's one of ours, since our subs dominate this area, but why the hurry? Perhaps it's going to rescue someone. Looks like it. Though we are only 175 mph on the airspeed meter, Hal informs us that we are going 314 mph across the surface, rolling right along, so we hold to our decision to stay at this altitude.

    Now we hear a commotion on the VHF, and Al calls our attention to it. There's a plane in trouble. It's Daredevil 6 -- that's Dawson! It seems that his No. 3 engine won't feather and is vibrating severely, it's catching fire and is vibrating the whole plane. They are preparing to bail out. We have trouble hearing the messages for there are so many disturbances on the air. Most of the talk is inconsequential with a lot of uhs, ands, wells, and buts, and here's Rocky, trying to get a message through, in emergency. Other planes are calling him and trying to help him. "The fire's out, we're going to stick with the plane a bit," we hear. Then "The plane's still vibrating so bad we don't know if it'll make it, might vibrate apart at this rate." We follow the conversation and now are relieved to hear that he has made it into Iwo.

After this another message of a plane in trouble comes through. It seems that a couple of engines are out and the landing gear damaged, so the crew bails out over Iwo. All traffic on the field is suspended until the men are safely on the ground. We are unable to see Iwo, and since our fuel seems adequate we go on to Tinian. We stay at altitude and let down 100 miles out, making the entire trip in 13 hours, the fastest we've ever made the round trip, and we have fuel to spare, apparently. Several broadcasts from the States, which Al gets on his Laison set, tell of this mission in great detail. We get a laugh over the representation of Hamamatsu as a strategic target, as though we were really "gunning" for it, instead of its being a "target of last resort".

We land uneventfully and go to the parking area. There we greet the boys and leave "Miss A. – '62" in their care. The plane appears to be in good shape, though the slow take-off had us scared. At the interrogation we learn that it was not a 6th Group plane that had ditched at take-off. We learn that of the 287 planes participating, 20 landed at Iwo, 3 were lost, and 1 ditched. Dawson left his plane at Iwo and the crew flew to Tinian with someone else.

After the critique of the mission the morale of the men is lower than ever. The Commanding Officer, who thinks that Dawson didn't send his distress messages properly, is giving Dawson and all of us a reprimand. He goes further to tell us that he's out to burn someone -- anyone who steps out of line. He makes no effort to give anybody credit for doing the job. Our thoughts of him and his threats do not bear repeating. Well do we remember that after we had cleared the pilot whom he unjustly accused, that he boasted to us he had just "evaluated" a man and would do the same to any one of us who might step out of line. We all knew that the pilot concerned had been cleared scot free and the C.O. proven to be wrong. He isn't scaring us when he threatens, but just making an unhappy situation worse.

Chapter 26 Tokyo

May 26, 1945 – Aborted Mission

"Miss America – '62 Quits"

We are on a DNIF status (duty not involving flying), partaking of the three day rest vacation, when the next mission goes out. Those flying are Jordan, Holton, Litchfield, Schad, Maki, Snyder, Parks, Meadows, Ramsey, Fortune, Lazin, and Boynton. Somehow we are just as glad not to be going on this one. Three of our plane's engines have close to 400 hours time on them and need some attention. "Miss A. '62" is getting tired, judging from the slow take-offs and cruising performance, and the crew is slowing down, too. There is no stimulus from the supervisory personnel. Our enthusiasm, or "eagerness" as the Army calls it, is worn down by the Group's constant internal dissension. Somehow the crews have always thought the mistakes and laughable incompetencies were just temporary and would change the next day, or the next mission, but now, after so long a time, it begins to look hopeless. Regardless of the competency up top, our Group keeps trying to put the left foot in the right shoe, and we feel the pinch. It is not the strain of combat that is further segregating the officers, men, ground and flight personnel. The continual conflict within the ranks is spoiling the wonderful spirit which everyone had at one time, facing a common foe with a common job to do. We know now how that spirit can be spoiled by one or more incompetent men in the top jobs of the Group.

The planes return from Tokyo, the target, and we learn that Fate, or Lady Luck, has laid a heavy hand on us. Two of the twelve do not return, John Boynton's crew and Joe Snyder's crew. Park's copilot, a new man to the Squadron, was killed outright over the target, when an attacking fighter angled a 20-millimeter shell though the cabin. On the return they were forced to land at Iwo with engine trouble and the plane crashed, breaking into three pieces, though somehow they got out. Maki managed to get to Iwo and crash-land. Fortune did the same, and he, too, lost a man. The other planes came back with many flak holes in them. It was as though the Japs were waiting for them. The 15,000 foot medium altitude in daylight made it ideal for their flak batteries. The renowned luck of our Group has vanished, so far as it pertains to our Squadron. Many of the other Groups did not have an unusually hard time. Ours just seemed to hit the tough going, as before we managed to dodge it. Again we have lost our hut mates. Joe Snyder and his officers, like Preston's crew before him, are gone, although we were not so close to these men as we were to Pres, Don, Lloyd, and Al. We wonder grimly if we should put up a Motel sign informing would-be tenants, "For Transients Only."

Shortly thereafter the Squadron Operations Officer, a good man, says he's thinking of scheduling us on a mission in our plane. I suggest that the plane should be getting the four-hundred hour inspection now because it's been losing power on take-off. After the last mission we checked to see at what speed other planes took off, and learned that each had at least 135 to 140, and we barely had 125. I point these things out and he counters with, "If we change the engines now you'll be taking off with three new ones later, and that's a chance, too.

Further, if you don't want to fly your own plane, then you'll be scheduled in someone else's." That does it. We'd rather fly in ours, I admit, but the plane should be getting the four-hundred hour inspection instead of flying. So we are scheduled to fly in "Miss A. '62" again. Now our plane has over 400 hours on the three original engines that remain. The standards were recently extended to permit this. Ordinarily engines were changed, regardless of their condition, at 300 hours. Evidently the strikes back home in those plants making B-29 engines are taking effect our here now. I know that our engines are losing power, witness the take-off, but there doesn't seem to be any choice. Nor do we feel any better when we see the briefed plans for the mission.

The target will be Tokyo and the course into the target, too, will be the same as that of the last disastrous mission. Of the 17 crews lost on the last mission, 2 were from our Squadron. Yet here we are to go out again on the same axis of attack, just as though the losses are negligible, as though it isn't necessary to plan the smartest axis of attack, where the flak and fighters will not be concentrated. Of course, when we try to reason it out we can't know all the factors that go into planning the mission, but it's hard for us to lose our friends and then sit quiet, unprotesting or unquestioning, when we see what appears to be a lack of care in the preparation of the mission. It is reminiscent of the time we were ordered to bomb in the sun, or those times, early in the game, when the planes were sent over the target, upwind, to hang there and be shot down. To us it seems that now, when we go in, the Japs know exactly where we'll strike because we're playing their game, the one they understand. A game in which we don't use the American horse sense that in the past has baffled and outwitted them.

In the first "blitz" we came in at unusual altitudes, changed the axis of attack from mission to mission, and kept them generally confused. Now we come in on the same heading, flying right over all the gun positions they've placed from our past attacks, flying the same course again -- the way they'd do it. In the past there have been indications of good homework by the planners. The changes from mission to mission fooled the Japs. Now the returning planes report that the Japs even have a battery of guns on Mt. Fuji to shoot at us along this path. Why isn't the heading varied, making the attack from the north or northwest? Anything to vary the routine. We're losing crews that might be saved. Perhaps, now that this theater is in the lime-light of the public eye, the missions can be less carefully planned, substituting quantity for quality. Possibly these questioning thoughts which the men have now are the result of not being told the situation. The Government doesn't tell the citizens what it's doing in war time, why should the Army tell us? We don't mind being bold, aggressive, brave, and all the rest, but this mission's plan looks foolhardy. This, in addition to the antagonism within the Group, has the morale of the men mighty low. It doesn't do any good to "gripe" any more.

It seems that this mission is designed again to knock out Tokyo. Rodenhouse takes over temporarily as Operations Officer and does a good job. What a change from the man who has been doing that job. We appreciate his serious, direct treatment of the mission, as though he's trying to protect us with information. He knows the dangers and how to handle the B-29. For the first time an experienced crew leader has a Group job. Ironically enough, it's because the former Operations Officer has been promoted to Deputy Group Commander, replacing the West Pointer we all liked. We suspect he was "removed" by the C.O. Why, we can only guess.

It seems that 600 planes will participate in this mission. Altitude out will be 8000 feet to Iwo, then to Oma-zaki, where landfall will be made. The bomb run will be at 79 degrees, the breakaway is to the northeast, and the trip home will be at 20,000 feet. The Intelligence Officer gives us some information on the strategic importance of the raid. Tokyo, it seems, has 15% of the labor personnel, which is equivalent to 15 German cities. The area to be bombed holds the R. R. Station, a telephone exchange, stockyards, supply depots, and the like. With pointer in hand, he goes on to intone how the various targets will stand out, and then pauses. Bill, looking at a flimsy, thoughtlessly mutters, "We'll stand out," and brings down the house. In the silence of the Major's weighty pause Bill's voice carries unexpectedly. Even the Major smiles as the fellows laugh and let off steam.

Down at the line we go through the usual checks of the equipment. We are resigned to the mission and the fellows joke about the expected flak and fighters. "Looks like we'll see some excitement, Nick," someone suggests. "I don't want any excitement, no sir, I got all I want at Shimonoseki! Why, they even threw up the kitchen sink! I saw Geisha girls go by with cook stoves and everything. We saw everything that night, and lots of things that weren't there, too, probably," Nick answers. Guess we all feel that way. Pete Harder comes by and takes our picture beside the plane. It should be a good picture, with full crew present.

We taxi out, everything under control. The scanners report that the bomb bay doors are open, which is not according to plan. The switch doesn't raise them, so Jake goes aft and tries to get them up. We are not particularly alarmed, since it's happened before. The catch on the doors is worn. We continue taxiing while others outside signal us, trying to tell us the doors are open, and we confuse the situation further by nodding and waving, so they think we're waving farewell to them. After several vain efforts to close the doors we try to taxi back by way of another Group's taxiway. As luck would have it, we meet one of their planes head-on, so we must turn around and retrace our course back to the service Apron. There a horde of specialists rush out to fix the trouble. They close the doors and tell us we're O.K., so we start out again. The doors drop open. Maintenance personnel see us this time and come out and fix them again. Now we line up for take-off. The other planes have gone on ahead and we're late, so we line up, release our brakes, and start the take-off. All four engines back-fire somewhat but we get 125 mph and are off the end of the runway. No. 4 continues to back-fire and the scanners report black smoke from the exhaust. As we continue to fly level the engines smooth out and the back-firing stops. Our speed for take-off was as bad as ever. Apparently we're not drawing full power, and we're heavy, 137,000 lbs. That's a load, even for good engines.

We settle down for the long run to the Empire. I reflect on the obvious dangers facing us. They seem partly unnecessary this time. It's as though we're thumbing our nose at the Japs telling them to come get us. Guess we're just not heroic. I can think of other ways to accomplish the damage without jeopardizing the crews this way. Obviously our trouble is that we use our heads too much, but that, too, is American. The Americans in the Revolution didn't stand out in the open in colored coats. They got behind trees and they were dressed to blend with the landscape. They used their heads to save their hides.

But the reverie is short lived. Nick calls, "No. 1 back-firing," as we hear the sharp explosions. No one has touched an engine control, it just started to back-fire. Nick tries auto-lean, the auto-rich fuel mixture, then back to auto-lean. We change power and RPMs, but the explosions get louder. "That's pretty violent," says Bill. At first the back-fire was regular, now it's irregular and more frequent. "She's just laying down and dying on us," I think, recalling that these three engines have gone over 400 hours, helping to pull us through the air over 80,000 miles -- a long and honorable service. But now we must do something with old No. 1. The violent back-firing is a sure indication of approaching engine failure, possible even of fire breaking out in the engine. "Let's feather it, Nick," I request. We feather the engine, trim the airplane for three-engine flight, and gingerly turn back towards Base.

In a path of moonlight we jettison the bombs so that we can see that they hit the water. The bombs ignite on impact, since they are fused for 5000 feet and that is our present altitude. We tell Bassett, who is a passenger with us on this mission, that this is the first air abort on our combat record. In fact, it's the first time we've aborted in the B-29 program, including our training program. We all feel that, considering the take-off as well as the past performance, "Miss A. '62" tried to give us warning. We don't like turning back, but tonight, after we're reconciled to it, we don't feel so bad. The plane flies well on three engines and we have no trouble landing. We tell Pat the trouble and fondly pat "Miss A." for protecting us. We are profoundly thankful that the engine didn't fail on take-off.

The next day we go down to the line to welcome the crews back. We are all tense, since something tells us that this was a rough one. Sure enough, Jordan comes in firing red flares -- wounded aboard. We greet them and Milt Garfinkle is carefully lowered. His foot was badly shot. The cabin of the plane is peppered with holes. We learn that a shell hit the engineer's instrument panel, and a control cable was out over the target. The autopilot saved the day, by replacing the severed manual control. Now Cooney comes in with part of the tail shot off and holes all over his plane. They appear serious and shaken. Fox does not return. We hear that Clay and his crew, from the 39th Squadron, bailed out over Iwo Jima. It seems that the Japs were waiting for them as we expected. Yet the element of chance was still there. Litchfield and Holton got through without damage, except a few small holes.

We learn that our plane had a defective valve in the No. 1 engine. The authorities finally decide to change the three engines. "Miss A. '62" will be ready to go again, queenly in her elegance. Between the two missions to Tokyo our Group has changed radically. Both manpower and planes are greatly diminished.

Chapter 27 Osaka

June 1, 1945 – No. 20

"Formation Flying Inside Clouds"

After a lay-off we are scheduled on a mission again. Our plane has three new engines and we have gladly put six house of "slow time" on them in order to break them in gradually in accordance with regulations. No other plane in the Group, so far as we know, built up over 400 hours on engines. Those were all combat hours, too, the most strenuous a plane can undergo, since it is heavily loaded and never spared. Our crew, since the last mission, has had an official rest of three days, an abortion, and an enforced rest of a week, waiting to be rescheduled.

No news has been received concerning John Boynton, Joe Snyder, Don Fox, and their crews. They are presumed lost. Maybe we'll never know what happened to them. We offer up silent prayers that all is for the best and that they'll get though, if still surviving. John's crew was flying old No. 1, their plane, which they acquired when we took No. 11.

Big news has come to us. It is hard to be calm. We are going home! Going home -- just think of it! Back to the U.S.A. It doesn't seem possible. May 27th I am summoned to the Squadron office and our Squadron C.O. informs me that my crew has been selected to go to the "Lead Crew School" in California, provided we want to go. My spinning head is sobered by this thought -- so we have a "choice". A choice in the Army is bad, you can't win. It is hard to be cool and collected now. I inquire, "What do you know about the school?" and learn that there is little known of the school, or what our future would be if we do not go. The Squadron C.O. states that we will have a rest leave attached to it, so that makes it look like a good bet. His personal advice is the old Army doctrine, "Take whatever you can get when you can get it." So it's agreed that I'll let him know our decision that afternoon.

Leaving the building I mull over the possibilities, and share them with Bill, Hal, and Jake, who are nearby. Realizing the importance of this decision, we discuss the possibilities. We are near the end of our combat tour, of 30 or 35 missions, after which we'd be sent home for good, or at least for a few months of instructing other crews before returning for another tour. Perhaps we'd never return again. If we go home now to the school we'd be coming right back afterwards, and perhaps would be required to fly a complete tour of 25 missions again. If we stay her now, at the rate missions are being accomplished, we'd be through within two months, allowing for a routine rest of 2 or 3 weeks in that period. The other crews are now going to Hawaii for their rest, then returning to finish their missions. If we go home we get our rest at home, and then come back to finish up. Further, if we go home there's the possibility we would be kept at home to instruct green crews en route to combat. Maybe the war would end in the meantime and we'd already be in the States. We discuss even the most far-fetched possibilities trying to make sure of our minds before we talk to the enlisted men.

Actually, this calm discussion is no reflection of our inner turmoil, and this one thought, "to go home". We have each already decided, but we behave rationally long after the mind is overthrown. Finally, with restrained grins, we decided that we're for home. Now let's see what the men say! We find them at their Quonset, killing time, and we quietly ask them to come outside. They suspect that we have something weighty to spill. "How would you like to go home?" I can't restrain a grin, thereby giving away my feelings, but they are aware that I'm not kidding, home is too serious a matter for kidding. While they stand dumbfounded I outline the proposition that the Squadron C.O. made and that we must let him know by afternoon.

As soon as they comprehend that we actually have the chance to go home there's but one answer -- "Let's go. I'll have my bag ready in 5 minutes." Dick acts as though he's going to get it. "Have a bag ready? I'm ready right now!" Nick says, in his worn-out khakis. "Let's go!" they all join in the joking. "There's no choice. Let's go." "Why not, here I come!" "George, you going back to the Glovers' Ballroom?" "Where's my hat?" "Hat! I'll go in my drawers!" "Oh man, let's pack."

After several minutes of laughter and chatter the men begin to inquire about the possibilities, just as we had. "Will we come back?" "Will it mean another tour?" "Do we get a rest in the States?" We give them what information we have and promise to talk to the Docs to find out our rest status. But the die is cast, and we know what the men want to do. We are glad they want to go home. We shouldn't be surprised, though, we all think alike. Our choice is bound to be their preference, too. We tell the Squadron C.O. our decision and he says that he thinks it will be a few days yet until the orders come out and we leave. We will be participants in the July class at Muroc, California, and we will have our rest leave at home before reporting at the school. So we leave, hoping that we'll get those orders soon. Every minute gained means time at home, since our rest at home comes before the school on June 29th.

We are still scheduled to fly, even while we are in the position of seeing Utopia just ahead. The Squadron C.O. and the crew all agree to keep it quiet while we continue to fly, and so ease the strain, but words gets around somehow. Various people ask, "Say, what's this I hear about you're going back to the States?" And we reply, "Don't know what you are talking about -- but keep it quiet, will you?" We are quite aware of the mission that faces us. We remember crews that had trouble on the verge of reaching home. The goal is so close now and the strain proportionally greater. We try to ease the situation by thinking that, actually, there is no difference now. Going home has been in our minds all along -- our goal -- only now it's closer. It's closeness shouldn't be bad luck, after all.

So we prepare for the mission in the same old way, but with lighter hearts. We see the crews listed: Jordan, Lazin, Alger, Meadows, Dawson, Litchfield, Ramsey, Hume, and Holton. We know that our plane is ready after the engine changes and the slow time. We broke her in as carefully as we would new rings in the old car at home. During the slow time we swung the compass again, so that it's accurate after the work that might have affected the deviation of the flux-gate compass. We also checked the magnetic compasses.

At the target identification, which is held at 1730 on the 31st, we pour over the photo mosaics, the charts, maps, radar pictures, and the problem of flying the course properly to accomplish the bombing correctly. There is not so much that is new to us now. The mainland and its many hills, rivers, bays, and flak batteries are well known. Jake points out the relationship of Osaka to the surrounding area of the Island of Honshu. It is located in the fourth bay, starting with Tokyo. Looking west from Tokyo Bay we see the next one, Eno Bay, where Numazu is located, the Ise-wan Sea, or Nagoya Bay, and the fourth, further to the west, where Osaka is situated. Osaka is at the northeastern extremity of the Inland Sea. This will be our first time to Osaka, since we had ground trouble with Fortune's plane on the previous attempt, and lost out on the Decoration for participating in the first "blitz", accomplishing only three of the four missions. Bill, Jake, Hal, Gabby and I are present at this meeting, the rest of the crew will be at the general briefing.

The combat crews are sorry to learn officially that the Deputy C.O. has left the Group and is now in Wing Headquarters. It's a big loss to us. We recall with pleasure the contacts we have had with this man. He was a good passenger on our Shimonoseki mission. But more important, he has the respect and regard of the whole Group, officers and men. He is a West Pointer, well-mannered yet forceful. He seems to consider the feelings of those about him, and as a result gets cooperation without threats. He supports the belief that we still hold, that a man can be high ranking and in a commanding position and yet be a good guy. We still think this possible, even in the face of our hardships and disappointments.

At one time, while it was being formed, that man was the Commanding Officer of this Group. We sometimes reminisce as to what it would have been with him at the helm. As it was, he had little actual authority in the Group, since he served as the second in command, under the present Commanding Officer. It's surprising that he has stuck it out this long without requesting transfer, or being removed because of his popularity and his disapproval of the methods of the C.O. As one of the many examples, we well recall the day he publicly congratulated our fine Chaplain, Pat Murphy, at the conclusion of the Sunday Service. On this occasion we were attending service at noontime, under a blazing sun, with a high wind from behind us that prevented our hearing the Chaplain very well, in addition to blasting him with coral dust. He was forced to hold the service in the open air theater instead of the enclosed briefing building -- the usual place -- which was not being used. The C.O. had ordered Pat to do so or else, so Pat tried to carry on outdoors. Finally he gave up and told us (though risking court martial by saying so) that the next time we would hold services elsewhere -- he'd see to that.

As we arose we saw the Deputy C.O. congratulate Pat for his stand, sympathizing with him. The men well know of Pat's unceasing struggle in his effort to combat the C.O.'s well known disinterest in religion, a disinterest which the men do not share. At every service the building or area was packed, with many standing. The men all attended the services when their duties permitted.

The C.O. would arbitrarily call another day of the week Sunday, or would not permit the men to take off from their work, even when possible. Pat continued to battle these difficulties, with the support of the combat crews, though there was little we could do to help except turn out for services whenever and wherever they were held.

The removal of this Deputy C.O. from the Group has resulted in the promotion of the Operations Officer, who is generally disliked. He is now the Deputy C.O., and we note that he and the Commanding Officer make a good (?) pair. Now our former Squadron C.O. is the permanent Operations Officer and conducts the briefings. We like this man, who unlike his predecessor (who received most of his experience in the training command and did not fly on the missions here) is a combat man with 50 combat missions behind him. He has flown here as well during his tour of duty at Guadalcanal. Our new Operations Officer even chats with us, knowing our outlooks, hopes, and disappointments, instead of living apart as do the others. He has the support of the men. It's easy to see that fact through the manner in which the men talk to him and about him.

At the briefing we are attentive and enjoy our new Operation Officer's presentation. We wonder if he will be permitted to keep his present job, or whether he will be transferred out of the Group. After the roll the Commanding Officer gives his talk of a general nature. We hear, unmoved, that we are "the best G -- D--- Group to come overseas", and what we'll do to the targets set up by the Bomber Command. "They set 'em up, we'll knock 'em down." Behind us we hear the comment, "Get that Lindbergh stuff!" by some crew member. The C.O. cites what a good job we did at Tokyo, and we think of the three crews it cost, who won't be around any more. We'll continue to do the job that our country expects, but we don't feel boastful. Only the Colonel feels boastful. He lives apart from us and stays on the ground.

Thinking of these men around me, I wonder what people mean when they speak of "the good soldier"? Is a man a good soldier when he stops doing his own thinking, stops defending the things he believes in, and blindly obeys orders, even against his common sense and better judgment? Yet we have been trained and told by the same Army, under which we are operating now, that we are Airplane Commanders and must safeguard our crews, that we are to "go to bat" for them. But we are required to fly a plane that is improperly loaded, and we must request the crew members to leave their positions so that we will have better balance. Or we see one of our fellow pilots unjustly accused and persecuted. Or a man is killed on take-off when an engine fails and he is written off as a pilot error. Are we good soldiers if we keep silent and don't try to protect ourselves, and our crews, by speaking out? The threat of a Court Martial is always over our heads. We realize the personal ambitions of our Commanding Officer and know that he is trying to get the job done for his own personal glory. He's not the man for the job, but what can we do?

The Operations Officer now states that we may have P-51s to escort us. We'd like to see them. The bomb load consists of 180 M-47 type bombs. The gas load will be 6800 gallons with 400 gallons of it as reserve. The assembly point for the formations will be Nishina-jima, and the reassembly point, in case bad weather scatters us, will be Muroto Cape, the southern tip of Shikoku. We learn a few facts about Osaka. It contains 30% of the manufacturing of the Empire and a population of three million. Fifteen percent of the heavy flak guns are made here ("Let's get 'em!" someone behind us says). 8.1 square miles have been burned out already on the previous incendiary attack there in March. There may be as many as 200 fighters to attack. The other information on radar, radio, and Air-Sea rescue is covered. The usual complement of rescue facilities will be available. The briefing ends with a prayer by the Chaplain, an important part of the meeting to those who fly.

We climb into the trucks amid the usual last minute assembling of canteens, guns, clip boards, and sponge seats, along with jostling and banter. We have the truck to ourselves and are not crowded this time. The fellows are feeling good, with thoughts of going home -- that's obvious. George finds the front seat empty and makes for it while Bill kids him about those pants. "Gotta wear 'em for luck, now" George answers. The baggy pants sag with the weight of gun and canteen. The bottoms, where abruptly cut with scissors, are frayed more than ever.

After the Personal Equipment room we go to the plane. It is parked in the far southwest corner of the area, a new hardstand, but only temporary. The plane is ready to go and we see the fellows sitting about -- one of the few times we've ever seen them stop working. Hank is working on No. 4 engine, grounding the mags, which keep firing after the switch is off. After preflight duties we join the fellow to chat. While we are talking, the entourage of visitors begins. This is now an established part of every mission. We appreciate it, since it is now well past midnight, and they might all be in the sack, sleeping. Ben Lay comes by, precariously hanging onto a Jeep, his chewing tobacco's in evidence and is making him sick, as usual. He feels it's the least he can do as a sacrifice for the send-off, so we don't fail to comment on it. Seem it's to bring us luck. Now our Squadron superiors come by to chat a bit. Jake Schad tears up with some last minute wit. As we're standing there chinning, the Commanding Officer drives up in his Jeep, with its multi-colored lights and assortment of radio antennas. We say that we'll be ready to go on time.

After almost two hours of sitting about, sleepy, we pull the props, crawl up the ladder, and slip into our seats, so familiar to us. I don't know whether that seat conforms to me, or me to that seat, but we certainly do fit. With the check lists completed we start the engines. They sound good and the instruments say they're working properly. We wave to the gang, release the brakes, and roll our sweet, ponderous baby out onto the taxiway. This will be our first take-off with the three new engines while carrying a full load. The ground crew knows this and spared no effort to check and recheck them. We, in turn, keep our eyes and ears attuned for indications of performance, good or bad. The scanners watch the exhausts of the engines. If you're going to balk, honey, do it now -- not on take-off. This time we're 40,000 lbs. heavier than on the test flight take-offs.

Lining up at 0308 we go through the accustomed routine and are rolling down the runway under full power. The engines are roaring and we see the airspeed needle keep swinging toward that take-off speed. We're off – "Gear up." Bill lifts the gear and calls the speed. Nick calls out the temperature. Jake's timing. The scanners call out the gear's position. Bill starts the flaps up at 165 and keeps them coming up gradually as the plane settles and picks up speed. At 190 Bill calls, "Flaps up." Nick calls, "High head No. 2, 250." Dick and Charlie come in with, "Gear and flaps up, engines look O.K." She's flying like a lady. Bill and I reflect, with amazement, that we had 140 when we left the ground and 150 over the end of the runway. Now we know how much power we were losing on those last few missions.

At 8000 feet we level off and fly instruments to get the feel of the plane, then set up the autopilot. With the chores done we talk over the take-off. We are both surprised at the difference. Nor was there a stronger than usual wind to give us greater air speed on this particular take-off. Instead of 125 to 130 mph we had 150 at the end of the runway. No wonder we had trouble on those last few missions and no wonder the loading became a critical factor sooner with our plane than with other planes. Many others have complained of trouble at take-off and with loading and cruise control. Evidently loss of power aggravates these difficulties. We realize now just how much the engineering department is in our debt. For a long time we've flown a plane that was not getting sufficient power. Apparently we were justified, as we contended, in holding that the plane should not be required to fly the missions scheduled beyond the inspection time at the 300 hour and 400 hour mark. Flying an underpowered plane with these heavy loads is not a healthy pastime. Well, we can just be thankful we weathered it safely.

The VHF catches my attention and Bill joins me. It seems that Happy 11 is in trouble behind us, just north of Saipan. They're bailing out. "Must be a fire," Bill says. Now we hear several planes that are at the scene of the bail out, trying to guide rescue facilities. We hear that two engines went out on the same side, and the heavily loaded plane was not supporting itself on the other two. It's a good thing he bailed out his crew, since at night, without balanced power to make a controlled ditching, he was at a distinct disadvantage. Probably it's just as safe to bail out a night as to ditch, anyway, because of the darkness.

Everything grows quiet -- the radio, the interphone. Daylight grows in the east and finally reaches the west as we approach Iwo. Hal computes a new ETA for the assembly point, Nishina-Jima, so that we'll know if we can make it at this speed. We do all right and arrive at the proper time, 0710. We are northwest of Chichi and Haha Jima of the Bonins. Holton, in No. 2, and Schwager in No. 15, arrive and we have the beginnings of a formation. George Schwager calls and states that his navigator is very sick, that they've given him morphine, but they may be forced to drop out of the formation at any time. Dick and Charlie call out other planes arriving in the area. As we close in on Holton we take the "B" flight lead and the other planes fill up the lead flight and ours. Now we have Schwager on the right, Hume on the left wing, and Cooney in the diamond. The lead flight has Holton with Ramsey and Lazin on the wings. Meadows arrives to take the diamond position in the lead flight. After 40 minutes of circling, assembling the formation, we straighten out on course for the reassembly point and target.

Dawson hasn't shown up.

The lead flight starts to spread out for comfort and cruise control's sake, and we do likewise, putting the plane on Autopilot. This makes it easier for the wingmen to judge their positions, since the autopilot makes fewer and smaller corrections than when we fly manually. Of course, we don't mind resting. So off we go for the Empire.

Looking at the other planes and thinking of the good boys in each one, I can't help but feel a certain joy in doing this job with these men. This is teamwork to the nth degree, and as we will probably not see it exemplified again in our lifetime. It hasn't just happened, it is the result of long practice, living together, bulling over the common subjects so that we grow to do them alike. The older crews have 20 missions now, and we know they are dependable. We don't mind flying on each other's wings. We are confident in their skill as in our own.

Schwager stays with us, evidently he will try to stick it out. Sefton must be mighty sick, possibly something he ate. Air sickness is no fun, and seldom has a question of degree. If you're sick, you're mighty sick -- or think you are. Dick and Charlie regularly call out the positions of the other planes in the formation. The spacing is good and constant. Ahead we see weather building up, but just how bad it is we can't tell. Nick says he's ready to transfer fuel any time, so we call Holton and tell him that we are going off the air while we transfer fuel. As is our custom, we turn off many of the electrical appliances in order to lessen the danger from the fuel fumes which accompany fuel transfer. After the fuel is shifted from the center wing section to the individual wing tanks we turn on the radios. We tell Holton that we're back on VHF again, and he acknowledges. We are fast approaching the weather, with clouds building above our level, and it appears to be solid.

On autopilot we have the most exact heading and speed that the lead planes are flying, so that if we penetrate the weather we'll continue to hold our relative position with the other planes -- at least we hope so. "Doesn't look so good," observes Higgy. Jake and I agree. According to the briefing, any weather encountered would be located further to the south. We go into a light type of stratus clouds that are not thick, and in a few minutes emerge on the other side. We comb the skies and Dick, Charlie, and Jonesy confirm our hopes, that the other planes are in their same relative positions.

Flying in clouds with other planes in the vicinity is always a strain. The imagination doesn't help, either. It's easy to picture some other plane straying off course and suddenly appearing, too late to prevent a collision. The mid-air collision is a dangerous accident, since it so frequently results in extensive damage, with subsequent loss of control. "Looks like it's getting heavier," Jake points ahead. We enter more stratus, thicker than before. Fortunately it isn't turbulent, which would necessitate turning off the autopilot, which holds us so steadily on course. Flying manually is not that accurate. From time to time we see the lead planes. We concentrate on keeping the same position with relation to Ramsey, since we figure he is doing the same with the leader, and as the plane behind us is doing with regard to us. Jake is sitting forward, peering through the nose. Bill and I aid in searching the clouds ahead. Dick, Charlie, Jonesy, and George are doing the same, watching for those behind us.

We break into the clear. Holton calls to the planes that we will begin to climb in 15 minutes, at 0925. By synchronizing our times with his, we'll all start climbing at the same time, keeping the same relative positions to each other. Conney can't hear Holton, so we relay the message. Again we hit the clouds and then break into the clear. Just before climbing we go into the clouds and it gets thicker, and the mist closes in so that even the wing tip is fuzzy to the sight. "24 43, Nick," and we start to climb, holding 500 feet a minute. We cannot see any other planes.

Frequently we hear other Squadrons calling, trying to hold their formations together. At various times we hear other planes giving their altitude in terms of "Heaven" (20,000 feet), or "base altitude" (bombing altitude -- 18,000 feet), and whether they are in the clear. Evidently the "soup" extends right on up. We hear nothing from our planes, and we hope that this big, old sky is big enough for all of us without any competition for the same space.

"Climb until breaking out on top," we hear Holton's voice calling. We continue to climb to 18,000 feet, 20,000 feet, and finally hit the frayed wisps of the top at 25,000 feet. Cloud country with mountains and valleys extends as far as we can see, everything white and clean in the sunlight. Looking about us in this land of no landmarks, we don't see anyone at first. Hal and Gabby check our position with the radar and we learn that we are to the right of course for the reassembly area. Making a correction, we fly on and in a few minutes see several planes converging toward the same area ahead of us. "There's No. 2," Jake exclaims, pointing to a plane crossing our path well ahead.

Since Ramsey has not appeared, Holton tells us to take the deputy lead, which we do. Gabby tests the radar set, since we may take the lead of anything that happens to Holton. Jake and Hal keep their material handy, in case they must do the lead duties for the formation. We are joined by other planes, except for Schwager and Hume. Perhaps Schwager turned back with the sick navigator. We don't know where Hume is. Evidently he was disconnected from the rest of us during the climb through the clouds. The would be understandable.

After several circles to the right we are settled down in a closer formation than that first, and we head for the departure point, putting us on course for the IP. Lazin is on Holton's left wing. In the "B" flight are Ramsey, Cooney, and Meadows. I have the controls, since the Leader is on my side. Bill prepares to open the doors and keeps the bomb release button handy on its extension cord. Jonesy, Dick, Charlie, and George are alert. George is in the tail. We're all set. Nick reports that the engines are O.K. Everyone has on his heavy equipment. Al is standing by on the Laison radio. I'm on the VHF and Bill stays with the crew on the interphone. I keep switching back and forth so that I know how the crew is going.

Smoothly, with little wing-dipping, bouncing, or jockeying, we head for the target. "Target's straight ahead," Hal reports. Down below, above the clouds which have lowered, there are two fighters, but they either don't see us or don't care to come up. That's good. "Flak at 1." "Flak at 11." Jake and Jonesy call out the burst ahead of us. We are close to the lead plane now, and we edge in a little closer so that the other planes can do the same. We've got a good, tight formation now, steady so that extra fuel isn't burned by the wing ships. Fire power is heavy in this arrangement. The wing flight is slightly higher than our flight, while the wing ships in both flights are slightly above the lead ship.

Holton's doors come open and we begin to time. After three minutes Bill opens ours and the plane jars. "Doors open," Higgy calls. Now we're only two minutes away, so we bring the nose of our plane abreast of the blister of the lead ship. Lazin comes forward, and the scanners call out the B-flight coming in closer. "Bombs away!" Jake and I bellow, but Bill has already started ours dropping. We can't see below. All we see are the white clouds about us and, somewhat lower and against them, the dark string of bombs.

Like so many cords of wood, the bombs pour out of the bomb bays of the lead ship and the left wing ship. The scanners report the other planes' bombs got away without trouble or delay. We've each dropped over 6 tons of bombs apiece -- 180 each. Oddly enough, the clouds clear away at this point and we are able to see glimpses of the target. Smoke obscures the fires so we can't see the extent of the damage, but we're certain that our bombs fell squarely on the city. The flak is light and we haven't seen any more fighters. Charlie reports that Ramsey's doors are open and Holton slows down so that he'll have no trouble staying up with us. We still are surprised not to be getting any more attention from fighters and flak. Possibly other formations just ahead of us had the trouble.

Now, with the important job behind us, we begin to figure the fuel and the return trip. We should be able to land after dropping the bombs instead of having such a long trip as an anticlimax, but we well know that we can't afford to let down on our effort now. It might make all the difference in reaching Base, if we figure the fuel correctly and are careful with our cruise control. The climbing to 25,000 feet caused us to use more gas than expected, far more than the "planners" figured that we'd use up to this point. Returning to Iwo, Nick and Bill keep figuring on the remaining fuel. We have lost sight of the other planes in flying our own navigation and saving those few extra miles that results from not adjusting our speed to that of someone else.

Approaching Iwo, Nick states that, according to the power settings we've used against the time used, we'll have 1200 gallons left. According to the gauges, which may or may not be right, we'll have 1400. Hal adds what he can about the expected weather between Iwo and Base, and we realize that we won't have any help from tail winds, but will be bucking a head wind. Our fuel is lower than before at this point and it takes close to 1500 gallons to make Base from Iwo. Iwo is open, so down we go. We can't take the chance.

We call the Tower -- "Walnut Tower, this is Daredevil 11, over the field at 20,000 feet, low on fuel. Request landing information." The Tower comes back with the message, "Roger, Daredevil 11, circle the field, we will call you." So we join the number of B-29s in the large circle of some 5 miles across. Our altitude is 1500 feet now and we get a bird's eye view of the field. "There's Suribachi," and with Jake we look at the 500 foot extinct volcano on the southern tip of the Island. There are two fields, where we see fighters lined up, and a few Navy planes. Also, the "Black Widow" which serves the radar night fighters in this area. Then in the center of the Island is the long runway that the B-29s use. Many B-29s are parked along the edge and on taxiways extending away from the runway. There are many damaged planes here, left from earlier raids by their crews. Some of them can be repaired, others have been pushed aside by bulldozers after they crashed on landing.

We continue to circle while the planes increase. If only the Tower would keep planes landing they wouldn't pile up so badly in the traffic pattern, but the field is kept open for emergency cases, with long periods when the runway is unused. A B-29 flies over the field, several objects drop from it and we see parachutes blossom below it. The crew calls out the parachutes as they open. The Tower is loudly warning all aircraft in the vicinity to stay clear of the field, and those on the field to remain motionless while the parachutes land. We see eight chutes in the air. Now we see a P-61 flying beside the B-29, almost in formation with it, as it makes a turn and heads back for the field. Three more men parachute from the plane. That means the whole crew is out. The plane flies north, empty now, out to sea. The P-61 begins to fire on it, pouring lots of lead into it. Finally, the B-29 gives up its straight course and gracefully banks to the right, goes into a dive and, with the P-61 firing into it, flies into the water. There goes somebody's pride and joy. I'd hate to leave "Miss A. '62" like that, yet I'd rather that than have an enemy fighter do it.

The parachutists have all landed on or near the Island, and traffic is resumed. We surmise that the B-29 had serious malfunctions that prevented landing it, in which case it was shot down after the crew left, rather than have it fly through these busy skies uncontrolled. Evidently the Tower will let us come in now. We keep calling, and after one and a half hours of circling we get a clearance and line up for landing. Ahead we see the planes lined up on either side of the runway. It's a crowded field. We settle in and touch the runway, which we find is extremely bumpy, more so than before. We shake and jolt, slowing down, then we turn around, taxi back and park.

It is hot and dusty. Planes with engines idling or roaring keep the loose volcanic top soil stirred up. The dust pall curls up to 20 or 30 feet in the air, and makes the heat stifling and oppressive. The Operations Officer of Iwo, our old Squadron Commander, comes by and seems glad to see us. We are given several forms and told that it is imperative that we fill them out. I make out the forms while Bill lines up the service, gas and oil. Meanwhile the gang steps over to an outdoor canteen to get coffee and doughnuts. Are they good! We realize how hungry we are. The strain of the flight and the lack of sleep and food are like a great weight on the shoulders. When it appears that it will take some time to get the service, I call Art from the nearby Dispensary. It turns out that he's not there, though on the Island, and that it's "Major" now. That's good news -- Art certainly deserves it.

Back at the plane "Miss A. '62" is getting the fuel, and we prepare to go. Art drives up to surprise us -- he's just learned that we are here. A sight for sore eyes, and that gold leaf, new and shiny! We fan the breeze and try to get caught up. Art says that he's going home, which is good to hear, since he's done more than his share, and his luck needs a rest. I tell him that we're going home, too. He suggests that we take a B-29 together, he'd like to be a passenger. We tell him that he's most welcome, but no such luck as our getting a plane to fly back. It seems that he gets a month rest leave on the way home in Hawaii and then will remain in the States. He may even be discharged because of his three years in forward bases, but he thinks he wants to stay with aviation.

Now Art tells us the sad news, which explains his haggard look. 28 fighters from his Group, 4 of them from his squadron, are missing as a result of today's flight. Through some oversight somewhere in the chain of command, the weather information given to the men at the briefing had been wrong. As a result, he and his fighters went out expecting good weather. 200 miles north they hit the severe turbulence of cumulo-nimbus clouds. They were forced to turn around and come back to Base. But 28 of the planes did not return. We sympathize. Art feels the loss keenly. He, himself, had gotten back very luckily, as he put it. We both agree that such mistakes shouldn't be made, not even once, particularly since the weather information is now available from planes which have just returned from the area covered by the prediction. Apparently it was just a mistake. And the fighters, because of their light weight, get bounced about so badly in heavy clouds that the pilots can't read the instruments.

After adieus, we get into the plane and taxi out, leaving the usual huge cloud of Iwo dust. What a place. The heat mixes sweat with dust until you think you can't get any dirtier. We feel sorry for the men stationed on this Island. On the take-off our new engines, and lack of a load, permit us to make almost a pursuit take-off. It's a different plane in its feel, when light.

We arrive home at 2040 on the ETA that Hal had figured. It's been one and a half days since we last slept. At the interrogation we recreate the mission for the paper work. We learn that all the planes in the Group returned home safely, though a number were forced to land at Iwo for refueling. We all are thankful that we have Iwo. Thirty-three aircraft of the Wing planes were damaged, so we know that once again our formation had it lucky.

The next day, as ordered, we attend the briefing. The Group Commanding Officer is present and his new Deputy. The latter presents the summary of the mission, giving us the interesting details of the flights of the various planes. After the general summary, one crew member made the remark, "How is it we never see any of our own fighters over the target?" He expresses the thought many of us, who have never seen a P-51 in the target area, have had. We'd certainly like to see them. The Commanding Officer takes the floor, and in a sharp tone tells us that they are there, even though we don't see them. That we can appreciate. Then he confidently goes on to outline the mission the day before, in terms of the fighter sweeps that were made over the target area beneath us, showing how this factor made the mission easier for us. I am sorely tempted to inform him that the fighters did not get up to Japan, but turned around and returned to their base because of bad weather. He apparently doesn't know this, but what's the use?

After straightening out our knowledge of the fighter support, the C.O. throws open the discussion for our suggestions for an SOP (a standard operation procedure) that could be used in frontal penetration, for use in weather such as we encountered on the mission. Several suggestions are made by men who participated in our formation, with regard to the manner in which we flew it. The formation was held together fairly well by holding the same heading and speed and broadcasting any change of plan, such as the announcement of the intention to climb in a certain time. But the Colonel points out that only 6 of the 8 planes had come through it together. Another points out that Schwager's navigator was ill, and that Hume, so he told us, had an autopilot malfunction which threw him off course before he could catch it, with the result that he lost the original heading. Therefore, our system of yesterday wasn't so bad. But the C.O. disapproves this with, "I want a plan that will solve all difficulties on this frontal penetration." That stops us, because we realize all too well that we haven't encountered any plan in flying that solves all difficulties, no matter what the particular subject. He believes that every move we make pertaining to a plane should be an SOP -- an infallible rule. From his many comments in the past it would seem that we should have a SOP manual instead of a head. We pilots feel that, on a basis of our training and combat experience, an SOP reduced to writing can never replace the considered judgments required at every move in a plane. We appreciate that standard procedures must be the basis, but there's a point beyond which all the SOPs in the world will do no good, and that point is where unusual situations require unusual judgment.

Our next critic is the Engineering Officer (who doesn't fly on the missions, either). He makes the suggestion to the pilots that they be more careful and go into Iwo less, since it's hard on the planes to land there in the dust. Now isn't that great! Why does he think we go there? The answer to that is that he should land at Iwo himself, and he would soon see that no one would land there who absolutely did not have to do so. It is hot and dusty. We are hungry, dusty, and tired, and stopping there takes hours, delaying our return to food, clean clothes, and sleep. The only reason we stop there is to prevent swimming part way home -- if we could survive. At Iwo the runway is hazardous, and planes line the runway, crowding even the plane that is landing or taking off. But despite the obvious retort to the criticism, none of the crew members answers. It just doesn't do any good to talk to these men. They don't go on the missions, yet they're running the show, so far as giving the orders.

We leave the meeting feeling a deep disgust and despondency over this conclusion to the mission. Ramsey and Cooney walk away toward the Quonset they share, shaking their heads. The fellows always have a joke to cheer each other up, but they all feel keenly the depression that results from doing the best job they know how, and then being criticized by those who don't understand. There is no hope of promotion, of harmony within the outfit, nor of respect for those who are running the Group. All the fellows want now is to get their missions over and go home. It seems too bad that so much of our trouble is caused, not by the enemy, but by the ignorances within our own outfit.

Now we have 20 behind us.

Chapter 28 Kobe

June 5, 1945 – No. 21

"Three Squadron Teamwork"

The days pass slowly, one by one. Where are the orders that send us to "Lead Crew School" and HOME? We "sweat out" the time and assure each other that we're ready to go at the drop of a hat. Others in the Group and Squadron ask about our plans. As if we know! We're still trying to keep it quiet, but somehow there's a leak. None of us will actually believe all this until we can look down between our feet and see U.S. soil, so the self imposed secrecy is protection to ourselves more than anything else. We're still flying, sweating out the long missions.

The mission board lists the crews going on the next one -- Schwager, Lazin, Alger, Meadows, Holton, Hume, Cooney, and Ramsey. Not a very large force, judging from our Squadron's participation. At the specified time Bill, Jake, Hal, and Gabby show up at the briefing building. We study the charts, maps, and mosaics, still wrinkled from the last mission. This time we're going to Kobe, which lies several miles only from Osaka, along the edge of the northeastern coast of the Inland Sea (the water there called the Izumi Sea). The MPIs (mean point of impact) of the various Groups are shown and ours is indicated in relation to theirs. It seems that the idea of this mission is to spread the incendiaries over the entire long, narrow area of the city of Kobe.

After the roll call the Commanding Officer comes in and we jolt to attention -- quite a strain with a lap full of assorted papers and equipment. In his talk, which gets the perfunctory attention of the men, he tells how "we" bombed out Tokyo and Yokohama and now are going after Kobe in like fashion, and, "We are the men that can do it. This is the best G -- D --- Group in the Twenty-First Bomber Command." His remarks remind us of a comment going through camp just now, pertaining to the brave High Command, who generally do not fly on the missions, but plan them, which is, "They'll fight to the last combat crew!" Our Commanding Officer is not one of us, and when he says "we" he only emphasizes the difference, which the men, sitting silently, recognize. One by one the men have realized that their suggestions are really not welcome, nor appreciated, so they become silent. Just fly your missions, take your chances, whatever they are, and let it go at that. Recompense comes in the crew endeavors in the feeling of satisfaction that comes from doing "your bit" in the plane, but it's hard to have a feeling of patriotism in a setup like this.

As the briefing goes on we see that this will be a big one. The four wings of the Command will participate. Each Wing will be represented by three or four Groups. Our Group will be the second Air Group over the target. Each Group will have 30 or more planes participating. In our Group there will be three Squadrons which will form in a column, with one minute intervals between them. The 24th will be the Third Air Squadron. There will be no secondary target. If Kobe's socked in with weather it will be bombed by radar. We will carry 31 E-46 bombs which are fused to ignite at 3000 feet, also a full load of ammunition. The gross load is expected to be 137,000 lbs.

"Miss A. '62" is one of those listed as carrying a strike camera to photograph the bombs dropping and striking the target. Base altitude for plane to plane communication will be 13,000 feet ("Base altitude plus or minus so many feet"). A weather plane ahead of the main striking force will broadcast the best altitude for assembly and the planes will then assemble at that altitude. We wonder about that arrangement, but accept it along with everything else. When the time comes, we'll have to do what circumstances dictate, anyway!

Bad weather is expected in the area at Nishina-Jima, so we'll go on to Japan and do our assembling there. The assembly point will be the area 15 miles due south of Shiono-Misaki, the farthest tip on Honshu extending south. Assembly will be accomplished while circling to the left. Communication during assembly will be on "A" channel VHF. The reassembly point will be Mirini-saki, the small island just south of Awaji Island. Departure time will be, for the 40th Squadron, 0804, for the 39th, 0805, and for the 24th, 0806. The IP will be Okino-shima, and the axis of attack on the target 26 degrees for 29 miles until "bombs away".

The best bombing altitude will be broadcast by a Master of Ceremonies over the target area, with code of "heaven" equaling 20,000 feet. Base speed for the Bombardier intervolometer will be 220 mph. The breakaway will be to the right, thereby dodging the flak, flying midway between Osaka and Kyoto. Details on the city of Kobe include heavy manufacturing equipment, and it is the 6th largest city, a seaport, and a railway center. There are 165 fighters located in the area, although there may be more shifted over from the other area after we have committed ourselves to that target.

In the Air-Sea rescue division we learn that there will be 4 subs, 2 destroyers, 4 superdumbos, and 5 dumbos. A "Flying Dutchman" (B-17 with droppable motor boat) will be standing by at Iwo. Ditching should not be attempted near any of the islands north of the Marianas, since it is known, definitely, that they are Jap held. Only the islands on either side of Pagan are friendly. The weather man tells us that there is a tropical storm located to the southwest of Tinian and that it is moving in this direction, but will not be at the field by the time we return -- we'll get back before it gets here. A warm front lies to the north of Iwo and will cause a good bit of weather and clouds of all types. For our help, in the future Terminal weather (weather at Base) will be broadcast every hour on the hour. The call signs of the planes over the target will be "Domino" for the weather ship and "Dragon Lady" for the Master of Ceremonies.

Down to the line we go, by the Personal Equipment and over to the plane. The permanent hardstand of the plane now is only a hundred yards away from the P.E. room -- very convenient. The plane is all ready. We stow our gear, except that kept out for the crew inspection, and complete the preflight chores. Bill finds that the weight of the plane is slightly over 139,000 lbs., 2000 lbs. heavier than the briefed weight, but our plane always weighs more than the briefed estimate. We have 14,000 lbs. of bombs this time.

After the chores we have time to sit down with the ground crew and talk.

The ground crew knows that we are going back to the States. We feel sure they'll miss us. We'll miss them, to say the least. It isn't possible to "thank" people like these, who spare no effort to make it easier and safer for us. We let them know every chance we get, how much we appreciate it -- but they know it. Pat, Red, Hank, and the newer member of the crew, Vito Merrell, all have something to say about home and the days in Grand Island. The usual subjects are covered -- things we're going to do back there, our families or wives or sweethearts, the things we'll eat, the places we'll go, all these things are mighty important to us now. We kid the boys that after their Army experience they'll be wanting to "sack up" when they get home. Pat throws in his occasional, distinctive, "Oh, hell yes!" with great vehemence. Vito claims I owe him some beers and that he's going to come around and collect. And so we ramble on, enjoying the banter.

Occasionally some of us get up to chat with the various dignitaries who drive up. There is the usual string of various maintenance personnel, checking to see if everything is all right. Vito witnesses a number of these people come up and hears me tell them variously that the plane seems to be all right. He says that it seems so routine and my affirmative answer taken so for granted that he wonders if it wouldn't be a bombshell to tell the next one who drops by that things are not right, so I agree. The next caller turns out to be the Group Ordnance Officer. He jocundly asks, "How's everything?" I answer, seriously, "Terrible. The bomb doors are inoperative, the bombs aren't fused and the arming wires are all too long. Everything's fouled up." His face drops and he looks quite pained and hurries back to the bomb bays. The fellows get a kick out of his surprise, but I begin to feel guilty, so I go back and allay his worries. He seems somewhat dazed as he drives off, like the look that we associate with too much time spent on Tinian.

We have a crew inspection, checking Mae Wests and parachutes following which we get our last ground exercise, pulling the props. After this hilarious activity, with a lot of kidding and argument, we get in the plane. The engines check O.K., and the crew members declare they're all set, each in his own position. I look out and wave to Pat, thinking of the last few words we exchanged while the other crew members were already aboard. "Pat, those guys are liable to taxi out and line up for take-off before they miss me, with a bunch like that, that does all the work, while I just ride along. I'd better get in before they leave me." Perhaps within our eleven man crew we have the secret of success of any organization. Have good men working together, delegated authority and responsibility each in his job. Whatever it is, in this smooth working team, it relieves me of a lot of work and I have time to think of our job in overall terms.

We taxi out two minutes after "Porky" Jordan rolls out of the hardstand across the taxiway. Our plane rolls and handles like a lady, the bomb load being evenly distributed between the bomb bays. This gives us a balance index of 26.5% of the MAC, which is a good index for our plane. We carry the incendiary bombs and a single fray bomb. The taxiway is fairly smooth and the oleo shock absorbers make the plane settle smoothly on the gear as we hit the bumps of uneven places. Turning right at the west end, we taxi along behind the other planes and fit in between those taxiing out from the next east-west taxiway as they feed into the west-end strip. We approach "B" runway, which now has a black top, just asphalted. We alternately stop and start as the planes move ahead to fill up the slack resulting from planes taking off. We pass "D" and are signaled onto "C". This means we'll be off in good time.

Before taxiing into take-off position Nick puts a generator on the cool engine and Bill lowers the flaps. At the same time Jonesy sees to the stowing of the "hot" guns, from vertical to horizontal position. The green light of the expediter (traffic man) goes on and in compliance we run up the engines gradually advancing the throttles to clear out the engines. When the flagman gives the signal indicating that the runway is clear ahead, we release the brakes. The four engines, now at 30 inches of manifold pressure, cause the plane to surge forward as soon as the brakes are released. Jake is the man who cross-checks to see that the runway all-clear signal is sent. The throttles are advanced while Nick closes the cowl flaps. The warning horn goes off, but stops as Nick gets the flaps closed. Bill begins calling out the air speed. As we reach 90 mph, which is the speed of no stopping, Bill reports that the engines' instruments are reading properly, and Nick substantiates this. This gives us a fair certainty that the engines will continue all right.

We continue to pick up speed and the plane gets lighter on the nose wheel. Rather than let it bounce on the nose gear, I hold it down with slight pressure and when we get to 135, let up on the pressure. The preset trim of the elevator control gets the plane gradually, and gracefully, off the ground. The usual leap into the air, that characterizes the B-29, is combated by turning the elevator trim to a further nose down attitude.

Bill lifts the gear as soon as we are airborne, to cut down on the terrific drag it causes, and the scanners are checking its progress retracting. We are now out over the water and all is well. Nick calls out the "high head" temperature, which is "250 on 1 and 4". This, too, is normal. Bill starts the flaps up at 155 and the plane gradually settles. By rolling back on the elevator trim, the plane holds itself level. We hold the 200 feet we have above the water while the speed builds up. It is quite dark. We see the water, shimmering just below, as we approach the light that extends south from Saipan three miles east of Tinian. The flaps are fully up and Bill immediately reduces the propeller speed from the 2800 take-off RPMs to 2400, while I pull off the power with the throttles to 43 inches. The hot engines are beginning to cool, Nick states, and all is well. After holding 204 mph for a short time for cooling purposes, we begin to climb and make almost 500 feet a minute. It was a good take-off (which means a safe take-off), since we were indicating 150 when we left the field behind. That's much better than the old engines gave us. More speed gives more control of the plane.

We climb on the take-off heading with Jake timing us, then we turn on the 70 degree heading for the specified number of minutes. This puts us well to the east of the Saipan traffic which is taking off. We finally pass Marpi Point on the north end of Saipan, still climbing with the other planes about us. Generally the distances between planes is good because of the staggered take-offs and timed legs flown after take-off.

We continue to climb, with the scanners reporting the positions of the other planes. Charlie, Dick, and Jonesy are all eyes, doing a nice job. Occasionally George, in the tail, gives us the position of planes behind us. The clouds are few and light so that we are "visual" most of the time. The plane handles nicely. This testifies to the fuel, oil and bombs being balanced properly. We reach our flight level and climb up an additional thousand feet so that we can lose a little altitude if necessary, yet hold our auto-lean power settings, which will save us fuel. We get the power to 2150 and 34 inches, with the boost backed off as low as possible. This cuts out the back pressure on the engines, which to a small degree cuts the power output. In this way we try to save fuel all the way. We are using more fuel than briefed. It is necessary to carry the power for longer periods than briefed, but this is customary. Evidently the conditions are not as ideal as anticipated. We are getting the power expected, since we climbed to altitude in less time than they designated. We are using up fuel saved now because we can't hold our speed straight and level without carrying more power than anticipated. Possibly the figures given to us on the cruise control paper work are wrong.

The plane feels good. After an initial period of flying on instruments to keep in practice, Bill takes it over and does the same. After an hour and a half the autopilot, previously warmed up, is engaged and flies the plane smoothly, always making the small corrections that clouds or rough air necessitate. Jake goes to sleep. It is late -- take-off was at 0113. Bill and I alternate sleeping, or just closing our eyes. The Benzedrine taken just after take-off always helps me to stay alert, but many times it doesn't interfere with sleeping.

The pin-point lights of the other planes give life to the darkness that swallows up land, water, and planes. The same darkness pervades the plane, except for the directionally pointed lights at each position, and many of these are out as the men sit in their darkened positions, trying to pierce the murkiness, looking for other planes or unusual lights. Any lights inside prevent outside visibility to a large extent because of the reflections on the glass. Gabby in the radar room, Hal at the navigator's position, and Al at his radio post have their lights on, the rest of the crew turn theirs on as needed. Mainly the purple-blue glow of the fluorescent lights does the work, illuminating the radiant dials of the instruments. In the "cockpit" (as it was called in the olden days) the fluorescent glows give a mysterious glow to the instruments, whose needles and calibrations seem to jump right out at you from the panel. They are easy to see.

Any light that is seen by us is known instantly to be a light from outside, so we are alerted for any nearby neighbors. The darkness and silence go well together as we seem to hang in space, each man quiet at his position. But the airspeed needle says 200 mph and calls attention to the powerful though quiet purr of the engines. With the propellers synchronized, eliminating the throbbing beat that occurs otherwise, the engines are like one. There is no sound of the terrific rush of air over the plane which accompanies such speed. When a window is opened at the pilot's or copilot's position, the hollow roar of the rushing air drowns out speech, sucks out nearby papers, and can easily break an arm or wrist thoughtlessly extended. But now, with the windows closed, all is quiet with only the purr, in the background, of the engines and the small, though continual vibration. We have wondered if this ever present vibration isn't one of the causes of the tiring effect of flying, even though we sit quietly and feel relaxed. But perhaps we're never relaxed. Whatever it is, it's surprising, when ending a mission, to try to sign the form (on occasion) and find the hand too shaky to write.

The darkness, miles, and thoughts rush by endlessly and uneventfully. Ahead we see flashes of lightening, though we can't tell how far it is. The lightening gives a glimpse of the cloud structure and we see that they are cumulous, building up to heights that we can't see. Yet the clouds seem to be independent, and beyond we see a number of similar lightening areas dotting the horizon. Such a sight as this may not be considered marvelous by many, but at least it's exclusive. No one else in the world can see this performance except those crews who are here in the darkness. And we may never see such a combination of natural phenomena after we leave this section of the world, and flying. But everyone, everywhere in the world, has this show going on about him in its varying aspects, and may or may not notice it. No doubt we are more aware of the natural forces -- clouds, wind, rain, hail, sleet, snow, turbulence, and gravity -- because we are a part of them. We can't escape into a warm living room out of the storm. But our cabin seems mighty homey and protective. Before too long we'll be trading it in for that living room, too. At present our footstool is the rudder bar, our cushion the headrest, and our lounging robe the emergency vest with rib-jabbing water tins.

Iwo comes and goes, obscured by clouds below our 7500 foot altitude. Just ahead we see a wall of clouds against the slightly lighter sky, and the crew members are alerted to fasten safety belts in case of turbulence. At 0446 we enter the clouds associated with the warm front. Bill wakes up with the first turbulence and we alternate flying instruments in order to spare the autopilot the heavy work that accompanies turbulence. Jake gives the outside temperature as "plus 5" which, changing the Centigrade to Fahrenheit, means well above freezing, so we don't expect icing in the clouds, nor do we have any. After 45 minutes we emerge into the clear again and breathe easier. We couldn't see a thing outside the plane in those clouds.

"Ready to transfer fuel," Nick reports, so we prepare for the transfer by turning off the radios. When the transfer is completed, Jonesy calls, inquiring about test-firing the guns. It's a good situation, considering the daylight and clear sky in which we see no planes, so Jonesy energizes the system and each man fires a short burst or two from his position. The guns chatter briefly -- quietly in the rear, noisily in front of us. George, Dick, Charlie, and Jake inform Jonesy that the guns are O.K., and Jonesy calls and reports that the guns are all right.

With so many clouds obscuring the water below us at intervals, it's hard for Hal to get the drift which enables him to hold our course and determine our actual speed, since the drift is vital in determining both. It's always tough for him, working with so many variables, and yet he knows that the crew, the other crews, and the top command expect him to get us there at the correct time for the assembly. Hal gives us his ETA for arrival and we see that it will put us there on time. Gabby turns on his radar set and we all put on our heavy equipment. We're approaching the assembly area and landfall just beyond. Properly hamstrung by the emergency vest, Mae West, parachute, flak vest, and dinghy underneath us, we are ready for the bombing run. We set our flak helmets nearby where they may be easily reached to put on at the last minute. The head is already heavy with headgear encasing headsets and oxygen mask attached.

Hal and Gabby determine that we are to the left of course. We make a large correction to the right, heading east. Our ETA runs out and we see ahead many planes circling in different directions at various altitudes. There they are, three squadrons of them, all having traveled 1400 miles, and arriving within several minutes of each other, each flying separately. It's a pleasure to be a member of a team like that. The confusion is lessened as we try to determine which formation is ours. We check our present altitude of 13,000 feet and see a formation circling left. That's it. We've heard several times over the radio while approaching that "Daredevil Amber" formation is assembling at 13,000 feet. We turn sharply inside the formation. The numbers of the planes verify that it's our formation. We come up rapidly on the inside and take the lead of "C" flight. Dawson drops back to let us in and then closes up on our right wing.

"Plane coming in on the left," Dick reports, and we see Litchfield take the left wing. Evidently he just arrived, and is too late to take his position in the lead flight. Other stragglers join on the right and the formation is complete. We see Ramsey (16), Lazin (14), and Holton (2), in the 1, 3, and 2 spots. The right hand "B" flight is led by Jordan in No. 3. On his right wing is Hume in No. 1 (replacing the plane lost, with Boynton), and Meadows in No. 10 on the left. In our flight we have Dawson in No. 9 on our right, and Litchfield in No. 4 on our left. In the diamond, the No. 4 position, is Schwager in No. 15. Crews and planes are thought of interchangeably, since they usually fly their own plane, and if not, we are aware of it and know who has the plane. This time most of the crews are in their own planes. Planes have personalities, dependent on their "feel", the way they handle, their balance, speed, and trim. Our plane is not a fast plane in this array, and trims slightly off-center, but has established the reputation as being a dependable old work-horse with few malfunctions. It is now among the first 2 or 3 planes in number of missions flown, despite it's early lay-off.

The formation heads for the reassembly point en route to the IP and target. To our right, and clearly visible below, is Japan, it's rugged country of miniature nature, standing out in the sunlight. Looking ahead we are amazed to see the two other squadrons. Considering the uncertainties of weather and navigation on the trip up, it is an example of precision, skillful teamwork, and luck -- the ever present factor in everything we do. It's surprising to see the formations come so close to the briefed plan. The scanners call out another flight of B-29s overtaking us. Now we have a fourth flight, taking the diamond position. They are stragglers from three outfits. Jonesy, Dick, and George report their numbers as X-2, B-2, and E-23.

Bill has the controls, since the lead flight is on his side and our flight is high this time. On our northeast bombing run we will be stacked against the sun, giving best visibility toward our most vulnerable spot. Jake hands me the bomb release extension and returns to his gunsight. We have proceeded up the channel between Honshu and Shikoku. Ahead is Awaji Island. We reach the IP and turn to the heading of 26 degrees, Bill carrying our flight well forward on the turn (so the lead flight won't get away from us) turning right.

The gunners are informed that we're on the bomb run. Ahead we see the thermal building up to our level. The heat of the fires underneath forces the air up, the moisture condenses, and so the straight pillar of clouds and smoke. It doesn't look so violent as other we've seen. Our course appears to take us to the right of it. Jake peers forward and he and Jonesy call, "Fighter at 12." It's coming toward us and the time required to announce it brings it much closer -- our combined rate of closure must be 500 mph. He's headed toward our flight. Jake fires. The cabin shakes as the four guns kick and we hear the cartridges fall inside the turret. Twin flames flicker on the fighter, now he is passing below the formation. Charlie gets in a short burst and he is gone. Apparently no one was damaged, at least noticeably, by the fighter.

"Flak ahead," Jake calls out as we notice concentrated areas of black puffs. Looks like the barrage type flak -- not so good. Ramsey opens his doors and we know we're getting close. Now the deputy's doors come open. The other planes open their twin sets of doors. "Bombs away," Bill shouts, seeing the bombs fall from the lead flight. Our bombs are falling and the plane is soaring, evidently they're getting away all right. The gunners call out large areas of smoke within the city, increasing while they watch.

The earlier formations are ahead, making their breakaway. The formation ahead is having trouble with fighters. We watch the small, fast moving objects, like terriers worrying great danes. They dive, climb, and wheel about the formation. Someone's in trouble. We see a B-29, without any smoke or visible damage, leave the formation, diving gracefully to the right in a shallow turn. Six fighters are on it, in and out, then they stop and fly along with it, but we lose sight of it below. Al is watching it through the open bomb bay and we wait to hear what he has to say.

Bill keeps the flight in close, and the gunners report the positions of the planes in our flight, and the formation. At this point no plane should straggle. The Japs jump the stragglers. There are many sad instances where B-29s were seen to go down with many Japs from all directions working them over. Those slightly behind now catch up and we're a tight formation. That gives us fire power that at a glance may scare the Japs off. All of our gunners would like a crack at a Jap fighter, but all of us know we're better off if they leave us alone. Getting one or several of them does not compensate the loss of one B-29 and crew -- not to us, at least.

Al calls on the interphone and mystifies us with his account. The B-29 appeared to be under control. The six fighters flew on all sides of it and the plane headed for the Kobe dock area, very low when last he saw it. We can't figure that one. It sounds as though the fighters were trying to force it to a certain spot, but that's hardly possible with gunners in the B-29 who could still fire. There must be condition we don't know. Good luck, fellows.

We are climbing, we notice, and are glad to see that Ramsey is using his head to dodge the concentrated flak. It's obvious that they had our altitude plotted correctly. The gunners report flak below us as we climb. Holding the formation together, we go up to 20,000 feet in our turn between Osaka and Kyoto. The flak consistently bursts below us. This climb was not briefed, but it's a good move, since we're going to return at 20,000 feet anyway, to get the benefit of a tail wind. Evidently, after our long suggestions of having us fly at altitude, the authorities are convinced that a return at altitude gains more in speed than it takes in fuel. Jordan and many of us have maintained this fact for a long time, but only in recent missions have the planners seen the wisdom of this. However, we return as we see fit, usually the result of the particular conditions that pertain at the time, and they are usually different each time.

As we loosen up Nick reports that we have 2500 gallons left. That should be enough to make it, based on our previous flights. Hal gives us his observations of the weather and winds that we can expect to encounter -- a combination of his briefed information and observations made on the flight up. We hear various ditching messages. Some planes are in trouble. We send out our unspoken hopes that they make it all right. There are subs in this area and B-29s rendezvousing with them that may be of help. In one case in the past a B-29 ditched beside a waiting sub, and the crew members, all eleven of them, got out safely.

These missions have changed greatly since the early days. When we arrived at Tinian and in the few weeks immediately after, the life of a crew, based on the records, was 15 missions, by that time the law of averages would have removed them one way or another. This we understood and accepted as the hazard of our business. Further, at that time it was not a question of whether you'd be forced to ditch, but only a question of when. We learned these things from the crews who were flying when we arrived, their thoughts and hopes then became part of our outlook on the war here. If you ditched, your chances of being rescued were slim, even if you were lucky enough to be located. Now we know that with the facilities available, and the organization between us and the subs, planes, and surface crafts, that we have a good chance of being located, and if located, a better than 90% chance of being picked up. It's a boost to the morale and we give thanks to the Navy boys who engage in this work.

It's one thing to hear the ditching messages and another to be the ones sending them. It's hard to think of this, our plane, going under water while we try to leave her. This cold, hard metal under my hand, that pulsates with life and has the acquired character and personality of "our plane", an extension of ourselves, does not seem destined for ditching, just as we hope that it isn't. Yet, there's someone else in trouble. They're jettisoning all moveable equipment, getting the emergency gear ready, preparing themselves, and calling for help to the rescue facilities. Buddy, you've got a lot of rooters hoping you make it, though they can't help you themselves. We don't hear the outcome -- they're too far away. As we approach Iwo we hear one of the "Daredevil" planes calling Walnut, asking for landing instructions. The radar man is dead. At 1200 we cross above Iwo and see the haven of refuge far below, looking too tiny to be of any help.

Nick states that in relation to other flights that caused us so much trouble, we have fuel to spare at this point, so we continue on to Base. 1600 gallons at this point we know is enough, barring any trouble, so we drowse and reminisce. "There's sack-land," Jake indicates dead ahead, and adds, "Isn't it beautiful?" Bill differs, "Give me the Golden Gate." Well, it may not be long and we'll see that most beautiful of countries. Saipan and Tinian are flanked by clouds -- a welcome sight. On arrival we circle the hardstand in a steep bank so the men can see the "Miss A. '62", and come in to land at 1520. Pat and the boys are there to greet us. "Did you give it to them?!" We give them a brief description of the flight, write up the plane's status in the Form 1, sign it, and depart in the truck.

At the interrogation we tell our story of the flight. We learn that so far as is known at this time, the plane lost out of the formation ahead of us was not one of our Group, but one from another outfit that tacked onto the formation going in. The next day we learn the facts from the Bomber Command twenty-four hour report, a synthesis of everything known of the mission. 9 planes were lost, 5 thought lost to enemy fighters, 3 to flak, and 1 operationally. 84 men are missing, 17 wounded, and 1 killed. 62 enemy fighters were destroyed, with 48 probably destroyed and 65 damaged. Among the observations of the returning crews were: a B-29 seen in a spin over the target exploded just off land after being hit by flak and rammed by a George-type fighter, 1 plane crashed at Iwo while landing, and 6 whose fate is unknown. Again we were lucky.

We are of age, with 21 behind us now.

Chapter 29 Osaka

June 7, 1945 – No. 22

"Iwo Jima"

After a night's rest we check in Squadron Operations and Orderly room, hoping that news has come through concerning our going home, perhaps even the orders. But there's no news, it's almost as though the whole matter were closed, and here we are practically standing on one foot, waiting to hear. We do notice that our crew has passed the 300 hours of combat flight time -- the first and only in the Squadron so far. We enjoy leading the pack. The crews are each desirous of getting the missions behind them and the other crews envy our having twenty-one behind us already. The average is around 19. But we're going home. Perhaps that's why we are being pushed fairly hard, the Squadron Operations Officer and the Docs figuring that we'll get a rest at home. Some of the crews have been sent to Hawaii, depending on their fatigue and strain. Mutch's crew and Park's crew are there at this time, and Fortune has just left.

The old routine of missions intermixed with sleeping and resting has almost buried the temporary vision of home, and the hopes fade further when we are scheduled for the next mission. On the mission board appear the names: Maki, Litchfield, Dawson, Meadows, Alger, Bassett, Rodgers, Cooney, Schwager, and Jordan. We make light of it and feel better. "Let's get one more before we go home, what you say?" and we return to our quarters to rest or gather equipment.

At the target identification we learn that this mission is designed to destroy the remaining portions of Osaka, and we go over the charts, maps, and mosaics again. The Commanding Officer at the outset passes on what he knows about the mission, stating that by pressing these attacks we'll force the Japs to quit before an invasion becomes necessary. We learn further that there will be fighter "escort" and this brings the usual titter. We've heard that so often, and have never seen the fighters. Most of us haven't seen an American fighter from our planes except in the vicinity of the Marianas or Iwo. We know that the fighters go to Japan, but the C.O. shouldn't call it an escort, rather diversionary. We realize they are busy strafing airfields below or engaging fighters elsewhere.

The new Operations Officer takes over and we settle down to absorbing the facts from his intelligent presentation. We learn that there will be three Squadrons in the Group and three Groups in the Wing. There is no secondary target, since the city of Osaka is a good radar target. We will have 6800 gallons of fuel and 179 M46 incendiary bombs plus one frag cluster, for explosive effect. The latter will reach the ground sooner, since the incendiary bombs ignite in midair and drop more slowly. Our total gross weight average will be 137,000 lbs. Our plane is among those which carry a strike camera.

Take-off will be to the east. The assembly point will be 15 miles to the west of Muroto-saki, the point of land extending farthest south from eastern Shikoku. The leader of our Squadron, Jordan, will trail red smoke at 19,000 feet in right hand circles. The time for leaving the assembly point will be 1257. The departure point is Wada-shima, an island south of Awaji Island, and the time for departure is 1306. The IP is Simoto, the tip of land extending west from Honshu into the Inland Sea. The heading into the target will be 54 degrees for a distance of 37 nautical miles. The breakaway will be on a heading of 102 degrees. The best return altitude will be 14,000 feet.

Now the Intelligence Officer states that, of the total area of Osaka (76 square miles), about 11 square miles has been burned out. Should it be necessary to bail out it might be wise to make a delayed chute opening. He recalls the story that we've heard in camp about the crew who bailed out over the target recently and an attacking fighter shot them as they parachuted. The bombing run will be a timed radar run. Air-Sea rescue will be very good, with 21 units participating. There will be 6 subs, 6 superdumbos rendezvousing with the subs, 6 dumbos, 1 tender, and 2 destroyers. The weather will not be very good between the Marianas and the target, for there is a cold front lying to the north of Iwo and there will be a cloud system with icing accompanying it.

The Operations Officer calls our attention to the fact that the fuel situation will be critical, since the reserve is 250 gallons. With a high altitude assembly we may require more than the expected amount. We appreciate the realistic manner in which he presents the facts to us. Apparently the fuel situation caught his eye when the directive came from higher headquarters and he is giving us the benefit of his observation -- a discernment his predecessor did not have. So again we are being pared down to the last gallon of fuel. A certain number of us will be forced to use Iwo, and if Iwo is closed -- ? But these are the plans and we have no choice. The time table will be, for us, the arrival of the lead plane at the assembly at 1219K, the main force at 1229K, and departure at 1251K.

At the plane we are fairly rushed, and have little time to chat while accomplishing the chores. In the midst of the activities the Commanding Officer drives up in his Jeep, which I immediately recognize from the rear of the plane. It has two green spotlights, a red spotlight, two radio antennas, "Commanding Officer" painted in yellow in several places, and a new plaque with his name and rank in large letters mounted on the lower windshield. "We're all set," I answer, and he drives to the next plane.

Pat tells us that he found a flak hole the size of his fist in the No. 1 engine nacelle after the last mission. Frequently there are flak holes in the skin, but we usually discover them immediately after we return. This one was located in an obscure place, so it was easy to miss. Odd that we missed it on the postflight inspection of the plane which we make after landing each time. Pat also calls our attention to an oil leak in No. 2 engine. He found that the gaskets were not replaced on several of the oil connections during the engine change, and that we may have a slight leak this time, but they haven't had time to fix it. The gasket is off the No. 2 rocker box, and thus the leak. He doesn't think that it is very bad, it hasn't leaked during the lengthy run-ups. We are glad to know about it, even though time does not permit fixing it.

Holton comes by. We kid him about this being a heck of a way to spend his rest leave of 3 days -- seeing planes off at 0330. Doc Schroeder comes by without his side-kick, Koltoon, who has gone to the States on emergency leave. He says that we'll have to take off at other times, these hours are wearing him down. We laugh and assure him that the time will be changed. Maybe the other crew members are feeling the nostalgia I feel already, facing our going home and leaving all this behind us -- of all things!

We climb in, heckling Nick about getting his check list started. Nick is usually the last one in his seat. Bill goes over the check list and I check the various levers and instruments to see that they're all right. Brakes, pilot's emergency cabin air pressure and gear door release, throttle over control, and the various engine controls located at the pilot's and copilot's positions -- they are found normal and ready to go. Nick completes his check list and the crew members state that they're ready to go, so we start the engines. Just like clockwork, each man does his job and checks in with me so we know that everything is operative and we're as ready to go as we'll ever be, yet it doesn't take long. It's almost a year now that we've been doing just this, and our teamwork is streamlined. The engines sound and look all right on the power check. We taxi out on time to the minute. This time we are flagged to runway "A". Since it's a "black top" we roll easily and pick up speed more quickly. We leave the field with 150 mph and the plane flying well.

From this point on the mission follows the general patterns of the past. We encounter bad weather north of Iwo, as expected. Usually at some point along the 1500 mile route we do encounter a stretch of bad weather, but we "barrel" right on through. The B-29 is a good plane on instruments, a good "weather" ship. We try to save fuel wherever possible, short of squeezing blood out of the turnip, and yet make good the assembly time. All goes well. Jonesy and the gunners test fire the guns after daybreak, and Nick transfers the fuel. We get into our heavy suits and wait for the hazy coastline to appear ahead. Much of the distance we've flown above a carpet of clouds and Hal can't get a ground speed or drift. At 1200 we arrive in the assembly area ahead of time, probably because of the wind being other than as briefed. All the way Hal made use of the winds' directions and velocities as the weather man said they would be. The low clouds prevented cross checking them after daylight. During the night there is no way to check the drift or ground speed visually.

Since we have some time to kill, we cut back on our power as far as we can and wait for the other planes. They soon appear, several of them ahead of time, too. Litchfield joins us as we wait for the leader, then Schwager. Finally, after a short wait, we see a plane ahead trailing red smoke and we make for it. Litchfield takes the deputy lead on Jordan's right wing. Schwager flies to the inside during the right hand turns, as leader of the "B" flight. Soon, as leader of the "C" flight, we have Cooney and Dawson on our wings.

We are still faced with the need of saving fuel for ourselves and our wingmen, so, instead of the standard procedure of flying to the left of the leader in the customary flight position, we carry the flight higher and behind the lead flight as it makes the right hand circles. In this way we are assembled in an auto-lean power setting, varying our forward position with relation to the lead flight by sliding more toward the inside of the turn or to the outside. Without touching our power increasing and decreasing speed, we are able to govern our forward speed guiding on Jordan. Born of necessity, we recognize immediately that this is a practical manner to handle the assembly problem of saving fuel and yet remaining close together.

Now our formation is joined. We see Maki and Rodgers with Schwager and Litchfield and Meadows with Jordan. In our flight we have Cooney in 14 and Dawson in 9. Only Bassett has not arrived. We see other formations in the area and are glad that we formed ours so easily with so many other planes around. At 1246 we stop circling and head for the tip of land so that we'll leave precisely at 1251. Ahead, between clouds, we see the wooded land of lower Shikoku, up whose eastern coast we're to fly. There is a low cover of stratus-type clouds covering much of the land, while the water is clear. It is a phenomenon that we've observed before. Bill and I alternate at the controls. We're the low flight and both of us can see the lead flight from our seats.

As we progress towards the IP Jake calls, "Looks like fighters ahead," and we see the small objects darting across the sky. "Fighter at 12," Jonesy comes in. "I've got the upper forward," Jake tells Jonesy. Here he comes, apparently attacking our lead flight. Several of the turrets of the other planes swing on him and fire. Now, in a rush, he's breaking away, diving behind the formation, too fast for George to get in a shot. We approach Awaji Island heading for the IP.

"Here comes another, 12 o'clock," calls Jake and he peers into his sight. The fighter starts high, dives to our level, and then comes straight in. It looks as though he's heading for our flight. Jake gets in a good burst, vibrating us all with the four guns. The fighter breaks away to our left. "He's smoking," George reports, but no one can get another shot at him as he enters the clouds. "Flak ahead," Jake calls out, and we see the smoke in the distance, pin-points which disappear while you look. Ahead we see clouds extending above our altitude, but we can't estimate their distance. We don't want to go into a cloud layer on the bomb run.

Jordan calls Litchfield and asks him to take the lead, since his radar is inoperative. Meadows crosses under, taking Litchfield's right wing, and then Litch moves forward, while Jordan drops back on his left wing. The change-over loosens the entire formation, and we're at the IP, but we pull the flights in tight again as the doors come open. At this point a B-29 formation, which had been well to one side before but has converged with our course, passes several hundred feet directly above us, crossing to our right on course for their point in the target area. We don't like it, as we look up into their open bomb bays, where the bombs may be seen ready for release, but we fly on. "There they go," Bill shouts and I push the release. Our bombs leave a fraction of a second behind the leader's. Our wing ships' bombs are falling, too, the scanners report. There seems to be no end to them as they leave the bomb bays of the lead flight. For almost half a minute they cascade from the open doors, 180 per plane. The extra power on our engines, with the doors open, is causing an unusual vibration of the plane, and it feels like one of the props is nicked -- perhaps by a shell. The vibration is quite noticeable. We close the doors and stay right in tight with the lead flight. Our planes seem to be all right, though all of them report a possible shortage of fuel. Nick announces that the No. 2 engine, which has been slowly but steadily leaking oil, is now down to 35 gallons remaining, having dropped from 68 gallons, and is going down faster now than at first. Nick figures the fuel remaining and we see it's going to be the old "squeeze play" to get into Tinian. Judging from the talk, the other planes are low, too. Well, it's the old story. Wonder who'll ditch this time. Maybe Iwo will be open.

About 15 minutes out from the target Al tunes in the San Francisco News Broadcast, and we hear the announcer mention the mission we are flying. He describes the flight as "A large force of Superforts flying from their Marianas bases have bombed Osaka." Then he goes on to say, "The Superforts had no opposition, there were no fighter attacks or flak. All planes returned safely to base." Well, that's great. Here we are, wondering whether we'll have enough gas to get home, and has us safely back at the base. Rather silly of one of us, isn't it? The flak we saw, and the fighters that attacked, must have been hallucinations on our part. We wonder for whom that broadcast is intended, and who's kidding who. Many times in the past we've been surprised over the news given the folks back home. But the Government's policy of denying accurate news to the public is no secret. So far as we're concerned, it's a mistake. They should be told the truth.

Staying at 20,000 feet, we reach the bad weather area north of Iwo and go into the long east-west line of clouds that reach well above our altitude. We turn off the autopilot and fly manually in the roughness of the up and down drafts. We are considerably shaken, but not more than anticipated. "Looks like we're picking up ice," Jake observes. Bill and I nod and look out at the engines and wings. Ice deposits are building up on the prop dome, the front of the engine cowling around the air-intake, and on the leading edge of the wings. The nose windows glaze over. Evidently it's adding to our weight or changing the shape of the wing, because we're slowing down. The ice is thick on the prop dome. So we start to let down, seeking an altitude where the ice will evaporate. At 17,000 feet the ice begins to leave the nose and we stay there until the ice is gone.

As we approach Iwo we check the estimate of fuel remaining, for the umpteenth time, and our general situation. Nick remains certain in his belief that we have 1200 gallons by figures and 1400 by the fuel tank reading. Hal estimates that we'll have head winds much of the way to Tinian, beyond Iwo, and it appears to be just a question of time until we must feather No. 2 for lack of oil -- it's down to 18 gallons, a loss of 50 thus far. Nick estimates that we should not go below 13 gallons in order not to hurt the engine, and also to be able still to feather it. Cooney calls and tells us that he's going into Iwo, being low on fuel. We acknowledge and tell him we're going to try to make home.

45 miles south of Iwo we are down to 13 gallons of oil and we feather No. 2. The big blades stop and we set up the other three engines and the trim of the plane for three wing operation. Our air speed falls from 185 to 165, and even jacking up the power doesn't give us the anticipated speed. Recomputing again, we see that there just isn't enough gas to make it, even assuming the amount of

fuel to be our maximum estimate. We decide to turn back and land at Iwo. The weather is clear there. We unfeather No. 2 in order to make a normal landing, and feeling sure that the few minutes more of operation will not hurt the engine. It wasn't heating from lack of oil at the time we feathered. As we turn back, the entire crew sounds relieved. Hal felt sure that the winds would be bad. Nick feels that the fuel might be lower than we thought. We all feel glad not to be taking the chance again. Al gladly relaxes after preparing to send the emergency messages necessary for our trip home. Al calls Tinian and tells the Base that we're going into Iwo.

We circle Iwo, calling Walnut, and explaining our situation. The Tower is hesitant to let us land until we tell them we absolutely can't go on, that we've tried and know we can't make it. Their reluctance to give us landing permission is explained by the field jammed with aircraft. Planes are jammed everywhere the eye can see on the central field, the B-29 strip. Even on the fighter fields there are B-29s. Bill whistles, "Look at that. Looks like the whole outfit. Hope the Island doesn't sink under the weight."

At 1820 we make the precarious landing, touching the runway between rows of planes parked just beyond our wing-tips on either side. The field is definitely in an emergency situation. As we follow the parking Jeep we roll slowly, carefully judging our wing-tips to avoid the planes. We are given the signal to cut our engines in the middle of the adjoining taxi strip. Before we can get out, a cleetrak with tow bar pulls and pushes the plane until we are parked between two other planes, whose wings almost touch our fuselage, as ours almost touches theirs. The nose extends over the edge of the narrow strip. On all sides of us the planes are jammed in, no effort being made to keep them free to move out and leave. The biggest problem is just to find enough soil on which to keep the plane's wheels.

After requesting service, including gas and oil, the crew takes off to find some chow. It's apparent that we'll be here for some time. I stay with the plane. Across the strip, in a small area where there are no planes, appears an amazing thing, a large scoop shovel loading trucks with steaming dirt. It seems that the soil being moved is steaming because this is a volcano upon which we are sitting. It is inactive, needless to say. A maintenance man, who has ceased to think this strange, answers my questions.

It begins to rain. For a few minutes it seems that a tidal wave is engulfing us from directly above. The clouds and the water itself prevent visibility beyond a few feet -- visibility zero-zero. Yet all the time the B-29s which have been serviced are taking off in order to ease the situation on the field, although taking off in this weather appears to be an extreme emergency in itself, unless there's less rain over at the runway.

Through the rain some bedraggled figures run toward the plane. The fellows seem to feel better for having some food inside them, despite the rain. Bill brings a sandwich and a beer for me. With a wry face I gladly gulp down the provisions. Seems like days since we last ate. An Operation Officer stops by to inform us that it will be a long time until service is available, perhaps not until morning, and that we should get some quarters and "sack up", awaiting our call when the plane is ready, so we troop off through the drizzle.

At a tent marked "Combat crews -- transients" we all go in together and draw two blankets, a towel, and a mess kit apiece. We also get a tent number. Through the mud we slosh into the tent that is to be our quarters, and find a couple dozen cots side by side, almost touching -- quite a squeeze. Dick, Al, Charlie, and George fall into the nearest cots with sighs. Nick tests one, "Ah, this one feels nice and soft." Gabby says, "I could sleep on the floor if I had to," but we feel glad that he -- and we -- don't have to. The two blankets are used in various ways to provide maximum padding and warmth. Jonesy has quietly collapsed, and Jake, Hal, Bill, and I do the same. It's a pleasure to lie down and rest again. On the outside the rain and mud is very discouraging, especially on a place so bleak, barren, and depressing as this hard-fought-for island. Bless the Marines.

The next morning, and it's hard to get up. Somehow during the night the cot has become a feather bed and caresses the weary flesh. But it's time to get moving, so we get up. After the dirt is wiped off face and hands with a few drops of water and the towel, we go over to the chow line for breakfast. There who should I see standing in line but John Coffman, an old friend, a fellow cadet during training days. What a treat! He looks mighty good. Tanned, perhaps a little more wrinkled about the eyes, but the same old, wise, philosophical outlook on life. He whittles while others worry. We talk like a couple of long-lost buddies. I introduce him to the fellows and we finish breakfast. Then, with adieus, we go our ways. We learn, however, that those in charge are not going to let us leave for awhile. It seems that the field is still tied up and the fighters are going out. So the crew members go their own ways, agreeing to meet back at the plane at 1100.

I find John, and since he isn't going anywhere in a hurry, we decide to do some sight-seeing. We walk off down the muddy roads toward the famous beaches and are amazed to find them so close to the point where the Marines assaulted. Why, a boy with a bee-bee gun or a 22 gun could be a threat at that distance. No wonder the Marines had such a struggle. The hill is pock-marked with shell fire, and the remnants of caves, pill-boxes, and foxholes. The Japs were really holed-in. We find that many piles of bags of rice are intact in the caves. A Navy man, noticing us sight-seeing, shows us a samurai sword, pistol, and flag belonging to dead Japs -- quite a grim looking set of souvenirs. The sword is pretty excellent material and workmanship. The flag has many Jap names, supposedly the men of the outfit to which its owner belonged, inscribed on it.

From here we go down to the beach itself, where we inspect a huge pile of debris, consisting of wrecked fighting equipment of various kinds. Further along the beach are the many wrecked ships and landing barges that are too big to move. The loose volcanic soil, that reaches above our ankles, has built about the wreckage. We are puzzled to see a man covering another man with this soil, and we learn that he is getting a steam bath from the hot ash, which is hot from the sub-surface heat. The water in this area is quite warm, too.

We wade through the loose soil and catch a ride in a jeep going toward Mt. Suribachi at the southern tip of the island. Along the way we see many of the Jap pill boxes, made of heavy reinforced concrete with two-foot walls. They are located so that the entire beach is covered by their point-blank fire. We just can't see how men could have run through that loose, volcanic soil, in the face of point-blank fire, to take the beach. The pill boxes have been burned out and some blown apart. We pass the 3rd and 4th Marines Division cemeteries and see thousands of white crosses. They would know how the beach was taken.

At the foot of the mountain we catch a ride in a jeep and up we go. The road is steep and winding, with a sheer drop-off and no railing. "Don't look back," John says as we hang on. 500 feet higher we look over the island. What a sight! There are the two beaches stretching north on either side of the base of Suribachi, flanking a narrow strip of land. Those are the Invasion beaches. John and I look in silence. All this happened while we lived in comparative luxury a few hundred miles to the south. This was the invasion for which we saw men practicing with planes, ships and barges off the western shores of our living area. Many of those ships are still here, sunk and unmoved on the approaches to the beaches. Now the island is a bee-hive of activity. The airfields are lined with planes, many vehicles are moving in all directions -- B-29s, B-17s, P-61s, P-51s, and Navy planes -- all lined up in great numbers. Large tent areas are seen, dotting the Island. John looks at the drop and shudders, "This is too dangerous, we'd better stick to flying."

We go back down the mountain and head for the field. There we say farewell, John going to pick up a plane that must be ferried back to Saipan, where he is stationed. He has 15 missions behind him and is going strong. The crew are all at the plane and have it ready to go, bless them. We climb in and fire up the engines. With so much power to burn, we make a pursuit take-off after we taxi out, zooming beside Suribachi and looking down into its activity. The old volcanic crater is filled with radar, radio, and allied equipment. Is this our last take-off in combat? We wonder if this is to be our last mission.

On the way back we lapse into silence, each with his own thoughts. Are we going to miss these missions, miss seeing the other men, all friends flying beside us in the planes? Are we going to dislike reading the news instead of participating in it? Are we going to be able to get along in the States, knowing what's going on over here? We all came out here voluntarily and wanted a full tour of duty behind us. Perhaps we haven't been scared enough yet to be glad to go home unquestionably and stay, but we're lucky to be leaving while our luck holds out.

Sitting here, reminiscing, it's easy to recognize that the "feel" of the plane is an inbred factor while flying now. I can feel the kicking of an engine and the subsequent yaw of the plane, almost subconsciously. The least bit of desynchronization of the props is noticeable and disturbing. There are the smells that are normal and those that are not, for instance, Hal's pipe and electric fires. There is the sense of "feel" that recognizes unusual vibrations. And the controls -- they have a "feel" to them. It is physical and it's mental, the latter deriving from the instruments' statement of the condition of the engines, and the trim tabs, indicating the balance of the plane around its three axes.

There is a peculiar mental alertness that accompanies flight. Anything that occurs either ahead or to the extreme sides alerts the system, even after the cause is gone, such as the flare of a match when half asleep, that brings one instantly alert. Any strange sound, smell, noise, or feel alerts the pilot and tells him that something is not right -- what is it? This situation in a plane might be compared to that on the ground if someone told you, "Now something's going to happen -- are you ready?" Perhaps that's why flying is so tiring. No matter what we're doing in the air -- even sleeping -- the subconscious watch-dog is alert, keeping us in a semi-awake condition all of the time. Somehow the nostalgia of this last flight -- if that's what it is -- keeps us busy recalling our many flying experiences and the men who shared them. Our mutual danger has knit a bond different from any other, just what it is I don't know.

The miles roll by and before long there's our home ahead. It's 0245 when we circle the field and set the big bird carefully on the runway. "Miss A. '62" still has a virgin tail-skid, so far as we are concerned, and it must stay that way. The ground crew saw us circle the field and are out to greet us as we taxi up to the hardstand. Pat directs us straight into the area, and we cut the engines. Now begins the unloading and banter with the crew. We're going to miss Pat and the boys.

At the interrogation we inquire about the results of the mission and learn that so far as they know all of our planes are accounted for. It seems that 98 of the B-29s were forced to stop at Iwo, most of them for refueling. It seems to us that this fact proves more than any preceding one, that the fuel allotted is not enough. We know what would have happened if Iwo had been closed and we couldn't have landed there. It doesn't seem to us that Iwo should be made part of a mission in that way, but should be kept distinctly for emergency landings, as we've been told it is.

22 missions down. ? to go. When do we go home?

Chapter 30 Stateside Interlude

"Off the Rock"

No sooner are the post-mission duties accomplished than we are asking the Sergeant in the orderly room if the orders have arrived. "Any news?" Comes the answer, "No news," to which he adds the obvious, "Ought to be here by now." We agree and extract the promise that we'll be notified as soon as they arrive. Having satisfied ourselves that nothing has happened in our absence, pertaining to the Stateside trip, we decide to "sack up". The men look tired. Only the excitement over our prospective return home has kept them going without more rest. The missions are very tiring, both mentally and physically. Each is almost a three-day affair, a day of preparation before the mission, the mission itself, and the post-mission activities while the effect of the Benzedrine wears off which includes unloading, interrogation, critique, and general resumption of regular hours. Many missions without a long enough announced rest and change progressively tire the men. Recuperation is not complete each time and the fatigue becomes gradually greater, or so the Doc has explained it to us. In our case the trip home has served as a further incentive, no doubt, and the fatigue was staved off. We agree that the rest at home will do the trick and we are given the assurance that our last flight before leaving is behind us. The crew is glad to learn this. We do not understand as the Doc does, just what fatigue is, technically, but we are glad to rest right now.

"Wish we could pack," comments Bill. "Or start clearing the post," Hal adds. We sit about the Quonset wondering where to start in preparing to leave. The other men know now that we aren't going to fly any more and don't hesitate to ask us about the impending trip. They understand how we felt about not caring to discuss it while still flying the missions. The consensus of opinion among the men is that we will not return. "They'll keep you there as instructors," Porky observes. "Sure, you'll be training Command Commandos, doesn't that make you happy?" jeers Clint Wride. He ribs us, knowing our distaste for the Training Command. "They won't send you back here for ten missions, or whatever it takes, for you to finish your tour," Charlie Lazin expresses what appears logical.

As the fellows hash our fate we begin to feel that maybe we will stay in the States, sure enough. In fact, there's no one who thinks we'll be returning, even though the "Lead Crew School" is, theoretically, to train crews who will come back here and lead formations on targets requiring precision bombing, regardless of weather. Rather, it seems logical to think, they would send a crew which has had only a few missions. They would have an idea of the work here, and a large number of missions to go before completing their tour of duty.

Feeling better after the observations of our neighbors, we start to go through our belongings, preparatory to packing. So far as we know there is no curtailment of luggage, so we begin to prepare what will be comfortable to carry and leave all the rest. For the next five days we are kept busy with a variety of activities, but all secondary to the long awaited orders. We can pack and unpack all day long -- like a girl first leaving home -- but nothing has significance without the orders.

Only with them can we move.

Squadron authorities give us a pamphlet considered highly significant, since it has been sent out by the school at Muroc. In it we learn that we are, under no conditions, to bring our families or cars -- there is no room for either. Further, neither heaven nor hell must interfere with our reporting there promptly on the 29th of June. These instructions are very depressing, but we worry about first things first -- getting orders and leaving the "rock".

Another parade is held in the dust and sweat, standing at attention or "at ease" for long periods, while the crews are awarded clusters to their air medals. Of greater interest are the nurses on the side-lines, who keep the heads in the ranks revolving.

The strain of waiting and joy of impending departure, plus sad farewells, culminate in two parties. The first is a joyous gathering of the officers of the various crews, whom we have known and worked with so long. Singing, joking, and visions of home figure largely in the proceedings. Fortune, Schad, Cooney, Mutch, and many others drop by to join Bill, Hal, Jake, and me for farewell banter. Ben Lay and Doc Schroeder even say "Hello", along with Bob Hall. Their repartee sparkles as usual, but is tinged with melancholia -- thinking of going home themselves. The second party is as meaningful as the first, though in a different way. We invite the ground crew over to our Quonset, since there is no place else for us to have a farewell chat. Pat, Red, Hank, and Vito drop by and regale us with stories about maintenance of the plane, their homes, and Army posts in the past. Everyone is aware of the solid bond established between us all, and we can only hint at what their work has meant to us, but they understand, we feel sure. It is hard to thank someone for repeatedly doing work, cheerfully and unceasingly, which has been a protection to your life -- possibly saved your life several times over. It is with sadness and nostalgia that we bid farewell to them.

The next few days our party is the center of recriminations and callings "on the carpet", since we officers entertained enlisted men in our quarters. In vain do I tell the Squadron C.O. there had been no rowdiness or back slapping, but only sincere farewells and best wishes, held in our quarters because there was no place else to entertain. The Squadron C.O. hated to call me down, that was obvious, but the Group C.O. had heard indirectly of the affair and had made it hot for him, so he had to pass it on to me. But this wasn't enough. The Group C.O. holds an "Officers Call" for all officers, and there he berates the entire outfit for conduct too friendly to the men. He doesn't realize that through it all we have the respect and friendship of these men, who will work for us as they never will for him. Nor have we actually overstepped Army discipline, we have strengthened it.

In our relationships, even at their most joyous, the enlisted men did not call me by my first name, but always addressed me by rank, "Lt. Alger, - - -." How well we, of the combat crews, have learned the inner most workings of the relationships of officers and men bound together, and now the C.O. lectures us on it! With in our crews we have worked together, joked together, been quartered together, lived day by day together, and almost died together, as an eleven man crew. And the C.O. lectures us on how to handle our relationships! He's just losing more ground. When, as the commander of the crew, the C.O.'s threat that because of the party we may not go to the States after all is told to me by the Squadron C.O., my answer is, "That's all right with us!" It really isn't, of course, but there's a point beyond which people don't shove you anymore. The Group C.O. can do as he likes.

By June 13th we are packed and ready to go. Our furniture has been passed on to others and we are living with one hand on our B-4 bag, ready to go. The orders come! But we can't go, there is no transportation available to take us. So we clear the post, which means visiting all the various departments, getting signatures. These certify that so far as each is concerned, we are free to go. Our orders state that we are II priority outside U.S. continental limits, which is mighty high, and are to be gone 30 days at the school, plus travel time. We are each allowed 65 lbs., with the exceptions for the navigator and bombardier, who must carry heavy professional equipment. They are allowed additional weight, 40 lbs. and 25 lbs. respectively. All of us have more luggage than allowed, but we haven't been told this before, so we decide to try to talk our way through. We think we're going home for good. The orders consider only the weight of flying equipment and a few personal clothes.

The orders are dated June 12th. It's apparent that this entire trip will be on our own time, since we get only the time remaining between our arrival and the 29th to spend at home. Through the semi-official grapevine we are told that we will go in the C-54 airplanes that are especially allotted to our Wing for transportation to the States.

The 13th turns into the 14th, and now the 14th is gone. Our fellow crews go out on a mission and we are left in a semi-deserted camp. Our unhappiness is augmented by the news that crews from other Wings, and even from a fellow Group nearby, have been gone for from one to two weeks already. On the 15th we are told to be ready to go within an hour, that we are to be picked up by a special C-47 at West Field, taken to Saipan to meet the C-54 and be on our way to the States. We make the fur fly, load onto a truck, and are away for West Field. Everyone is in high spirits. At West Field there is no plane. After three hours we catch a ride on a C-47.

At Saipan no one has heard of us, and we are given cards to fill out, which will be filed away until some transportation shows up. All space is taken by the wounded of Okinawa. To our inquiry about the C-54s assigned to our Wing, we get a laugh. "They're all in the States, won't be back for 10 days." So that's that. We get quarters, as instructed, and wait, and wait. We are told that it will be several days at least. Rather than die a lingering death, we get in touch with the Navy and are promised a ride out that night. So here we are, at midnight, bag and baggage, including "Gyro", our only mascot since "Turbo" went a-courting and never returned.

So it is that on June 17th we get aboard the PB4Y and taxi out into Saipan Harbor for take-off. During the flight, after a not too sad farewell to the Marianas, we sleep, read, talk, and play cards. But, though dead tired, I can't sleep from the strain of trying to get a ride for the crew, so I visit the flight deck of the plane and talk to the pilot about flying and the Navy way.

At Kwajalein tragedy strikes. The Naval port officer insists, at the pilot's request, that "Gyro" be off-loaded. "The authorities at Hawaii won't like it and then the pilot will be burned for it," the port officer unfeelingly states. We debate, quoting the Army Air Forces Magazine, which makes a fuss over flying mascots of the service which mean so much to the men. We dicker, plead, and argue. Finally, as we are all about to be off-loaded for such temerity, we are forced to agree or give up the crew's chances of even a short visit at home. So off Gyro goes. It's a pathetic moment when we leave the dock. Gyro is straining at the leash to accompany us, whimpering and crying, while the crew stoically or tearfully watch in silence from the port holes. Just before departure my eyes felt damp, watching Hal and Jake hug and pat Gyro for the last time. A card was affixed to his collar reading, "My name's <u>Gyro</u>!" and then the Squadron and Group names were written, with address on Tinian, "Please send me there."

We fly on to Johnston Island, arriving the middle of the next night. From there we go to Honolulu, after a very slow flight. After going through customs we get quarters at Hickam Field and register. Immediately it's the same routine of getting a "ride" to the States. The authorities change our priority from a II to a III. We protest. They remain adamant. We explain our long delay already, but we can't mention our rest at home, because they would delay us all the more, so we emphasize the importance of the school and arriving there immediately. We use every plea ever thought of and the next night we get away at 0130 on a C-54. It is June 19th. No one has rested or eaten regularly, and I feel tense and tired. Guess the others are "bushed", too. They look to me to get the rides and I can't let them down.

Despite resurgent twinges of air-sickness in the rough clouds, I daydream over the proximity of the U.S.A. The others, each in his own way, silently or noisy, do the same. Higgy gestures out of his southern window, through which we have been scanning periodically for hours. U.S.A.! Stretching south of us far ahead is a hazy line -- the coast. So we're home at last, we made the round trip after all! Everyone happily kids the others. It's dream-like in its glory. The next few minutes, as we fasten our seat belts, look out the small windows, and prepare for landing, are a buzz of excitement. "There's the Golden Gate!" "There's Frisco." "No, San Francisco," someone corrects. That first glimpse of U.S. soil after months of Jap landscape will not be forgotten. The majesty of the big hills, rugged scenery on a grand scale, is a sharp contrast to the small quality of Japan. And this city of skyscrapers, that has never been bombed! What a beautiful place this city and surrounding country is. How fortunate we are to come home to this. How lucky we are to have survived. How lucky to have such a country to come to. Almost dizzy with excitement, and now quiet with thought, everyone settles down ready for landing at Hamilton Field. Once again we touch U.S. soil. We are home again. But now we must get home -- each to his own locality.

Again the fight for priority and attention begins. "No, you must wait until tomorrow. The Officer in charge has gone home," a Captain at the terminal informs us. "Wait, it's only ten to five. We've got to get started home!" These and other argumentative comments are passed. After bickering and cajoling we reach an agreement by calling the officer in question at his home. He agrees to permit us to go ahead if we'll leave our addresses where the orders can be mailed that must accompany us after reaching the U.S.

Bill, Hal, and Jake take off after getting low Army priorities. They have a ride over to the Airline Terminal. The rest of us dispose of our flying gear by checking it, so it will be sent to us at Muroc. The seven of us remaining, Nick, Al, Gabby, Jonesy, Charlie, George and I try to locate Dick Bush, who was sent ahead of us at Honolulu on an earlier plane. There is no message from him, so we assume that he had a ride and has gone on to Cleveland, his home.

While the men get some food I try to turn our Army priority into a ride by ATC to our various homes. So it is that after midnight we get a ride to Sacramento, from which such long flights are originated. While the others get some sleep, I remain at the Terminal Office with some magazines, so that I'll be first on the scene when the morning shift arrives. The C.Q. (Charge of Quarters) fails to awaken the men and the miss the first ride out. There is great argument and gnashing of teeth. It seems they thought we had already gone, despite our reminders and cards on file and my sitting there in the office. At 0930 the others catch a ride while Jonesy and I wait for another plane. We say farewell, "Have a good time at home!"

At Hamilton Field the authorities had advised us not to try to get home and back to Muroc in the short time remaining. He explained the transportation difficulties, and that men have waited for days for a hop that only took them part way, stranding them in some remote location from which they couldn't get a ride. Nothing daunted, we went right ahead trying, and thus far are going good. We have a low priority, thanks to the XXIst Bomber Command not caring whether we got some time at home or not. However, thus far, through our own efforts we're doing all right.

Jonesy and I are told that there are no rides to Oklahoma or Dallas from Sacramento, that we must go to Los Angeles and see what we can do there. We are ready to spare no effort, so we take the offered ride to Los Angeles. Dead tired, I go through the verbal routine again, explaining and begging and pleading -- trying to convert the low domestic priority into a ride. We know that with the short time remaining a train or bus is out of the question, even if we could get a seat. Since there are just the two of us, we are put on the loading list of a plane a short time later, and despite all the verbal "It's impossible" told us thus far, are on our way to Tulsa. It's just a question of not being "bumped" now by someone with a higher priority. Good fortune is ours and we stay on, landing at Tulsa at 10:30 that night. We say farewell and Jonesy goes on his way to Drumright, his home. The next morning I catch an early Airlines plane to Dallas. There Peel and our daughter greet me. It's the end of a journey, temporarily at least. How wonderful is the homecoming! No doubt the rest of the crew members are approaching their homes or have arrived now, too. George may still be a long way from Boston.

The seven days of little rest, sleep, and irregular, scanty food have taken their toll and the time home between June 22nd and 27th went mainly to recuperation. During that time I send a wire to the Commanding Officer of the Muroc school, as I had told the crew I would do: "RE LEAD CREW SCHOOL JUNE 29TH TRANSPORTATION DIFFICULTIES DELAYED THIS CREW 6 DAYS ON FLIGHT HOME. CREW MEMBERS NOW EN ROUTE HOME TO MASSACHUSETTS PENNSYLVANIA GEORGIA NEW YORK OHIO. FLIGHT SURGEON SPECIFIED THIS DELAY INTENDED AS REST PRIOR TO REPORTING MUROC JUNE 29TH POSSIBILITY OF SOME CREW MEMBERS HAVING ONLY 2 DAYS AT HOME BEFORE RETURN TO MUROC. 15 DAYS GIVEN US TO REACH THE STATES HOME REST AND RETURN TO MUROC IS INSUFFICIENT CONSIDERING DELAYS AND STRAIN OF TRAVELING. MEN APPEARED MORE NERVOUS AND TIRED THAN EVER. SERIOUSLY RECOMMEND AND HOPE YOU WILL GRANT US ADDITIONAL TIME? SEVERAL DAYS MORE. IF AFFIRMATIVE I CAN NOTIFY CREW GIVING NEW REPORTING DATE."

Hopefully I waited. The answer when it came, 4 days later, read "EXTENSION OF TIME DISAPPROVED." Brief and to the point. Now began my personal struggle. Should I relay this information as it stands or countermand it, knowing the state of affairs and willing to risk my future, by telling the men to take the extra week they were promised, the time we should have had through leaving Tinian earlier, like the other crews. The many considerations weighed me down, spoiling my brief moment with my family, and finally I wired the men the only answer I could: "TIME EXTENSION DISAPPROVED. SEE YOU AT MUROC JUNE 29TH UNLESS SICK." Maybe they would read in between the lines.

An ironical incident flavored these days of uncertainty, of joy and sadness with wife and child. A wire from Tinian came stating that since June 11th I was a Captain. Oh hollow joy! They could have it, for just a few days more at home. The entire bitter promotion situation recalls itself. Long ago, in the States, the C.O., realizing our long service in grade, told us, "There'll be promotions as soon as you prove that you can fly the B-29 and handle your crew. Wait a couple of months." It mattered not that the promotion in several cases had been earned before, over 15 to 25 months of work in grade, and had not been awarded because at the time promotions were frozen temporarily. So we waited. Later the inquiry was made again. "Wait until we get overseas, besides the tech order calls only for a 1st Lieutenant to pilot the B-29." He well knew that even the tech order permits higher rank for flight leaders, or for those men whom he wants to promote on any one of a dozen different bases.

After we arrived overseas we waited. "Colonel, how about a promotion?" we finally inquired. "Wait until you've proven yourself in combat," was the answer. So we did, some dying in the attempt. Still no promotions, except for the top few close associates of the C.O. We called attention to it plenty, but tried not to let it embitter us. So now, after the travail of 22 missions, and well over two years in rank, the promotion comes through. It doesn't mean what it should anymore.

On June 27th, when the opportunity for a flight out of Love Field appeared, I took it, again saying goodbye to wife and baby. It's either hello or goodbye all the time. It was out of the question to go to St. Louis to visit my parents -- there just wasn't time.

In Los Angeles at the bus station from which the Muroc bus departs, others of the crew turned up: Bill, Charlie, Dick, and Jake. The bus station is jammed with crew members from the 40 crews that we learn are here for the class. Most amazing of all is the large number of women who are accompanying their husbands. We recall the pamphlet about the school which was given to us and decide that they haven't been enlightened as yet on there being no families or cars allowed at the school.

The fellows are happy to see that I've been promoted and extend congratulations. Every member of the crew has been promoted. Hal, Jake, and Bill are 1st Lieutenants, Nick is a Master Sergeant, Jonesy is a Technical Sergeant, and Al, Gabby, Dick, and George are Staff Sergeants. Charlie is our only Buck Sergeant and he deserves a promotion. Most of the promotions were awarded according to tech order specification, sent out from Washington, not according to merit or length of service. Most combat crew members deserved them through merit anyway.

The bus finally deposits us at Muroc, on the edge of the Mojave dessert. It is about 106 degrees, which we learn is the normal daily heat. Shimmering waves of hot air rise from the ground. It is very dry so that, despite the heat, we are not damp, the perspiration evaporating rapidly. "Lovely spot, eh?" Jake observes. "Lovely," Dick agrees.

After getting quarters my first stop was at the office of the Commanding Officer, whom I found to be a different man from the head of the Muroc Field. We come under the direction of the XXI Bomber Command, not the C.O. of the Field. He listens quietly to my comments on the condition of the men, and sympathizes heartily. However, he points out, "My hands are tied, since my instructions come from the Bomber Command. If I could, I would give your crew some time off." He continues, "As it is, why don't you go ahead with the program here, and then if the men appear to be too tired, we'll make some changes. Furthermore, I want you to know that there will be some time off during the program, and then at the end there will be seven days or more for the best 20 of the 40 crews. In the meantime, go to the Flight Surgeon and tell him the situation and see if he can be of help." So my statement that the men may be too tired to fly safely is answered, kindly, by agreement, but for us to go ahead and fly anyway. At least he may remember us and be lenient if any of the men are late.

The Flight Surgeon chats with me awhile, and then on my case history card states that "This man should have three weeks rest before returning to flying." He points out that all he can do is recommend, that the old story of a Flight Surgeon having control of whether the men fly is only a myth, despite its appearing in

Army regulations. A Flight Surgeon is taking a terrible chance if he goes against the will of his Commanding Officer. I realize his position. After all, why should he jeopardize his position by opposing his C.O. because of us, even if we are deserving. His instructions from the XXI Bomber Command come first, and though he has an outside channel by contacting the Surgeon General, who supervises the work of all Doctors, he could do so only by opposing the Commanding Officer of the particular command in which he is located. That takes guts!

There are few men in the Army who will buck their superiors, thereby jeopardizing their future in the Army and even the success of their whole civilian life after getting out of the service. The Army is a hard and implacable master. Realizing this fact, I take leave of the Flight Surgeon, but not before mulling over the cases awaiting attention in the ante room with whom I stop to talk. Some of the men, just arriving at Muroc from the 50th Wing, came from India and China to Tinian. Some have survived crashes and flown as many as 31 missions, yet on arrival at Muroc they learn that the Flight Surgeon can be of no help in taking them off flight status for awhile. Some have been overseas on combat status for three years.

This situation is further explained by the arrival and departure of General LeMay, who leaves instructions for the crews. These are presented to us by the C.O. of the B-29 department. He carefully explains to us that everyone at this school is here to fly, and that no one will remain in the States, regardless of his condition. If a man breaks a leg, or has any other ailment, including combat fatigue, he will remain here flying with his crew, or if he will not fly, he will be sent back to the Marianas for disposition. This plain talk shows us the error of any crew member choosing not to fly with his crew. He will be replaced by another man from some other crew, and then will be sent back to the Marianas anyway. However, much of the worry over our crew is allayed when the crew is scheduled for the first "processing". Much to my surprise everyone is present, no one missing or late. And George, Gabby, Jake, Al, Jonesy, Nick, and Hal look rested, more so than when we parted.

So we have a crew together and I mention the various things the C.O. told me, including the time off during the course and the final reward for the best crews. The crew agrees to try to do their best and get the vacation at the end. Contrary to our instructions, we find that many of the other crew members have their wives with them, and their cars, and have taken all available living quarters, so we hasten to correct the situation. Bill, Al, Jonesy, and I contact our better halves in Georgia, Pennsylvania, Oklahoma, and Texas, respectively, and request them to come out.

Meanwhile we start the daily program of work. Every other day we go to ground school, and fly the alternate days, so that every day is a full day. It's a stiff schedule, particularly since we walk everywhere we go, and that runs into miles daily on this big desert field. Because of the disappointments thus far, we wonder whether we did the smart thing in coming home, after all. The instructors are combat veterans themselves, and they try to keep the course practical. We study the techniques of radar bombing, none of them new to the crew, but we gain a little insofar as the practice improves our teamwork and coordination on the radar bomb runs. From the instructors we learn that we are at the school by mistake, as we suspected all along, since the school is intended to train newer crews, who will have a longer time overseas after their return. So it looks like a comedy of errors all the way around, only no one is laughing, except ruefully, over Army ways.

On the flights we bomb, through use of radar, the various aircraft plants in and around Los Angeles and Burbank, and other city targets, thereby getting practice under similar conditions to those involved in bombing Jap cities and targets therein. We work hard, trying to please the instructors, toward getting that high rating and the time off.

Meanwhile our wives arrive and they are quartered in Army barracks, after a certain amount of friction with the authorities. There is no town near the field. Some of the wives are placed in an old parachute building. Married life becomes a series of dates, after which, in the evenings, goodbyes are said and we part. What a way to live! But we all enjoy their presence. One evening we reserve a large table at the local restaurant (30 miles away) in Lancaster. The crew and the four wives have a gala dinner and champagne party, which is the high spot in our social season. At other times we go into Los Angeles overnight and enjoy the night spots.

We are almost acclimated to the 106 degree daily afternoon temperature now. We feel lucky not to be under the 3rd Air Force jurisdiction. One of their regulations concerns drilling. Permanent personnel must drill two hours a week, regardless of the heat. During an afternoon session a Wac dropped dead. Such a regulations seems inadvisable at a desert station.

As the end of school approaches we feel the ominous farewell hanging over our heads again. Peel, Marie, Betty, and Mary Alyce are mighty good about it, and try not to be despondent after our original high hopes of being home for awhile, if not for good. They are particularly unhappy over our having so little time at home before the school. They have learned that many of the crews arrived at their homes in the States several days before we left Tinian, almost two weeks more time than we had. They can't understand it, though we try to explain. But we're not sure, either. As the school ends for us we learn that crew 2409 has been rated as No. 2 out of the 40 crews, second to a crew from another Wing that had 31 missions overseas. We eagerly plan what we are going to do with the time off. Should we go to Los Angeles? Should we go to Lake Arrowhead? We expect that the time off which we did not take, during the month's school, will be added to the time at the end.

As we approach the end we realize that we have as extensive acquaintance with California from the air, particularly Los Angeles and San Francisco areas. What a lovely country! There are the mountains, the ocean, the desert -- and they may all be seen at once. Mt. Whitney, Mt. Shasta, Mt. Rainier, all guarding the rugged ranges along the coast. Washington and Oregon are likewise pretty from the air, with large tracts of timbered land.

The last events transpire quickly. We learn that for half of the crews there will be no time off at all, but that the day after the last class they will leave for Hamilton Field. For the other half -- the 20 best adjudged crews -- there will be two days off, then all men will entrain for Hamilton Field on a troop train. They cannot provide their own transportation or stay with their families by having them on the train. By this time we feel groggy from low blows and are beyond the point of even protesting anymore. We try to make the last two days count, and then once again here we are, saying goodbye, leaving our wives to shift for themselves. This leave taking is harder than the first. We asked so much of Lady Luck last time, to take us over and to bring us home. Now here we are, doing it all over again.

After three false starts, thanks to Army management, and three goodbyes, we leave by troop train. The trip, we find, takes over twice as long this way as it would have taken if we had motored with our wives. As we leave, Hal hands me the last letter to reach me at Muroc, and I find that it's news from Tinian, written by Pete Fortune. My! It's good to hear from him, to find out how the fellows are doing. It's the only authentic information to reach us from combat since we've been here, so the other fellows crowd around.

Now we learn the bitter side. Porky Jordan and crew are missing, lost on their 33rd mission, only two missions short of going home. However, there is a possibility that the crew got out, since the plane flew straight for some time after catching fire, leading those in other planes to hope that the crew escaped. At the time they were about 100 miles north of Tokyo. Other than this, Pete describes the missions as being routine, knocking out the smaller cities of Japan, and a lot easier than the former raids on Tokyo, Nagoya, Osaka, Kobe, and Shimonoseki. Once again we feel that we are a part of the Pacific and not the United States, and resign ourselves to the truth, which we have tried not to believe, that we are going back!

At Hamilton we hear the news through the San Francisco papers that an atom bomb has just been dropped on Japan, at Hiroshima. As the power of this bomb is delineated in the papers we find it hard to believe. This is a little too much like Buck Rogers. We know what effort it takes on the part of many to lay waste a whole city, and here this bomb is supposed to destroy the entire city. Just one plane, just one bomb. "Well, if that's how it is, they don't need us," observes Bill, and we agree, thinking that they already have ten times the number of crews there to do the job.

We have a hearty meal at the Hamilton Officers' Club and revel amid a vast assortment of courses to choose from at the buffet, clean tablecloths, shiny silver, china dishes, and neat uniforms. In the lounge are overstuffed chairs and carpets. Not many of these things are known overseas -- so far as we are concerned! One of our greatest treats on returning, in retrospect, was the first overstuffed chair, encountered at Johnston Island, and the first silverware, china, flowers, and tablecloths, found at Hickam. How wonderful these things are.

We are not surprised to find that the high command has seen fit to make us high priority on the return trip, so we are hustled straight back -- nothing like the trip east. All of us laugh over those who are going over for the first time. Just as we did, they are awaiting planes, too, eager, impatient to be gone, and armed like commandos with knives, guns, and allied equipment of their own choosing, items which have no use once overseas, except on the beachheads.

The time comes, as come it must. With heavy hearts we file onto the C-54 and strap ourselves in. Off to Hawaii. Once again we depart from the Golden Gate, but I haven't the heart to watch it slip by, as the others are doing. August 8th we are at Hickam, arriving at midnight. We are told not to leave the post, so we walk about the beautifully landscaped base, visit the P-X, and eat at the Club. "Russia's in the war," Jake points out, and we scan the headline. Perhaps now we'll use Russian bases and shuttle-bomb. We talk over the possibilities. The next day we're off again, this time in a C-47. We fly directly to Kwajalein. In the brief period here we try to trace Gyro, but there's no record of him, other than the expressed belief by several who recall him, that he was sent back to the Marianas, so we hope to find him on Saipan. The trip to Saipan is uneventful. We immediately get quarters, the same we had before going home, and sink again into familiar surroundings. We might just as well not have been home, so natural does it seem to be back in the Marianas.

We encounter Jake Schad, "Spook" Sedden, and Clarence Rein who are on their way to Hawaii for a rest before returning to finish their missions. They tell us more news about the Group and Squadron -- in fact, the whole Group. Porky was one of the originals and was almost finished with his missions when it happened. Popular among the men, even the Commanding Officer of the Group is quieter now that Jordan is gone, thus observes Schad. We get a big piece of news when we first hear about Pete Fortune and his crew. "You mean you haven't heard about Bulgy's experiences?" Schad inquires. "No, how could we," I remind him. "Well, it seems that Pete's plane was loaded with "hot" gasoline at Iwo, when we stopped on the way up for refueling for the longest mission yet, mining on the other side of Japan, near Russia. Anyway, it seems that on the way home everything was all right until well south of Iwo. Bulgy's tanks started dropping in quantity mighty fast until they were almost empty, so he and his crew wasted no time. They got out while the fans were still turning." "They all bailed?" Jake inquires. "That's right, and all are O.K. except for the engineer, who almost drowned trying to get his Mae West inflated," Schad adds. Schad goes on to describe how the rescue boat picked them all up within a couple of hours. We all express amazement over his good luck. It's always tough to locate men down in the water. They are hard to see, even when nearby. But to find all eleven, safe and sound, that must be a record.

While we are chatting we hear a terrific whooping and hollering across the way. Being sounds of an unusual nature we listen and hear repeatedly, "The War's over!" Boy, they must be looped for sure. Schad says, "What the hell - -" and gets up to investigate, but I am too tired and disgusted for foolish pranks now, and lie down on my cot. Now we hear firearms being fired all over the Island, way in the distance. What is this, anyway? War over! That's not possible. It just isn't possible. But Bill, Jake, and Hal are moving toward the front of the Quonset, so I join them. We hear snatches of a broadcast. The announcer sounds excited, as though he were at a football game. Gradually the whooping and hollering take effect on us. Far distant cries are mingled with those near by. Sounds like the whole Island is going berserk. Our unsettled, depressed outlook on the world, after our string of misfortunes, makes us suspicious of everything, particularly good news. But finally we begin to wonder if we shouldn't accept the possibility and find it's easier to believe than we thought. If so, everybody's worries are over, including our own. Jake keeps repeating, "I don't believe it," half aloud, half to himself, and we go back to our cots and try to get some sleep. It'll keep, if it's true. We won't lead with our chins by accepting it ourselves, we'll wait and see.

August 11th, when we arise and have breakfast, we hear that the news about the war being over is confirmed, but the dickering is still going on about the terms. It's still too revolutionary, in our way of thinking here, to accept it, so we shelve the idea and go back to the unhappy task of getting a ride over to Tinian.

A C-47 takes us back to Tinian and then a truck deposits us in the old surroundings, 8000 miles from home, again. As we are greeted by the fellows they seem amazed that we're back. Even the authorities claim that they didn't expect to see us again. Well, that makes us stupid all the way around. Maybe we should have hid out somewhere in the mountains of the west. It seems that crews that went back after we did were detained in the United States. But here we are, and that's that. No sense torturing yourself over what might have been. What a confounding situation. We were sent to the States by mistake, we are returned by mistake. Those receiving us at both ends are surprised to have us, and yet we are powerless to help ourselves. About all we know is that we're here, not in the United States, and that's that.

We are absorbed into the routine again. Again we adjust ourselves to our new "old" surroundings. The trip becomes like a high pressure dream, and we adopt the way of thinking and mode of life required, as easily as putting on the old sunglasses, and the appearance of things differs again. We think about going on the next flight, not going into Los Angeles. It is not a question of getting a milk shake, but whether we'll get Spam again. The tablecloths have changed into board tops. The china is metal ware. Instead of reaching for the wallet all the time, we leave it in our foot locker. The singing commercials and windy advertisements are replaced by continual music form Saipan, or short skits, or news of Japan. We don't think in terms of meeting the wife, autos, shiny shoes, razor-edge pants, parties, jukeboxes, drugstores, first of the month bills. No. We think in terms of when do we go home, are we scheduled to fly, is our plane in condition, are the crew members ready to go, what curved ball can we expect from the Army and supervisory personnel this time, how about borrowing your Jeep, let's take a swim, let's have a beer, and what do you think's going to happen now?

We are happy to learn that "Miss America – '62" has been flying steadily, adding another 15 missions to her string, and now running even with another plane for top honors in the Squadron. She now sports a black bottom -- for camouflage purposes. It's a happy occasion when we see Pat, Red, and Vito again. They are still working on the plane and they give us the history of events since our departure. The plane has been fine, with no damage worth mentioning. The Commanding Officer of the Group surprises me greatly by welcoming me (as representative of the crew), saying that he is glad to see us back. He requests that I submit a summary of the Muroc training to him, together with a criticism, which I gladly agree to do.

Meanwhile, the peace rumors are being mangled by radio announcers in the States. We listen carefully and read the teletyped news that comes in from Bomber Command headquarters. None of the men in the camp has any sympathy for the Governmental Representatives who are hesitating over accepting the peace. This disgust is engendered, mainly, by the tough talk of those at home who bravely pledge us to fight further, unless the Japs come across with the proper terms quickly. It isn't that the men here aren't brave and don't want to trounce the Japs, but it's the feeling that those who don't have to do the fighting are being the toughest, quick to commit us to more fighting, when the Japs have admitted that they're ready to quit.

We move into a different Quonset hut, instead of our old abode. Now we reside among the trees in "Jester's hut", the place where Schad and his crew lived. Hal takes Rein's place, Bill takes over Spook's and I take Schad's. Jake lives next door. So we take up housekeeping again, only this time we don't even unpack our bags -- not because we're going anywhere for some time to come, but because it feels less permanent if the belongings aren't completely put away, as you might do preparatory to a long stay. We share the Quonset with Charlie Holton's crew and Bob Hume's officers. We quickly learn the news that Johnny Hart and "Quiz" Qualizza of Charlie's crew have over 30 missions, since they have flown with another crew while Charlie has been Operations Officer. Donnell, the Group's other West Pointer and a good man, finally gave up bucking the Supervisory personnel and got a transfer to another outfit.

As for Hume, who thought that the missions were going to be easy, he has found out the hard way, we learn, and he frankly admits he changed his thinking mighty fast after one particular mission. It seems that he joined a strange B-29 formation, not being able to find his own Group, and went over the target, with fighters making passes at the formation. He started the bomb run as a part of a three ship flight in a three flight formation. In short order the leader of the flight and the other wingman were shot down by the fighters and he was left alone to close up the gap and continue on, while the fighters continued to work them over. He admitted afterwards that he adopted a new outlook and became prayerfully thankful that his crew was spared. Now the fellows kid him about his abrupt change of mind, but we realize that at the time it wasn't funny.

In the course of getting settled again we catch up on the news. Charlie Lazin and crew, having completed 35 missions, are on their way home. Charlie never did get a promotion -- tough luck! Pete Fortune's crew, after their bail out and rescue experience, are to go home as soon as transportation is available. Schwager, Litchfield, and Maki are in the thirties and will be eligible to return home soon. Dawson's crew is now with another Group, having been transferred to help form a new Squadron. Some of the crews are split, part still flying, part holding ground jobs. Of this number we learn that Parks is the Mess Officer now, and keeping the men happy through hard work and out-talking them. Ramsey is the Engineering Officer, doing so well that he set a record for the best Group maintenance. Mutch is still carrying on at the old stand; as Squadron Adjutant. Concerning the replacement crews, Cooney and Meadows are crowding 30 missions now, well ahead of the others, Bassett is in the States at the Lead Crew School for the August class, Hume is plugging along with almost 20 missions, Rodgers is plugging right along with somewhat less, Sapp is preparing to go to the States for the September class of the Lead Crew School, and the remaining two, Moschau and Howett, are just well started. P.E. Jones and our crew are even up, having lost the same amount of time in the States.

So that's how we find the Squadron affairs. The Squadron has been doing quite well, considering the standpoint of loss and casualty, although the loss of Jordan's crew is felt far more than is indicated by a paperwork recount.

Chapter 31 Kumagaya

August 15, 1945 – No. 23

"One Too Many"

The days between the 12th and 14th are filled mostly with talk and speculations about the end of the war. It is easy to criticize the Government, so we do, seeing only our little world, conditioned by the news broadcasts. We are at a loss to understand the hesitancy over settling the peace -- we're ready to quit, and how! Now we hear that the Japs want to keep their Emperor, so that makes for more discussion. Most of us agree that the surrender should be unconditional, yet we want to eat our cake and have it, too. In short, we don't particularly care to go on any more missions, but we want no back-talk from the Japs.

"Gyro" is still missing. Though we occasionally see Cockers that resemble him, arousing our hopes, none of them are our one and only. We've given up hope of finding Turbo, but Gyro was the homebody of the two. He liked to be with us. On Saipan we found no trace of him. Now on Tinian, with its 60,000 men, there's not much chance of finding him. But Hal and Jake don't give up hope.

Charlie Holton informs us, "Pat Murphy's still in the States. Don't know when he'll be back." It seems that Pat was called back to attend a court martial and it's taking more time than expected. We remember the eager First Base that Pat played, his down to earth religion that made him one of the boys, and his stimulating Sunday services. Everyone misses Pat. We learn further, that the Chaplains who have filled in, have had a tough time. In one instance the C.O. sent the Deputy C.O. to the Chaplain to request him to change his prayers, that they weren't war-like enough. The Chaplain pointed out that he was using a standard Army-Navy prayer before the missions. But that wouldn't do. The upshot of the entire situation was hard feelings all the way around, and nothing accomplished. The Chaplains, while they are under a C.O. and must obey, have the backbone to stand up against unfairness to a certain extent. Their high calling apparently gives them moral courage. In their relating of the incident to us we could see that the men were amazed over the C.O. thinking he could dictate to a Chaplain.

"Is the war over yet, Hal?" Bill inquires as Hal returns from the Intelligence room where we get the news broadcasts from home. "It was five minutes ago, no telling what's doing by now," Hal answers. We've given up trying to keep abreast of the developments which change back and forth. One minute the announcer leaves not a particle of doubt in our minds that the peace is definite, the next there's a new turn to events. We finally decide that it must be over, and we stop trying to hear each broadcast. Big League ball teams are on the Island for exhibition games, so everyone goes to see the games. Then there's the swimming at the newly improved "Yellow Beach". The nurses turn out en masse, too, and it's quite a sight. It comes mainly under the heading of sight-seeing, not swimming. However, the excavated pool on the coral ledge that extends well out to sea is quite suitable for swimming without fighting the waves. The current endeavor centers about picking the "Peach of Yellow Beach", and Cooney, Hall, Mutch, Farrell, Juskiewicz, Ramsey -- in fact, all of us, are busy cataloging "probables" as we appraise the nurses in Stateside bathing suits. At first glance you might think we were at a coast resort back home. In the usual Army fashion, there is a separate beach for the enlisted men, known as "South Beach", where there is an even larger attendance. Swimming and shell hunting are popular pastimes.

On the 13th, as we go about our washing of sox and light housekeeping, we are informed that there is a mission going out tonight. "Wait a minute. Don't you know the war's over?" observes Jake to Sergeant Belleville at Operations. "I do, but they don't," he answers, nodding toward Headquarters. "Someone's got their wires crossed, must be a mistake," one of the men declares, and we agree. However, the horrible doubt remains. Maybe it isn't over. And we realize that it is a jolt to start thinking in terms of missions again after the happy basking in a peace-time atmosphere. Perhaps we would have been better off not to have accepted all this peace talk. Now we must revise our outlook again. No one knows anything beyond a message from higher headquarters stating that a mission will go out tonight, so be ready. The Group officials are in a fog, too. Someone way up top is pulling strings and has closeted himself to do so. Even the radio announcers at home don't know it. They continue to talk about the peace, saying that the President will officially announce the end of the war over the radio, himself, -- and here we are being told to prepare to go on a mission.

Tired of it all, we rest up and await developments. Night approaches, we eat chow. Still no news. "Think we ought to go bomb tonight, Ben?" I ask Ben Lay, Squadron Intelligence Officer. "No, why don't you stay home tonight. It's such a waste of time. You need your rest, we'll go to the show," he replies. "Well, all right. If it's a good show we'll change our plans," and we continue the joshing in the usual vein. After dark we are told that the mission is postponed. Once again we breathe easier. Surely it's over now. Maybe they're just threatening the Japs. The next day the situation is unchanged. We hear that the mission has not been canceled, and the planes are loaded, ready to go. Now we are told that the mission will go out this afternoon, definitely.

Realizing that someone up the line thinks we are going, I reflect on our situation. Undoubtedly we are at the peak of our ability as a crew, after a solid month of flying and practicing the specific techniques used on the missions. There was a lot of dead wood in the work, to be sure, but the practice was beneficial. We got more out of it because of the extensive combat experience behind us. We know the importance of knowing the job. Those training flights permitted us to practice the techniques which are used only once on a mission, when there's no time for practice. Since our earlier training in the States was shy much of the radar work, the Muroc flights permitted learning the bombing procedures on radar runs so well they could be done without effort -- almost unconsciously. Since our return, we are aware that the Atom bomb has not stirred up excitement here that it did in the States. Most of the men see no difference, since their status is unchanged. Little information has been circulated concerning its nature, and it does not apply to our work. If and when a mission goes out it will be in the usual manner, with the usual bomb load of incendiaries or General Purpose High Explosives, two whole bomb bays full.

The destruction in Tokyo and the other cities where the low level "blitz" fire raids laid waste is still the most devastated area of Japan. Besides, to accept the Atom bomb unconditionally makes light of the hard work that the bombing has required thus far, at great expense in lives and equipment. So the men are quite "leery" of the Atom bomb and depreciate its significance. Right or wrong, the men all feel that the damage was done, and the Japs beaten, before the Atom bomb, and not as a result of it. So they are quick to dislike the impression, caused by the newly arrived outfit that came over to drop the Atom bombs, that they won the war for us -- sort of a high and mighty attitude.

The announcers at home still seem to think the war is over. Yet we prepare for the mission, assembling our gear after our long combat lay-off. The crew members all look well and are equally puzzled over the strange set of affairs. We attend the briefing, feeling almost like spectators, collecting the information flimsies, distributing them to the various specialists, and listening to the men presenting the briefing. We learn that should "the war be over" while we're going up to the target, the code word "Utah" will be broadcast and that will mean to come home. The target will be the small town of Kumagaya, 40 miles north of Tokyo, where several roads and railroads come together. Our path will skirt Tokyo, to the east, thence turning toward the target on a west heading. Withdrawal will be to the west and south, so that we'll miss the western outskirts of Tokyo. None of the crews believe all this, however. Everyone is too sure that the war is over, and that includes ourselves. But we go through the motions, as though putting on a dress rehearsal for the top command. We'll probably be recalled before take-off.

Down at the line we talk to Pat, Red, and Vito in between chores, and learn that the plane is flying all right. It returned from a test hop only a few minutes before our arrival, that's why the delay in loading. Apparently it will be nip and tuck to have the plane ready on time. The deadline for take-off is 1800. The fuel is loaded but the bombs are slow going. As we wait, an engineering representative drops by to check the plane, and mentions that the broadcast just heard stated that the war is over and that the President will broadcast the news himself. But no orders have come telling us to return to the area. Looking over toward Meadows plane, whose crew is also scheduled this time, we are surprised to see no activity at all. At the Personal Equipment room we are told that he has gone back to the area, thinking that the news broadcast was the official war's end, an automatic cancellation of the mission. Maybe he's right, but we'll go ahead until we get different orders.

At 1800 we pull the props through, realizing that we won't get off before the deadline. It would look mighty "fishy", considering our known dislike for this trip, if we stop now because of going beyond the deadline, so we go ahead. Across the field on the far runway we see planes of another Group taking off. This outfit, we are told, is going on a mining mission to Japan. They're in a peculiar position, too. Mighty strange strategy, we think, to sow mines at war's end, that may sink our own ships in peace time. No doubt our Navy will be in the Japanese area soon, if they are not already there.

The crew members take their stations, we wave goodbye and taxi out. The engines sound good. The power check was excellent. All the check lists have been accomplished and we know that, technically speaking, we are ready to go. We've got to stay "on the ball", considering that current events don't change our heavyweight take-off, and the reality of accomplishing this mission. Maybe this is a war of nerves, at least our nerves are in on it, whatever it is. The crew goes about the old routine. Seems like we've been doing this a lifetime or two. Seeing the old sights, following the old routine, is akin to the strange feeling that comes over one occasionally. "I've done this before." In our case we have no trouble remembering when it was -- seems like we've always been doing just this.

"Al, hear anything?" Is the frequent question when we wonder if the code word is being sent. "No, not a sound," comes the answer. Darkness settles. We continue on, heading 330 degrees, to the north-northwest, past Iwo, over the long stretches of blackness beyond Iwo, and now we are within an hour of the target. Sill no "Utah"! The plane flies well, Nick transfers the fuel. We don our heavy battle equipment. The turrets are energized, the men at their stations. We are ready to go in on the target.

"Navigator to pilot, turn on a 279 degree heading in 2 minutes," comes Hal's message, warning us of the approach of the bomb run. "Turning to 279 true in 2 minutes, Roger," I answer. "Ready to turn -- turn!" Hal directs, and we turn "Miss A. – '62" on course for the target. I steel myself for the run and try to keep busy with the instruments and controls, keep the mind occupied. "There it is, fire dead ahead," Jake calls out. "O.K., gunners, keep your eyes open," I unnecessarily advise, and they acknowledge, one by one. Gabby and Hal are scanning the radar scope for the tell tale landmarks while Jake checks his bombsight, after turning on the switches. Then he swings the bombsight back into its stowed position while Jonesy covers the forward area with the top turrets from his position. Hal and Jake work together on the run, timing the distance out, and then the sighting angles. "Lord stick with us," I beg and then I go through the Lord's Prayer again, which is my old standby. There's the old thermal, the fires below, and the billowing clouds of smoke. Is that flak exploding? Are those tracers and small arms fire from below? Look at that thermal -- will we have to go through it? It's too late now, the code word won't help. We're almost there and the city has been badly hit already. Evidently the other planes have dropped their load, we were late in taking off. Wonder if those Japs thought the war was over, too, before the planes arrived!

Down below it's perfectly dark, as though the fires were burning the blackness, not buildings. The flames don't light up the area as they did in the past. Can't see any land. Even the plane is semi-dark. Hal and Jake are talking the monosyllables of the bomb run. Jake is hunched over the sight. The bomb doors are open and the crew is awaiting the release point. Even the silence of the interphone seems fraught with meaning, as though we can hear the breathing and thought of each member at his station -- waiting. Close to the fires now we see that we're going into the thermal. "Check safety belts, it may be rough in the thermal," Bill announces as a precaution. He holds his set of controls, along with me, so that we're ready for any required maneuvers. The autopilot is on, but disengaged. "Bombs away!" Jake calls, as the plane tries to climb.

We hold the plane steady, going into the thermal. The boiling smoke looks mean, but inside it doesn't seem very rough. We come out on the other side of the smoke under control, and begin our breakaway to the left. "Several bombs hung up in rear bay," Dick calls. Jake toggles the switches, then goes aft to check. "B-29 below," Charlie calls just as we catch sight of another plane about 100 feet below us. Bill and I wrack the plane up into a bank to the right, then back to the left. "Bombs are falling," Dick reports from the blister. We are glad to get rid of them now, while we're still over Jap soil, where they'll do some good. The old forces of habit keep asserting themselves! The gunners stick with their guns, scanning the darkness around us. Bill takes the controls while I lean back. My arms and hands are shaking, and sweat is running down inside my clothes even though it's cold, and we've been sitting quietly at the controls. I realize that I've been gripping the controls so hard that I'm worn out.

As we approach the southern edge of Jap landscape, a low stratus-type cloud completely covers the sky beneath us, appearing almost a carpet on the ground from this altitude. Gabby calls, "You ought to see the shipping down there!" His radar scope clearly shows such objects. "Can't begin to count 'em, they're in groups of 2s and 3s and everywhere," Hal joins in with amazement at the terrific quantity of shipping. They are not moving as we pass overhead. They know who we are, no doubt.

Hal gives us the heading "home" and we begin to remove our equipment. "Al, did you hear anything on the radio?" I inquire, still wondering about that "Utah". "No sir, not a word," he replies. We dispose ourselves comfortably in our various positions for the long run home. This is for the last time, surely.

While silence prevails, and we are free to reflect again, I think about this mission. Do the others feel as I do? I can't relax, my hands are still shaking and weak. I feel dead tired. What's the matter with me? The billowing smoke above the orange glow, surrounded by utter blackness. The old familiar scene came to life again for those few minutes tonight. The heavy gear on my shoulders seemed to weigh down my mind, and all the time, as we approached the target, my right leg kept shaking uncontrollably, no matter how hard I willed it otherwise or pushed the rudder pedal or tried to keep my mind occupied. Actually, we had little or no opposition, but in the fire and explosions I could see the fighters of Shimonoseki, the flak and thermal of Tokyo, the searchlights of Nagoya, Osaka, and Tokyo. I prayed, the most sincere in a long line of combat prayers, and wondered if we'd get away safely. Did the others feel this way? Everyone did his job in the routine manner. I could hear them over the interphone. It's good they couldn't hear my thoughts or they would have been surprised to know how scared was their "Airplane Commander". Is it our lay-off and return to the States? Is it the state of current events? Whatever it is, the strain is beginning to tell. Something's wrong. I feel tired and scared beyond anything experienced before. I've had enough!

Weak, and almost sick to my stomach, I gradually relax and begin to enjoy the rest. That darn right leg, vibrating on the rudder, as it did that night on take-off when Steel's plane was burning on the runway. A man can't fly with a vibrating leg, can he? Of course not. O.K., let's stay home and enjoy the peace from now on. My thoughts trail on endlessly while we cruise homeward. The interphone is quiet, probably many are catching naps. Bill's clothes rustle and I open my eyes to see him looking intently ahead. "Looks like weather ahead," he indicates lightening which shows heavy surrounding areas of cloud. We watch the lightening as it lights up the sky to show the structure of the clouds. They were not bad coming up, and according to the weather information there is only a weak "front" of weather lying across our path. Before we reach this area we encounter lighter type clouds without severe turbulence, but which cut our visibility considerably.

As we continue on the turbulence increases. "Fasten your safety belts, looks like mean weather," Bill warns the crew as he wakens them, after we see the threatening clouds. Very soon we learn, without a doubt, what type of cloud it is -- a thunderhead or cumulo-nimbus, as it is named, the kind we always detour when possible. The plane pitches and banks violently, and Bill and I wrestle the controls in an effort just to keep the wings semi-level. Flashes of lightening are frequent, brilliantly lighting the cabin. The power is frightening as the plane wrenches its way along. Bill and I concentrate on the instruments. The rain beats on the plane -- noisily against the glass, until it appears that we're encased in a thick sheet of water, piled up in front of the plane a foot or two. A solid water wall through which we are bulling our way. It's impossible to see outside the plane. The windows are covered with heavy torrents of water, whose currents may be seen through the glass.

The rain decreases somewhat, though the turbulence remains violent. Sharp cracks hit against the plane like fine gravel. Now it's ice. Wonder if our wings have any ice, but we can't see. It's all we can do to keep the plane level. Evidently we're still flying since the airspeed indicates 200 mph, and the altimeter is not racing around. As we think we are getting out of the cloud we encounter the lightening section. Our fluorescent lights are on "bright" and we concentrate on the instruments, regardless of the brilliant flashes about us. There is a blinding flash and a thud outside my window! "We've been struck by lightening," races through my mind. The intensity of the light blinds me -- I cannot see. The flash seems to continue. I hold the controls neutral, helpless to keep the plane level if it gets off. Giddy, I squeeze my eyelids tightly together, trying to restore sight. Some grainy, visible blackness seems to slide by, as though I am reeling after spinning rapidly and stopping. I can feel Bill on the controls with me, since they are remaining rigidly centered. We hold tight, waiting for returning sight. Several seconds pass, as the plane continues to buck. Let's hope the plane averages out on an even keel.

Slowly, the fluorescent lights become visible and the instruments come out of the blackness into their old positions. Bill's shaking his head. Appraising the instruments, I see that we've been turning, so I right the plane and pick up the original heading. The turbulence decreases and we are hitting the rear of the cloud. Everyone is chattering on the interphone about the lightening. It seems that each man thinks the plane was hit just outside his own position. There seems to be little doubt that the plane was hit. Once again "Miss A." has demonstrated her sturdiness. The violence was second only to the thermal that we encountered over Tokyo, but this time it continued, trying to wrench the wings off the plane. Why it didn't is a wonder to us. Perhaps the manufacturers know the reason.

Daylight comes, finding us in clear weather. We "sweat out" the last few miles, which always seem the longest. Anatahan appears in the distance, from there we see Saipan. Since our return a new approach is in use, so we call "Bromide" control on Tinian, requesting "room service", which means we want clearance to land. We are instructed to proceed to the North Field. As we come over the field we switch to Lotus Tower and receive landing information. Down at the parking area we see the tiny "blue room" where Pat, Red, and Vito wait, beside the hardstand. Landing is effected safely and we taxi into the hardstand. We are greeted with hands clasped overhead in the old congratulatic sign. Getting out of the plane we learn that the war is over, officially. The President having announced it just a few minutes before our arrival. "You say the war's over again?" we inquire jokingly. "It's _officially_ over this time," they reply.

We take our time loading the gear into the truck, laughing and joking with the boys. They tell us that Meadows finally went. He and his crew thought the war was over and had returned to the area, only to be sent back to their plane. While we are talking Meadows taxis in, and waves as he passes. Our Group was scheduled to be the last to bomb the target, and we were the next to last plane in the Group, so we must have been the next to the last plane to bomb Japan. Later we find this to be true.

Not finding any interrogators about the area, we skip interrogation and get some food. Sleep is out of the question -- too much too talk about, so we clean up and chat with the fellows in our Quonset, then go to visit other Quonsets, where a great deal of palaver is going on.

As we happily realize that the war is over, we remember those of the Squadron who are not with us. God willing, we have come through safely. If only Boynton, Preston, Snyder, Jordan, and their crews were here to share it. We think of them as our second selves. It could have been us, not them. We are humble that we are permitted to live on. Perhaps that alone obligates us to make the most of the years ahead.

"Miss America -- '62" stands in the hardstand, by the "blue room", just as pretty and substantial as ever, albeit with a black bottom. 43 missions and 800 hours. How we would like to take her home, to complete the round trip with the crew and ground crew as passengers, but that's a pipe dream. It's too much to expect, even though "Miss A." is so obviously old and weary, ready to be taken as are all the old planes. We would like to lay her to rest in the States where she belongs in her old age.

So long, "Miss America -- '62".

Chapter 32 Post War Combat

The game is over, the other team is licked, and it's time to be going home. For the first few days the happy glow of peace lights up the faces of everyone. It is a happy, secure feeling. Nothing more is needed than this realization that there will not be any missions going out again, no flak, fighters, thermals, or heavy take-offs. Good humor springs from the hearts of the men. But the fertile human brain and active imagination will not permit indefinite contentment. What was jest before becomes food for thought, discussion, bets and rumors. "When do we go home?" VJ Day parties are frequent until everyone has attended several at least. Home is the all-engrossing subject of conversation, including the activities that will occupy each on return.

Points are the central qualification for those who have not flown 35 missions. They are computed and recomputed. How many points for length of service, for overseas duty, for children, for awards, for campaign stars? Which category are you in? A, B, C, D, and on down the line. No sooner is one system set up as a basis for discharge than it is repealed and another substituted. The central difficulty of all the systems, we finally learn, is the lack of transportation. Many men who qualify under a system and get ready to leave, find that leaving is another proposition entirely. That 7000 miles of water is something of a problem. The Army solves this in its own fashion by telling those who are eligible that they are free to leave _if_ they can get their own transportation -- a near impossibility. Eagerness turns into despair, and despair to bitterness as home comes no closer. Initial disappointments make the men cagier, and more suspicious of the daily write-ups in the Wing newspaper, which outlines the current point system. Having points means eligibility for discharge but discharge is accomplished in the States, not her. First, where's the transportation?

Occasionally some with extra gumption, recalling that all they need is transportation, brave the representatives of various transportation facilities and the conversation goes like this, as we know from experience: "How about passage to the States?" This is asked of the Navy Port Control Officer. "Got any room?" "Sure, be glad to put you on the list, but it must be O.K.'d by your Wing headquarters transportation department." "Have you boats going?" "Yes, one leaving Sunday, and several next week." So, up to the Wing transportation office. Here you overhear, while waiting for the attention of the officer in charge, that a lot of trouble has been caused by those men, eligible to go home, coming to this officer, when in reality they should go through channels, that is, have their Group Adjutant speak for them. If this knowledge doesn't deter you, and you inquire, you are promptly told to tell it to your Group Adjutant instead of coming there. They'll deal with him.

Not licked yet, you go to the Navy Flight Operations, and inquire about a seat home to the States in a Naval plane. "Well, we don't have much right now. Generally the seats are filled with Navy men. Of course, if you are here when a plane leaves with a vacancy - - - - ? Why don't you try those B-29 Groups. We understand that they fly people home." By that time you don't feel like pointing out that you are from a B-29 Group. You have a choice then, to return to your

Group and wait or stand there in the Naval Operations indefinitely, assuming you are not required to be present in your own outfit. Occasionally the myth is kept alive. "Hey, did you hear that so-and-so got a ride with the Navy?" "No foolin'! Doesn't his brother run one of the Seabee outfits?" "Well, yes, guess he does -- but maybe there'll be some more rides available." So the hardy soul, like his brethren, returns to meditation and hopes that somewhere, somehow, a ride will turn up. The situation is not helped by the confident announcers at home, who daily state that so many thousands of men a day are being discharged in the States, with less than half the service and points of the men here.

A furious battle of paper work occurs in a last rush of applications for awards. Some of us have been interviewed previously for the D.F.C., which is awarded on a basis of 22 missions. Our crew was further eligible for an award, we were told, as a result of our 6th Mission to Nagoya, when we bombed the target with our electrical equipment inoperative. In the feverish flurry of awards being given to many whom the men do not consider deserving, we lose stomach for the whole thing, and tell our Intelligence Officer to forget it so far as we are concerned. So we discard the additional award, wondering what some men are going to tell the folks back home, after they've received those phony citations. Perhaps they only want the awards because each is worth 5 points under the point system, that maybe the added points are needed to make them eligible for discharge. The whole situation is most unsavory, particularly to those in the Intelligence Department who are forced to write up and submit the false superlatives and exaggerations which clothe the individuals concerned, in an effort to make them appear deserving.

Faced with lots of spare time, the combat crew members turn to activities such as landscaping the yards of the Quonsets, reading the books of the newly formed library (real books, many best sellers), playing cards or ping-pong, chatting at the Service Club or Officers Club, swimming, visiting friends in other outfits about the Island. We are occasionally buoyed up by someone's good fortune. Schad and crew in Hawaii are sent back to the States, rather than returned to Tinian. Rodgers and crew are sent back to the States in a B-29 to get school books, but the general rumor is that he'll not return himself. The Wing Commander goes home. The C.O. of our Group goes home, taking a new B-29 loaded with his personal goods and several of his eligible friends. Everyone is getting out who can -- that is, who has the transportation, and leaving the others to shift for themselves. We are not surprised, of course, to see our C.O. leave so soon. Only a few days before he had told us that "'We' will be out here quite a while yet, men."

Seeing so many leave by special transportation, our hopes rise when we learn that 5 of our old planes will be sent home. Immediately we assume that our crews will take them. It doesn't work out that way. Instead of our taking "Miss A. -- '62" home, a strange crew is sent from Guam, who have less experience and fewer combat missions, to take the plane back to the States. It is with sadness that we see this occur. Pat, Red, and Vito will miss the old gal, but Miss A. is getting old, maintenance will be more difficult.

Meanwhile, there is a small amount of flying going on, as the planes are test-flown after maintenance, and the flight personnel get their required flying time for monthly pay. August 30th we are surprised to learn that a large formation of planes will be sent from the Group, as part of a "Show of Power" to Japan. Some of the crews are eager to go, those who need another flight or two to make them eligible for shipment home, and those who are newly arrived and do not have many missions to their credit, but some of us are not enthusiastic. The war is over, and our luck strained thin. Why fly the long trip, which never fails to produce accidents or ditchings, just to impress some of our higher "brass" or the Japanese. The Japs, best of all, know what our power is. However, if it must be so, let those who are eager to go make the flight. So it is that some of us request to stay behind, thereby causing hard feelings with higher authorities. There are plenty who do want to go, so we don't feel bad. Later when the Prisoner of War supplies are flown to Japan, we know that this is a worth while endeavor. A number of trips are made, dropping out supplies by parachute to awaiting prisoners. Several B-29s are lost through ditching, parachutes dragging behind the plane, and faulty loading, but our Group manages to get through unscathed.

Schwager and crew goes home, followed by Litchfield's crew. Crews with 35 missions are getting the priority now, in the available transportation. Bill Reed goes, and Holtzclaw, both on a mission basis. Maki's crew follows, as Maki volunteers to go to Iwo to act as Operations Officer. Various local formation flights become frequent duties, passing in review for high-ranking authorities who are leaving to go home, or just arriving to take over command. Tinian, Guam, and Saipan -- the formations pass in a stately review, and they do look pretty, but many of us have had enough flying for now. The formation, with bad weather, and heavy traffic in the area, is always a gamble and occasionally someone pays with his life.

The last flight of Crew 2409 is made on September 14th, when we fly in a local formation. The last trip together means something to us, but the uncertain leadership, plus the new crews flying along with us instead of the old gang, make it a little too thrilling. Bill takes over the crew while Gabby and I retire, preparing for departure home. We are the first eligible in the crew.

Pat Murphy returns from the States and is an inspiration to the men, bucking up the homesick spirits and keeping many busy with the construction of the new Chapel. After months of working, pleading, arguing, and failure, Pat has been granted permission to have a Chapel, and the lumber to build it.

The feeling of dissatisfaction because of lack of transportation to take those who are eligible home for discharge, culminates in the minds of those waiting on "Navy Day" in New York. Because of the announced lack of ships they can't get a ride, yet previously there were daily reports of the Naval vessels leaving for home partly empty. It leaves a bad taste in everyone's mouth, as do the News broadcasts that announce the terrific size of the United States Merchant fleet. Still there is no transportation here for lack of ships.

Various classes are held in school fashion teaching mechanics, pre-law, accounting, history, math, and other subjects. Ben Lay, our popular Intelligence

Officer, conducts the law class, flavoring the subject with Texas language and humorous illustrative cases. Ben, Doc, Schroeder, Srebro, and others more obviously homesick than the rest, are the butt of the jokes. "When you going home, Ben?" is the usual question. "Any day now, only the authorities don't seem to know it," Ben drawls ruefully. In the evenings frequent bull sessions spring up concerning business opportunities back home, or the good points of various localities. "Now you take the great Northwest, that's the only place." "Aw, go on, give me good old Pennsylvania." "Now if you fellows really want to see some good country, come to Denver." And so on.

We argue about how everyone will adapt himself to civilian life again. We wonder whether some of the men will be bitter all their lives because of the unfairness encountered in the Army. Raised in a democratic county where "all men are equal", with free speech, free action, and minds of their own, they are plunged into the totalitarian, dictatorial world of the Army with its gross mistakes, mismanagement and lack of freedom. It is apparent that some of the men have been seriously affected by the experience, and harbor terrible grudges that will harm themselves and others. We conclude that being a civilian again, with a job, will change that -- if jobs are to be had.

War-time dislikes are aired with many a disgusted sigh. The strikes and labor situation while we needed airplane engines, the black market, the attitude of some at home who want "Life the same as usual", griping about pay, food shortage, and transportation, the great war-bond drives and the redemptions thereafter. "How about the Hotels where you couldn't get rooms while the traveling salesman could?" says one. "They didn't care how they treated you." Or, "Well, that's true of merchants generally. No one had to 'sell' anything -- just take the customer's money," came another observation. The talk also covers the housing trouble, prices, and the cost of living for traveling Army personnel. From here the talk goes to Army red tape and "rank consciousness" and polishing the apple. Motion pictures get their share, too, with many a remembrance cited of the insipid glamour, unreal super-super presentation, and the general lack of reality or sincerity. Politics, forms of government, political parties, the "pork barrel" -- all share the limelight with many heated comments pro and con. After the shooting clears away we agree that the Government won't improve until the people, who are in it, do. The final analysis is that human nature is what causes war and poor government, and that these things will not be changed until human nature changes, or is made to do so. The battle is "within" people -- or should be.

Inevitably, women creep into the conversation, and then the sharp demarcation between married men and bachelors becomes evident, the number of each being the deciding factor as to what course the conversation follows. Usually it winds up with the latest pictures of the off-spring, somewhat self-consciously produced, for general scrutiny.

In early October Gabby leaves, going to Saipan to await a boat at a larger deportation camp. Shortly afterwards I receive my orders to report there likewise. The rest of the crew, with fewer points, are uncertain when they will leave, though the prediction generally made now is that the transportation is going to pick up rapidly. So, on departing, I have hopes that all will be home by Christmas.

Amid the many farewells, Hal writes an entry in his diary under October 8th, "This is the end of our crew as a unit and therefore the end of the record of the daily comings and goings of an air crew during that arduous period of Army life called a combat tour. The occasion is both sad and happy: Sad in that a fine team is broken up, old friends will be separated, happy because the various members of the crew are going back to their homes and loved ones. All that remains is to say goodbye and good luck and to hope that a continuation of this record would show happiness and success for everyone."

So long, team mates.

> "May the grace of the Lord Jesus Christ, and the love of God, and the fellowship of the Holy Spirit be with you all." 2 Cor. 13:14

GOD BLESS AMERICA

2012

Chapter 33 Appendix

1945

January

Sun	Mon	Tue	Wed	Thu	Fri	Sat
	1	2	3	4	5	6
7	8	9	10	11	12	13
14	15	16	17	18	19	20
21	22	23	24	25	26	27
28	29	30	31			

February

Sun	Mon	Tue	Wed	Thu	Fri	Sat
				1	2	3
4	5	6	7	8	9	10
11	12	13	14	15	16	17
18	19	20	21	22	23	24
25	26	27	28			

March

Sun	Mon	Tue	Wed	Thu	Fri	Sat
				1	2	3
4	5	6	7	8	9	10
11	12	13	14	15	16	17
18	19	20	21	22	23	24
25	26	27	28	29	30	31

April

Sun	Mon	Tue	Wed	Thu	Fri	Sat
1	2	3	4	5	6	7
8	9	10	11	12	13	14
15	16	17	18	19	20	21
22	23	24	25	26	27	28
29	30					

May

Sun	Mon	Tue	Wed	Thu	Fri	Sat
		1	2	3	4	5
6	7	8	9	10	11	12
13	14	15	16	17	18	19
20	21	22	23	24	25	26
27	28	29	30	31		

June

Sun	Mon	Tue	Wed	Thu	Fri	Sat
					1	2
3	4	5	6	7	8	9
10	11	12	13	14	15	16
17	18	19	20	21	22	23
24	25	26	27	28	29	30

July

Sun	Mon	Tue	Wed	Thu	Fri	Sat
1	2	3	4	5	6	7
8	9	10	11	12	13	14
15	16	17	18	19	20	21
22	23	24	25	26	27	28
29	30	31				

August

Sun	Mon	Tue	Wed	Thu	Fri	Sat
			1	2	3	4
5	6	7	8	9	10	11
12	13	14	15	16	17	18
19	20	21	22	23	24	25
26	27	28	29	30	31	

September

Sun	Mon	Tue	Wed	Thu	Fri	Sat
						1
2	3	4	5	6	7	8
9	10	11	12	13	14	15
16	17	18	19	20	21	22
23	24	25	26	27	28	29
30						

October

Sun	Mon	Tue	Wed	Thu	Fri	Sat
	1	2	3	4	5	6
7	8	9	10	11	12	13
14	15	16	17	18	19	20
21	22	23	24	25	26	27
28	29	30	31			

November

Sun	Mon	Tue	Wed	Thu	Fri	Sat
				1	2	3
4	5	6	7	8	9	10
11	12	13	14	15	16	17
18	19	20	21	22	23	24
25	26	27	28	29	30	

December

Sun	Mon	Tue	Wed	Thu	Fri	Sat
						1
2	3	4	5	6	7	8
9	10	11	12	13	14	15
16	17	18	19	20	21	22
23	24	25	26	27	28	29
30	31					

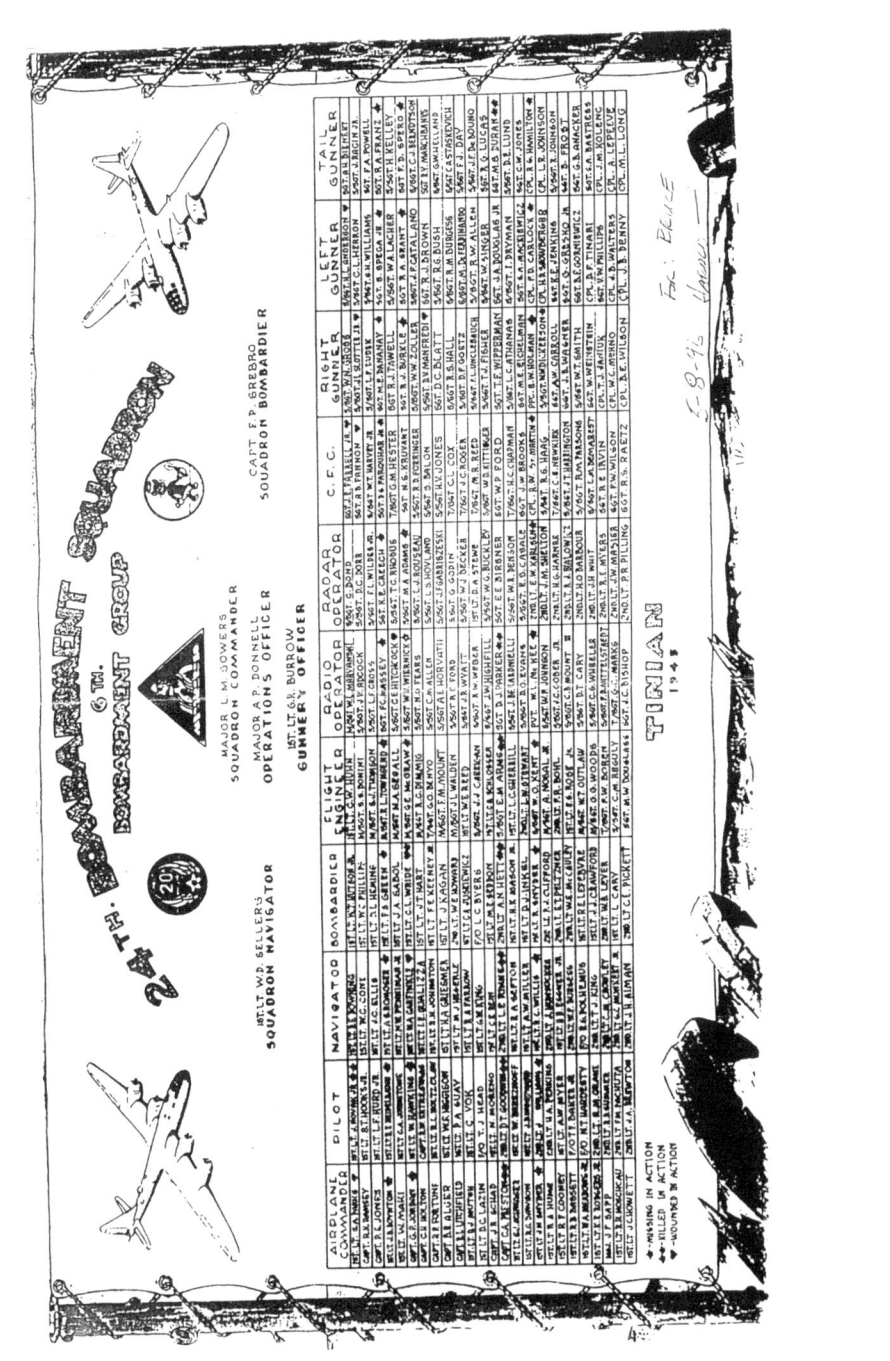

20th Air Force Patch

Distinguished Flying Cross

Two Air Medals

Asiatic Pacific Campaign with 3 Battle Stars

World War Two Combat Medal

Efficiency - Honor - Fidelity

Della Mae Patterson (Wife), Priscilla Alger (Wife), Bruce R. Alger - Commander and Pilot, Dick Patterson - Crew Chief - Head Mechanic

Steven Alger (Son), Priscilla Alger (Wife), Bruce R. Alger - Commander and Pilot, Jill Alger (Daughter)

Dick Patterson - Crew Chief, Bill Higgison - Pilot, Bruce Alger - Pilot and Commander, Jill Alger - Miss America '62, Al Horvath - Radio Operator, Harold V. Jones - CFC (Central Fire Control), Hal Griesemer - Navigator

Bruce R. Alger, Jill Alger, Priscilla Alger (Wife), Warren Bailey - Curator, Fairfield Air Force Base Museum, California

Parts from Original Miss America '62

REUNIONS SUMMARY

CREW 2409-6th GROUP - 313th WING - 21st BOMB COM. - 20th AIR FORCE

WHEN HOST?HOSTESS	WHERE	TIME ELAPSED	NUMBER PRESENT
1) Oct. 13-15/89 Mount	Princeton IL Wyanette	44 yrs+ 2 Mo.	7
2) May 17-19/91 Griesemer	Reading, PA	19 Months	8
3) Sept.10-13/92 Jones	TAFB Fairfield, CA	16 months	5
4) Oct, 7-10/93 Higgison Horvath	Morrow, GA	13 Months	6
5) June 16-19/94 Alger	TAFB CA Fairfield	8 Months	6
6) May 3-5/96 Patterson	Grove City, PA	23 Months	7
7) Sept.26-28/97 Jones	Tulsa, OK	16 Months	5
8) April 26-28/99	Pigeon Forge, TN	19 Months	3 + 2

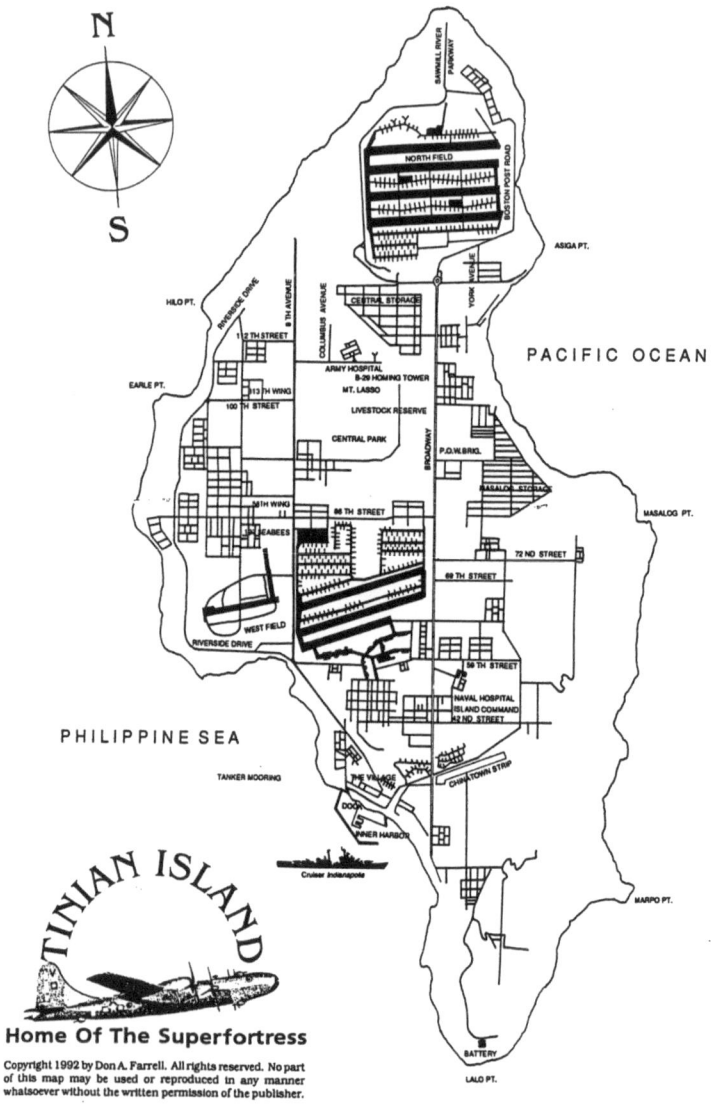

Viola Ann Koss
37470 Barkridge Circle
Westland, MI 48185

May 22, 1994

Bruce Alger
101 Rainbow Drive, #1731
Livingston, TX 77351

Dear Bruce:

I really enjoyed speaking with you about the upcoming June dedication. I truly regret, however, that we are unable to attend the dedication, and to meet you and the other crew members in person.

This was such a surprise, and I'm so proud to be included in the history of "MISS AMERICA '62".

As we discussed, I've attached a copy of the letter I wrote to Warren Bailey.

Sincerely,

Viola Ann Koss

Viola Ann Koss
37470 Barkridge Circle
Westland, MI 48185

May 22, 1994

Warren Bailey
President, Travis Air Force Base Historical Society
P. O. Box 1565
Travis AFB, CA 94535

Dear Mr. Bailey and the Crew of "MISS AMERICA '62":

    Since our conversation, I've been filled with memories of wartime and of Americans working together toward the common goal of winning the war. The emotional atmosphere of the Detroit based Chrysler defense plant, where "MISS AMERICA '62" had her beginnings , was charged with determination, hope, faith and American pride. The work force was predominately women whose mission was clearly that of supporting our troops...our loved one's ...and each day, as our shift would end, we knew that we had done everything we could physically do to bring our men home. I can say without reservation that our hard work was only exceeded by our prayers.

    It was my job to install the interior fuselage padding in the B-29's. However, prior to installation, I would inscribe a Good Luck message and identify myself, so that every B-29 I worked on silently carried my prayers for safe return and victory. I am delighted to know that my prayers for the crew of the "MISS AMERICA '62" were answered!

    My husband, Bill and I were married in 1942. Two months later, Bill enlisted in the Army Air Corps. I worked at the defense plant in 1943 and 1944, occasionally taking a leave of absence to join my husband, who was a crew chief for the B-17's. We were stationed at George Field, Illinois; Bainbridge Field, Georgia; and Barksdale Field, Louisiana. After the war had ended, Bill returned to Detroit and was hired by the Detroit Fire Department where he enjoyed a successful career of 33 years, retiring as a Battalion Chief.

Family has always played an important role in our lives. I have one brother and Bill came from a family of nine. My brother and four of Bill's were also in active duty in WWII, all returned safe and sound. We have truly been blessed with strong family relationships that deepen as each year passes.

Bill and I have two daughters. Carol, our oldest, recently retired from Ameritech as a Division Manager, and currently has her own consulting and distribution business. Carol and her husband, Gordon, have been married for 24 years. Gordon works for Electronic Data Systems and had three years of active duty in the Marine Corps including twenty two months of combat in Viet Nam. Jane, our youngest, and as Gordon would say, " the most courageous member of our family", is legally blind. Jane's personal determination and zest for life has allowed her to achieve just about anything she's wanted to do, from cross-country skiing to joining Carol and Gordon in their business.

I regret that we will not be able to attend the dedication ceremony. However, it gives me great pleasure to write one more time:

"Good Luck" to the crew of "Miss America '62", my prayers are with you.

Sincerely,
Viola Antkoss

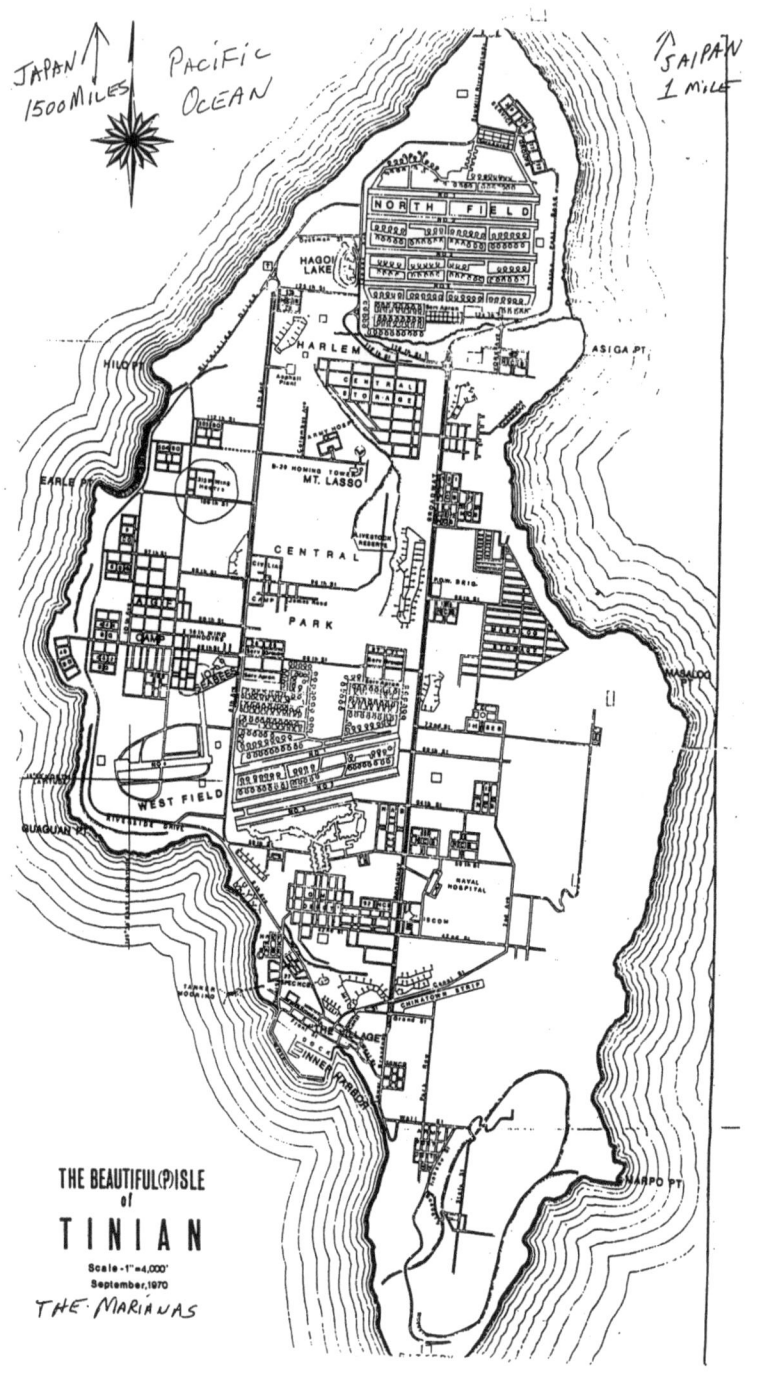

MILITARY

Saipan's own D-Day recalled

This was a horrible, horrible battle. The Japanese have come back and buried their dead. They have memorials all over the island. But the park is our first real memorial for the Marines.

Nancy Weil
Saipan memorial organizer

Associated Press

SAIPAN, Northern Mariana Islands – President Clinton wasn't there. Nor were any other heads of state or lines of satellite dishes and TV trucks.

But for the 50th anniversary of D-Day in Saipan – a fierce, three-week battle that helped end the war in the Pacific – there is finally a fitting memorial for the U.S. Marines who died there.

"The trees will have to come later," Froilan C. Tenorio, governor of this U.S. commonwealth in the Northern Mariana Islands, said as he spread a stack of blueprints out on a table in his office. "But, after all these years, I think that we are finally going to have something."

That something is American Memorial Park, a $4.5 million project Saipan's leaders have mulled over for years, but never got around to building until Tenorio gave the plan a push after he took office in January.

Memorial organizer Nancy Weil said she was disappointed that, considering all the pomp and ceremony afforded to Normandy last week, Saipan's 50th is going virtually unnoticed by many Americans.

"Americans are so biased toward Europe," she said. "This was a horrible, horrible battle. The Japanese have come back and buried their dead. They have memorials all over the island. But the park is our first real memorial for the Marines."

Construction workers labored around the clock for three weeks to prepare for Wednesday's anniversary, pouring concrete for the park's amphitheater, setting up fairgrounds and erecting a wall listing the names of thousands of Americans who died in the assault on Saipan.

Saipan is the second-largest island in the Marianas chain, about 3,800 miles west of Honolulu and 1,600 miles south of Tokyo. It was at the fringe of the Japanese empire during World War II, but today is under U.S. jurisdiction.

D-Day on Saipan came early on June 15, 1944, when the Marines' 2nd and 4th divisions landed on its southwestern beaches under heavy fire from Japanese artillery and antiboat guns. By nightfall, more than 1,500 Americans had died.

Before the island was secured on July 9, 71,034 U.S. troops would come ashore, and 3,100 would die along with 300 Chamorro natives and almost all of the 30,000 Japanese defenders.

A crowd watches as a B-29 is welcomed into the exhibits at the Travis Air Force Base Museum on Saturday.

Daily Republic/MIKE McCOY

Travis shows off restored B-29

By Matt Peiken
of the Daily Republic

TRAVIS AFB — Peter Summer, Bruce Alger, Bill Higgison and others recalled their time aboard the bomber as if it were yesterday. And in a way, it was.

Air Force officials on Saturday turned the clock back 50 years, unveiling a restored Boeing B-29 Superfortress that helped bring about Japan's surrender in World War II.

In a dedication ceremony luring about 300 veterans, family and history buffs to the Travis Air Force Base museum, men who served on the plane's first two missions said they owe their lives to the bird they'd dubbed "Miss America 1962."

"It's like a dream, but a dream come true," said Higgison, who piloted the plane's first mission, from Tinian Island to Japan. "Once you leave a plane, like we did in '45, you never think about seeing it again. When I left that B-29, I never wanted to see another one again. But five years ago, when I heard they located that plane in the desert, I couldn't wait to see it. They've done a miraculous job of restoring it, almost to how I remember it."

In 1956, the Air Force turned over most B-29s used during World War II to the Navy for weapons testing. Restoration of this particular plane started in 1985, when museum volunteers rescued it from China Lake Weapons Center in the Mojave Desert.

Though most of the plane was intact, volunteers rebuilt the nose and combed the country for other parts. They worked from photographs to restore an interior that, in

See B-29, Page 3

B-29: Unveiled

Continued from Page 1

one crewmen's eyes, was a shambles just two years ago.

Surviving crew from the first two missions regaled themselves and Saturday's audience with battle tales and tribute's to the B-29's capabilities. One member estimated that the craft they rode in might have dropped the final bomb of World War II.

"When we flew these planes in missions, we came in tight and very close," said Alger, a captain who led the plane's first mission. "Imagine the fire-power one plane could put out. But in a group, it was just a curtain of lead. It was quite a war bird. But the fact we're alive and here is the greatest feat of all."

"To get a feel for what we went through, practically everything they portrayed in the movie 'Memphis Belle' was the same as we saw it," added Al Horvath, a radio operator with the plane's first crew. "But that was a B-17 they had in that movie and we

were much more controlled and business-like. There were fires and a lot going on, but everything was calm."

Higgison, who came from his Atlanta home for the ceremony and crew reunion, attributes that to the B-29's cutting-edge machinery. Charlie Crowley, who navigated the plane's second mission, called it "a marvel of American science and ingenuity."

"Of course, in today's environment, it would be primitive. But it was the most advanced technology at the time," Higgison said. "The sophistication of the gunnery was the most advanced anybody had ever seen. The gunners had their hands on remote-controlled sighters instead of the guns, themselves. We knew our gunners had been well-trained and it was comforting to know we had better protection from other fighters."

Crew members named the plane "Miss America 1962" in honor of Alger's daughter and other girls born in 1944, the year

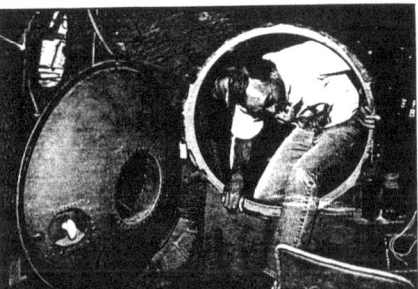

John Poynter, from Sacramento, ducks through a hatch while walking through the B-29.

plane was built.

The name was a brand of hope — by 1962, those girls would be eligible for the famed pageant that crew optimistically planned to see.

Crew at Saturday's ceremony signed their names to the bottom of an oil painting by aviation artist Rhu Bigay, who immortalized "Miss America 1962" in a work still in progress.

June 24, 1994 ♦ TAILWIND ♦ 3

Photo by Mike Dial

Miss America '62 Unveiled
Brig. Gen. Howard J. Ingersoll, 60th Airlift Wing commander, and Linda Alger unveil Miss America '62. The dedication ceremony Saturday morning featured the B-29 bomber that was restored by volunteers from the Travis Historical Society. The plane, which was named in honor of Alger's birth, is on display at the Travis Air Museum.

Brig. Gen. Howard J. Ingersoll, 60th Airlift Wing commander at Dedication, June 24, 1994

Miss America '62 reborn at Travis

Patti Rogers
Contributing editor

A B-29 bomber hasn't called Travis home since the 1949-58 Strategic Air Command years, but Saturday, the Travis Historical Society will unveil "Miss America '62" with all the fanfare of a long lost friend.

For almost 10 years, members of the society have put in over 12,000 volunteer man-hours restoring the 1944-circa bomber that will become one of the Travis museum's static displays.

The aircraft will be welcomed to the museum fleet by a host of special guests including two grandchildren of "the architect of the Air Force," Gen. Henry H. "Hap" Arnold. Also present will be six members of the aircraft's original crew, who flew 23 missions in the aircraft, and five members of the second crew, who flew 15 missions. Adding to the history of the day will be the woman whose birth contributed to the aircraft's name.

RESTORATION BEGINS

The old bomber's journey to Travis began in 1984 when the historical society learned of some B-29s being stored at China Lakes Naval Weapons Test Facility in Southern California. Bringing the worn aircraft back to Travis was a chore, said Warren Bailey, president of the Travis Historical Society.

"The aircraft was so far out on the test range it had to be pulled by a road grader across the desert floor. Then a volunteer team spent about 15 days disassembling it so two C-5s and 10 trucks could bring the pieces to Travis," said Bailey.

The team removed the engines, the outer wing panels, the vertical and horizontal tail assemblies, and disassociated the fuselage from the wing in order to prepare it for the return voyage.

The museum's restoration hangar housed the disassembled B-29 for the next several years while it underwent refurbishment. As the layers of paint were removed, the plane's identity was revealed. Markings indicating the plane's former unit, the 6th Bomb Group, appeared. Other markings aligned the plane to the 24th Bomb Squadron. The restoration team then found a reunion group who identified several members of the original crew and a mini-reunion was held at Travis in 1988 for those who chose and flew Miss America '62 from Tinian Island in 1945.

TOWARD COMPLETION

From that point on the restoration project took hold. By 1992 the exterior was nearly 100 percent complete. For the last two years a team of about seven volunteers took on the intense task of bringing the interior of the Superfortress to restored status.

And these history sleuths couldn't have been more pleased with what they uncovered. Near the navigator's seat, tucked under the installation blanket is the inscription, "To the G.I.'s good luck," which was written by Viola Ann Kolinski who installed installation blankets in B-29s at the Omaha, Neb., factory in 1944. She had left her address and phone number, and the restoration team immediately started to search for her.

"She was so excited when we tracked her down," said Bailey. "She said it was very nice after all these years to be recognized for what she did. Due to an illness in the family she won't be able to attend the dedication, but she sends her regards to all." Miss America '62 will be altered slightly so the inscription can be seen by everyone who visits.

However, the bombers namesake will be in attendance. The original crew, known as the Alger Crew No. 2409, chose

Photo by Mike Dal
A museum patron gets a sneak preview of the B-29 Superfortress "Miss America '62" that will be dedicated in a formal ceremony Saturday. The aircraft's namesake will be at the ceremony as well as two of Gen. Harold "Hap" Arnold's grandchildren.

the plane off the ramp at Tinian Island and set out to name her. The commander's wife had just given birth to a daughter and that sparked an idea.

"One of the crew members suggested she represent all the little girls born that year, and he came up with the idea that they would be eligible to be Miss America in 1962. Hence Miss America '62 was born, and she will be at the dedication ceremony," said Bailey.

Saturday concludes years of dedication by a group of people who are paid only with the pleasure of others. Bailey feels this way, "To give your time, skill, frustration and joy and see the progress being made and know you had a hand in it, is one of the greatest feelings in the world.

Miss America '62 flew her last bomb mission against Japan and was still flying the day the Japanese surrendered. After World War II she was assigned to the Bahamas as a weather reconnaissance aircraft.

NO MORE WAR

Crew

To the crew of my mate

Who flew together not knowing their fate.

God brought them home at the war's end,

All safe and sound to family and friend.

Years later God allowed them to reunite,

To reminisce about their courageous fight

To save the world so that we're here to say

We remember you on this holiday.

We're very grateful that all of you flew

In that magnificent Miss America '62.

An original poem by Helen Kagan

www.ingramcontent.com/pod-product-compliance
Lightning Source LLC
Chambersburg PA
CBHW041350290426
44108CB00001B/3